HER MAJESTY'S NAVY

VOL. III.

LORD NELSON.

Her Majesty's Navy.

LOWERING THE ENSIGN AT SUNSET.

VOL. III.

HER MAJESTY'S NAVY

INCLUDING

ITS DEEDS AND BATTLES

BY

LIEUT. CHAS. RATHBONE LOW, F.R.G.S.

(Late Indian Navy)

AUTHOR OF "HISTORY OF THE INDIAN NAVY," "LIFE OF LORD WOLSELEY," ETC., ETC.

With Coloured Illustrations

BY W. CHRISTIAN SYMONS AND W. FRED. MITCHELL

VOL. III.

The Naval & Military Press Ltd

Published by

The Naval & Military Press Ltd
Unit 5 Riverside, Brambleside
Bellbrook Industrial Estate
Uckfield, East Sussex
TN22 1QQ England

Tel: +44 (0)1825 749494

www.naval-military-press.com
www.nmarchive.com

In reprinting in facsimile from the original, any imperfections are inevitably reproduced and the quality may fall short of modern type and cartographic standards.

CONTENTS.

VOL. III.

CHAPTER I.

PAGE

Battle of Trafalgar—Nelson's Plan of Battle—Collingwood opens the Attack—The *Victory* engages the *Bucentaure* and *Redoutable*—Lord Nelson is wounded—Details of the part taken by each Ship in the Battle—Last Moments of Lord Nelson—The Gale after the Battle—Fate of the Prizes—Obsequies of Nelson—Some Account of the Services of the *Victory* 1

CHAPTER II.

Sir Richard Strachan's Victory over Dumanoir's Squadron—Gallant Defence of the *Arrow* and *Acheron*—Capture of the *Psyche* by the *San Fiorenzo*—Loss of the *Cleopatra* and her Recapture—Lieutenants Yeo at Muros, and Pigot at St. Mary's River—Capture of the *Marengo* and *Belle Poule*—Loss of the *Blanche* and *Calcutta*—Capture of the *Didon* by the *Phœnix*—Sir John Duckworth's Victory off San Domingo—Capture of the *Impétueux* and Fate of Admiral Willaumez's Squadron—Sir Sydney Smith at Naples—Services of the Boats of the *Pique* and *Renommée*—Exploits of Lord Cochrane—Loss of the Indiaman *Warren Hastings*—The *Blanche* and *Guerrière*—Services of the Navy on the Coast of Cuba—Capture of French Frigates by Sir Samuel Hood's Squadron—Surrender of Cape Town—The Expedition to the La Plata—Capture of Copenhagen—Admiral Duckworth in the Dardanelles—The Abortive Expedition to Egypt—Captain Brisbane at Curaçoa—Capture of the *Lynx* by the Boats of the *Galatea*—Repulse of the Boats of the *Spartan*—The *Weasel* off Corfu—The *Windsor Castle* Packet and the French Privateers 33

CHAPTER III.

The Naval Situation in Europe in 1808—Capture of the Russian seventy-four *Sewolod*—Action between the *San Fiorenzo* and *Piémontaise*—Services of the Navy on the Coasts of Norway and Denmark—Death of Captain Conway Shipley—Some Cutting-out Expeditions and Boat Actions—The *Seahorse* and Turkish Frigate—The *Sémillante* and *Terpsichore*—Fighting in Danish Waters—The *Amethyst* with the *Thetis* and *Niemen*—Destruction of French Ships in Aix Roads by Lord Cochrane—The Expedition to the Scheldt—Frigate Actions in 1809—The *Spartan* with a Squadron off Naples—Boat Actions in the Adriatic, and with Danish and Russian Gunboats—Loss of the *Junon*—Capture of French Colonies—Death of Lord Collingwood—Frigate Actions in 1810—Repulse at Palermo—Loss of three Indiamen—Captain Willoughby at Jacolet—Capture of *Réunion* and *Isle de la Passe*—Loss of Four Frigates off Grand Port, in Mauritius—Loss of the *Africaine* and *Ceylon*, and Recovery of the latter—Capture of Mauritius and Amboyna—Captain Cole at Banda-Neira—Actions with the Boulogne Flotilla and on the Coast of Holland—Defeat of the Danish Expedition to Anhalt—Loss of the *St. George, Defence,* and *Hero*—Captain Hoste's Victory off Lissa—Action between Single Ships in 1811—Capture of the *Pomone*—Action off Madagascar—Capture of Java—Frigate Action in 1812-14—Capture of the *Rivoli* and French Frigates—Conclusion of the War 56

CHAPTER IV.

The War with the United States—The *President* and *Little Belt*—*President* and *Belvidera*—The *Guerrière* and *Constitution*—The *Frolic* and *Wasp*—The *Macedonian* and *United States*—The *Java* and *Constitution*—The *Peacock* and *Hornet*—Capture of the *Chesapeake* by the *Shannon*—Loss of the *Dominica* and *Boxer*—Capture of the *Argus*—Boat Attacks in Chesapeake Bay—The Fighting on the Canadian Lakes in 1813—Capture of the *Essex*—the *Epervier* and *Peacock*—Loss of the *Reindeer* and *Avon*—The Expedition to Washington—Captain Gordon at Alexandria—The Attack on Baltimore—The Fighting on the Canadian Lakes in 1814—The Operations near Mobile and on Lake Borgne—Capture of the *President*—Loss of the *Cyane, Levant, Penguin,* and *Nautilus* 97

CHAPTER V.

Biographical Notices of some distinguished Admirals and Captains of the Revolutionary War—Captain John Harvey—His Gallantry and Death in the Action between the *Brunswick* and *Vengeur*—Captain Robert Faulknor—His glorious Death on board the *Blanche*—Captain Richard Bowen—His Career and Death at Teneriffe—Some Account of Sir Andrew Douglas—A brief Notice of Earl Howe—Also of Lord Graves and of Lord Duncan; of Captain Hood, who fell when in command of the *Mars*; and of Captains John Cooke and George Duff, who were slain at Trafalgar 119

CHAPTER VI.

A brief Notice of Lord Nelson's Career—Also of some of the most celebrated Commanders of the British Navy during the War with France: Sir Thomas Troubridge—Captains Hardinge and Lydiard—Lord Gardner—Lord Collingwood—Lord Bridport—Lord Hood—Sir Samuel Hood—Lord Keith—Sir Sydney Smith—Earl Howe—Lord Duncan—Earl St. Vincent—Sir John Louis—Sir John Duckworth—Sir Charles Cotton—Some of Nelson's most famous Captains and other Officers 157

CHAPTER VII.

Lord Exmouth's Victory at Algiers—Details of the Action—Some Particulars of the *Queen Charlotte, Canopus,* and *Implacable*—The Battle of Navarino—Defeat and Destruction of the Turkish Fleet—Anecdotes of the Battle—The Syrian War—Capture of Sidon—Bombardment of Acre 209

CHAPTER VIII.

Expeditions against the Pirates of the Persian Gulf in 1809 and 1819—Capture of Ras-ul-Khymah—Expedition against the Beni-Boo-Ali Arabs—The first Burmese War—Operations on the Irrawaddy—The first Chinese War—Capture of Chusan and the Bogue Forts—The Navy on the Seaboard of China and on the Yang-tse-Kiang—Captain Harry Keppel and the Pirates of Borneo—The second Burmese War—Capture of Rangoon—Other Operations of the War—Forcing of the Parana River in South America—Actions with Slavers—The Persian and New Zealand Wars—A brief Survey of Arctic Exploration—Sir Edward Parry's Voyages towards the North Pole—Sir James Ross's Discoveries in the Arctic and Antarctic Regions—Sir John Franklin—Expeditions in Search of the great Explorer—McClure and the North-West Passage—Collinson's Voyage in the *Enterprise*—McClintock discovers traces of the Franklin Expedition 229

CONTENTS.

CHAPTER IX.

The War with Russia—Expedition to the Black Sea—Bombardment of Odessa—Siege of Sebastopol—The Expedition to Kertch and Yenikale—Commander Lyons, of the *Miranda*—Expedition to Kinburn—Operations in the Baltic—Capture of the Forts of Bomarsund—Commander Lyons at Kola—The Failure at Petropaulovski—The Baltic Fleet in 1855—Bombardment of Sweaborg—The Indian Mutiny—Services of the *Shannon* Brigade at the Relief and Siege of Lucknow—The Indian Navy Detachments serving on Shore 265

CHAPTER X.

The China War of 1856-60—Action at Fatshan Creek—The Operations off the Peiho—Repulse of Admiral Hope before the Taku Forts—The Abyssinian and Ashantee Expeditions—The Naval Brigade in South Africa—The Defence of Ekowe—The War in Egypt—The Seizure of the Suez Canal—The Bombardment of Alexandria—The Naval Brigade at Suakin—The Nile Expedition—Conclusion 277

CHAPTER XI.
(SUPPLEMENTARY.)

The *Matériel* of the British Navy in 1892—England's Responsibilities and the Condition of the Fleet—The Transition from Wooden Ships to Ironclads—British Ships-of-war of the Past and Present—The Guns of our Day—The Naval Defence Act of 1889, and the New Programme of Shipbuilding—The *Royal Sovereign*—Some other Battle Ships—Our Cruisers—Our Torpedo Flotilla—Comparison of British with Foreign Navies—The *Personnel* of the Navy—Our Reserves 311

LIST OF ILLUSTRATIONS.

VOL. III.

	PAGE
LORD NELSON	*Frontispiece*
LOWERING THE ENSIGN AT SUNSET	*Vignette*
THE "VICTORY"	*To face page* 20
"CAPTAIN"	52
A BOARDING PARTY	76
H.M.S. "THRUSH"	100
2ND CLASS PETTY OFFICER	124
AT THE BREECH-LOADING GUN	148
H.M.S. "SPEEDWELL"	172
SIGNALLING	196
LIEUTENANT AND SIGNAL BOY	220
LANDING ORDER	244
H.M.S. "BLENHEIM"	268
SHIP'S COOK	300
H.M.S. "ROYAL SOVEREIGN"	332
ROYAL NAVAL ARTILLERY VOLUNTEERS	340

HER MAJESTY'S NAVY.

CHAPTER I.

Battle of Trafalgar—Nelson's Plan of Battle—Collingwood opens the Attack—The *Victory* engages the *Bucentaure* and *Redoutable*—Lord Nelson is wounded—Details of the part taken by each ship in the Battle—Last Moments of Lord Nelson—The Gale after the Battle—Fate of the Prizes—Obsequies of Nelson—Some account of the services of the *Victory*.

LORD NELSON—having given expression, in his beautiful prayer, to his gratitude to the Almighty for affording him the opportunity of destroying the naval power of France and Spain, thus conducing to the establishment of peace and the safety of his beloved country, and enjoining humanity on the crews of his fleet—disposed of his private affairs, and then, quitting his cabin for the last time, visited all the decks of the *Victory*, and, addressing the men at their quarters, cautioned them to take aim and not throw away a single shot. On his return to the quarter-deck, Captain Blackwood expressed to Nelson the anxiety of his lordship's friends lest his conspicuous dress, with the orders glittering on his breast, might attract the fire of the enemy's sharpshooters, and prayed him to shift his flag to the *Euryalus*, or allow the *Téméraire* to go ahead of the *Victory*. To this he said, with a significant smile to Captain Hardy, "Oh, yes, let her go ahead." But at the same time he had no such intention, and, indeed, hailed Captain Harvey, commanding that ship, to keep his place, nor would he permit a yard of canvas to be shortened.* The *Victory*, therefore, kept her station and led the fleet into battle.

* When the *Téméraire* ranged up on the *Victory's* quarters in order to pass her and lead, Lord Nelson hailed her and speaking, as he always did, with a slight nasal intonation, said, "I'll thank you, Captain Harvey, to keep in your proper station, which is astern of the *Victory*."

The wind was so light, that although the British ships had studding-sails set on both sides, they only made three knots an hour. Apprehensive that the enemy might run for the port of Cadiz, which was about twenty miles on the lee bow, his lordship signalled to Admiral Collingwood, "I intend to pass through the van of the enemy's line, to prevent him from getting into Cadiz." The reversed order of their line having brought the shoals of San Pedro and Trafalgar under the lee of both fleets, the *Victory* made the signal for the British ships to prepare to anchor at the close of the day. Lord Nelson was pacing the deck when he remarked that some signal yet appeared to be wanting, and added, "Suppose we telegraph that 'Nelson expects every man to do his duty.'" Captain Blackwood suggested whether it would not be better to substitute the word England, when Lord Nelson rapturously exclaimed, "Certainly, certainly," and at about 11h. 40m. the signal, so well known to every Englishman, "England expects that every man will do his duty," was hoisted at the mizen-top-gallant-masthead, and was greeted with three cheers by every ship in the fleet.

"Now," said Nelson, "I can do no more. We must trust to the Great Disposer of all events, and the justice of our cause. I thank God for this great opportunity of doing my duty." He now sent the captains of the frigates to their ships, and as Blackwood shook him by the hand on leaving, saying he hoped to come back soon and find him well and in possession of twenty prizes, Nelson replied, "God bless you, Blackwood, I shall never speak to you again."

The British fleet bore down with the wind on the port quarter, in two columns, led by the *Victory* and *Royal Sovereign*, which were about two miles apart, the former having directly ahead of her the *Bucentaure*, Villeneuve's flagship, with the *Santissima Trinidada* as her second, ahead; and Collingwood, with the lee division, bore down on the *Santa Anna*, Vice-Admiral Alava's flagship, while the *Principe de Asturias*, bearing the flag of Admiral Gravina, the Spanish Commander-in-chief, was the rearmost ship of the hostile fleet.

It was just about noon that the *Fougueux*, the second astern of the *Santa Anna*, fired the first gun upon the *Royal Sovereign*, which was considerably ahead of the ships of her division, and thus commenced the action. Immediately the British Admirals hoisted their flags, and every ship, the St. George's, or white, ensign, and in order to prevent confusion in the heat and smoke of battle, a Union Jack at their maintop-mast-stay, and another at their fore-topgallant-stay, while the *Victory* carried at her main-topgallant-mast-head, Nelson's customary signal, "Engage the enemy more closely."

The enemy's fleet replied by hoisting their national colours, and the Admirals their flags.

Soon after noon the *Royal Sovereign*, then close up to the *Santa Anna*, poured into her the whole of her port broadside, the guns being double-shotted, and with such terrible effect, that, as the Spanish officers afterwards acknowledged, nearly 400 of her crew were placed *hors de combat*, and 14 of her guns were disabled. With her starboard broadside, similarly charged, the *Royal Sovereign* raked the *Fougueux*, but owing to the distance, with little effect. It was just as the *Royal Sovereign* was passing between these two ships, that Vice-Admiral Collingwood called out to his captain, "Rotheram, what would Nelson give to be here?" And by a singular coincidence, showing how completely the minds of these two great seamen were in sympathy, Lord Nelson, the moment he saw his friend in his enviable position, exclaimed, "See how that noble fellow, Collingwood, carries his ship into action." Having passed under the stern of the *Santa Anna*, the *Royal Sovereign* put her helm a-starboard and ranged so close alongside of her, that the guns were nearly muzzle to muzzle. But the *Royal Sovereign* soon found that she had more than one opponent to contend with, as the *Fougueux*, having bore up, raked her astern, while ahead, about 400 yards, lay the *San Leandro*, which raked her in that direction, and on her starboard bow and quarter, within less than 300 yards, were the *San Justo* and *Indomptable*. At length, observing that three or four British ships were fast approaching to the support of their gallant leader, the four two-deckers, one by one, drew off from the *Royal Sovereign* and left her to combat solely with the *Santa Anna*. For upwards of fifteen minutes the *Royal Sovereign* was the only British ship in close action, but now the *Belleisle* came up, and firing a broadside into the lee-quarter of the *Santa Anna*, bore away for the *Indomptable*.

Lord Nelson directed the *Victory* to be steered towards the bow of the *Santissima Trinidada*, his old opponent at the battle of St. Vincent, but it was not with the intention of attacking her, as a Spanish Rear-Admiral, whatever the force of his ship, was considered an unworthy object, while a French Vice-Admiral commanded the fleet, and his lordship was of opinion, and the sequel proved that he was correct, that Villeneuve was in one of the two or three ships next astern of the four-decker. Slowly the *Victory*, with studding sails set on both sides, bore down on the enemy's line, Nelson anxiously trying, with his glass to his sound eye, to descry the flag of the French Commander-in-chief, though he could distinguish nothing. It was about twenty minutes past noon that the *Bucentaure* fired her first shot at the *Victory*, but it fell short. A second soon followed, and others in quick succession, the *Bucentaure* having now come within range. As soon as this was perceived, several of the enemy's fleet opened fire upon the *Victory*, which now sustained such a cannonade as few ships have encountered. Still the flagship pursued her way silently, as from her position no guns could be brought to bear, but it was a trying time for the gallant crew, as officers and men began to fall without having the excitement of working the guns to occupy them.

Mr. Scott, the Admiral's secretary, was killed while speaking to Captain Hardy, and as the *Victory* had got within 500 yards of the port beam of the *Bucentaure*, her mizen-topmast was shot away, and her wheel was knocked to pieces, so that the ship had to be steered in the gun-room by the first lieutenant, Mr. Quilliam, and the master, Mr. Atkinson. Now a double-headed shot killed eight marines on the poop, and wounded several others, and so, under this iron hail, the gallant old ship stood bravely on at a rate of speed, owing to the wind having died away, of not more than a knot and a half an hour. Presently a round shot, passing through four hammocks, stowed in the nettings, struck the launch on the booms, and the fore-brace bits on the quarter-deck, and passed between Lord Nelson and Captain Hardy, whose left foot was bruised by a splinter. Doctor Beatty says in his "Narrative," "They both instantly stopped, and were observed by the officers on deck to survey each other with inquiring looks, each supposing the other to be wounded. His lordship then smiled and said, 'This is too warm work, Hardy, to last long,' and declared that through all the battles he had been in, he had never witnessed more cool courage than was displayed by the *Victory's* crew on this occasion."

At this time the ships closed around the *Bucentaure*, and the enemy's line was divided nearly in the centre, fourteen being in the van and nineteen in the rear, with an interval between them of about 1,200 yards. Captain Hardy, thereupon, represented to the Admiral the impossibility of passing through the group of ships around the *Bucentaure*, without running on board one of them, when his lordship quickly replied, "I cannot help it. It does not signify which we run on board of. Go on board which you please. Take your choice."

At length, when 20 men had been killed and 30 wounded, and the studding sail-booms had been shot away, and her sails riddled, the foresail being almost stripped from the yard, the order was given to open fire, as the *Victory* passed under the stern of the *Bucentaure*. The 68-pounders, mounted on the port side of the forecastle, each charged with a round shot and a canister, containing 500 musket balls, were discharged right into the cabin windows of the French flagship, and were followed by the whole broadside of 50 guns, double or treble shotted. So close were the ships at the time that the *Victory's* port main-yard-arm touched the vangs (steadying ropes) of the *Bucentaure's* gaff, and the guns' crews were nearly suffocated by the smoke that blew back into the *Victory's* port holes, while Lord Nelson and others on the quarter-deck were covered with dust from the crumbled woodwork of the *Bucentaure's* stern. As in the case of the *Royal Sovereign*, French officers placed the effect of this tremendous broadside on board Admiral Villeneuve's flagship, as "nearly 400 men" killed and wounded, and 20 guns dismounted.

Close ahead, ready to return the fire which the *Bucentaure* was quite incapacitated from doing, lay the *Neptune*, of 80 guns, and as the *Victory's* bows opened clear of the *Bucentaure's* stern, she poured into her a destructive raking broadside, which caused considerable damage below and aloft, and then setting her jib, ranged ahead in order to prevent the *Victory* falling on board of her. But Captain Hardy had decided to close with the *Redoutable*, which had been firing into the flagship with her foremost guns, and porting his helm, ran foul of the French seventy-four. Presently the *Victory* dropped alongside the *Redoutable*, and her starboard fore-top-mast studding-sail boom-iron hooked in the leech, or outside edge, of the latter's fore-topsail, when the two ships fell off from the wind, the *Victory's* lower deck guns almost touching the side of the *Redoutable*, which had closed most of her lower deck ports. In this position the *Redoutable* used her main-deck guns and musketry from her open ports and her tops on the deck of the *Victory*, which retaliated with her middle and lower deck guns chiefly, and the boatswain cleared the French ship's gangways by discharging the starboard 68-pounder carronade loaded with a heavy charge of canister.

Now happened the sad event which resulted in the death of England's greatest and most cherished hero. Lord Nelson, accompanied by Captain Hardy, was unconcernedly pacing that portion of the quarter-deck, about twenty-one feet in length, bounded abaft by the wheel, and forward by the cabin companion, when just as the pair faced about, the Admiral was seen to fall on his knees with his left hand touching the deck. As the captain of the *Victory* stooped to assist him, the Admiral fell on his left side, exactly on the spot where his secretary had fallen, and, indeed, Mr. Scott's blood dyed his master's uniform.

Eagerly Captain Hardy expressed a hope that his lordship was not severely wounded, but the answer he received must have struck a chill to his brave heart.

"They have done for me at last, Hardy."

"I hope not," rejoined Captain Hardy, encouragingly.

"Yes," said his lordship, "my backbone is shot through."

A musket ball had passed through the left shoulder, and descending, had lodged, as he too truly said, in the spine. The wound was mortal, and the gallant sufferer from the first entertained no illusion on this point. It had been inflicted by one of the small-arm men in the mizen-top of the *Redoutable*, which was only about fifteen yards distant. Under Captain Hardy's instructions, a sergeant of marines and two seamen tenderly bore their revered chief below to the cockpit, where, lying on a midshipman's cot, he was attended to by the surgeon of the *Victory*, Dr. Beatty, who has written a detailed description of the circumstances of the great seaman's death. We will now revert to the incidents of the battle, giving an account of the services of each individual ship.

The *Royal Sovereign* was joined, after fifteen minutes' close action with the *Santa Anna*, by the *Belleisle*, which, after a single broadside, passed on. Lord Collingwood's flagship was closely engaged with the Spanish three-decker, which, at the end of an hour and a quarter, had lost all three masts, and 45 minutes later, at 2.15, the *Santa Anna* struck her colours. Her opponent had suffered to an almost equal extent. At the time of the surrender, the *Royal Sovereign's* mizen-mast went over the side, and soon it was followed by the main-mast, and the foremast was left in a tottering condition, and stripped of most of its rigging. Her loss was one lieutenant, the master, a marine officer, two midshipmen, and 42 seamen and marines killed; and two lieutenants, a marine officer, four midshipmen, a master's mate, the boatswain, and 85 seamen wounded. The *Santa Anna's* loss was much more severe, and among the dangerously wounded was Vice-Admiral Alava.

The *Belleisle* passed through the enemy's line abreast of the *Fougueux*, and pouring a broadside into the *Santa Anna*, and exchanging several with the *Indomptable*, she first engaged, at long range, the *San Juan Nepomucino*, which shot away her main-top-mast, and then entered into close action with the *Fougueux*, which collided with her on the starboard beam. The *Belleisle* soon lost her mizen-mast, but the *Mars* coming up, the *Fougueux* dropped astern. At 1.30 the French *Achille* took up a station on her port quarter, over which the wreck of the mizen-mast lay masking her after guns, and the *Belleisle* also received the distant fire of the *Aigle* and two other ships, so that the British seventy-four had a hot time of it. Thus surrounded, her mainmast was shot away, and fell over the poop and port side, completely disabling her guns. At 2.30 the French *Neptune* placed herself across the starboard bow of the *Belleisle*, and soon her foremast and bowsprit were shot away by the board, and she lay a bare and helpless hulk on the water. But there was no thought of surrender on the part of Captain Hargood and his brave crew, who displayed a Union Jack fastened at the end of a pike, and, at length, between 3.15 and 3.25, the *Polyphemus* interposed between the *Belleisle* and *Neptune*, the *Defiance* took off the fire of the *Aigle*, and the *Swiftsure*, passing close under her stern, the crews cheering each other, engaged the *Achille*, which soon lost her main and mizen topmasts. The *Belleisle* now ceased firing, and Captain Hargood, being close to the Spanish 80-gun ship *Argonauta*, which had surrendered, sent his only remaining boat on board to take possession. In the desperate conflict she had so nobly maintained, the *Belleisle* had two lieutenants, one midshipman, and 30 men killed; and one lieutenant, a marine officer, two master's mates, two midshipmen, and 86 seamen and marines wounded. The ship's hull was battered to a fearful extent. Her three masts and bowsprit were shot away, as also all her boats, except the pinnace, and her figure-head and anchors.

The *Mars*, the ship next astern of the *Belleisle*, suffered severely from the raking fire of four ships, and became engaged with the *Pluton*, while her stern was raked by the *Monarca* and *Algesiras*. Presently the *Tonnant* came to her assistance, and the *Mars*, which had become unmanageable, owing to her damaged condition aloft, fell off before the wind, receiving the fire of the *Fougueux's* starboard broadside and a raking fire from the *Pluton*. At this time a round shot struck Captain Duff, carrying off his head, and throwing his body in the gangway, and also killed two seamen standing behind him. Lieutenant Hennah assumed command, and, soon afterwards, other ships coming to her assistance, the *Mars* was relieved from further molestation by the *Fougueux* and *Pluton* standing off. Besides her captain she had lost a master's mate, two midshipmen, and 25 men killed; and two lieutenants, her master, captain of marines, five midshipmen, and 60 seamen and marines wounded. The *Mars* had her main-top-mast and spanker-boom shot away, all her masts were badly wounded, and the foremast subsequently went over the side, and her hull was much shattered. The *Pluton's* loss was about 300, out of a complement of 700 men.

The *Tonnant*, after assisting by her fire the ships surrounding the *Mars*, ran under the stern of the *Monarca*, into which she poured a raking broadside, and hauled up alongside the Spanish seventy-four, which dropped astern and struck her colours, but soon rehoisted them. The *Tonnant*, which had lost her fore-top-mast and main-yard, porting her helm, ran on board the *Algesiras*, while with her port guns she fired at the *Pluton* and *San Juan*. The battle raged with great fury between the antagonists, locked in deadly embrace, and soon the *Tonnant* had her main and mizen-top masts shot away, and the French seventy-four, her foremast. An attempt made to board the *Tonnant* was frustrated by the fire of her marines, and at 2.15, just as her main and mizen-masts went over the side, the *Algesiras* surrendered. Fifteen minutes later the *San Juan* hailed that she had struck, and a jolly boat, the only one that would float, with an officer and two men, was sent to take possession, but a shot sank her, and Lieutenant Clement and his companions were with difficulty saved. The *Tonnant* lost one midshipman and 25 seamen and marines killed, and among the 50 of all ranks wounded were Captain Tyler (severely) and three other officers. The *Algesiras* had upwards of 200 casualties, among the mortally wounded being Rear-Admiral Magon, who had been previously wounded in two places, but refused to leave the deck.

The *Bellerophon*, following some distance in the wake of the *Tonnant*, crossed the enemy's line under the stern of the *Monarca*, which, having rehoisted her colours after engaging the British 80-gun ship, attacked her on the port bow and the *Aigle* on the starboard, while she also received the fire of three other ships. The *Bellerophon* soon showed the effects of this concentrated cannonade. Within half an hour her main and mizen-top masts were shot away, and the sails caught fire. Captain Cooke was killed, when the command devolved upon Lieutenant Cumby; the master was slain about the same time, and the musketry fire from the *Aigle*, which was near enough for her people to throw hand grenades from the tops, swept the decks of the British seventy-four. Nevertheless all attempts to board were repelled, and the *Bellerophon* remained unconquered when the *Colossus* drew off the fire of three of her opponents, and the *Aigle* dropped astern, and, though unmanageable, she even compelled the *Monarca* for the second time to haul down her colours, when she took possession of the prize. The *Bellerophon* lost, besides her captain and master, one midshipman and 24 men killed, and the captain of marines, one master's mate, four midshipmen, the boatswain, and 116 seamen and marines wounded. The three lower masts and most of the yards were badly wounded, her main and mizen-top masts, and much of her rigging, were shot away, and her hull and decks were much damaged. Her opponents suffered no less severely, the *Aigle* losing nearly two-thirds of her crew, including her captain and first lieutenant among the killed.

The *Colossus*, receiving the fire of two or three of the enemy's ships, was laid alongside the French *Argonaute*, which, after a hot cannonade, managed to clear herself and get away, with a loss, according to French accounts, of about 160 killed and wounded. At this time Captain Morris lost a leg above the knee, but applying a tourniquet, refused to go below. The *Colossus* now engaged the *Swiftsure*, and also the *Bahama*. Soon the former dropped astern, when the British seventy-four devoted her attention solely to the *Bahama*, which surrendered, after losing her main mast. Again the *Colossus* engaged the *Swiftsure*, and brought down her mizen-mast, and as the *Orion*, in passing, gave her a broadside which shot away her main-mast, the French seventy-four surrendered. In hauling up to take possession of her prizes, the *Colossus* carried away her wounded mizen-mast, and during the following night, had to cut away her main-mast, thus leaving her with only the fore-mast, which was shot through in several places. In addition, her hull was shattered, her anchors and three boats were destroyed, and, as in most of the ships, some of her guns were disabled. The *Colossus* lost 40 killed, including her master, and besides her captain, she had two lieutenants, a marine officer, one master's mate, eight midshipmen, the boatswain, and no less than 146 seamen and marines wounded. But she took a striking revenge on her adversaries, as besides the loss inflicted on the *Argonaute*, the *Bahama* and *Swiftsure** had each nearly 400 men placed *hors de combat*, among those killed being the captain of the Spanish seventy-four, and both ships were reduced to the condition of wrecks.

The British *Achille*, sailing close astern of the *Colossus*, engaged the *Montanez* to leeward, and on her sheering off, stood towards the *Belleisle*, then lying totally dismasted and engaged with three of the enemy's ships. But the *Argonauta* barred her passage, and a close action ensued, lasting an hour, when the Spanish 80-gun ship surrendered, but before the *Achille* could take possession, her namesake and the *Berwick* came up, and the latter, interposing between her and the *Argonauta*, a deadly duel commenced between these well-matched opponents. At the end of an hour the British seventy-four triumphed, and the *Berwick* hauled down her colours. The former lost one midshipman and twelve men killed, and two lieutenants, two marine officers, one master's mate, three midshipmen, and 51 men wounded. She had also suffered considerably in her hull, and all her masts and bowsprit, though standing, were much injured by shot. The *Argonauta* is stated to have lost nearly 400 in killed and wounded, including her captain (dangerously), and the French *Achille*, all whose masts were in a

---

* In both the French and British fleets engaged at Trafalgar, were ships bearing the names of *Swiftsure*, *Neptune*, and *Achille*.

tottering state, had 51 killed including her captain, and nearly 200 wounded. We will now deal with the operations of the ships of the weather column, led by the *Victory*, which got into action some time after Lord Collingwood's division.

Lord Nelson received his mortal wound at 1.30, from a musket-ball from the mizen-top of the *Redoutable*, and so destructive was the fire from the ship's tops and deck that within a few minutes, nearly 50 officers and men were shot down on the upper deck, and the guns here were mostly abandoned. But the lower and middle deck batteries were hotly engaged, the port guns firing distantly at the *Bucentaure* and *Santissima Trinidada*, while the starboard guns, charged with three shot, were making great havoc on the decks of the *Redoutable*. "A circumstance in this situation," says Beatty, "showed in a most striking manner the cool intrepidity of the officers and men stationed on the lower deck of the *Victory*. When the guns on this deck were run out, their muzzles came in contact with the *Redoutable*'s side, and, consequently, at every discharge there was reason to fear that she would take fire, and both the *Victory* and *Téméraire* be involved in the flames. Here was seen the astonishing spectacle of the fireman of each gun standing ready with a bucketful of water, which, as soon as the gun was discharged, he dashed into the enemy through the holes made in her side by the shot."

Within a few minutes after Lord Nelson fell, the fire from the *Redoutable* almost cleared the upper deck of the *Victory*, the men still effective being engaged carrying below their wounded shipmates. Encouraged by the apparently defenceless state of the flag-ship, Captain Lucas, the gallant commander of the French seventy-four, directed his men to board her, but Captain Hardy, who, with Captain Adair, of the marines, and one or two officers, still remained on the poop and quarter-deck, called up his men from below, and, after an exchange of musketry, the French seamen abandoned the attempt. In repelling this daring assault, Captain Adair and 18 men were killed, and Lieutenant Ram (mortally) and Midshipman Westphal—who survived to attain high rank and a great age—and 20 men were wounded.*

At this time the hardly-beset *Redoutable* found herself opposed to yet another antagonist.

The *Téméraire* was close in the wake of the *Victory*, and, soon after the latter had raked the *Bucentaure*, opened fire on the *Neptune* and *Redoutable*, and when the flag-ship

---

* Captain Adair was killed by a musket-ball in the neck, and the two wounded officers were struck by a cannon-shot, which, from the oblique direction it took, must have been fired from one of the *Redoutable*'s main-deck guns pointed upwards.

closed with the latter, Captain Harvey hauled up to pass through the enemy's line, receiving so heavy a raking fire from the *Neptune* that his foreyard and maintop-mast were shot away, and his foremast and bowsprit much damaged. The British three-decker continued to bring her port guns to bear on the *Redoutable*, which was still engaged with the *Victory*, and about 1.40, the French seventy-four fell on board the *Téméraire*, whose crew immediately lashed her bowsprit to their main rigging, thus enabling them to pour a raking fire into her. According to the French accounts "the effect of this fire was terrible upon the crew of the *Redoutable*, who were assembled on the forecastle, gangway and quarterdeck. Nearly 200 were placed *hors de combat*. The brave Captain Lucas, although wounded, remained on deck." The fore-shrouds and channels of the *Redoutable* were now in flames, which communicated to the fore-sail of the *Téméraire*, but they were extinguished in both ships by the exertions of the fore-castle men of the three-decker, assisted by the crew of the *Victory*, which also had been on fire in the booms. All resistance having now ceased on board the *Redoutable*, Captain Hardy despatched two midshipmen and a party of men to assist in subduing a fire which had just broken out afresh.

The *Victory* disengaged herself from the French seventy-four about 2.15. Her loss had been heavy while receiving the raking fire of a division of the enemy's ships when bearing down to the scene of battle, and from the cohorns and musketry fire from the *Redoutable's* tops. Besides the Commander-in-chief and his secretary, Captain Adair, and Lieutenant Ram, she had killed two midshipmen, the captain's clerk, 32 seamen and 18 marines. The official account placed the wounded at 59 seamen and nine marines, exclusive of two lieutenants, two marine officers and three midshipmen, but, in addition, says Dr. Beatty, the boastwain and 26 men reported themselves to him as wounded after the returns had been made up. The *Victory* lost her mizen-top-mast, and her fore and main-masts, with all the yards and the bowsprit, were badly injured, and all her running and standing rigging was cut to pieces, and her hull was much damaged.

It is interesting to compare the authentic narrative of the action between the *Victory* and the *Redoutable*, as received in England, with the French official account, written by Captain Lucas, the officer commanding the seventy-four. In many points the writer was incorrect, as in saying that, before the fall of Nelson, the British flagship ceased firing, because she could offer no further resistance. The musketry fire of the *Redoutable* was alone destructive, and she was overmatched by the English three-decker long before the *Téméraire* came alongside, and she surrendered to the boarders from Captain Harvey's ship. Nevertheless, Captain Lucas and his brave crew performed their duty manfully, and Admiral Villeneuve wrote to him:—"Had all the captains acted in like manner to you, the battle would not have been indecisive for an instant, and no one knows this better than myself." After giving an account of the manœuvring of the two fleets before the battle, Captain Lucas says that his proper place in the line was third ship from the admiral, but it seems that the two which should have been in front of him were, either from mismanagement or bad sailing qualities, unable to get into station, and, accordingly, at the last moment he closed up, and, as he puts it, " ordered his bowsprit to be placed on the poop of the *Bucentaure*." He then goes on to say :—

" At half past eleven the enemy's fleet hoisted its colours; those of the *Redoutable* were done in an imposing manner, the drums and fifes playing, and the marines presenting arms as the flags were hoisted. The enemy's column, which was directed against our fleet, was now on the port hand, and the flagship *Bucentaure* began firing. I ordered a number of the chief gunners to mount on the forecastle, told them to notice how many of our ships fired badly, and found that all their shots carried too low. I then commanded them to aim at dismasting, and above all to aim well. At a quarter to twelve the *Redoutable* began to fire with a shot from the first battery, which cut through the foretop-sail yard of the *Victory*, causing it to lay over the fore-mast of the *Redoutable*, whilst shouts of joy resounded in all our batteries. Our firing was well sustained, and in less than ten minutes this same ship was deprived of her mizen-top-mast, fore-topsail, and main topgallant-mast. We kept so close to the *Bucentaure*, that several times they cried to me that I should run her down; in reality the bowsprit of the *Redoutable* touched the crown of her poop slightly, but I assured them they had nothing to fear. The damage done to the *Victory* did not at all change the daring manœuvring of Admiral Nelson, he repeatedly persisting in trying to cut the line in front of the *Redoutable*, and threatening to run us down if we opposed. The proximity of this ship, followed by the *Téméraire*, instead of intimidating our crew, only increased their courage, and to show the English admiral that we did not fear his fouling us, I had the grappling irons hoisted on all the yards. The ship *Victory*, not having succeeded in passing the stern of the French admiral, ran foul of us from stem to stern, and sheered off aft in such a way that our poop lay alongside her quarter-deck. From this position the grappling irons were thrown on board her; those from the stern parted, but those forward held on, **and one** broadside was discharged, which resulted in a horrible slaughter. We continued to fire for some time, though many were delayed in loading our guns, through not being able to bring them to bear on the ports, which were closed by the flank of the *Victory*, but by means of the firearms through the port holes we prevented the enemy loading. At last they ceased firing on us. What a day of glory for the *Redoutable* if she had only had to fight the *Victory!*

"After her batteries, not being able to resist us longer, had at length ceased firing, I had the trumpets sounded, which was the signal to our men for boarding. She gave a similar order, and her officers sprang at the head of their company, as if it was only an exercise. In less than a minute our decks were covered with armed men, who dispersed themselves on the poop, netting and shrouds. Then began a heavy fire of musketry, in which Admiral Nelson fought at the head of his crew. Our firing became so rapid and was so superior to his, that in less than a quarter of an hour we caused that of the *Victory's* to cease. More than two hundred grenades were thrown on board her, the decks were strewn with the dead and wounded, and Admiral Nelson was killed by the firing of our musketry. Very soon after this the topsides of the *Victory* were deserted, and she ceased firing, but it was difficult to board her, because of the motion of the vessel, and the height of the third battery. I, therefore, gave the order to cut the supports of the mainyard, thus to cause it to serve as a bridge. A midshipman and four seamen sprang on board by means of the anchor of the *Victory* and we observed there was no one left in the batteries. At the moment when our men were hastening to follow, the ship *Téméraire*, which had noticed that the *Victory* fought no longer, and that it would be captured without fail, came full sail on our starboard hand, and we were subjected to the full fire of her artillery.

"It is impossible to describe the carnage produced by the murderous broadside of this ship; more than two hundred of our brave men were killed or wounded; I was wounded also at the same time, but not sufficiently to prevent me staying at my post. Not being able to attempt anything at the side of the *Victory*, I ordered the rest of the crew to place themselves promptly in the batteries and fire at the *Téméraire*, from the guns her firing had not dismounted. The order was carried out. By this time we were so damaged, and had so few guns that the *Téméraire* opposed us with great advantage. A short time afterwards another ship, whose name I forget, came and placed herself on the stern of the *Redoutable*, and fired on us at pistol range. In less than half an hour our ship was damaged in such a manner that it looked nothing but a heap of *débris*. In this state the *Téméraire* hailed us to surrender and cease prolonging a useless resistance. I ordered some soldiers who were near me to answer this by firing, which was done with great alacrity. Almost the same moment the masts of the *Redoutable* fell on the English ship, the two topmasts of the *Téméraire* fell on board us, our whole poop was stove in, the rudder, tiller, sternpost, quarter-galleries, and the steering gear were broken into bits, the decks were pierced with the fire of the *Téméraire* and the *Victory*, and all our guns were shattered or dismounted by the broadsides of these ships. In addition to this, one 18-pounder gun of the second battery, and one 32-pounder carronade on the forecastle had burst, and killed and wounded a great many of our men, both sides of the ship, with the port-lids and ledges, were cut to pieces, and four of our pumps were broken, as well as our quarter-deck ladder, which rendered communication between the batteries below and the upper deck very difficult. All our gangways were covered with the dead, buried beneath the *débris*, and a large number of wounded were killed, too, on the main deck.

"Out of the crew of 643 men we had 522 *hors de combat*, of whom 300 were killed, and 222 wounded, nearly all the staff among them. Of the remaining 121, a large number were employed in the hold, and handing powder, so that the batteries and decks were absolutely deserted, and we were unable to offer the least resistance. No one that had not seen the state of the ship *Redoutable*, could ever form an idea of its condition. I know of nothing on board that was not cut to pieces with cannon-shot. In the midst of this terrible slaughter those heroes who had not succumbed to their wounds, cried, " Long live the Emperor! we are not taken yet. Does the Commander still live ?" Our helm about this time took fire, but happily nothing else did, and we succeeded in quickly extinguishing it. The ship *Victory* fought no longer. She occupied herself only with getting clear of the *Redoutable*, but we were cut to pieces by the cross fire of the *Téméraire*, by whom we were still engaged, and by the ship which fired on our stern. Unable to parry it, and not seeing any of our ships, which were all too far to leeward to come to our assistance, I waited no longer to surrender, as the leaks were sufficiently large to ensure our going to the bottom, and as soon as I had satisfied myself of this, I gave the order to strike our flag, and it came down by itself by the fall of the mizen-mast. We were then abandoned by the ship which fired on our poop, but the *Téméraire* continued to fire on us, and did not cease until her men were obliged to do so by having to work at extinguishing the fire which had broken out on their own ship. A short time after, the *Victory* and *Redoutable*, which, with the *Téméraire*, were connected through their masts having fallen across each other, being deprived of the use of their helms, formed a group which drifted at the mercy of the wind and ran foul of the ship *Fougueux* which, having fought against several of the enemy's ships, was abandoned by them without having struck her flag. She was completely unrigged, and no longer capable of being steered, and finding herself boarded by the *Téméraire*, was beyond making any resistance. Nevertheless, her brave captain, Beaudoin, made some efforts to do so, until he was killed in her vain defence, and his second in command being wounded at almost the same moment, some men of the crew of the *Téméraire* jumped on board and took possession."

The remainder of the narrative describes how, after a long struggle to keep her afloat, the *Redoutable* went down so suddenly that a large number of her wounded were drowned.

We have given an account of the doings of the *Téméraire*, the ship next to the *Victory* in the weather division, up to the time when she was lashed to the *Redoutable* on one side, the flag-ship being closely engaged on the other. At this time the *Fougueux*, which, after quitting the *Belleisle*, had stood across the space between the *Santa Anna* and the *Redoutable*, neared the British three-decker, with the object of raking or boarding,* and received, within a range of 100 yards, her full starboard broadside. The effect of this crushing discharge was terrific, and the *Fougueux*, about 2 P.M., ran foul of the *Téméraire*, some of whose men immediately lashed her fore-rigging to one of their ship's anchors. Thereupon Lieutenant Kennedy, accompanied by a party of two officers and 26 men, boarded in the port main rigging, and the French sailors being driven below, the *Fougueux* became the prize of the *Téméraire*. On her quarter-deck were found Captain Beaudoin mortally wounded, and the second captain, who was severely wounded in the brief struggle for mastery. It was at this time that the *Victory* cast off from the *Redoutable*, whose main and mizen-masts came down, the wreck of the latter falling over the poop of the *Téméraire*, and across the spar acting as a bridge, a party of her crew, led by Mr. Wallace, the second lieutenant, made their way on board and quietly took possession.

The *Téméraire* lost a captain and lieutenant of marines, one midshipman, a warrant officer, and 43 seamen and marines killed; and a lieutenant, a marine officer, one master's

---

* French ships carried larger crews than British ships of the same class. Thus the *Téméraire*, though a three-decker, commenced the action with only 600 men, while the *Fougueux*, a 74-gun ship, had a complement of 700.

mate, the boatswain and 71 men wounded. She lost her mizen-mast, main-topmast, foreyard, and fore and main topsail yards, and her fore and main masts and bowsprit were so badly wounded as to be unfit to carry sail. All her rigging was cut to pieces, and among injuries to her hull, eight feet of the starboard side of the lower deck was stove in, and both her quarter galleries carried away when coming into collision with the two French seventy-fours.

Of these, the casualties sustained by the *Redoutable* have already been given in Captain Lucas's official account. She had lost her fore and main masts, bowsprit and fore-topmast from the fire of the three deckers, which she had so gallantly sustained, her rudder was shot away, her hull riddled in every direction, and 20 of her guns were dismounted and one had burst. The *Fougueux* had suffered but little in comparison, only some 40 of all ranks being killed and wounded, including her captain among the former, and her first lieutenant among the latter.

The *Neptune*, next in the British line, became engaged, about 1.45, when she raked the *Bucentaure*, shooting away her main and mizen masts, and committing great havoc on board. Closely following in her wake, the *Leviathan* poured in her fire within 30 yards of the *Bucentaure's* stern, and the *Conqueror* did likewise, and then hauling up on her lee quarter, shot away her fore-mast. Thus fearfully mauled, the French flag-ship, which had been raked by three ships in succession, hauled down her flag, and was taken possession of by a party of five men from the *Conqueror*, under Captain Atcherley, of the marines, to whom Admiral Villeneuve handed his sword as a token of surrender. But considering that this honour should be conceded to Captain Israel Pellew, his commanding officer, Captain Atcherley secured the key of the magazine, which he locked and placed under charge of two marines, taking with him the French Commander-in-chief and his two captains, and pulled to the *Mars*, the *Conqueror* having proceeded in chase, where the French Admiral was received by Lieutenant Hennah, the acting commander, Captain Duff having been killed.

The *Neptune*, after raking the *Bucentaure*, passed under the stern of the *Santissima Trinidada*, raking her also with such effect that her main and mizen masts went by the board. Laying herself alongside the huge Spanish four-decker, the *Neptune* brought down her fore-mast, but her attention was called off by the approach of some of the enemy's van-ships, which, bearing up, raked her with great effect. The dismasted four-decker was not taken possession of until the close of the action, when the *Prince* took her in tow.

The *Neptune* sustained a loss of ten killed, and one officer and 33 men wounded, but her damages aloft were not very severe. The *Conqueror* lost her mizen-topmast and main-top gallant mast, and her fore and main masts and all her rigging were much cut up. Her loss had been only one killed and two officers and seven seamen wounded, but when Admiral Dumanoir's squadron, at the close of the action, hauled to the wind, a round shot killed her first and third lieutenants, Messrs. St. George and Lloyd. The *Bucentaure* was dismasted and much cut up in her hull, and lost upwards of 400 officers and men, including among the latter, Admiral Villeneuve and his flag captain.

The *Leviathan*, standing in close in the wake of the *Neptune*, and ahead of the *Conqueror*, after pouring in a raking broadside into the *Bucentaure* and the *Santissima Trinidada*, stood towards the French *Neptune*, which evaded a conflict, but about 3 o'clock, she found a more worthy antagonist in the *San Augustin*. Captain Bayntun poured a broad into the starboard quarter of the Spanish seventy-four, at a range of less than 50 yards, which brought down her mizen-mast, and ran her on board, the jib-boom catching the British seventy-four's main rigging. The Spaniards were soon driven below by a hot fire from the poop carronades and decks of the *Leviathan*, and the third lieutenant, Mr. Baldwin, boarded at the head of a party of men and carried the ship. The prize was then lashed to the British seventy-four, which soon after received the passing fire of the *Intrépide*. The *Leviathan*, which had only four killed and one midshipman and 21 men wounded, was a good deal cut up aloft in her rigging and spars.

The *Africa*, 64, which, when the action began, was broad on the *Victory's* port-beam, nearly abreast of the van-ships of the enemy's line, exchanged broadsides with the van division, and at 3.20, engaged the *Intrépide* for nearly 45 minutes, when the *Orion* came to her assistance and took off the fire of the French seventy-four, which had almost silenced her. In less than a quarter of an hour the *Orion* shot away her opponent's main and mizen-masts, and about 5 o'clock, on the approach of the *Ajax* and the *Agamemnon*, the *Intrépide* hauled down her colours, having lost nearly 200 in killed and wounded.

The *Orion* lost only one seaman killed, and two midshipmen and 21 men wounded, and had her main-topsail yard and main top-gallant mast shot away. The *Africa*, which was so opportunely succoured, had her three lower masts and bowsprit too badly injured to stand, and her main-topsail yard was shot away, and all her spars and rigging much cut up. Out of 490 men she lost 18 killed, and one lieutenant, the captain of marines, two master's mates, three midshipmen and 47 seamen and marines wounded.

Meantime, obedient to the signal that they were to take part in the action, the ten ships of the enemy's van, not yet closely engaged, about 2.30 were endeavouring to wear or tack, and on completing the manœuvre, one Spanish and four French ships, under Rear-Admiral Dumanoir, hauled their wind on the starboard tack, and the remaining five kept away as though to join Admiral Gravina, then to leeward of the rear, in escaping. The *Britannia, Agamemnon, Orion* and *Ajax* got among the latter division and exchanged broadsides with them, but the only ships that remained to engage were the *Intrépide*, which, as already described, surrendered to the *Orion*, and the *San Augustin*. The *Britannia* had one lieutenant and nine men killed, and her master, one midshipman and 40 men wounded. The *Ajax* had only two killed and nine wounded, and the *Agamemnon* two and eight respectively. None of the three ships suffered very materially below or aloft.

The division, under Admiral Dumanoir, which hauled to the wind, consisting of the *Formidable*, flagship, *Duguay-Trouin, Mont Blanc, Scipion*, and *Neptune*, in making off, passed at a distance the *Victory, Téméraire*, and *Royal Sovereign*, all of which lay almost helpless on the water, while these five ships were practically intact. They exchanged a few distant shots with the *Victory*, and one or two broadsides with " the fighting *Téméraire*," which lay, with her two prizes, the *Redoutable* and *Fougueux*, alongside, but no attempt was made to attack these ships or turn the tide of victory. The *Minotaur* and *Spartiate*, the rearmost ships of the weather column, gave them an opportunity to engage by lying to, and exchanged broadsides with the four foremost ones; and succeeded in cutting off the *Neptune*, 80, which gallantly defended herself for over an hour, and surrendered at 5.10, the last ship to do so, having lost her mizen-mast and fore and main topmasts. In this affair the *Minotaur*, which lost her fore-topsail yard, had three men killed, and her boatswain, one midshipman and 20 wounded. The *Spartiate* had likewise three killed and 20 wounded, including her boatswain and two midshipmen.

The *Dreadnought*, one of the ships of Collingwood's (the lee) division, got into action about 2 o'clock with the *San Juan Nepomucino*, which had been hotly engaged with several ships, and had struck to the *Tonnant*, but got away, and was now supported by two Spanish ships and the *Indomptable*. The *Dreadnought* ran on board the *San Juan*, which hauled down her colours, and passing on, engaged the *Principe de Asturias*, which, however, succeeded in effecting her escape, though Admiral Gravina, the Spanish Commander-in-chief, lost an arm from a round shot and died of the wound. The British ninety-eight lost seven killed, and one lieutenant, two midshipmen and 23 men wounded. The *San Juan* was greatly shattered and had nearly 300 casualties, including her captain, who was mortally wounded.

The British *Swiftsure* succeeded, about 3.30, in bringing the French *Achille* to action, and a running fight ensued, in which the *Polyphemus* took part. At the end of about forty minutes the French seventy-four, having lost her mizen-mast and foreyard, ceased firing. The *Swiftsure* had her mizen-top-mast shot away, and lost nine men killed, and one midshipman and seven men wounded, and the *Polyphemus* had only six casualties.

The *Revenge*, in crossing the bows of the *Aigle*, fouled her jib-boom, and poured a couple of broadsides into her, but when standing on, received the fire of Gravina's flagship, which, assisted by three seventy-fours, all almost fresh ships, continued to fire into her until the *Dreadnought* and *Thunderer* arrived to her assistance, when the three-decker and others made off.

The *Revenge* had been severely handled. Her masts and bowsprit were shot through, and her hull was riddled with cannon shot, while she lost two midshipmen and 26 seamen and marines killed, and her captain, master, one lieutenant, the captain of marines, and 47 men wounded.

The *Defence* got into action with the *Berwick* at 2.30, and, when the latter hauled off, and engaged the *Achille*, to whom she finally surrendered, attacked the *San Ildefonso*, which struck to her at the end of an hour, having lost quite one-third of her crew. The *Defence* had her main-mast shot through and received much damage aloft, besides losing seven men killed and 29 wounded. The *Thunderer*, which came so opportunely to her assistance, when attacked by the *Principe de Asturias*, engaged her and the French *Neptune*, in conjunction with the *Dreadnought*, until they retreated, the Spanish three-decker having lost in her partial engagements with several British ships, a lieutenant and 40 men killed, and 107 wounded, including Admiral Gravina and many officers, while her main and mizen-masts were so much injured that they went over the side. The *Thunderer* suffered but little, and had only four men killed and two officers and ten men wounded.

The *Defiance*, one of the ships that had engaged Gravina's flagship, ran alongside the *Aigle*, which had suffered a good deal in her engagements with five or six other British ships, and attempted to capture her by boarding, but the boarders were driven off. She then took up a station within half pistol shot range, and plied her with her guns until the *Aigle* surrendered. The *Defiance* had her masts shot through and her hull and rigging were much cut up. She had one lieutenant, a midshipman, her boatswain, and 14 men killed, and her captain, two master's mates, two midshipmen, and 48 seamen and marines wounded. The *Aigle*, which had defended herself with gallantry throughout the day against her numerous enemies, lost 270 officers and men killed and wounded, and was much shattered in her hull and aloft.

The *Achille*, which had been engaged in succession with her British namesake, the *Belleisle*, *Swiftsure*, and *Polyphemus*, and lost her mizen-mast, main-top-mast and foreyard, caught fire, when every effort was made by the *Prince*, the last to engage her, and other British ships, to rescue the crew, but the service was a dangerous one, owing to the French ship's guns going off, and about 5.45 the *Achille* blew up, and her gallant captain, who had been wounded, and 500 men, out of 700 forming her crew, perished.

Thus, of the nineteen ships, forming the allied rear, eleven were captured, one was destroyed, and seven escaped. Of the fourteen ships, composing their van division, inclusive of the *Redoutable*, only three were captured in the line of battle, but of the remaining eleven, three were taken after they wore out of the line, and eight only escaped. Of the eighteen lost, half, including the *Achille*, were French ships, and nine French and six Spanish escaped, of which four French got away to the southward, and eleven, five being also of that nationality, all much shattered, with all the frigates and brigs, succeeded in reaching Cadiz. The battle, which commenced about noon, was at its height about 1.30; at 3 the firing began to slacken, and about 5, wholly ceased, with the exception of the *Achille*, her destruction, forty-five minutes later, being the last incident of this memorable engagement, which had such far-reaching consequences.

We will now turn to the cock-pit of the *Victory*, where the life of the hero, to whom is due the credit of this great success for the arms of England, was slowly ebbing away. It was a sad, but sublime, scene that was presented in that dark recess of the lower-most deck, beyond the water-line, whither was borne the sound of the guns booming overhead, which, at any other time, would have been the sweetest music to the ears of the dying seaman, and even now, though painful to his distracted head, brought a fervent expression of thankfulness to his lips.

THE VICTORY
(LAUNCHED 1765.)

After receiving his wound, as he was being carried down the ladder from the middle deck, says Dr. Beatty, in his "Narrative," his lordship observed that the tiller-ropes were not yet replaced, and desired one of the midshipmen stationed there to go up on the quarter-deck and remind Captain Hardy of that circumstance, and request that new ones should be immediately rove. Having delivered this order, he took his handkerchief from his pocket and covered his face with it, that he might be conveyed to the cock-pit at this crisis unnoticed by the crew. An examination of the wound soon showed that it was mortal, and Lord Nelson himself appears, from the first, to have entertained a similar opinion. His sufferings from pain and thirst were manifestly great. He frequently called for drink, and to be fanned with paper, making use of the words: "Fan, fan," "drink, drink." It was about 2.35, or over an hour after Lord Nelson had received his wound, that Captain Hardy found leisure from his anxious duties on deck, to comply with the frequently repeated request of the Admiral, to visit him in the cock-pit.

"They shook hands affectionately," says the surgeon, "and Lord Nelson asked: 'Well, Hardy, how goes the battle? How goes the day with us?

"'Very well, my lord!' replied Captain Hardy, 'we have got twelve or fourteen of the enemy's ships in our possession; but five of their van have tacked, and show an intention of bearing down on the *Victory*. I have therefore called two or three of our fresh ships around us, and have no doubt of giving them a drubbing.'

"'I hope,' said his lordship, 'none of our ships have struck, Hardy.'

"'No, my lord,' replied Hardy, 'there is no fear of that.'

"Lord Nelson then said, 'I am a dead man, Hardy. I am going fast, it will be all over with me soon.'

"Captain Hardy returned to the deck after a few minutes, and soon after, the *Victory* opened her port guns upon Rear-Admiral Dumanoir's squadron passing to windward. The concussion of the firing so affected Lord Nelson, that he called out: 'Oh, *Victory*, *Victory*, how you distract my poor brain!' adding, after a pause, 'How dear is life to all men!' Soon the *Victory* ceased her fire, and after an interval of about fifty minutes from the conclusion of his former visit, Captain Hardy descended a second time to the cock-pit. Lord Nelson and Captain Hardy shook hands again, and while the captain retained his lordship's hand, he congratulated him, even in the arms of death, on his brilliant victory; which, he said, was complete, though he did not know how many of the enemy were captured, as it was impossible to perceive every ship distinctly. He was certain, however, of fourteen or fifteen having surrendered.

"His lordship answered, 'That is well, but I bargained for twenty,' and then emphatically exclaimed, 'anchor, Hardy, anchor!'

"'I suppose, my lord,' said the captain of the *Victory*, 'Admiral Collingwood will now take upon himself the direction of affairs?'

"'Not while I live, I hope, Hardy,' cried the dying admiral, and at the same moment, endeavoured ineffectually to raise himself from the bed. 'No,' added he, 'do you anchor, Hardy.'

"Captain Hardy then said, 'Shall we make the signal, sir?'

"'Yes,' answered his lordship, 'for if I live, I'll anchor.' In about a quarter of an hour after Captain Hardy had quitted the cock-pit, Lord Nelson became speechless, and expired without a struggle or a groan at 4.30 P.M."

Lord Nelson's last articulate words were, "I have done my duty. Thank God for it." What nobler expression—and well justified by his life's history—could come from the lips of a dying man! Thus the hero passed away, with the *Victory's* guns thundering a *requiem* above his head, and the cheers of his men ringing in his ears, as ship after ship struck her colours, and the greatest naval battle recorded in history, not even excepting Salamis, Actium, or Lepanto, was consummated.

Nelson was one of those great spirits to whom the world concedes an undisputed pre-eminence. As Shakespeare stands at the head of poets, and Napoleon of soldiers, so the immortal Nelson remains peerless among sailors. And no voice has yet been raised to deny him the pride of place in his profession which, in the case of the poet, some may claim for Dante or Homer, and in that of the soldier, for Alexander or Hannibal, Cæsar or Wellington. The professional skill and dauntless gallantry that brought him into prominence at St. Vincent, found a grander field for display at the Nile and Copenhagen, and culminated in the last great victory, which left him nothing more to win in his profession. With the Navies of France and Spain annihilated in the remarkable battle which crowned his life, his work was done, and his triumphant death at the moment of victory, was a fitting termination to an unrivalled career.

As soon as Lord Nelson had breathed his last, Captain Hardy sent Lieutenant Hills, in the only remaining boat, to the *Royal Sovereign*, to report to Admiral Collingwood, and shortly afterwards, accompanied by Captain Blackwood, of the

Euryalus, who had arrived on board, proceeded in the frigate's boat to the *Royal Sovereign*, where he acquainted Collingwood with Nelson's dying order that the fleet and prizes, having regard to the danger of a lee-shore in the gale he apprehended, should be brought to an anchor. But the new Commander-in-chief exclaimed, "Why it is the last thing I should have thought of," and refused to entertain the proposal. The result proved the correctness of Lord Nelson's judgment.

The aggregate British loss at Trafalgar was 449 killed and 1,241 wounded, a total of 1,690, of which no less than 1,452 fell to the share of 14 out of the 27 ships engaged. The *Colossus* came first with a loss of 200, then the *Victory*, with 159, of whom the list of killed, 57, was the heaviest in the fleet. The *Bellerophon* came third with only nine less than the flagship; then the *Royal Sovereign*, with 141, followed by the *Belleisle*, with 126, and the *Téméraire*, with 123, of whom 47 were killed, the same number as in Admiral Collingwood's flagship, these two coming after the *Victory* in the number of slain.

The aggregate loss of the allied fleet cannot be correctly indicated beyond the details already given.

At six in the evening of the eventful 21st October, Admiral Collingwood shifted his flag into the *Euryalus*, which took the *Royal Sovereign* in tow, Cape Trafalgar being at this time distant eight miles to the south-eastward. Many of the British ships had lost one or more masts, and few were in a condition to carry sail, while of the 17 prizes, eight were wholly dismasted, and some were in a sinking state. To add to the danger of the situation, night was coming on, the wind began to rise, the shoals of Trafalgar were but a few miles distant, and the ships were in 13 fathoms of water, on a lee-shore. The wind freshened during the night, and during the following day, but through the skill and activity of the British seamen, the 13 prizes that remained under way, four of which were dismasted, having anchored off Cape Trafalgar, were towed to the rendezvous.

The *Redoutable*, being in a sinking state, the *Swiftsure*, which was towing her, about 5 P.M. brought off part of the prize crew and 150 Frenchmen in her boats. Later in the evening she cut adrift the prize, whose stern was under water, and about daybreak on the morning of the 23rd, again sent her boats, which rescued 50 people, making in all 170 saved, including 70 out of the 222 wounded, but the remainder of the men, some hundreds in number, with 18 of the prize crew, went down in the ill-fated ship. The *Fougueux* drifted on to the rocks and was wrecked with the loss of all on board, except about 25 persons, among the drowned being 30 men of the *Téméraire*, her prize crew.

The *Algesiras*, which surrendered to the *Tonnant*, had a prize crew of two officers and 48 men, and owing to the loss of all her masts, her position soon became critical after she parted with the 80-gun ship. The French crew, numbering 600, were secured below the hatches by gratings, but the handful of British seamen were only sufficient to guard the prisoners, and no steps could be taken to jury-rig the prize. Throughout the following day the *Algesiras* drifted on to the rocks at Cape Trafalgar, and in the evening, Lieutenant Bennett felt constrained to release his prisoners to save the ship. They no sooner came on deck than they put the prize crew in confinement, and having rigged up some spars, took the ship into Cadiz, whence the prize crew were returned to Admiral Collingwood by the Governor. The *Buçentaure*, having on board a party of men from the *Conqueror*, drifted towards the shore, and on the following day was wrecked, but all, or the greater portion of those on board her, were saved by the boats of a French frigate, only, however, to meet a watery grave within forty-eight hours.

On the 23rd, a squadron, consisting of the *Pluton, Indomptable, Neptune, Rayo,* and *San Francisco de Asis*, with five frigates and two brigs, put to sea, from Cadiz, with the object of recovering some of the prizes that had been cut adrift by the British ships, and the frigates succeeded in recapturing and taking into port the *Santa Anna* and *Neptuno*. But disaster overtook the combined squadron. On the following day the *Indomptable*, 80, was wrecked on the north-west point of the Bay of Cadiz, and of 1,100 or 1,200 souls on board, including nearly 500, the survivors of the crew of the *Bucentaure*, only 100 are stated to have been saved. The *San Francisco*, which had anchored, parted her cables at the height of the gale, and went ashore, but the greater portion of her crew were saved. The *Rayo*, of 100 guns, anchored off San Lucar, and rolled her masts overboard. Here she was discovered by the *Leviathan*, which took possession of her, and standing on, in company with the *Donegal*, 74, Captain Pulteney Malcolm, from Gibraltar, boarded the *Monarca*. Captain Bayntun, finding the Spanish seventy-four in a sinking state, removed nearly the whole of her men, and all the English prize crew, and it was well he did so as she went ashore during the gale of the ensuing night. The *Rayo* also drove ashore, and of the prize crew of 107 officers and men, put on board by the *Donegal*, 25 were drowned, and the remainder were made prisoners by the Spaniards.

The continuance of the heavy weather determined Admiral Collingwood to destroy some of his prizes, and accordingly, the *Santissima Trinidada* was scuttled and sunk, when 28 of the wounded perished. The *Aigle* drifted into Cadiz Bay on the night of the 25th, and went ashore, but by great exertions, the few remaining prizes, together with the British fleet, of which the *Royal Sovereign* and *Mars* had lost their fore-masts in the gale, were anchored to the westward of San Lucar. Here the *Intrépide* and *San Augustin* were burnt and the *Argonauta* sunk, but the *Berwick* drove ashore and struck on the shoals, when about 200 men perished in her.

If proof were wanting of the seamanlike prevision of Lord Nelson in directing the fleet to anchor at the close of the action, it was afforded by the circumstance that the *Defence*, which, together with her prize, the *San Ildefonso*, anchored the same evening, rode out the gale in safety, and two other prizes, the *Neptune* and *Bahama*, were also preserved by the same means. The fourth and only remaining prize that was saved, the *San Juan Nepomucino*, not having suffered so much aloft in the engagement, weathered the storm. Thus, of the nineteen ships captured, including the *Rayo*, the *Achille* was burnt by accident, fourteen were recaptured, lost, or destroyed, and four only were saved as trophies of the great victory. The loss of life, both during the engagement, which fell chiefly on the fourteen ships most hotly engaged, and after the battle by the wreck of the prizes, was almost unexampled, and the latter exceeded that after Rodney's victory over the Count de Grasse on the 12th April, 1782, when 3,500 perished and one or two prizes only were brought in safety to England. The victory was in every way most honourable to the British Navy, as the allied fleet was more numerous, thirty-three to twenty-seven British, and the aggregate rated number of guns, 2,626 to 2,148, was fully one-sixth in excess.

On the 30th October, Admiral Collingwood was joined by the *Canopus*, 80, *Queen*, 98, and the 74-gun ships, *Spencer* and *Tigre*, which Lord Nelson had detached to Gibraltar, under Admiral Louis, for water, and to escort a convoy up the Mediterranean. The *Victory*, towed by the *Neptune*, arrived on the 28th at Gibraltar, where she found the *Belleisle*, and after a partial refit, the renowned flagship, carrying the body of her late Admiral, preserved in spirits, sailed for England, and cast anchor at Spithead on the 4th of the following month. The body, placed in a coffin made from a fragment of the *Orient*, which blew up at the Nile, was conveyed round to Greenwich, and lay in state for three days in the Painted Hall in the Royal Naval Hospital. On the 9th

January, 1806, the interment took place in St. Paul's with every accessory of pomp, and amid demonstrations of mourning by the entire nation.

> "Let the bell be toll'd,
> And a deeper knell in the heart be knoll'd,
> And the sound of the sorrowing anthem roll'd
> Thro' the dome of the golden cross."

The Prince of Wales, all the King's sons, the Ministers, and a crowd of naval officers stood around the coffin as it was lowered to its resting-place under the dome of the national Cathedral, but the most interesting feature of the ceremony was the presence in the procession of the sailors of the *Victory*, whose grief found vent in tears. It is related that, as the coffin disappeared, they, with one accord, tore his flag, the Union Jack of the *Victory*, to pieces, each one retaining a fragment as a memorial of his beloved commander.

An earldom was conferred on the hero's heir, his brother. Collingwood was made a peer with a pension of £2,000 a year. Rear-Admiral the Earl of Northesk, who, with Collingwood, lies beside his chief in St. Paul's, was made a Knight of the Bath, and Captain Hardy was created a baronet. The first lieutenant of the *Victory*, and of the *Bellerophon* and *Mars*—whose captains had been killed in the action, when these officers assumed command—and also the lieutenants in temporary command of the *Ajax* and *Thunderer*, were promoted to the rank of post-captain, and the second, third, fourth, and flag-lieutenants of the *Victory*, the first and second lieutenants of the *Royal Sovereign* and of the *Britannia*, and one from every other ship, were promoted to the rank of commander.

This was the last great naval battle of the war. Napoleon henceforth gave up all idea of wresting the sovereignty of the seas from this country, and relinquished at the same time his scheme for the invasion of England. Not even could he secure the "six hours'" command of the Channel, which he considered sufficient to ensure the success of his favourite project. The brave seamen, who guarded our native seas, held too strict watch and ward to permit any further attempt to be made on the security of their country, and Nelson did not die in vain, for in his last great fight he shattered beyond recovery the naval power of France and Spain.

Some account of Nelson's famous flagship in his last great fight will fitly conclude our account of Trafalgar. Since the days of Elizabeth, and before the defeat of the Spanish Armada, in 1588, says Lieutenant Wharton, of the Navy, in his "History of the *Victory*," the British Navy has had on its list a ship of that name. The immediate predecessor of the existing *Victory* was a noble three-decker of 110 guns, which, as described in a preceding chapter, was lost in a terrible gale off the Casketts, near Alderney, in 1744, when Admiral Sir John Balchen and over 1,000 men perished, as is chronicled in the marble cenotaph in the north transept of Westminster Abbey. The present *Victory* was launched on May 7th, 1765, at Chatham Dockyard, and was built from the designs of Sir Thomas Slade, then Surveyor of the Navy. Her extreme length is 226½ feet; her beam, 52; and tonnage, 2,162. Her armament in 1778 was :—

Lower deck	30 long 32-pounders
Middle „	30 „ 24 „
Main „	32 „ 12 „
Upper „	12 „ 12 „
Total	104 guns.

Some changes were subsequently made in her armament. In 1793, four 32-pounder carronades were substituted for an equal number of twelves on the upper deck, and six 18-pounder carronades were added on the poop, making her total number of guns 110. These latter were, however, removed, and in 1803 two 68-pounder carronades were placed on the forecastle instead of two 32-pounders. Thus the weight of her broadside at Trafalgar, from 52 guns, was 1,160 pounds, not half that of some of the modern turret-ships.

The *Victory* was first commissioned on March 15th, 1778, when war with France became imminent, by Captain Sir J. Lindsey; and, on May 16th, Admiral the Hon. Augustus Keppel, commanding the Channel fleet, hoisted his flag on board her at Portsmouth. Admiral Keppel sailed from St. Helen's on June 8th, with twenty-one sail-of-the-line and six frigates and sloops, having Sir Robert Harland and Sir Hugh Palliser as his vice-admirals. The *Victory* returned to St. Helen's after her first cruise on June 27th, but Admiral Keppel proceeded to sea on July 19th, with thirty sail-of-the-line, to encounter Count D'Orvilliers, who was cruising off Brest with thirty-two ships and twelve frigates. A partial action ensued on July 27th, when the enemy succeeded in effecting their escape into Brest. Our ships suffered much in their rigging, at which the French seamen chiefly aimed, and the *Victory* had at one time six ships of the enemy firing on her, and was much cut up in hull and aloft. Out of the total of 113 killed and 373 wounded, the *Victory* had 11 and 24 respectively, being the greatest loss sustained by any single ship, with the exception of the *Formidable*. Admiral Keppel returned to port, and again proceeding to sea on August 23rd, anchored at Portsmouth two months later.

On June 16th, in the following year (1779), Sir Charles Hardy hoisted his flag on board the *Victory*, and proceeded to sea with thirty-seven sail, but was forced to return to Spithead as he encountered off Scilly the combined French and Spanish fleets, numbering no less than sixty-seven sail-of-the-line, and thirty frigates. But the enemy effected nothing, and Sir Charles Hardy cruised in the Channel till the end of the year. On his death in May, 1780, Admiral Geary hoisted his flag on board the *Victory*, and sailed early in June for Brest with twenty-nine ships-of-the-line, but owing to the sick-list of the fleet having swelled to 2,500 men, he returned to Spithead in August.

The *Victory* flew in succession the flags of Rear-Admiral Drake, third in command of the Channel fleet, and of Vice-Admiral Parker, and carried the broad pennant of Commodore Elliot, but saw no service until Rear-Admiral Kempenfeldt hoisted his flag as fourth in command of the fleet. In December that gallant officer, while detached with twelve sail and five frigates, intercepted a convoy of French ships carrying troops and stores for Count de Grasse, in the West Indies, and though they were protected by a superior fleet of nineteen sail-of-the-line, he cut off a division of fifteen transports, sunk four frigates, and beat off every attempt of the enemy to recapture his prizes, which he brought into Plymouth. Kempenfeldt shifted his flag in March from the *Victory* to the *Royal George*, and on the 29th the gallant admiral and 900 of his men met the tragic fate immortalised in Cowper's noble lines. At that time the *Victory* lay close to the *Royal George*, at Spithead, and her boats picked up many of the survivors.

Lord Howe, on being appointed to the command of the Channel fleet, selected the *Victory* as his flagship, and sailed on September 11th, 1781, with thirty-six sail-of-the-line and a large convoy of transports, laden with troops and every kind of stores and supplies for the relief of Gibraltar, which was stoutly held by General Elliott against 40,000 men, with a powerful train of artillery, assisted by forty-eight French and Spanish sail-of-the-line and ten floating batteries, carrying 154 of the heaviest ordnance known. The relief achieved, the *Victory* returned to Portsmouth, where she arrived on November 10th, and on the signature of peace with France in the following January, the three-decker was paid off on February 27th, after having been nearly five years in commission.

War being expected with Spain, the *Victory* was commissioned in June, 1790, and carried the flag of Lord Howe, until he transferred it to the *Queen Charlotte*, when Lord Hood succeeded him, but she was paid off in the following year. Lord Hood again selected the *Victory* as his flagship, in May, 1793, soon after the war broke out with France, which was destined to add the most glorious chapter to the naval annals of this country. Lord Hood sailed for the Mediterranean with six two deckers and five frigates, and effecting a junction with Admiral Hotham's division, proceeded to Cadiz and Gibraltar, and thence to Toulon, which was surrendered by the French monarchical party, who were in dread of the Red Republicans, whose sanguinary acts during the Reign of Terror form so terrible a page in the history of the French Revolution. Toulon was occupied by a combined force of British and Spanish troops under the terms of a convention, but the city was soon invested by a powerful army of 40,000 National troops. The seamen from the fleet worked the batteries with indefatigable courage, but the city became untenable, and was abandoned. During these operations the *Victory's* men served in the batteries on shore with conspicuous gallantry, and suffered considerably.

In January, 1794, the *Victory* was nearly lost in a heavy gale, while proceeding to Corsica to assist the Royalists in that island, and the fleet and transports accompanying her were scattered. She participated in the bombardment of Bastia, by the seamen of the fleet, acting as a naval brigade, a success due chiefly to the extraordinary energy and skill of Captain Horatio Nelson, then commanding the *Agamemnon*, to whom Lord Hood confided the arrangements. When the refusal of the British Generals Dundas and D'Aubant to afford military assistance, is taken into consideration, the result achieved by a handful of seamen may be regarded as almost unparalleled. Well might Nelson write:—"When I reflect on what we have achieved, I am all astonishment. I always was of opinion, have ever acted up to it, and never have had any reason to repent it, that one Englishman is equal to three Frenchmen."

The *Victory's* men were also engaged at the siege of Calvi, when Nelson was again to the fore, assisted this time by some troops, under General Stuart. The *Victory* landed seven of her 32-pounders, which were worked in battery by her crew, several of whom were killed and wounded before the town surrendered, after a siege of fifty-one days. In November, Lord Hood proceeded to England in the *Victory*, and after she had been thoroughly refitted, his lordship, whose health had been much impaired, rehoisted his flag in April, but only to haul it down a few days later, when she sailed for the Mediterranean as a "private ship," that is, without an admiral's flag.

Rear-Admiral Man hoisted his flag on board the *Victory* on the 8th July, and during the pursuit of the French fleet off Hyères, her excellent sailing qualities brought her into contact with their rear, while the *Britannia*, Admiral Hotham's flagship, and most of the fleet, were miles astern. On this occasion, assisted by the *Culloden* and *Cumberland*, she captured the *Alcide*, 74, which blew up with nearly all hands, her own loss being only five killed and 16 wounded. In October, 1795, Admiral Man shifted to the *Windsor Castle*, and Vice-Admiral Linzee hoisted his flag on board the *Victory*. Two months later, the new Commander-in-chief, Sir John Jervis, selected her as his flagship, and cruised about between Minorca and Toulon with thirteen sail-of-the-line, watching the French fleet, which would not venture out to sea.

The naval strength of the two powers was changed when, in 1796, Spain joined France against us, and Sir John Jervis found that he had only fifteen sail to cope against the united fleets, amounting to thirty-eight ships-of-the-line. Corsica was evacuated in November, and then Admiral Jervis proceeded to Lisbon. On the 14th February, 1797, the *Victory* carried his flag at the memorable battle off Cape St. Vincent, which gave him his title. On the 28th March, Lord St. Vincent shifted his flag from the *Victory* to the *Ville-de-Paris*, a new three-decker which had arrived with the other ships to reinforce the Mediterranean fleet, and on the following day, the *Victory* sailed, in company with the Admiral, for Cadiz, where Nelson was blockading the Spanish fleet. Here some of her crew participated in the night attacks and bombardment with boats and mortar-vessels, undertaken at Nelson's suggestion, and under his orders. On the approach of winter the fleet returned to Lisbon, and the *Victory* was sent home with the prizes captured on the 17th February, and was paid off at Chatham on the 26th November, after a long and eventful commission of five years.

For two years the gallant old three-decker was employed as a prison hospital ship, but her well-known sailing qualities induced the Admiralty to refit her for sea, and on the declaration of war with France, on the 29th April, 1803, Nelson selected her as his flagship on the Mediterranean station. She was commissioned by Captain Sutton, and, on the 16th May, arrived at Spithead, where his lordship awaited her. She sailed on the 20th, and two days later was off Brest, where Nelson expected to meet Admiral Cornwallis. After waiting for the latter one day, Nelson, who was chafing at the delay, struck his flag on board the *Victory*, and, proceeding on board the *Amphion*, frigate, continued his course for the Mediterranean. The *Victory*, having communicated with Admiral Cornwallis, followed Lord Nelson, and, capturing on her way the *Ambuscade*, formerly an English frigate, anchored at Gibraltar on the 12th June. On the 9th of July she was at Malta, and on the 30th, joined the squadron of five ships off Cape Sicie, where Nelson once more shifted his flag into her, bringing with him Captain Thomas Masterman Hardy, who exchanged with Captain Sutton.

For eighteen months nothing of importance occurred in the history of the *Victory*, she being employed, in conjunction with a squadron, averaging nine sail-of-the-line, in watching the French fleet of eleven ships in Toulon. The three-decker carried the great Admiral's flag at his crowning victory. The news brought by Captain Blackwood, of the *Euryalus*, frigate, on the 2nd September, of the arrival at Cadiz of Admiral Villeneuve, on the 21st August, induced Lord Nelson to offer his services to the Admiralty, and at 8 A.M., on the 15th September, the *Victory*, accompanied by the *Euryalus*, sailed from Portsmouth to the southward. On the 28th she arrived off Cadiz, and on the 21st October took place the great battle in which she played so prominent a part, and had 159 officers and men killed and wounded, including the immortal Admiral, who had so long hoisted his flag on board her.

The *Victory* managed to weather the gale which broke out on the night of the 22nd October, but on the 25th her sails were split, and her position became critical; she was, however, ultimately taken in tow by the *Neptune*, and arrived at Gibraltar. Having been refitted, she sailed on the 3rd November, accompanied by the *Belleisle*, and after a stormy passage, cast anchor at Spithead on the 4th December. From thence she proceeded to Sheerness,* and Lord Nelson's flag, which had been flying half-mast high ever since his death, was now lowered, and the *Victory* went into Chatham, where she was paid off on the 16th January, 1806, and thoroughly refitted.

In 1808, when a fleet of eleven sail was fitted out to assist Sweden against the designs of Russia, Sir James Saumarez hoisted his flag on board the *Victory*, and she sailed for the Baltic in March of that year. Sir Samuel Hood, with three ships, engaged a Russian squadron, and chased them into Rogerswick, and on arriving at this port, the *Victory*, in company with the *Goliath*, silenced a battery, but was unable to prosecute her success, owing to a gale of wind, which drove the British squadron to sea.

* During the passage, Mr. Devis, the painter of the well-known picture of the "Death of Nelson," which is now on board the *Victory*, took portraits of all the personages depicted, and sketched the spot where Nelson died, so that the picture may be regarded as a faithful memorial of that event.

On the approach of winter, Sir James Saumarez proceeded to England, and struck his flag on the 9th December. The *Victory* at once proceeded to Corunna, and assisted in bringing home the army of Sir John Moore.

In April of the following year, Sir James Saumarez rehoisted his flag on board her, and in that year, and again in 1810, resumed command in the Baltic. Cronstadt was blockaded, but the fighting was entirely confined to the gunboats and ships' boats of the squadron, as the Russians, according to the tactics they followed in 1854-5, would not venture out of port.

Early in 1811, the *Victory* was employed in assisting to carry a reinforcement of 6,500 men to Sir Arthur Wellesley, then blockaded at Torres Vedras by Massena, after which she again proceeded to the Baltic, where she was employed as Sir James Saumarez's flagship between the months of April and November, in the years 1811 and 1812. Though the boats and smaller vessels of the squadron were actively employed at Hango Head, in the Gulf of Finland, and at other places, the *Victory* was not engaged. She was paid off in November, 1812, and since that date the historical old three-decker has not left her moorings at Portsmouth.

From the year 1825 to 1869, the *Victory* was the flagship of the Commander-in-chief at Portsmouth, but as, sometimes, as many as 1,500 seamen were berthed in the guard-ship, the admiral's flag was finally struck in that year, and hoisted on board the *Duke of Wellington*, which has more accommodation.

Though she is now kept only as a show ship, under the charge of a boatswain and a few men, on every succeeding anniversary of the day of her chief glory, the noble old ship is decorated with a wreath of laurel at each mast-head. On the Trafalgar day of 1844, Her Majesty, observing the wreaths, visited the ship, and viewed the spot where Nelson fell, and the cockpit in which he died. Very many thousands of his countrymen have made a pilgrimage to this shrine, dedicated to the memory of the man whose chief thought was his country's weal, and his only incentive, "duty." From this retrospect of the services of the *Victory*, it will be seen that she was the favourite flagship of our most famous admirals, from Admiral Keppel in 1778, to Sir James Saumarez in 1812, a selection mostly due to her excellent sailing qualities.

CHAPTER II.

Sir Richard Strachan's Victory over Dumanoir's Squadron—Gallant Defence of the *Arrow* and *Acheron*—Capture of the *Psyche* by the *San Fiorenzo*—Loss of the *Cleopatra* and her Recapture—Lieutenants Yeo at Muros, and Pigot at St. Mary's River—Capture of the *Marengo* and *Belle Poule*—Loss of the *Blanche* and *Calcutta*—Capture of the *Didon* by the *Phœnix*—Sir John Duckworth's Victory off San Domingo—Capture of the *Impétueux* and Fate of Admiral Willaumez's Squadron—Sir Sydney Smith at Naples—Services of the Boats of the *Pique* and *Renommée*—Exploits of Lord Cochrane—Loss of the Indiaman *Warren Hastings*—The *Blanche* and *Guerrière*—Services of the Navy on the Coast of Cuba—Capture of French Frigates by Sir Samuel Hood's Squadron—Surrender of Cape Town—The Expedition to the La Plata—Capture of Copenhagen—Admiral Duckworth in the Dardanelles—The Abortive Expedition to Egypt—Captain Brisbane at Curaçoa—Capture of the *Lynx* by the Boats of the *Galatea*—Repulse of the Boats of the *Spartan*—The *Weasel* off Corfu—The *Windsor Castle* Packet and the French Privateers.

A FEW days after the battle of Trafalgar, Admiral Rosilly arrived at Cadiz to supersede Villeneuve in the command, but he found only four disabled ships, besides the *Hero*, 74, in which he hoisted his flag. Four other ships, the *Formidable*, 80, and the seventy-fours *Mont Blanc*, *Scipion* and *Duguay-Trouin*, under the command of Rear-admiral Dumanoir, stood for Rochefort, when, on the 2nd November, in the latitude of Cape Finisterre, they fell in with the *Phœnix*, 32, Captain Baker. This officer commenced firing guns to attract the attention of a squadron, under Sir Richard Strachan, cruising here to intercept the Rochefort squadron of five sail, under Admiral Allemand, which, since its escape in July, had been committing great depredations on British commerce. The following were the ships in question, excluding the *Bellona*, 74, which parted company and took no part in the succeeding action.

80		*Cæsar*	.	Captain Sir Richard Strachan.
		Hero	.	,, Hon. Alan Gardner.
74	{	*Namur*	.	,, Lawrence Halsted.
		Courageux	.	,, Richard Lee.
36		*Santa Margarita*	.	,, William Rathbone.
32		*Æolus*	.	,, Lord William Fitzroy.
38		*Révolutionnaire*	.	,, Hon. Henry Hotham.

An animated chase ensued, but the *Phœnix* and *Santa Margarita* so harassed the enemy that, at noon of the 4th, Dumanoir, finding an action unavoidable, hauled up and awaited his persistent enemy. The *Cæsar* began the engagement by opening fire on the *Formidable*, and the *Hero* and *Courageux* attacked the *Mont Blanc*, the *Namur* being stil ten miles astern. A running action now ensued, and the *Duguay-Trouin*, in the van, received a destructive fire from the *Cæsar* and *Hero*. The latter, about two, again came up and engaged the *Scipion*, whose main-topmast she shot away, when the French seventy-four dropped to leeward, where she was engaged by the *Courageux* and the frigates *Phœnix* and *Révolutionnaire*. The *Hero*, pushing on, engaged the *Formidable* until the *Namur* came up, when she made sail after the *Mont Blanc*. At three o'clock the French flagship, being much shattered, and the *Cæsar*, which had repaired damages, having taken up a position to attack her, hauled down her colours, when the *Namur* took possession. A few minutes later the *Scipion* also surrendered. The *Duguay-Trouin* and *Mont Blanc* made sail to escape, but were overhauled by the *Cæsar* and *Hero*, and, after twenty minutes' close action, the former surrendered to the *Hero*, which had played the most prominent part in the action.

The British loss was 24 killed and 111 wounded, of which Admiral Strachan's flagship had four killed and 25 wounded, and the *Hero*, a marine officer and nine men killed, and three officers and 48 men wounded. Both these ships received considerable damage in their hulls, while the *Cæsar* lost her main-topgallant-mast, and the *Hero*, her fore-topsail-yard. The French loss, which was very heavy, was placed at 730. The *Formidable* had 200 killed and wounded, including the admiral among the latter; the *Scipion* the same number, her captain being wounded; the *Mont Blanc* had 180 casualties and the *Duguay-Trouin* 150, including her captain wounded. All the squadron were so greatly shattered aloft by the deadly and accurate British fire that, soon after the conclusion of the action, the only masts left standing were the foremasts of the *Formidable* and *Mont Blanc*. Thus it happened that, out of the eighteen French sail-of-the-line present at Trafalgar, only five, now blockaded in Spanish ports, were left.

The fate that befell the unfortunate Villeneuve was wrapt in mystery. On obtaining his release on parole, he returned to France, to meet the wrath of an incensed Emperor, and was found stabbed to death in his bed, but whether by his own hand or other agency was never cleared up. The four captured ships were added to the British Navy, when the *Formidable* was renamed the *Brave*, and the *Duguay-Trouin*, the *Implacable*, but the latter and the *Scipion* were the only ships that went to sea. Sir Richard Strachan was invested with the ribbon of the Bath, the first lieutenants of the squadron were promoted, and all the officers and crew received the thanks of Parliament.

During the year 1805, in which all other naval events are overshadowed by the great victory at Trafalgar, some frigate actions and others occurred which merit brief chronicle. The sloop-of-war, *Arrow*, of 28 guns and 125 men, and the *Acheron*, bomb-ship, of eight guns, beside her two bombs, and a crew of 67 all told, when convoying thirty-four sail of merchantmen from Malta, encountered, and were engaged by, the frigates *Hortense*, of 48 guns and 350 men, and *Incorruptible* of 42 guns, and 640 men, including troops. The British ships did their utmost to protect their convoy, of whom thirty-one escaped, but after a long and spirited action, continued on the following day, were compelled to strike, the *Arrow* having had 40 casualties, including 13 killed, and the *Acheron* 11. In proof of the determined resistance they made, the *Arrow* sank at the termination of the action, and the *Acheron* was so shattered that her captors burnt her.

A spirited action was fought, with a more favourable result, off Barbados, between the British 16-gun brig *Curieux*, Commander Bettesworth, and the privateer *Dame Ernouf*, of the same force, in which the latter was compelled to haul down her colours, after losing 30 killed and 40 wounded out of 120 men, more than one-half her crew, and the brig five and four respectively, among the former being an officer, and the latter included the captain, who received a musket-ball in the head.

A furious action at short range was fought in the East Indies between the *San Fiorenzo*, Captain Henry Lambert, mounting 42 guns, and the *Psyche*, carrying 36 guns. The fight lasted from eight in the evening to midnight, when the *Psyche* surrendered, having lost her second captain, with her lieutenants, and no less than 54 men killed and 70 wounded, out of 240 forming her crew. The *San Fiorenzo*, which was of slightly superior force, with a complement of 253 men, had 12 killed and 36 wounded, so that the engagement was of a specially sanguinary character, and Captain Bergeret, the same officer who had engaged the *Wilhelmina*, is entitled to the highest honour for his stubborn defence of his ship.

The advantage as regards force was on the side of the enemy during the duel, fought in the West Indies, between the *Cleopatra*, 38, Sir Richard Laurie, and the *Ville-de-Milan*, 46. The two ships kept up a running fire under a strong wind and heavy sea for some hours, and the *Cleopatra* was getting the best of the fight, when an unlucky shot jammed her wheel, so that she became unmanageable. The French frigate thereupon bore up, and striking her about the quarter-deck, attempted to board. But her men were repulsed, when they brought so heavy a musketry fire to bear upon her decks that they cleared them, and soon after five, the action having lasted nearly three hours, the captain of the *Cleopatra*, which was greatly shattered in her hull and rigging, hauled down her colours. Out of only 200 men, mustered at their quarters, the British frigate had 20 killed, and her three lieutenants, master, marine officer, one midshipman and boatswain, and 30 seamen and marines, wounded, two mortally. The loss of the *Ville-de-Milan*, which had 350 men on board, was not ascertained, but her commander, Captain Renaud, was killed, and the second captain was severely wounded.

But the officers and crew of the French frigate did not long enjoy their prize, as, a few days later, the 50-gun frigate, *Leander*, Captain Talbot, hove in sight, and the *Cleopatra* and her captor, after a show of resistance and an attempt to escape, were fain to surrender in succession, their crippled condition, under jury-masts, rendering resistance and flight alike impossible. The prize was taken into the service under the name of *Milan*, and the command bestowed on Sir Robert Laurie, while his first lieutenant, Mr. Balfour, was promoted.

Worthy of mention was the action between the sloop *Reindeer*, of 18 guns and 121 men, Commander Coghlan, and the *General Ernouf* (formerly the British sloop *Lily*), having 20 guns and a crew of 160 men, if only for the tragic fate that befel her. After an action within pistol-shot range the privateer blew up, when only 55 men were picked up, floating on fragments of wreck. Captain Coghlan was the same gallant officer who, some years before, had performed an almost unexampled feat of successful daring in cutting out the 10-gun cutter *Viper*, having a crew of 87 men, at the head of only 21 British officers and seamen. It has been said that on this occasion the French captain hailed the *Reindeer* in English, demanding that she should strike, when Coghlan replied "that he would strike, and d——d hard too."

Lieutenant Oliver, of the *Bacchante*, landed with a party of about 35 men on the coast of Cuba, near Havannah, and in the most gallant manner, in open day, escaladed and carried a tower garrisoned by 30 Spanish soldiers, on which were mounted three long 24-pounders. A tender of the *Hercules* also performed good service off Saint-Domingo, and, forcing on shore, set on fire, after a spirited action, a Spanish schooner of seven guns and 96 men.

Many other brilliant affairs took place at this time in the West Indies, in which Spanish vessels were cut out; and on the coast of Spain, off Muros, Lieutenant Yeo, of the 38-gun frigate *Loire*, Captain Lewis Maitland, greatly distinguished himself by an act of conspicuous daring. While the frigate engaged a fort, mounting 12 long 18-pounders, he landed with 50 officers and men, and finding an outer gate open, dashed into the works, and after a severe hand-to-hand conflict, during which the lieutenant killed the governor, the garrison, consisting of 22 Spanish soldiers and about 100 of the crew of the French privateer *Confiance*, at anchor in the harbour, fled in confusion, when the British colours were hoisted on the fort, which was blown up. This was an achievement of which too much cannot be said in praise, but the gallant Yeo, with the modesty that generally characterises the brave, made no mention in his report to Captain Maitland of an act of individual prowess. The privateer, mounting 24 guns, and another smaller one were taken quiet possession of, and the *Confiance*, on being brought to England, was commissioned by Lieutenant Yeo, with the rank of commander.

Lieutenant Pigot did good service on the coast of Florida, with the boats of his ship, the *Cambrian*, capturing a Spanish privateer schooner of 14 guns and 60 men, after a short resistance, and the frigate also took a French privateer, mounting 10 guns and a crew of 90 men, in charge of which Mr. Pigot was placed. This officer proceeded two miles up the St. Mary's River, and, in the teeth of a hot fire, recaptured an English merchant-ship, having a prize crew of 50 men, and took a privateer of six guns and 70 men. In this service Lieutenant Pigot received three musket-balls, and lost two men killed and 13 wounded, including two officers. For his gallantry Mr. Pigot was deservedly promoted.

An unfortunate occurrence took place in the loss of the *Blanche*, Captain Mudge, to a French squadron between Jamaica and Barbados. The British frigate, carrying 44 guns and a crew of only 215 men, was overhauled by the *Topaze*, of the same force but having 340 men on board, two 20-gun corvettes, and a 16-gun brig, and after an engagement lasting two hours, Captain Mudge struck his colours. The *Blanche* lost eight killed and 15 wounded, and was stated by her captain to have become "a perfect wreck" at the close of the action, when she had eight feet of water in her hold, and it is certain a few hours later she went down. But Commander Baudin did not reach France, whither he was bound, in safety with his prisoners, who were distributed among the ships of the squadron. About 200 leagues from Rochefort the *Camilla*, 20, Commander Taylor, discovered the brig *Faune*, which was captured and taken to England, together with 22 of the *Blanche's* crew she had on board. The *Goliath*, 74, Captain Barton, in company with the *Raisonable*, 64, Captain Josias Rowley, on the following day, the 15th August, sighted the *Topaze* and two corvettes, which separated, and one succeeded in effecting her escape, but the *Torche* was captured, having on board 52 of the crew of the British frigate. The *Raisonable* chased the *Topaze*, and exchanged some shots with her, but she succeeded in making her escape to Lisbon.

Here Captain Mudge was released, and on his return to England, was tried by a court-martial and honourably acquitted of all blame.

On the 16th July, 1805, the Rochefort squadron, consisting of five sail-of-the-line, one of 120 guns, and three frigates, under Rear-Admiral Allemand, put to sea, with the object of intercepting the *Illustrious*, 74, which was convoying a fleet of 200 merchantmen from the West Indies. Two days later she captured the *Ranger*, 18, Commander Coote, and fell in with the *Calcutta*, 56, Captain Woodriff, having in charge a few ships bound from the East Indies to Europe. The *Calcutta*, which had been successfully engaged earlier in the day with the *Armide*, a French 40-gun frigate, one of the Rochefort squadron, finding herself near the *Magnanime*, 74, endeavoured to disable her as the only chance of escape. But the superior fire of the French seventy-four completely unrigged her, and on the approach of the other ships, Captain Woodriff hauled down his colours. The *Calcutta*, which was formerly an Indiaman, carried a crew of 343 men and boys, of whom six were killed and six wounded. By her meritorious defence she enabled the *Illustrious* and her convoy to effect their escape.

In the East Indies, Admiral Linois, with the *Marengo*, 80, after his brush with the *Centurion*, in Vizagapatam Roads, accompanied by the *Belle Poule*, 40, had a partial engagement with the *Blenheim*, 74, flagship of Sir Thomas Troubridge, who had been sent to supersede Sir Edward Pellew in the command to the eastward of Ceylon, and had at this time a convoy in company. The gallant Troubridge succeeded in beating off the enemy, when Admiral Linois steered for Simon's Bay, quitting which on the 10th November, he cruised with his squadron (now reduced to the *Marengo* and *Belle Poule*, the *Atalante* having been lost) along the African coast near Cape Lopez and Prince's Island, whence he made sail for St. Helena. From this island he steered for France, and in March, 1806, just three years after quitting Brest for his memorable cruise in the East Indies, was unlucky enough, when near this haven of safety, to encounter the squadron of Sir John Borlase Warren, consisting of the *Foudroyant*, 80, flagship, the *London*, 98, Sir Harry Neale, and the 38-gun frigate *Amazon*, Captain William Parker. The *London* quickly overhauled and got alongside the *Marengo*, which, however, managed to shake off her formidable antagonist and made sail to escape. The *London* a second time overtook Admiral Linois's flagship, which, after a running fight of a few hours, struck her colours, having experienced a loss in the action, out of a crew of 740, of two officers and 61 men killed, and 82 wounded, including the admiral and his son, and the captain (all severely). The loss of the *London* was one midshipman and nine men killed, and 22 wounded, including two officers. The broadside weight of metal of these two ships was not so unequal as to deprive the British three-decker of credit, being 958 and 907 pounds respectively. About the same time the *Belle Poule* surrendered to the *Amazon*, having lost six killed and 24 wounded.

In the Philippine Islands the British frigate *Phaeton* and brig *Harrier* engaged the *Sémillante*, the only remaining one of Admiral Linois's ships now in the East Indies, which lay under the protection of a battery near Manilla, and the brig suffered considerably in her rigging, while the *Sémillante* lost, it was said, 13 killed and 36 wounded.

An action, displaying some of the best qualities of British seamen at this time—good gunnery, discipline, and smart seamanship—took place near Cape Finisterre on the 10th August, between the *Phœnix*, Captain Baker, of 42 guns and 245 men, and the French frigate *Didon*, carrying 46 guns and having a crew of 330. The *Didon*, confident of success from her superior strength, began the action at 8.45, and after much manœuvring and broadside firing and mutual raking, the two ships came in contact. The crew of the *Didon* attempted to board, but were beaten back, and Captain Baker, with much difficulty and at some sacrifice of life, owing to the fire of the French marines, directed into his stern windows, at length succeeded in transporting a main-deck gun and placing it in the cabin window next the quarter. By the first discharge no less than 24 of the crew of the *Didon* were placed *hors de combat*, as its fire swept the ship's deck from the starboard bow to the port quarter. Meanwhile the enemy's musketry fire was kept under by the marines of the *Phœnix*, stationed on the gangway. At length the two ships parted, and, after engaging in a heavy cannonade with their yard-arms touching, separated to repair damages. The sails of both the combatants hung in ribbons, and the *Phœnix* had lost her main-topsail-yard and gaff, while the *Didon's* main-topmast had been shot away, and as she lay repairing, her foremast went over the side. About noon the British frigate, having finished refitting, made sail and took up a position on her adversary's weather bow, when the latter struck her colours. She had lost 27 killed, including her second captain, and 44 severely wounded, while her successful antagonist had 12 killed, including the second lieutenant and a master's mate, and 28 wounded, among whom were a marine officer and two midshipmen.* The prize, whose mainmast had followed the foremast, was towed into

---

* One of these youngsters was in the act of sucking an orange, when a musket-ball, after passing through the head of a seaman, perforated both cheeks, without injuring a tooth.

Plymouth, but on the way twice narrowly escaped recapture from a French fleet. The action reflected great distinction on the officers and crew of the British frigate, but for some reason, Captain Baker only received the distinction of the Bath ten years later, when that Order was enlarged after the peace.

Before the close of the year 1805, the *Cyane* (late a British ship), of 26 guns and 190 men, was recaptured, after a gallant resistance, by the 36-gun frigate *Princess Charlotte*, Captain Tobin, to which, having been disguised as a merchantman, she had given chase; and the *Libre*, of 40 guns and 280 men, was taken by the British frigates *Loire* and *Egyptienne*, after a spirited resistance, in which she lost 20 men and all three masts.

For the year 1806 Parliament voted 120,000 seamen and marines. In January, in consequence of the receipt of intelligence that eleven sail-of-the-line and four frigates had escaped from Brest, two British squadrons put to sea, one of seven ships, under Vice-Admiral Sir John Borlase Warren, and the other of six, under Sir Richard Strachan, who was ordered to proceed to the Cape of Good Hope to reinforce an expedition sent to effect the reduction of that important Dutch settlement. In the preceding December the *Arethusa*, 38, Captain Charles Brisbane, sighted two French squadrons, the French fleet having been broken up the better to prey on British commerce in the West Indies and elsewhere, and soon after fell in with a squadron of six sail-of-the-line and two frigates, commanded by Vice-Admiral Sir John Duckworth, who had been to Teneriffe and as far south as the Cape de Verde Islands in quest of Admiral Allemand's squadron of five sail, which had captured the *Calcutta*. Duckworth descried Admiral Willaumez's squadron of six line-of-battle ships and two frigates, and gave chase, which, however, he discontinued at the end of thirty hours, when the *Superb*, flagship, commanded by Captain Goodwin Keats, whose brilliant services we have often described, was almost in a position to bring the enemy's rearmost ships to action. The British admiral detached the *Powerful*, 74, to reinforce Sir Edward Pellew in the East Indies, and, steering for the West Indies, on the 12th January, anchored at Barbados.

Acting on intelligence, on the 1st February, Admiral Duckworth set sail for the city of Saint Domingo, accompanied by the *Northumberland*, 74, flagship of Rear-Admiral Hon. Alexander Cochrane, and the *Atlas*, Captain Pym, of the same force, and found at anchor a French squadron of five sail-of-the-line and one frigate, part of the Brest fleet, under Rear-admiral Leissegues. The latter slipped his cables and stood out to sea, when a running engagement ensued. The *Spencer*, Captain Hon. Robert Stopford, succeeded in bringing the *Alexandre*, 80, to close action, while the remaining ships continued their course. The *Alexandre* received the fire of the *Canopus*, 80, Rear-Admiral Louis, and the *Donegal*, 74, Captain Pulteney Malcolm, as they crossed her bows, when all her masts went by the board, and she hauled down her flag. Meantime the *Northumberland* and *Superb* engaged the three-decker *Imperial*, flagship, and the *Donegal*, having received the submission of the *Canopus*, turned her attention to the *Brave*, 74. The *Atlas* attacked the *Jupiter* of the same force, until Captain Malcolm, again disengaged, ran her on board, receiving her bowsprit over his port quarter, where it was secured by a hawser. Thereupon the *Jupiter* surrendered, and the *Donegal*, sending on board a prize crew, took her in tow, while the *Acasta*, frigate, took possession of the *Brave*. The *Atlas*, after engaging the *Jupiter*, proceeded to aid the admiral in the attack on the *Imperial* and *Diomède*, 74, alongside of which she dropped and closely engaged until the *Spencer* came to her assistance. The great three-decker was chiefly engaged with the *Northumberland*, which lost her mainmast, aided by the fire of the *Superb*, and at a later period of the *Canopus*, but she managed to escape from her foes, but only to run ashore when her only remaining mast went by the board. The *Superb* now joined the *Atlas* in engaging the *Diomède*, which soon after ran aground, when all her masts went over the side.

Thus, within two hours, the five ships composing the French squadron were all captured or driven ashore, but the frigate and a corvette escaped. The *Imperial* was considered the finest man-of-war afloat, and carried at this time 130 guns with no less than 1,200 men, while the aggregate strength of the French crews was placed at 4,260. The British loss was 74 killed, of which the *Northumberland* contributed 21, including one midshipman, the *Spencer*, 18, and the *Donegal*, 12, of whom one was a midshipman. The wounded numbered 246, the *Northumberland* coming first with 79, including eight officers, the *Superb* having 56, including eight officers, the *Spencer*, 50, among whom were her captain and three officers, and the *Donegal*, 33, of whom four were officers.

The French losses, on the other hand, were severe, and according to a letter from Sir John Duckworth, the *Alexandre* had 300 casualties, the *Brave*, 260, and the *Jupiter*, 200. The losses of the *Imperial* and *Diomède* were not stated by the British admiral, but by French accounts the three-decker had 500 killed and wounded, including among the severely wounded the first and second captains. The *Diomède* was said to have had 250 of her men *hors de combat*. The crews of these ships, with the exception of about 150 from the *Diomède*, managed to effect their escape to the shore, and the British frigates succeeded in setting on fire and destroying both ships as they lay on the rocks. The *Alexandre* was dismasted and was so riddled with shot as to be only kept afloat with difficulty.

The victory off Saint Domingo was creditable to the British crews engaged, though obtained by a slightly superior force. Of the seven ships of the former, the *Agamemnon*, Nelson's old ship, now commanded by his friend, Sir Edward Berry, was a small sixty-four, while the five ships of the enemy included a man-of-war that was equal in strength to any two of those opposed to her. The thanks of Parliament was voted to the victors, and the usual promotions took place, while Admiral Cochrane, who had so gallantly closed with the three-decker, received the Bath, and Admiral Louis was created a baronet.

Meanwhile Admiral Willaumez, one of whose ships, the *Veteran*, was commanded by Prince Jerome Buonaparte, arrived with his squadron off Cape Town, which he found in the hands of the English, when he stood for the South American coast, and thence made his way to the West Indies, where his chief anxiety appeared to be to avoid an engagement with Sir Alexander Cochrane's squadron, while himself preying on British commerce. Off the Bahamas Prince Jerome quitted the quadrons without leave and sailed for France, which he reached in safety, having on the way captured six merchantmen, and been chased by a British squadron, which he, or rather the capable officer in charge of him and his ship, managed to elude. Prince Jerome as a naval officer was a failure, not less conspicuous than he later proved himself to be as King of Westphalia, and when commanding the division at Waterloo which attacked Hougoumont. Willaumez now stood for the coast of Newfoundland, but was overtaken by a violent gale, when all his ships were dismasted and scattered, and his flagship, the *Foudroyant*, 80, steered for Havannah, off which he engaged and drove off the British 44-gun frigate *Anson*, Captain Lydiard. The *Foudroyant* was refitted at this Spanish port, and Admiral Willaumez, setting sail, succeeded in reaching Brest in safety. Sir Richard Strachan, who had been sent in pursuit of him, returned to Plymouth, but again set sail for the West Indies in search of the French admiral, and on the 14th September, the seventy-fours *Belleisle* and *Bellona*, and the frigate *Melampus*, sighted the dismasted 74-gun ship *Impétueux*, off Cape Henry, on the coast of the United States, which ran herself on shore, and hauled down her colours. She was taken possession of by the frigate, and, after her crew were removed, was burnt. Two others of the disabled French ships, the *Patriote* and *Eole*, reached Annapolis, whence the former managed to effect her escape to France, but the *Eole* was broken up, as was also the *Valeureuse*, frigate. The *Cassard*, 74, stood for Rochefort, which she reached in safety, and thus, including the *Veteran, Foudroyant*, and *Patriote*, four ships of this squadron returned to France, and three failed to do so.

During the summer of 1806 all the five ships-of-the-line at Cadiz, under Admiral Rosilly, were ready for sea, with six Spanish ships, which were blockaded by Lord Collingwood, but some French frigates succeeded in escaping from that port, though an 18-gun brig, accompanying them, was chased and captured by the 38-gun frigate *Hydra*, Captain Mundy, without their firing a shot in aid, so anxious were they to evade the British squadron. Lord St. Vincent had succeeded to the command of the Channel Fleet, superseding Admiral Cornwallis, and the Mediterranean was clear of the French flag, though its European shores were overrun by Napoleon's armies, and, in January, King Ferdinand of Naples, for the second time, was forced to take refuge on board a British ship-of-war, and was conveyed in the *Excellent*, 74, to Palermo. Before the end of March General Massena was in possession of the whole kingdom of Naples except Gaeta, the defence of which was assisted by a British squadron, under that able and indefatigable officer, Sir Sydney Smith, who landed and succeeded in capturing the island of Capri, off Naples.

It was owing to Sir Sydney's persuasion that General Stuart, commanding the British troops in Sicily, was induced to invade Calabria, on the 1st July, with 4,800 men, at the head of whom, two days later, he totally defeated General Regnier at the battle of Maida, one of the most complete and brilliant victories gained up to that time by British arms. The result to the French was the loss of all the forts along the coast, and their evacuation of Calabria, but the success was ephemeral, and after the fall of Gaeta, the whole of that province was recovered, with the exception of Scylla, which was held by a British garrison, and with the town of Messina, on the opposite side of Faro, gave them the command of the Straits.

Numerous were the acts of gallantry of British officers and men wherever they met the enemy, among them the cutting out of the *Raposa*, of 12 guns and 75 men, off Campeachy, by the boats of the *Franchise*, frigate, under the command of Lieutenant Fleming; and of three luggers in the port of Avillas by the boats of the armed brig, *Colpoys*, under Lieutenant Usher.

The *Pique*, 36, Captain Ross, performed some good service in the West Indies, but not without sustaining considerable loss. She sighted and brought to action two French brigs, and fell foul of one of them, when she threw a party of four officers and 25 men on board, and stood towards her consort. But the crew, taking up a sheltered position, opened so heavy a fire on the boarders that they killed an officer and eight men, and wounded three officers and 11 others. Thereupon the *Pique* sent a boat's crew on board, who speedily carried the vessel, and standing on, she overhauled the second brig, which surrendered. Both these prizes were commissioned as British cruisers. The frigate's boats also cut out two armed Spanish vessels, and drove ashore a French privateer. Off the coast of Spain the *Renommée*, Sir Thomas Livingstone, engaged and brought off a 12-gun brig, lying under the protection of some batteries, and, under the name of *Spider*, she was taken into the Navy, and proved of much service. The boats of the frigate and of the 18-gun brig *Nautilus*, under the command of Lieutenant Sir William Parker, boarded and cut out a schooner, which was protected by a battery and the fire of 100 soldiers on the beach. The same officer, whose name is so prominent in the annals of the British Navy, brought out of a port in Majorca, several armed native craft.

Lord Cochrane, now in command of the *Pallas*, lying off the Gironde river, sent his boats, under the command of Lieutenant Hansell, to cut out two French brigs, which lay under some batteries, twenty miles above the point to which the frigate could reach. In spite of every obstacle the boats of the *Pallas* succeeded in capturing, after a stout resistance, one of the brigs, named the *Tapageuse*, of 14 guns and 95 men, but the other lay too high up the Gironde to be attacked. While his boats were absent Lord Cochrane chased and drove on shore two French 20-gun corvettes and a brig of 16 guns. A few weeks later, his lordship landed detachments of seamen, who destroyed the signal stations on the coast. Lord Cochrane reconnoitred the French squadron of five sail-of-the-line and five frigates, which lay in Aix roads, and, on one occasion, engaged the 44-gun frigate *Minerve* and three brigs, which stood out to drive off the *Pallas*. Nothing daunted, his lordship, by skilful manœuvring, got between the *Minerve* and the shore batteries, and after engaging her at close quarters, ran her on board. But in the collision, the *Pallas* carried away her fore-topmast, jib-boom, and fore and main-topsail yards, and was so shattered aloft that her antagonist succeeded in making her escape. In this her commander had not much to congratulate himself, as the *Minerve* was nearly double the size of the *Pallas*, and carried six more guns and over 100 more men. The daring displayed by Lord Cochrane was only less remarkable than on the occasion of his capture of the *Gamo*, when in command of the *Speedy*.

With almost equal temerity Captain Prowse, commanding the *Sirius*, 36, attacked, off Civita Vecchia, a French flotilla, consisting of the corvette *Bergère*, of 19 guns and 189 men, three brigs, one carrying 18 guns and the others 12, and several smaller vessels. The *Sirius* closely engaged the squadron, having an aggregate of 97 guns, and at the end of two hours, the *Bergère* hailed to say she had surrendered. The remainder of the vessels succeeded in making their escape, some being disabled.

One of the most praiseworthy events of this long and sanguinary war, was the defence made by the East India Company's trading-ship *Warren Hastings*, carrying 36 guns and 138 men and boys, against the French frigate *Piemontaise*, of 46 guns and a crew 385 in number. The enemy overhauled the Indiaman, which was homeward bound, and commenced the action at 10.30 within musket-shot range. Five times the *Piemontaise* hauled off, only to renew the attack, until the merchantman was reduced to the condition of a wreck; but still the gallant commander, Captain Larkins, and her crew, who could only set a main-topsail on their ship, continued the unequal conflict until the mizen-mast fell on board, disabling the guns on the main-deck, and the lower-deck caught fire. As further resistance could only occasion useless slaughter, Captain Larkins hauled down his colours at 4.50, having lost an officer and six men killed and 13 wounded, including four officers. The victors disgraced themselves by treating their prisoners with great inhumanity, and five officers, including the captain, were wounded in cold blood.

The boats of the *Minerve*, Captain George Collier, performed good service on the Spanish and Portuguese coasts, and twelve boats from a British squadron, cruising off Rochefort, cut out a 16-gun brig, lying in Verdon Roads, at the entrance of the river Gironde. The boats were under the command of Lieutenant Sibley, of the *Centaur*, 74, Commodore Sir Samuel Hood, who was severely wounded by sabre and pike when in the act of boarding the brig, which had a crew of 86 men. She was captured after a severe struggle, in which the British loss was a lieutenant, a master's mate, and seven men killed, and four lieutenants, a master's mate, and 34 men wounded. The brig was brought out in triumph, but a boat belonging to the *Revenge*, containing a midshipman and 19 seamen and marines, was sunk by a large shot from the battery, when the crew succeeded in gaining the shore, where they were made prisoners.

During the year 1806 a ship was added by capture to the British Navy, which was destined to be lost to it, a few years later, in a memorable action during our brief and not very glorious war with the United States of America. This was the *Guerrière*, of 50 guns and 317 men, which was captured about midnight on the 19th July, after an action of three-quarters of an hour, by the *Blanche*, Captain Lavie, carrying 46 guns and having a crew of 265 hands. There was nothing of special interest in the action, and the *Blanche* suffered only a trifling loss in men and *materiel*, while the French frigate lost 20 killed and 30 wounded, and her masts, rigging, and hull were much shattered, owing to the excellent gunnery of the *Blanche's* crew, a quality it had been well their successors had displayed a few years later. Captain Lavie was knighted for this success, and his first lieutenant received promotion.

In the East Indies, the *Greyhound*, 32, Commander Elphinstone, and 18-gun brig *Harrier*, Commander Troubridge—son of the famous officer, the friend of Nelson and Jervis, who soon after, together with his ship, met with a tragic fate at sea—engaged a 36-gun Dutch frigate, with two large armed merchantmen and a 14-gun brig, cruising in the Java sea. After a well-contested action the ships struck their colours, the brig alone escaping. The frigate had eight killed and 33 wounded, including her captain (mortally), two lieutenants, and five other officers.

In February, four French frigates, which had succeeded in putting out to sea from Rochefort, shaped their course for the West African coast, thence steering for the West Indies. Here they were sighted and chased by the *Mars*, 74, Captain Robert Oliver, which succeeded in compelling the *Rhin*, of 40 guns, to haul down her colours, her consorts having abandoned her to her fate with a pusillanimity not often found among French naval officers.

The "saucy *Arethusa*" of the song, formerly commanded by Sir Edward Pellew, and now by the equally active Captain Charles Brisbane, in conjunction with the *Anson*, 44, Captain Lydiard, chased the Spanish 34-gun frigate *Pomona*, under the protection of some batteries about six miles from Havannah, and coming to an anchor, one abreast of some Spanish gunboats, and the other alongside the *Pomona*, engaged the enemy. The gunboats were soon all destroyed or driven ashore, and the frigate surrendered, having lost her captain and 20 men killed, and two lieutenants and 30 wounded out of her complement of 347. The fort at this place fired red-hot shot from her eleven 36-pounders, which set the *Arethusa* on fire, and the British frigate sustained a loss of 34 killed and wounded, including, among the latter, Captain Brisbane, one lieutenant, and a marine officer. The prize was purchased into the Navy under the name of the *Cuba*. Off the Cuban coast also, the *Bacchante*, 20, Commander Dacres, and the 18-gun sloop, *Stork*, Commander Le Geyt, with the schooners *Supérieure*, *Flying Fish*, and *Pike*, rendered good service in cutting out the enemy's armed vessels and privateers. Commander Rushworth, of the *Supérieure*, was especially successful with the three schooners, and landing with 53 men about two miles from Batabano, a port on the island, defeated a small Spanish force, captured a fort mounting six 18-pounders, and took possession of six vessels lying in the harbour.

Near St. Malo, the *Constance*, 22, Captain Burrowes, with the 16-gun brig *Sheldrake*, Commander Thicknesse, and gunboat *Strenuous*, Lieutenant Nugent, succeeded in capturing the armed storeship *Salamandre*, of 26 guns and 80 men, but during the action the *Constance* got aground under a heavy battery, and had to be abandoned, after losing her captain and seven men killed, and her first lieutenant, boatswain, and 14 others wounded, exclusive of 38 taken prisoners. Not being able to bring the corvette off the enemy set her on fire.

While cruising off Rochefort, in September, with six ships-of-the-line, Sir Samuel Hood sighted five French frigates which had escaped from that port, bound for the West Indies. The commodore gave chase and his flagship, the *Centaur*, 74, came up with the frigates *Gloire* and *Armide*, when the latter, after a spirited resistance, struck her colours. Soon after, the *Minerve* surrendered to the *Monarch*, 74, Captain Lee, and the *Indefatigable* to the 74-gun ship *Mars*, Captain Lukin, which also overtook the *Gloire*, and compelled her to haul down her flag. The *Centaur* and *Monarch* had nine killed and 29 wounded, among the latter being Sir Samuel Hood, whose arm was shattered, necessitating amputation. Of the captured frigates, three of which suffered severely in hull and rigging as also in loss of men, the *Gloire* mounted 46 guns, and the three others, 44, and they each carried, inclusive of troops, about 650 men, besides valuable stores of arms and ammunition. They were all added to the Navy, but the *Minerve* was rechristened the *Alceste*, and the *Indefatigable*, the *Immortalité*.

Disaster quickly followed disaster, to the French flag, since the day of Trafalgar. After the losses sustained in the action with the squadrons of Sir Richard Strachan and Sir John Duckworth, and Admiral Willaumez's unfortunate cruise to the West Indies, there was the capture of the four fine frigates off Rochefort, and now the frigate *Presidente*, 44, was taken. She formed one of a squadron from Lorient, despatched to prey on British commerce on the West African coast and in the West Indies, and was returning to Europe when chased by a British squadron, to which she hauled down her colours.

The Dutch Navy also lost, off the coast of Java, a 36-gun frigate, which, under the name of *Java*, was a few months later lost, with all hands, when on her way to the Cape of Good Hope. The British 36-gun frigate, *Caroline*, Captain Rainier, engaged her in the most gallant manner, although she was in company with a corvette of 14 guns, and a brig and an armed ship. The action lasted half an hour, but it was most disastrous to the Dutch frigate, which had 50 killed and wounded out of her crew of 270. In the following year the *Psyche*, 36, Commander Pellew, son of the gallant admiral commanding on the India station, captured, near Samarang, where they had run themselves ashore, an armed merchantman, a corvette of 24 guns and 150 men, and a brig of 12 guns and 70 men; and by his persevering efforts all three prizes were got afloat. For this spirited service Captain Pellew was knighted. Admiral Sir Edward Pellew now arrived from Malacca with the seventy-fours *Culloden* and *Powerful*, frigates *Caroline* and *Fox*, and four sloops, to effect the capture or destruction of two 68-gun Dutch ships that had escaped from Batavia, and taken refuge at Grassie, on the river Sourabaya, at the eastern extremity of Java. This service he effected without firing a shot, and the ships were burnt.

Early in the year 1806 England acquired the important Dutch possession of Cape Town and Colony. Some eight years before, the settlement had been captured, only to be surrendered at the peace, but the British Government, resolving to retake this valuable station on the route to India, despatched Commodore Sir Home Popham, with a squadron of three 64-gun ships, one of 50 guns and two frigates, to dispossess the Dutch. Forming part of the expedition was a fleet of transports and Indiamen, having on board 5,000 troops, under Sir David Baird and General Beresford, which were disembarked at Saldanha Bay. On the 6th January, after some severe fighting, the Dutch Governor of Cape Town capitulated, and the Colony came under the British flag. Accompanying the troops was a detachment of seamen and marines, under Captain Byng of the *Belliqueux*, who rendered good service.

A few weeks after this capture, the French 40-gun frigate *Volontaire*, forming one of Admiral Willaumez's squadron, which he had detached to the Cape, unaware of the Colony having changed hands, anchored in Table Bay, and was captured. She had on board 217 men of the 2nd and 54th Regiments, whom she had taken out of a transport she had captured, and these prisoners, to their great joy, found themselves unexpectedly released. The prize was added to the Navy under her own name.

Sir Home Popham, with the concurrence of Sir David Baird, took upon himself to undertake an expedition to Buenos Ayres and Monte Video. Embarking the 71st Regiment and some artillery, under the command of General Beresford, they sailed from Table Bay, and being reinforced at St. Helena, on the 25th June a body of 1,630 men, including a detachment of seamen, was landed about 12 miles from Buenos Ayres, which, after a skirmish, was surrendered on the 2nd July. But the inhabitants rose upon the invaders, and General Beresford, after losing 165 men, killed and wounded, was compelled to surrender. Sir Home Popham now blockaded the port until the arrival of reinforcements, when he took possession of Maldonado, but the Admiralty disapproved of his unauthorised action, and he was tried by court-martial at Portsmouth in March, 1807, and "severely reprimanded."

Rear-Admiral Stirling arrived to supersede Commodore Popham, and the troops, now reinforced and commanded by Sir Samuel Achmuty, stormed the town of Monte Video, assisted by a detachment of about 300 seamen and marines landed from the fleet, and some 600 more who were engaged in transporting guns and stores to the front. In the operations the army had 192 killed and 421 wounded, and the Naval Brigade three and 24 respectively. General Whitelocke, who had arrived with 5,000 men, now assumed command of the soldiers, and Rear-Admiral Murray of the squadron, when the former undertook the capture of Buenos Ayres, the failure to effect which, and the surrender of 2,500 troops, forms one of the most discreditable chapters in our military history. In this *fiasco* the Navy had no share.

The year 1807 is chiefly memorable in naval annals for our expedition against Copenhagen, in which the Army carried off the honours, and the forcing of the Dardanelles by Sir John Duckworth's squadron. On the 26th July, Admiral Gambier, (who commanded the *Defence*, under Lord Howe, in his great victory) having his flag in the *Prince of Wales*, 98, sailed from Yarmouth roads, with sixteen line-of-battle-ships, and being joined by several others, the fleet ultimately numbered no fewer than twenty-five sail-of-the-line and forty frigates, exclusive of 377 transports, having on board 27,000 troops, under Lord Cathcart and Sir Arthur Wellesley, afterwards the great Duke of Wellington. A demand made for the surrender of the Danish fleet was rejected, and the first shot was fired on the 14th August, when, without a declaration of war, the *Comus*, of 32 guns, attacked and captured, after forty-five minutes' action, the frigate *Frederickscoarn*, of like force, with the loss of 12 killed and 20 wounded. Two days later a portion of the troops was disembarked at Wedbeck, midway between Elsinore and Copenhagen, where Admiral Gambier arrived on the 17th with sixteen sail, and a state of war now ensued, the Danish king having issued a proclamation, laying an embargo on all British ships. On the 23rd and following days an engagement took place between three of our sloops, five bomb-vessels, and seven gun-brigs, with ten launches fitted as mortar-boats, and the Danish gunboats, assisted by the great Trekronen pile-battery, mounting 68 guns, besides mortars, which, with the citadel, a pile-battery in advance of it, and the arsenal battery, the whole mounting 174 guns and 25 mortars, formed the city's sea defences.

On the morning of the 2nd September the British batteries on shore opened fire, and the bomb-vessels began the bombardment, which continued for twenty-four hours. Again it recommenced on the following evening and during the night of the 3rd, 4th, and 5th, by which time the city was set on fire in several places. At length the governor requested an armistice, and, on the 7th September, terms of capitulation were arranged,—the British commissioners being Sir Arthur Wellesley, Sir Home Popham and Colonel Murray,—by which the fleet was surrendered to the British commanders, Lord Cathcart and Admiral Gambier, who were also placed in temporary possession of the citadel.

Thus, with a loss of only 56 killed, 179 wounded, and 25 missing, the capital of Denmark was gained and the enemy brought to submission. In nine days the fourteen sail-of-the-line in the harbour were fitted out by British seamen and towed into the roads, and a few weeks later the remaining three, with ten frigates, fourteen sloops and brigs and five gunboats, were removed, and the naval arsenal cleared of all stores, which filled no less than ninety-two transports. By the 20th October the embarkation of the British army was completed, and, on the following day, the fleet sailed from Copenhagen with the prizes and transports in three divisions. The enterprise was not one for which much glory could be said to accrue to the victors, who were in overwhelming strength, and the chief sufferers were the inoffensive inhabitants, 305 of whose dwellings were wholly destroyed, while the loss of life among them, inclusive of the combatants, was stated to be 2,000. Nevertheless, the Services received the thanks of Parliament, and Admiral Gambier was created a peer, Lord Cathcart received an English peerage, and the two senior military officers and the second in command of the fleet, Vice-Admiral Stanhope, were made baronets.

The most arduous task, that of preventing reinforcements crossing the Little Belt, from Holstein into the island of Zealand, was performed by Commodore Keats, with his usual thoroughness and success. One of the immediate consequences of the state of war that arose between Denmark and this country, was the acquisition of the island of Heligoland, off the mouth of the Elbe, which capitulated* on the 4th September to Rear-Admiral Macnamara, who had under his orders the *Russell*, 74, and the 32-gun frigate, *Quebec*, Lord Falkland.

The second important naval undertaking of 1807, was that against the Dardanelles by Sir Thomas Duckworth, an officer who had commanded the *Orion*, 74, on the "glorious first of June," and inflicted the defeat on the French squadron off St. Domingo. The Dardanelles is a channel 36 miles long, and little more than three-quarters of a mile broad at its narrowest part, where are the castles of Sestos and Abydos, which form the chief protection to the passage leading to Constantinople. Sir Thomas Louis had reconnoitred this channel in December of the previous year, with three ships-of-the-line and some frigates, on board of which, in the following January, embarked the Russian and British Ambassadors and all the British merchants from the capital. Admiral Duckworth, having his flag in the *Royal George*, 100, arrived off Tenedos on the 10th February, when he had under his command eight sail-of-the-line, two frigates, and two bomb-vessels, and without loss of time, on the following day he weighed anchor and stood for the Dardanelles, but the wind being adverse, brought to an anchor again. Here, on the 15th, a great disaster befell the squadron in the total destruction by fire of the *Ajax*, 74, Captain Hon. Henry Blackwood, when she blew up, and 250 souls perished.

The wind changing, the squadron weighed on the 19th, and stood through the channel, receiving an ineffective fire from the castles, which was returned, when the loss experienced was six killed and 51 wounded. Sir Sydney Smith, having his flag in the *Pompée*, with the *Thunderer* and *Standard*, and the two frigates, engaged a redoubt armed with heavy guns and the Turkish squadron lying a little above Abydos, and speedily silenced their fire, when all the ships, consisting of one of 64 guns, a frigate of 40 guns, two of 36, and one of 32, with four corvettes, ran on shore on the Asiatic side of the channel, where they were destroyed by the boats from Admiral Smith's ships.

Sir John Duckworth, instead of anchoring off the capital, influenced, doubtless

* As is well known, Heligoland was made over to the German Emperor in 1890.

by the ambassador who was on board, brought to eight miles from the city whence, on the 21st, he sent a demand to the Sublime Porte for the surrender of the Turkish fleet, but he failed to carry out his threat, that, in the case of non-compliance, he would lay the city in ashes. The Turkish Government, urged on by General Sebastiani, Napoleon's ambassador, then all-powerful at the Porte, brought into play all the resources of procrastination and dissimulation, always at the disposal of Orientals, and, on the 1st March, the admiral swallowed all his brave professions and weighed anchor on his return to Tenedos. The castle of Abydos was passed early on the 3rd, and before noon the British squadron was out of reach of molestation, having completed its inglorious mission. The defences had been improved since they passed up, and most of the ships were hulled by stone-shot, weighing 800 pounds, the total loss being 29 killed and 138 wounded. Among the former was Captain Kent, of the marines on board the *Canopus*, and Lieutenant Belli, of the *Royal George*. One stone-shot lodged in the mainmast of the *Royal George*, and another from Sestos entered the lower deck of the *Standard*, where it killed four seamen, and caused an explosion, badly wounding a lieutenant and 46 others.

During the month of March an expedition, even more ill-starred, so far as the military result was concerned, was despatched to Egypt, for which the Navy supplied the *Tigre*, 74, Captain Hallowell; the *Apollo*, 36, Captain Fellowes; and the 16-gun brig *Wizard*, Commander Palmer. The troops, 5,000 men, were landed at Aboukir, and on the 21st March the city of Alexandria was surrendered. But this was almost the last success, and the troops, being overpowered by numbers, after losing about 1,000 of their number, were re-embarked in the transports.

Coerced by Napoleon, the Prince Regent of Portugal issued a proclamation on the 20th October, shutting his ports against British ships, upon which Sir Sydney Smith was despatched, with nine sail-of-the-line, to the Tagus. Here he enforced a rigid blockade, and demanded either the surrender of the fleet, or that the Royal Family should retreat to Brazil. The Regent accepted the latter alternative, and the members of the House of Braganza, with about 18,000 inhabitants, set sail from Lisbon in the Portuguese fleet, consisting of eight ships-of-the-line, and eight other vessels, with twenty armed merchantmen. Escorted by the British fleet, the armament steered for Brazil, and, on the 6th December, Sir Sydney Smith returned with five sail, leaving Commodore Moore, with the remaining three, to see them in safety to Rio. On the 30th November, the day after their departure, Junot entered Lisbon at the head of the French Army,

CAPTAIN

and Admiral Smith, who was reinforced with five sail from England, kept watch off the Tagus, where a Russian squadron of nine ships had taken shelter, that Power having declared war against England on the 2nd December preceding. In consequence of the French occupation of Portugal, Rear-Admiral Sir Samuel Hood, with four sail-of-the-line and four frigates, having on board some troops, under General Beresford, appeared off Funchal, in the Madeiras, which surrendered without resistance.

One of the most gallant feats of the war was the capture of the Dutch settlement of Curaçoa, by that intrepid officer, Commodore Charles Brisbane, with four frigates, the *Arethusa*, carrying his broad pennant, and the *Latona*, *Anson*, and *Fisgard*. Sailing from Jamaica on the 24th December, at daybreak on the 1st January, 1807, he made his appearance off the port with his boats in tow, and, anchoring in position for engaging the heavy forts and two Dutch ships, wrote a summons to the governor, on the capstan of his ship, whose jib-boom was over the wall of the town, to surrender the place, and giving him "five minutes" to accede to his demand. No notice being taken of this peremptory procedure, at 6.15 the British squadron opened fire, and after a few broadsides, the commodore, at the head of a portion of his crew, boarded and captured the Dutch frigate, a party from the *Anson*, Captain Lydiard, securing the second ship. This effected, they pulled for the shore and carried the fort of Amsterdam, with equal sailor-like promptitude, and the citadel, some minor forts and the town were all seized. There still remained Fort République, situated on a high hill, but at the sight of 300 English bluejackets and marines marching up in their rear, the commandant hauled down his flag, and thus was acquired the whole island of Curaçoa. Altogether this exploit is one of the most remarkable recorded in history, and its success is almost inexplicable except on the ground of its suddenness and daring. Commodore Brisbane received the honour of knighthood, and the first lieutenants of the *Arethusa* and *Anson* were promoted.

During the year 1807 a gallant feat was achieved by the boats of the *Galatea*, 38, off Caraccas. Captain Sayer sighted the French brig-of-war *Lynx*, of 14 guns and 161 men and boys, and as she made off with her sweeps, the wind being light, he resolved to attempt to capture her by boarding. She was at this time hull down, but six boats, with seamen and marines, under command of Lieutenant Coombe, pushed off at 2 P.M., and after a pull of seven hours, under a burning sun, about nine o'clock, five boats, with five officers and 65 men, had arrived within pistol-shot of the enemy. Every preparation being made, the crews, with a hearty cheer, dashed for the brig, and a desperate struggle ensued. The British seamen were repulsed by a heavy fire of musketry and from the guns trained aft, but a second time they made the attempt to board, when they succeeded in gaining the deck. In five minutes they had carried all before them, and the survivors were either driven below or had taken refuge aloft. In achieving this brilliant success, equalled by few and scarcely excelled by any in our naval annals, the British experienced the loss of Lieutenant Waller and eight men killed, and Lieutenant Coombe (severely in the thigh of the leg he had previously lost), two masters' mates and 19 men wounded. The *Lynx* had a lieutenant and 13 men killed, and her captain, first lieutenant (both severely), four other officers and 14 men wounded. The prize was purchased into the service as the *Heureux*, there being one of her name in the Navy, and Lieutenant Coombe commissioned her.

This heroic officer, however, did not long survive his good fortune as, in the following year, he was killed while engaged in cutting out a vessel from a harbour in the island of Guadaloupe. With the daring that distinguished him, Commander Coombe had boarded, and carried, with only his barge, manned by 19 men, a two-gun schooner, having a crew, 39 all told, but the prize and a brig, captured by Lieutenant Lawrence, grounded, when a heavy fire was brought to bear on them from the shore. A 24-pound shot struck the gallant officer, who fell, exclaiming, "I die contented. I die for my country." Lieutenant Lawrence was also wounded, but succeeded in bringing out the captured vessels.

An attack on the fort of Samana, in the island of St. Domingo, the haunt of privateers, was made by the 32-gun frigate *Mediator*, Captain Wise, formerly an Indiaman, the *Bacchante*, 20, Captain Dacres, and a schooner of 12 guns, captured shortly before by these two ships. With this object the *Mediator* was disguised as a merchantman, and the prize hoisted French colours, when the three vessels, without exciting suspicion, managed to anchor close to the fort, which, after a cannonade of four hours, was carried, the British loss being two killed and 16 wounded. Lieutenant Watts, of the *Comus*, 20, with three boats, succeeded in cutting-out an armed felucca, which lay under the protection of a fort in the Grand Canary island, though he was severely wounded in several places, for which act of gallantry he was promoted.

But not equally successful was Captain Jahleel Brenton, of the *Spartan*, 38, when off Nice, in his attempt to carry by boarding a polacre ship. Seeing her becalmed, and taking her for an unarmed merchantman, he despatched his boats with 70 men, under the two senior lieutenants, Weir and Williams, to secure her. But the ship was fully prepared to receive them, having her boarding nettings up, and all hands ready to offer resistance. The result was a sanguinary repulse, in which both the lieutenants and 26 men were killed or mortally wounded, the remainder, with the exception of seven, being also wounded.

Scarcely more fortunate was the 18-gun brig *Curieux*, Commander Sherriff, having a crew of 100 men, in her action with the French privateer *Revanche* (formerly a Liverpool merchant ship), of 25 guns and 200 men. After a close action of an hour, in which the brig became unmanageable, owing to her braces and tiller ropes being shot away, the *Revanche* ran into her, and her crew made an attempt to board, but were driven back. Captain Sherriff being killed, Lieutenant Muir assumed command, and soon after, the ships separated, and the *Revanche* made sail and escaped. The *Curieux* lost, besides her commander, seven killed and 14 wounded.

Some record should be made of the spirited manner in which Lieutenant Drury, of the *Hydra*, 38, with 50 seamen and marines, cut out, under a heavy fire, three polacres which lay in the harbour of Begur, on the coast of Catalonia. The party first landed and captured a battery, manned by French soldiers, and mounting four 24-pounders, and then boarded the vessels and brought them out, for which act of gallantry Lieutenant Drury was promoted.

Captain Clavell, of the brig *Weasel*, of 18 guns and 120 men, was enabled to render an important service to his country at this time. After the treaty of Tilsit, the Russians surrendered Corfu to the French, who sent a detachment to take possession. But the *Weasel*, when cruising off the island, encountered three vessels, on which she fired, when they ran upon the rocks, and three others in the offing she captured, on board of which were found 250 French soldiers. Destroying one of these, she set sail for Malta with the two remaining, and brought them to Valetta.

A gallant exploit was performed in the West Indies by the packet *Windsor Castle*, Commander Rogers, of eight guns and 28 men and boys, in capturing a French privateer, mounting seven guns of larger calibre, and having a crew of 92 men, after an action, the desperate nature of which was attested by the losses on both sides. Having defeated an attempt of the enemy to board, Captain Rogers in turn sprang on the privateer's deck and forced her to surrender. His own loss was three killed and 10 severely wounded, and that of the enemy, 21 and 33 respectively. Few equally intrepid actions were recorded in this war, and none more meritorious.

CHAPTER III.

The Naval Situation in Europe in 1808—Capture of the Russian seventy-four *Sewolod*—Action between the *San Fiorenzo* and *Piémontaise*—Services of the Navy on the Coasts of Norway and Denmark—Death of Captain Conway Shipley—Some Cutting-out Expeditions and Boat Actions—The *Seahorse* and Turkish Frigate—The *Sémillante* and *Terpsichore*—Fighting in Danish Waters—The *Amethyst* with the *Thetis* and *Niemen*—Destruction of French Ships in Aix Roads by Lord Cochrane—The Expedition to the Scheldt—Frigate Actions in 1809—The *Spartan* with a Squadron off Naples—Boat Actions in the Adriatic, and with Danish and Russian Gunboats—Loss of the *Junon*—Capture of French Colonies—Death of Lord Collingwood—Frigate Actions in 1810—Repulse at Palermo—Loss of three Indiamen—Captain Willoughby at Jacleot—Capture of *Réunion* and *Isle de la Passe*—Loss of Four Frigates off Grand Port, in Mauritius—Loss of the *Africaine* and *Ceylon*, and Recovery of the latter—Capture of Mauritius and Amboyna—Captain Cole at Banda-Neira—Actions with the Boulogne Flotilla and on the Coast of Holland—Defeat of the Danish Expedition to Anhalt—Loss of the *St. George*, *Defence*, and *Hero*—Captain Hoste's Victory off Lissa—Action between Single Ships in 1811—Capture of the *Pomone*—Action off Madagascar—Capture of Java—Frigate Action in 1812-14—Capture of the *Rivoli* and French Frigates—Conclusion of the War.

NOTWITHSTANDING the losses experienced by the French fleet at Trafalgar, and, since that great battle, in the numerous disasters they had suffered, so great were the exertions of the French Emperor that, early in 1808, his fleet consisted of upwards of eighty ships-of-the-line. For the service of the year the House of Commons voted supplies exceeding 18 millions, including pay and maintenance for 98,600 seamen and 31,400 marines, which numbers were increased, in 1809, by the addition of 15,000 seamen. Profiting by the temporary absence of Sir Richard Strachan's blockading squadron, Admiral Allemand escaped, with five sail-of-the-line, from Rochefort, and arrived at Toulon, whence, on the 7th February, Admiral Ganteaume sailed, with ten battleships and three frigates, for Corfu, and having succeeded in eluding Lord Collingwood, who went in search of him, cruised along the coast of Africa, Sicily, and Sardinia, and cast anchor in Toulon Roads on the 10th April.

Lord Collingwood now sailed for Gibraltar and Cadiz, to assist the Spanish patriots, who had thrown off the yoke of Napoleon's brother, Joseph, and one of his first efforts was to compel the surrender of Admiral Rosilly's squadron of five sail-of-the-line and a corvette, which had been long shut up in Cadiz by the British fleet. The latter, hitherto so persistent and implacable an enemy, was now welcomed in all the ports of the Peninsula as a deliverer, and the British officers and seamen exerted their energies to drive the French out of the seaports of Spain. Portugal soon followed the example of her neighbour, and then commenced the great war in the Peninsula, which, begun at Roleia and Vimiero, was only ended at Vittoria and the battle of the Pyrenees by the immortal military genius this country was so fortunate as to possess in this crisis of European affairs. In landing the British troops, under Sir Arthur Wellesley, and in the subsequent operations, Admiral Sir Charles Cotton was of great service, and, by one of the terms of the convention of Cintra, which was due to his insistance, the Russian squadron, of nine sail-of-the-line and one frigate, lying in the Tagus, was made over to the British Admiral, and their crews conveyed to Russia.

The conclusion of the treaty of Tilsit, between the Czar Alexander and the Emperor Napoleon, had been followed by a declaration of war, and as this involved Russian hostility towards Sweden, Sir James Saumarez, with his flag in the *Victory*, and having as his rear-admirals Sir Samuel Hood and Sir Richard Keats, sailed for the Baltic, with eight seventy-fours, two 64-gun ships, and five frigates. Sir Samuel Hood, having his flag in the *Centaur*, 74, with the *Implacable*, of the same force, commanded by Captain Byam Martin, was in company with the Swedish fleet of ten sail and five frigates, when he sighted and gave chase to a Russian squadron of nine sail and eight frigates. The British ships outsailed their consorts, and the *Implacable* succeeded in overhauling and bringing to action the *Sewolod*, 74, which she compelled to strike, after a brisk action of less than half an hour. But the Russian admiral bore up to her assistance, and the *Implacable* was obliged to sheer off. A Russian frigate took the *Sewolod* in tow, but was compelled by the two British ships to cast her off, when the *Centaur* ran her on board, and raked her with terrible effect, as the bows of the Russian seventy-four swept along her starboard side. The *Sewolod's* bowsprit was now lashed to the *Centaur's* mizen-rigging, and at length, after a gallant defence, and the *Implacable* having ranged up to within 300 yards, she struck her colours. During this double duel the *Implacable* had six killed and 25 wounded, the *Centaur* three and 27, including among the latter her first lieutenant, and the *Sewolod* lost no less than 48 killed and 80 wounded in the first action, and had 180 casualties in the second. The prize having taken the ground, and all efforts to bring her off being unsuccessful, she was set on fire and destroyed.

Rear-Admiral Keats, a most capable officer, also rendered distinguished service at this time by the measures he adopted to ensure the neutrality of the Danish town and forts at Nyborg, in the island of Funen, while he effected the embarkation of 6,000 Spanish troops stationed here, and 4,000 in Jutland, who were desirous of quitting the service of Napoleon, and returning to their native land.

The most remarkable frigate action during the year 1808, was that between the *San Fiorenzo*, Captain Hardinge, of 40 guns and 186 men, and the *Piémontaise*, carrying 46 guns and a crew of 366, besides 200 Lascars to work the sails. This was the same ship that nearly two years before had captured, after a desperate and protracted resistance, the Indiaman *Warren Hastings*, but her officers and crew found more than their match when engaged with a man-of-war of inferior strength. At the time she was sighted by the British frigate, the *Piémontaise* was engaged in the congenial task of chasing, off the coast of Ceylon, some Indiamen, but now she abandoned her anticipated prey and made sail to escape. Shortly before midnight on the 6th March the *San Fiorenzo* brought her to action, but within ten minutes she made sail to escape. On the following morning she was overhauled by her persistent adversary, who again brought her to action. At the end of two hours the *Piémontaise* discontinued firing and again sought to escape, leaving the British frigate so much cut up aloft as to be in no condition to give chase.

The *San Fiorenzo*, having repaired damages, made sail in pursuit, but lost sight of the enemy, though at daybreak on the morning of the 8th March, she was once more seen about four leagues distant. The *San Fiorenzo* gave chase, and, owing to her superior sailing qualities, was able to force her unwilling opponent to accept the gage of battle. At 4 P.M. the frigates, passing on opposite tacks, opened fire at a range of eighty yards. By the second broadside the gallant Captain Hardinge, who has before been mentioned in these pages, was killed, when the command devolved upon Lieutenant Dawson, who continued the action for an hour and fifty minutes, when the *Piémontaise*—having her rigging and sails cut to pieces, and her three masts and bowsprit badly wounded, with a great proportion of her crew *hors de combat*—hauled down her colours.

The total British loss during the three days was 13 killed and 25 wounded, including one lieutenant severely. The victory was, however, dearly purchased by the death of her captain, a truly chivalrous and heroic officer, who, though young in years, had given promise of great professional distinction. The *Piémontaise* had 48 killed and 112 wounded, including some of the Lascars, who were of no account as fighting men. Soon after the action the three masts of the prize went over the side, and in this helpless state she was towed to Colombo, where the remains of Captain Hardinge received interment.

Good service was rendered on the coast of Spain by the *Emerald*, under her first lieutenant, Bertram, in capturing and destroying a French schooner of eight guns and 70 men, but the duty was not performed without considerable loss, the *Emerald* having nine men killed and 15 wounded, including four officers, of whom one was Lieutenant Bertram. The *Childers*, Commander Dillon, carrying 14 twelve-pounder carronades and 65 men, gallantly engaged, off the Norwegian coast, and beat off the Danish 20-gun brig *Lougen*, with a crew of 160 men, but a few months later the latter succeeded in capturing, after a prolonged resistance, the *Seagull*, Commander Cathcart, a brig of 16 guns and 94 men. In effecting this the *Lougen* was materially assisted by six Danish gunboats, each armed with two long 24-pounders, which, taking up a raking position on each quarter, were enabled, owing to a calm, to use their guns with great effect. The *Seagull*, when she hauled down her flag, had five feet of water in her hold, and sank soon after. Her loss was a lieutenant, master, and six men killed, and her captain (severely), first lieutenant (dangerously), and 18 men wounded. Both Commanders Dillon and Cathcart received promotion to post-rank for the gallantry they had displayed, though in the case of the latter officer it was without avail.

In these waters also, the British 64-gun ships *Stately*, Captain Robert Parker, and *Nassau*, Captain Campbell, chased, and forced to strike, a Danish seventy-four, but she grounded at the close of the action, and as the breeze was freshening, and they could not get her afloat, she was set on fire and destroyed. The loss of the two British ships was only five killed and 45 wounded, and that of the enemy 55 killed and 88 wounded, out of a complement of 576. Excellent service was also performed by five boats of the *Daphne* and *Tartarus*, under the command of Lieutenant Elliott, and by the boats of the *Falcon*, commanded by Mr. Ellerton, master, in cutting out and destroying numerous Danish craft, lying under the protection of batteries.

The 32-gun frigate *Tartar*, Captain Bettesworth, attempted an attack on the town and batteries of Bergen, in Holland, but, owing to the wind having fallen light, she became exposed to a heavy fire from some gunboats and shore guns, without at first being able to return it, during which her gallant commander and a promising young midshipman were killed. The Dutch frigate *Guelderland*, the object of the *Tartar's* search, was, a few days later, sighted by the 38-gun frigate *Virginie*, Captain Brace, which brought her to action one dark night, and at the end of an hour and a half, having shot away her masts, forced her to haul down her colours, with the loss of 25 killed and 50 wounded.

In another quarter, on the Spanish coast, near Cadiz, the *Alceste*, 38, Captain Maxwell, *Mercury*, 28, Captain Gordon, and 18-gun brig *Grasshopper*, Commander Searle, stood in shore and attacked about twenty gunboats, convoying some vessels and a train of artillery on the shore, and the brig especially displayed daring in standing close in and engaging some batteries. Meanwhile, Lieutenant Stewart, of the *Alceste*, made a dash for the convoy with the boats of the two frigates, and brought out seven tartans from under the muzzles of the guns. A few weeks later, the gallant commander of the *Grasshopper*, who was accompanied by the 14-gun brig *Rapid*, Lieutenant Baugh, chased two Spanish vessels, convoyed by four gunboats, which took refuge under a battery near Faro, in Portugal. These enterprising officers engaged and silenced the fort, captured two of the gunboats, drove the others ashore, and took the vessels, whose cargoes were valued at £60,000.

Not equally fortunate was the attack made by Captain Conway Shipley—with eight boats from his own ship, the *Nymphe*, 36, and 18-gun sloop, *Blossom*, containing about 150 officers and men—on the large brig *Garrota*, of 20 guns and a French crew of 150 men, lying within pistol-shot of the guns of Belem Castle on the Tagus. It was about 2.30 in the morning that, with a strong ebb tide against them, the *Nymphe's* gig, with Captain Shipley on board, was the first to get alongside the brig, which was fully prepared to give them a warm reception. This daring officer, springing into the fore-rigging, was in the act of cutting away the boarding netting, when he received a musket-ball in the forehead, and fell dead into the water. By some mischance, the boats boarding on this, the port, side, fell foul of each other, and were swept astern by the tide, running seven knots an hour, owing to the freshets; and as the boats of Captain Pigott's division could not make headway, the enterprise was abandoned.

The next affair we have to chronicle was distinctly discreditable to the British crew concerned. The 18-gun brig, *Carnation*, Commander Gregory, having brought to action in the West Indies the *Palinure*, of 16 guns, fell on board her, but owing to Commander Gregory and most of his officers being killed, no attempt was made to carry her by boarding. Encouraged by this lack of enterprise, the French took the offensive, and soon the *Carnation* became the prize of the *Palinure*, having lost, besides her captain, the master, purser, and eight men killed, and 30 wounded (15 mortally), including both her lieutenants (severely). A portion of the crew, though called upon by the boatswain, now in command, refused to support him, and were subsequently tried by court-martial at Martinique, when 32 seamen and marines were convicted of cowardice, and sentenced to fourteen years' transportation to Botany Bay, and a sergeant of marines was hanged at the yard-arm. It was seldom, indeed, in the annals of our Navy that so disgraceful a charge was brought home to British seamen, and the punishment was exemplary. The *Palinure* was captured a few weeks later by the 32-gun frigate *Circe*, Captain Pigot, after a gallant resistance, in which, out of her surviving crew of 79 men, she lost seven killed and eight wounded.

About the same time the French 14-gun brig, *Pilade*, was captured by the *Pompée*, 74. Both these cruisers had, before these events, been engaged by the British 18-gun sloop *Gorée*, and 12-gun brig *Supérieure*, but without result, though the enemy lost on that occasion eight killed and 21 wounded. Excellent service was performed by the 16-gun brig *Wizard*, Commander Ferris, in engaging the *Requin*, of the same force, and chasing her for 88 hours, during which the vessels covered a distance of 369 miles, until the French brig took refuge under Port Goletta, in Tunis. The *Bacchante* and *Griffin* rendered good service, and also the 36-gun frigate *Unite*, in the Gulf of Venice, where she captured an Italian 16-gun corvette and two brigs, which lost heavily, and drove a third ashore. The two taken were added to the Navy. Captain Hoste, of the *Amphion*, 32, also displayed marked enterprise in attacking the French storeship *Baleine*, armed with 26 guns, as she lay at anchor in the Bay of Rosas, under the protection of some batteries which kept up a hot fire on the frigate. Again, the boats of the 22-gun ship *Porcupine* cut out two large polacres on the coast near Civita Vecchia, and drove a third ashore. These services were not effected without some loss, and Lieutenant Price, in command of the boats, received promotion, and Lieutenant Smith was favourably mentioned.

A more extended notice is due to the gallantry with which Captain Stewart, of the *Seahorse*, of 42 guns and 251 men, engaged the Turkish frigate *Badere Zaffer*, carrying 52 guns and 543 men, which was accompanied by the *Ali Fezan*, of 26 guns and 230 men. The former sought to board the British frigate, which Captain Stewart prevented by the smart handling of his ship. The small Turkish frigate, now interposing, came in for a share of Captain Stewart's attention, and a broadside, poured in at close range, played havoc on her decks, when she made off from the scene of conflict, and the *Seahorse* was left alone to deal with her more formidable adversary. Again the Turkish crew attempted to board the British frigate, which, shooting ahead, brushed against her jib-boom and bowsprit, and poured a tremendous discharge of grape from her stern-chase guns, which cleared her forecastle, crowded with the boarding party. Thus the action went on all night, until the guns of the *Badere Zaffer* were reduced to silence. But her captain made no sign of submission, and with daylight Captain Stewart ranged up under her stern and poured in a broadside. Finally the Moslem commander was compelled to haul down his colours from the stump of the mizen-mast, and the ship was boarded and taken possession of. The decks presented a dreadful scene of carnage, no less than 170 of her crew having been killed, and 200 wounded, while her mizen-mast and fore and main-topmasts had been shot away and she was much shattered. The *Seahorse*, on the other hand, had only experienced a loss of 15 men, of whom five were slain. In January of the following year (1809), peace was restored between England and Turkey.

Some notice must now be directed to the East Indies, where the *Sémillante*, the remaining one of Admiral Linois' squadron when he returned to France two years before, was blockaded in Mauritius, by the British frigate *Pitt*, 36 (afterwards called the *Salsette*), Captain Bathurst, (who fell at Navarino nearly twenty years later), and the *Terpsichore*, 38. Early in 1806 the latter parted company, and steered for Ceylon, and the *Sémillante*, accompanied by the *Bellone*, privateer, put to sea. They were chased by the *Pitt*, but eluded her, and after a cruise, in which they made prizes of some merchantmen, Captain Motard regained Port Louis in safety. After completing repairs the *Sémillante* again set sail, accompanied by the *Bellone* and another privateer, the *Henrietta*—both of which were soon afterwards captured by English cruisers—and took eight merchant-ships, with cargoes valued at a million and a quarter sterling. During the following year (1807) the *Sémillante* was scarcely less fortunate, having captured three richly-laden vessels on the way to China, and, as before, succeeded in taking them in safety to Mauritius. In March, 1808, when cruising off Ceylon, she, however, "caught a Tartar" in the *Terpsichore*, Captain Montagu, which was disguised as a merchantman. The British frigate permitted her to approach within one hundred yards, and then opened fire upon her, which, however, was not very effective, as, owing to her age and weakness, she had left at Madras most of her upper-deck guns, so that at this time she only mounted 26 twelve-pounders and two six-pounders. The *Sémillante* evaded every attempt of her antagonist to close, and at length she made sail, having reduced her to a condition of helplessness, her rigging and sails being cut to pieces, and all her masts badly wounded. But the persevering officers and men of the *Terpsichore* so smartly repaired damages that a day or two later they again sighted the enemy. After five days' chase, the action was renewed, but the crew of the *Sémillante*, by throwing overboard some of her guns, and otherwise lightening her, managed to distance their pursuer.

During the fighting, but chiefly owing to an explosion caused by some combustibles thrown by the enemy when at close quarters, the *Terpsichore* lost, out of 180 men, one lieutenant and 20 men killed and 22 wounded. The loss of the *Sémillante*, which mounted 40 guns and had a crew of 300 men, is not known, but Captain Motard, a most enterprising officer so far as preying on an enemy's commerce was concerned, was severely wounded. Having repaired damages, she embarked a cargo valued at seven millions of francs, and with the good fortune she had always experienced, in February, 1809, managed to enter a French port in safety.

The French naval commanders at Mauritius were not equally chary of engaging a foe when the odds were much in their favour, as was proved when the *Canonnière* (formerly a British frigate), of 48 guns and 526 men, including 70 soldiers from the garrison, stood out of Port Louis harbour to engage the *Laurel*, a small vessel not half her tonnage, carrying 30 light guns and a crew of 144 men. Though Commander Woollcombe accepted the challenge, the disparity was too great for him to hope for success, and the *Laurel* struck her flag when she was in a helpless condition from the enemy's superior fire. On the 12th April, 1810, this ship, renamed the *Espérance*, while on her way home from Mauritius with a valuable cargo of colonial produce, was encountered off the French coast by the 32-gun frigate *Unicorn*, Captain Kerr, when she struck her colours, and was restored to the Navy list.

Not less gallant and unsuccessful than the resistance offered by the *Laurel*, was that of the French corvette *Jena*, of 18 guns and 150 men, which was engaged off the Sandheads by the 36-gun frigate *Modeste*, Captain Hon. George Elliot, and for an hour sustained the superior fire of her conqueror. The *Jena* was purchased into the Navy as the *Victor*, but she was subsequently retaken. The *Canonnière*, armed with 14 guns, and laden with a cargo valued at £150,000, sailed from Mauritius for Europe towards the end of 1809, and on the following 3rd February, when close to Belleisle, on the coast of France, was sighted by the *Valiant*, 74, Captain Bligh. After a seven hours' chase the *Valiant* overhauled the ship, now renamed the *Confiance*, when she hauled down her colours.

In Europe some loss was occasioned by the Danish gunboats, which, since the surrender of the ships-of-the-line in the previous year, represented their navy. Some of these craft would surround British convoys, in Danish waters, during calm weather, when the small men-of-war escorting them were almost helpless. On one occasion, the *Tickler*, gun-brig, was captured after a stubborn resistance, during which, out of 50 men, she had 14 killed and 22 wounded, and the gun-brig *Tigress* was taken by sixteen gun-vessels, and the *Turbulent* by another flotilla. The 18-gun brig *Cruiser*, Lieutenant Wells, however, beat off twenty armed boats and gun-vessels, for which that officer received promotion, and a fortnight later, the *Africa*, 64, Captain Barrett, with the greatest difficulty succeeded in repulsing a flotilla of twenty-five large gun and mortar boats, and seven armed launches, the whole carrying 80 heavy guns and 1,600 men. The engagement lasted from three till nearly seven, when darkness put an end to the conflict, but it is allowed that had there been two hours' more calm and daylight, the *Africa* must have either surrendered or been sunk. As it was, she had nine men killed, and the captain, five officers, and 47 men wounded.

There were few more brilliant actions in the war than those in which Captain Michael Seymour, commanding the *Amethyst*, of 42 guns and 261 men, captured the French frigates *Thetis* and *Niemen*, of superior force. It was on the 10th November, 1808, that the *Thetis* was sighted near Lorient, when all sail was made in chase. The action commenced at 9.15 in the evening, and the two ships engaged in close conflict, broadside to broadside. In attempting to cross her opponent's bows, in order to rake her, the *Thetis* fell on board, but the ships soon separated, and, shortly after, the *Amethyst* succeeded in raking the enemy. An hour and a quarter after the commencement of the action, both ships lost their mizenmasts, and about eleven, the *Thetis*, having suffered terribly from her opponent's fire, endeavoured to board, but was received with such deadly broadsides that she gave up the attempt. Locked in a close embrace, the action was continued until about twenty minutes past midnight, when the enemy's fire, having been completely silenced, the men of the *Amethyst* boarded and took possession. Soon after this event both the remaining masts of the prize went over the side, and on the arrival of the *Triumph*, 74, and *Shannon*, 38, Captain Broke, the latter took her in tow. At the close of the action the British frigate was so pierced by shot-holes that she had three and a half feet of water in her hold, and her loss was a marine officer and 18 seamen and marines killed, and five officers (one mortally) and 44 men wounded. The *Thetis* was much shattered in her hull, besides losing all her masts, and out of a crew of 436, had her captain and no fewer than 134 men killed, and 102 wounded.

The high state of discipline to which Captain Seymour—a famous name in our naval annals—had brought his crew, and their skill in gunnery, received on the 12th April in the following year a further illustration. On that day the *Amethyst* engaged the *Niemen*, of 46 guns and 339 men. The chase lasted all day, and about half an hour before midnight, having arrived sufficiently close to the French frigate, Captain Seymour opened fire with his bow-chasers. Gradually the two frigates neared each other, and about 1.45 A.M. the *Amethyst* ranged close alongside, and, exchanging broadsides, passed ahead, bore up, and raked the *Niemen*, then bracing sharp up on her lee bow. An hour after, the two ships fell on board each other, but, shaking herself clear, the *Amethyst* got on her adversary's weather beam. The *Niemen* lost her mizenmast and maintopmast, when she ceased firing, as did also the British frigate, and soon afterwards, the latter carried away her mizen and main masts, and the *Niemen's* mainmast also went by the board.

Unfortunately at this time the British frigate *Arethusa* came up, and the *Niemen*, after receiving a few rounds from the new arrival, struck her flag to her, but she was fairly the prize of the *Amethyst*. At the time of the action the latter had a crew of only 222 men and boys, of whom she lost eight killed, and two marine officers, the boatswain, and 34 men wounded. The *Niemen*, which was much cut up in her hull, lost 47 killed and 73 wounded, and her remaining mast went over the side on the day following her capture. Both the *Thetis* and *Niemen* were purchased into the Navy, the former under the name of *Brune*, and Captain Seymour received a baronetcy, while his first lieutenants in both actions were promoted.

During the year 1808, Lord Cochrane, then in command of the *Impérieuse*, rendered admirable service on the coast of Catalonia in harassing the French; and his repulse of an assault made by them on Fort Trinidad, one of the defences of Rosas, in the north-east corner of Spain, was a very brilliant exploit. A detachment of seamen and marines from the 74-gun ships *Excellent* and *Fame*, who temporarily garrisoned the citadel of Rosas, also served with credit and repulsed the enemy. In the West Indies the small islands of Marie Galante and Désirade, lying close to Guadaloupe, were captured by a small squadron under Captain Selby, of the *Cerberus*. On the other hand, the boats of the *Wanderer*, 18, and two British schooners, suffered a disastrous repulse when attempting, with an insufficient force, to storm the fort on the island of St. Martin, when Lieutenant Spearing was killed, together with six men, and 30 others were wounded.

In July, 1809, Commodore Beresford, with the *Cæsar*, 80, the 74-gun ships *Defiance* and *Donegal*, and the *Amelia*, 38, engaged three 40-gun frigates, which had taken shelter under the batteries at Sable d'Olonne, and forced them to cut their cables and run ashore, where they were wrecked, having lost in the action 24 killed and 51 wounded.

A French squadron of nine line-of-battle ships and four frigates, lying in the roads of Isle d'Aix, was blockaded by Admiral Stopford with eight ships, until the arrival of Lord Gambier, who assumed command, having under his orders eleven sail, besides frigates and small vessels. It was determined to make an attempt, from his anchorage in Basque Roads, to destroy the enemy's squadron by fireships, and Lord Cochrane, still in command of the 38-gun frigate *Impérieuse*, was selected to undertake the hazardous duty. His lordship joined the British commander-in-chief on the 3rd April, and immediately eight transports, of the thirty then in company, and the *Mediator*, storeship, were fitted as fireships, and three explosion vessels were also prepared under his immediate inspection. A week after his arrival twelve fireships arrived from the Downs, and these, together with the *Etna*, bomb-vessel, were placed under Lord Cochrane's orders, and also a squadron of six frigates and twelve smaller vessels. The British fleet of eleven sail-of-the-line lay some eight or nine miles distant from the French squadron, ready to co-operate if necessary, though the assistance they actually afforded was *nil*.

Admiral Allemand anchored his ships in two lines, about 250 yards apart, the van ship distant about 640 yards from the southern extremity of Isle d'Aix, where were some batteries, while further protection was afforded by a formidable boom, half a mile in length—composed of cables, $31\frac{1}{2}$ inches in diameter, secured by anchors, weighing five and a half tons, and flanked by buoys — which was thrown across the channel leading from Basque to Aix Roads.

On the night of the 11th April, at 8.30, the *Mediator* and the other fireships cut their cables and made sail, and two out of the three explosion vessels, one * conducted by Lord Cochrane in person, assisted by Lieutenant Bissell and four seamen, proceeded towards the roads of Isle d'Aix. These two vessels were ignited within less than three-quarters of a mile of the French line, and several fireships were ignited and abandoned prematurely, but others were admirably conducted, especially the *Mediator*.

* This vessel carried 1,500 barrels of gunpowder, with between 300 and 400 shells and thousands of hand grenades.

This ship, the largest and heaviest of the number, broke the boom, and Captain Wooldridge was so determined to do his duty effectually that he was severely scorched, and all nearly perished by the explosion. Five or six other fireships were properly employed, being towed to the attack by boats, the crews of which displayed great daring. The frigates lying nearest within the boom immediately cut their cables, and, making sail, fell back within the enemy's line, which had opened fire upon the fireships. The *Regulus*, 74, and *Ocean*, 120, which were the first ships grappled by these craft, cut their cables, and though the former escaped with slight damage, the three-decker ran aground, and was again assailed by a fireship, when the flames spread to her, notwithstanding every effort of the crew.

At this time, says the writer of a letter on board Admiral Allemand's flagship, quoted by James, the line-of-battle ships, *Tonnerre* and *Patriote*, fell on board her. At length they succeeded in booming off the fireship, and on another coming towards them, they opened fire, cutting away her mainmast and compelling her to sheer off. The *Ocean* lost about 50 men, and the *Cassard* had five killed and 15 mortally wounded by a shot from one of the fireships. The latter, and all the French fleet, except the *Foudroyant*, cut their cables, and by midnight, when the scene was of surpassing grandeur, the sky being reddened by the flames, and the darkness lit by the discharges of the guns, the whole of the remaining thirteen ships were aground.

When daylight broke, the *Ocean* was seen lying in the mud. About 500 yards from her lay the *Varsovie*, 80, and *Aquilon*, 74, on a rocky bed, and close by them, the 74-gun ships *Regulus* and *Jemappes*. The *Tonnerre*, 74, had thrown her guns overboard, and cut away her mainmast to get afloat, but was bilged, and the *Patriote*, *Tourville* and *Calcutta* (a captured Indiaman) lay in the mud, and the four frigates were also ashore. The French ships, therefore, though not actually lost, were helpless, and could have been destroyed had Lord Cochrane's proposals to Lord Gambier been adopted. That enterprising officer communicated to the Commander-in-chief their condition, and signalled to the *Caledonia*, flagship, "Eleven on shore, only two afloat," and again, "Half the fleet can destroy the enemy." But Lord Gambier lost precious time, and then weighed, only to re-anchor again before noon, about six miles from the grounded ships. He then sent the *Etna*, bomb, covered by three gun-brigs, to bombard the enemy's fleet, when the *Foudroyant* and *Cassard*, the only ships still afloat, cut their cables, and made sail for the Charente, but both took the ground on the shoal at its entrance. Aided by the flood tide, one of them succeeded, by dint of great exertions, and throwing overboard quantities of guns and stores, in getting afloat, and Lord Cochrane, despairing of receiving assistance from his chief, without orders got under weigh in the *Impérieuse*, and made sail towards the *Calcutta*, *Varsovie* and *Aquilon*, which were striving to join their consorts. In order to force the admiral to co-operate, he hoisted the signal, " The ship is in distress and requires to be assisted immediately," and, standing on, at two o'clock, anchored on the starboard quarter of the *Calcutta*, and opened fire on her, and also occasionally on the *Varsovie* and *Aquilon*.

Lord Gambier thereupon despatched the frigates *Pallas*, *Indefatigable*, *Aigle*, *Emerald* and *Unicorn*, to his assistance, and later, the seventy-fours, *Valiant* and *Revenge*. Before these ships came up, the *Calcutta* ceased firing, and the crew abandoned her, when the two French seventy-fours, after sustaining for some time the fire of the British ships, to which they were only able to reply from their stern-chase guns, hauled down their colours. Soon after, the *Calcutta* blew up, as did also the *Tonnerre*, which had been set on fire by her crew on quitting her. The only English ships to suffer were the *Impérieuse*, which had three killed, and two officers and nine wounded, besides being a good deal cut up, and the *Revenge*, which had 18 casualties, chiefly from the fire of the batteries on Isle d'Aix. The greatest sufferer of the enemy's ships was the *Varsovie*, which lost 100 men, and the captain of the *Aquilon* was killed by a round-shot, while sitting in the boat beside Lord Cochrane, from one of the *Tonnerre's* guns which accidentally went off.

In order to destroy the *Ocean* and four other ships-of-the-line which were lying aground at the entrance of the Charente, three transports were hastily converted into frigates, and Admiral Stopford, in the *Cæsar*, with these in company, stood towards them. But the *Cæsar* grounded, and as the wind was unfavourable, about two in the morning of the 13th, Admiral Stopford made sail to return, and nothing was done beyond setting fire to the *Aquilon* and *Varsovie*, both of which were destroyed. Lord Cochrane remained with the *Pallas*, Captain George Seymour, when the admiral, with the ships-of-the-line, made sail from Little Basque Roads, and despatched the *Etna* and the gun-brigs to attack the four ships aground, which they did, the *Beagle* especially displaying gallantry in the manner she brought her fire to bear on the *Ocean*, which could only reply from her stern-chasers; but on the tide falling, they all returned to their anchorage, which the *Impérieuse* and *Pallas* were unable to leave in order to assist them, owing to the velocity of the tide and the direction of the wind. Lord Cochrane remained where he was, in the hope of having an opportunity to attempt the destruction of the grounded ships, but in compliance with orders from Lord Gambier, his lordship, on the afternoon of the 14th, rejoined the British fleet in Basque Roads, and, on the following day, sailed for England. As for the French ships aground, the *Ocean*, on the 16th, managed, by throwing overboard all her guns, and also the *Cassard*, to get up the Charente. The *Indienne*, 40-gun frigate, being immovable, was blown up by her commander, and, ultimately, the *Foudroyant*, 80, and seventy-fours, *Tourville* and *Regulus*, were got afloat and joined their consorts at Rochefort.

Lord Cochrane received the Order of the Bath for the great services he had rendered, but he intimated to Lord Mulgrave, the First Lord of the Admiralty, that he should oppose from his place in Parliament any vote of thanks to Lord Gambier, whereupon the latter applied for a court-martial. This was given him, with the result that the court not only acquitted him of the charge of "neglect or delay in taking effective measures to destroy the enemy's ships on shore," but added that his conduct "was marked by zeal, judgment, ability, and an anxious attention to the welfare of his Majesty's service." This verdict was not supported by public opinion, or by the majority of the naval profession, and it would seem that Lord Gambier displayed anything but zeal or enterprise in the destruction of the French ships aground.* Cochrane alone was entitled to credit for the results obtained by the insufficient means placed at his disposal, and the destruction of three French ships-of-the-line and the *Calcutta*, armed *en flute*, by the gallant captain of the *Impérieuse*, was a very brilliant exploit, while the conduct of Commander Wooldridge, in the *Mediator*, displayed coolness and courage of a high order. The vote of thanks to Lord Gambier was carried in the House of Commons by 161 votes to 39, and without a division.

The captains of some of the French ships were tried by court-martial, with the following results:—The commanding officer of the *Tonnerre* was acquitted, of the *Tourville*, sentenced to two years' imprisonment and to be cashiered, of the *Indienne* to three months' confinement, and the captain of the *Calcutta* was condemned to death, and suffered execution on board the *Ocean*.

* What the opinion of Napoleon was may be gathered from O'Meara's "Napoleon in Exile," when the ex-emperor said:—"Lord Cochrane could not only have destroyed them, but he might and would have taken them out had your admiral supported him as he ought to have done. For in consequence of the signal made by Allemand to the ships to do the best in their power to save themselves, they became panic-struck and cut their cables. The terror of the *brulots* (fireships) was so great that they actually threw their powder overboard, so that they could have offered very little resistance. The French admiral was an imbecile, but yours was just as bad. I assure you that, if Cochrane had been supported, he would have taken every one of the ships. They ought not to have been alarmed by your *brulots*, but fear deprived them of their senses, and they no longer knew how to act in their own defence."

In May the British Government despatched an expedition to Walcheren, which came to an unfortunate termination, owing to the fever which decimated the army. The naval portion consisted of thirty-seven sail-of-the-line, with over two hundred other vessels of war, and four hundred transports. The primary object was the destruction of the enemy's ships in the Scheldt, consisting of ten seventy-fours ready for sea, besides those building at Antwerp, and also of the dockyards and arsenals there and at Flushing, which had been ceded by Louis, King of Holland, to his brother the French emperor.

The operations that ensued were conducted almost entirely by the army, but a squadron of seven seventy-fours, under Sir Richard Strachan, and several bomb-vessels and gunboats, assisted by their fire in reducing the defences of Flushing, which surrendered on the 15th August, and was the only success attained in this unfortunate campaign. A brigade of seamen from the fleet also served in the shore batteries at the bombardment of Flushing. The conduct of operations was not remarkable for either audacity or celerity, as may be gathered from the famous epigram descriptive of the action of the military and naval commanders.

> "The Earl of Chatham, with his sword drawn, stood waiting for Sir Richard Strachan;
> Sir Richard, longing to be at 'em, stood waiting for the Earl of Chatham."

The year 1809 was almost uneventful as regards any important successes achieved by the Navy, but in the Mediterranean, where Lord Collingwood continued to hold the command, Rear-Admiral Martin, when chasing some ships and transports, despatched from Toulon to throw supplies into Barcelona, drove ashore the *Robuste*, 80, flagship of Rear-Admiral Baudin, and the *Lion*, 74, which were abandoned by their crews and set on fire and destroyed. To effect the capture of eleven transports and armed vessels, which had taken shelter under the batteries in the Bay of Rosas, Lord Collingwood sent Captain Hallowell with the seventy-fours, *Tigre* and *Cumberland*, the frigates *Volontaire*, *Apollo*, and *Topaze*, and the brigs *Philomel*, *Scout*, and *Tuscan*. Under the orders of Lieutenant Tailour, of the *Tigre*, the boats pushed off and, with cheers, boarded and, notwithstanding a heavy fire, succeeded in capturing the whole of the eleven vessels, which were either brought off or burnt at their moorings. The British loss in effecting this gallantly executed service, was 15 killed, including one lieutenant and a master's mate, and 55 wounded, among whom were the gallant Tailour, who received his well-earned promotion, four lieutenants and three midshipmen. The islands of Zante, Cephalonia, and Ithaca, of the Ionian group, surrendered without opposition to a combined British military and naval force, Corfu having previously been wrested from the French.

As in previous years, some gallant services were rendered by ships and boats in action with the enemy. The brig *Onyx*, of 10 guns and 75 men, captured, after a spirited action, the Dutch brig *Manly*, of 12 guns and 94 men, and the prize, which formerly belonged to the British Navy, was restored to the service, while both Commander Gill and Lieutenant Garrett, first of the *Onyx*, received promotion. Near the Texel, the *Aimable*, 32, Lord George Stuart, took the French corvette *Iris*, of 24 guns and 140 men, after a brief running fight, and she also was purchased into the service under the name of *Rainbow*. The 38-gun frigate *Loire* captured the *Helen*, of 20 guns and 160 men, after a close action of twenty minutes; and in the West Indies, the *Cleopatra*, 32, Captain Pechell, *Jason*, 38, Captain Maude, and *Hazard*, 18, Commander Cameron, after a chase, drove the *Topaze*, 40, to take shelter under a battery in Guadaloupe. Here she was closely attacked by the *Jason* and *Cleopatra*, the *Hazard* engaging the battery, and was compelled to haul down her colours, having sustained a loss of 12 killed and 14 wounded, out of a complement, including 100 soldiers, of about 430 men. She also was added to the Navy, under the name of *Alcmene*. The French frigate *Junon*, 46, when chased by the *Latona*, 38, and brig *Supérieure*, carrying then only four guns, found herself confronted by the *Horatio*, 46, Captain Scott, which brought her to action. Running alongside of the enemy, the two frigates became closely engaged, but the *Junon*—having disabled her adversary aloft by her fire, by which also the captain and first lieutenant were seriously wounded, when the command devolved on Lieutenant Hon. G. Douglas—managed to shake off her adversary. But the *Latona* now came up, and the 18-gun sloop *Driver*, when, finding escape impossible, and her masts having gone over the side, the French frigate hauled down her colours. The *Horatio*, out of 270 hands, had one midshipman and six men killed, and besides her captain and first lieutenant, the wounded included two other officers and 28 men wounded. The *Junon* had 130 casualties, out of a crew numbering 323, including her gallant commander, mortally wounded, and was added to the Navy list under her own name.

On the other hand, the service suffered a loss in the *Proserpine*, 32, Captain Otter, which, cruising near Toulon, was captured by the 40-gun frigates *Penelope* and *Pauline*. One frigate took up her station on the *Proserpine's* port, and the other on the starboard quarter, and in half an hour their fire had reduced her to the condition of a wreck, so that she had no option but to strike. Captain Otter remained a prisoner in France until the conclusion of the war in 1814, and on his release was tried by court-martial for the loss of his ship, and honourably acquitted. But this ill fortune was more than counterbalanced by the capture of the *D'Haupoult*, by a British squadron, after a long chase off Martinique. The French seventy-four was in company with two others, which, with three frigates, had managed to make their escape from Lorient, and when her consorts eluded pursuit, was persistently chased by the *Pompée*, 74, Captain Fahie, with which were the 18-gun brigs *Recruit* and *Hazard*. These latter she managed to shake off, but the frigates *Latona* and *Castor* took up the pursuit, and the latter, engaging her, gave time to the *Pompée* to come up, and eventually the French seventy-four, now a complete wreck, hauled down her colours, after a running fight lasting fifty-five hours. The *Pompée* lost her boatswain and eight men killed, and three officers, including her captain and first lieutenant, and 27 wounded, and the *Castor* had seven casualties. The *D'Haupoult*, out of her complement of 680, had between 80 and 90 killed and wounded. During the chase, Commander Charles Napier, of the *Recruit*, who earned great distinction in the war and afterwards, specially distinguished himself by the pertinacity with which he hung about the seventy-four, giving and receiving her fire at close quarters; and, in reward for his gallantry, Sir Alexander Cochrane, who had his flag on the *Neptune*, 98, one of the chasing squadron, appointed him to the command of the prize, which he commissioned under the name of the *Abercromby*.

At the same time the *Felicité*, of 14 guns and 174 men, when escaping from Guadaloupe, was overhauled by the *Latona*, and struck her flag; and her consort, the *Furieuse*, mounting 20 guns, and having a crew of 200 men, was brought to action, a few weeks later, by the sloop-of-war *Bonne-Citoyenne*, of 20 guns and 127 men, Commander Mounsey. The former was in the act of taking possession of a prize she had made when sighted by the British sloop, which, after a chase lasting all night, succeeded in getting alongside, and commenced the action at pistol-shot range. The battle was furiously contested for nearly seven hours, both ships being greatly crippled aloft, but at length, when the *Bonne-Citoyenne*, having expended nearly all her powder, had taken up a position athwart her hawse, with the intention of boarding, the *Furieuse* hauled down her colours. The British ship, whose main and mizen masts went over the side after the action, had only six casualties, but her antagonist, which had five feet of water in her hold, and was dismasted, had 35 killed and 57 wounded, the greater portion dangerously, including her captain, two lieutenants, and three midshipmen. She was navigated with difficulty to Halifax, and was bought into the

Navy, and commissioned by Captain Mounsey, who was posted for his gallantry, and his first lieutenant was also promoted.

Good service was rendered in the Gulf of Venice, off Pesaro, by Captain Jahleel Brenton, with his ship, the *Spartan*, and the *Amphion* and *Mercury*, and by the boats of the *Scout*, under Lieutenant Battersby, in capturing the fort of Carri, between Marseilles and the Rhone, for which he was promoted. Not less gallant was Captain Griffiths, of the *Topaze*, 36, in engaging two French frigates off Paxo, near Corfu, which left him the honours of the action, and of Captain Staines, of the corvette *Cyane*, of 32 guns and 175 men, who, in company with the 18-gun brig *Espoir*, and some British and Sicilian gunboats, was attacked off Naples by the French ships, *Ceres*, *Fama*, and a flotilla of gun-vessels. The wind falling light, the *Cyane*, notwithstanding her inferiority, manned her sweeps and stood towards the *Ceres*, carrying 42 guns and 350 men, which she engaged at half pistol-shot range. But ultimately she was compelled to haul off, being reduced to the condition of a wreck aloft, and having forty-five shots through her side. In this action she had two men killed and 20 wounded, among whom were her captain (who lost his arm out of the socket), both her lieutenants and one midshipman. The *Cyane* was brought out of action by her master and sailed for England to be refitted.

In May of the following year, when Captain Brenton was cruising off Naples in the *Spartan*, Murat, the usurping king, embarked 400 troops on board the French frigate, *Ceres*, and corvette, *Fama*, of 28 guns and 220 men, and sent them out, with seven 8-gun brigs and seven gunboats, each mounting a long 18-pounder, with the object of boarding and bringing into port the British frigate. This was a formidable squadron for a single ship, carrying 46 guns and 258 men, but then the latter were British seamen, and their commander one of the most enterprising officers in the Navy. When within pistol-shot range the *Spartan* poured in a treble-shotted broadside, causing terrible carnage among the troops on her antagonist's deck, drawn up in readiness to board. She also engaged in succession the *Fama* and brig. At one time the *Spartan* was in a condition of much danger, as the breeze had fallen, and she was surrounded by the enemy's ships and gunboats, but the wind again freshened, and the frigate was so well handled by her gallant commander, who was severely wounded, that she cut off her opponents. With the exception of the brig, which struck her colours, they steered for Naples, but in so crippled a state from her fire that they had to be towed back by the gunboats. In the action the *Spartan* had an officer and nine men killed, and her captain, first lieutenant (who was promoted) and 20 men wounded. The French acknowledged to a loss of 30 killed, including the second captain of the *Ceres*, and 90 wounded, exclusive of the loss experienced by the brig. To return to the events of the year 1809.

The boats of the *Amphion* under Lieutenant Phillott, with 70 men, stormed a battery between Venice and Trieste, in the most gallant manner, and turned the guns on some gunboats, which were taken and burnt, for which exploit Mr. Phillott received promotion. The boats of her consort, the *Mercury*, under Lieutenant Pell, did equally well, cutting out a gunboat from the port of Ruvigno, and the gallant officer in command, who had previously lost a leg in his country's service, was wounded in two places. The 38-gun frigate, *Melpomene*, Captain Warren, one dark night was attacked by twenty Danish gunboats in the Great Belt, and had a difficult task in beating off his numerous opponents, each of which carried a long 18- or 24-pounder. Her loss on this occasion was five killed and 29 wounded, and she was so much shattered that, on her return to England, she was not again commissioned for sea.

Our ships in the Baltic were also frequently engaged with the Russian gunboats and batteries. The boats of the *Bellerophon* carried a fort off Hango, mounting four 24-pounders, and an attack by the boats of a squadron on a flotilla of eight Russian gunboats was conducted with conspicuous success. Seventeen boats from the 74-gun ships, *Bellerophon* and *Implacable*, the *Melpomene*, and *Prometheus*, 18, carrying 270 officers and men, under command of Lieutenant Hawkey, first of the *Implacable*, proceeded on this duty, and, regardless of the fire of the enemy, who were ready to receive the attack, these gallant British seamen, without firing a shot, boarded and captured the whole flotilla with the exception of one, which succeeded in escaping. Twelve merchant-vessels, under their protection, laden with supplies for the Russian army, also fell into their hands, and one armed ship, which was burnt, the others being brought out. In this brilliant exploit Lieutenant Hawkey was killed, with the words, "Hurrah! push on! England for ever!" on his lips, and Commander Martin declared, not without warrant, that his death was a calamity to his country. The loss incurred was two lieutenants, one midshipman, a second master, and 13 seamen and marines killed, and 37 wounded. The Russians had 63 killed, and of 127 prisoners, 51 were wounded, exclusive of others who escaped ashore, while many were drowned.

Not less sanguinary and hardly-contested was the resistance of four Russian gunboats in the Gulf of Finland to an attack made on them by seventeen boats of the British squadron, under Commander Forrest, of the 32-gun frigate *Cerberus*. The attack commenced at 10.30 in the evening, and was successful, three of the gunboats, each mounting two long 18-pounders, and having an aggregate of 137 men, and an armed brig, with a crew of 23, being brought off. The British loss was a lieutenant, marine officer, and midshipman, with six men killed, and Captain Forrest, one lieutenant, three midshipmen and 46 wounded. The enemy acknowledged to a loss of 28 killed and 59 wounded. Commander Forrest was promoted for his gallantry on this occasion.

Very gallant, but unhappily unsuccessful, was the resistance offered by the British frigate *Junon*, 46, Captain Shortland, to two French ships of equal force, and two armed vessels mounting each 20 guns, and laden with troops and military stores for Guadaloupe. The frigates stationed themselves on either side of the *Junon*, while the armed transports took up a position ahead and astern, and the soldiers on board kept up a destructive musketry fire. Captain Shortland was dangerously wounded, and died after much suffering; and the *Junon*, having made a gallant resistance of forty-five minutes, during which time the action had been conducted yard-arm to yard-arm, hauled down her colours. She was so much shattered, both in her hull and aloft, that her captors set fire to her, and out of 224 all told, she had 20 officers and men killed and 40 wounded. The two frigates had 21 killed and 18 wounded. The two armed transports separated from the frigates, and being chased by the *Blonde*, 38-gun frigate, and some other ships, took refuge under some batteries in a cove in the island of Guadaloupe, where they anchored broadside to the sea. Here they were attacked by the British squadron, and captured, and the batteries were stormed or silenced, but not without considerable loss, Commander Cameron, of the *Hazard*, and the first lieutenant of the *Blonde*, together with seven men, being killed, and 22 wounded.

Four French frigates, *Venus*, *Manche*, *Caroline*, and *Bellone*, succeeding in escaping from the blockaded French ports, reached the Indian seas, where, with Mauritius as a base of operations, they committed serious depredations on British commerce. The *Caroline*, of 46 guns and 330 men, encountered in the Bay of Bengal three Indiamen, homeward bound with rich cargoes, and, after an obstinate resistance, two of them, the *Streatham* and *Europe*, having most of their guns dismounted and being greatly shattered, were compelled to surrender, but the *Lord Keith* managed to escape. During the year, Commander Willoughby, of the 18-gun sloop *Otter*, an officer of distinguished enterprise and gallantry, cut out a lugger from under the protection of some batteries in Mauritius, and an important service was rendered by the capture of St. Paul, in Isle Bourbon, where the *Caroline* had taken shelter. To effect this, 368 troops from the British garrison of the adjacent island of Rodriguez, under Colonel Keating, with 236 seamen and marines from the squadron, under Commodore Rowley, of the *Raisonable*, 64, led by Commander Nesbit Willoughby, were lan'ed about seven miles from St. Paul, and in a few hours succeeded in capturing the batteries, while the ships, standing in, compelled the *Caroline* and her two prizes to cut their cables and drift ashore, whence they were hove off without having sustained damage. The total British loss was only 15 killed and 58 wounded. For his gallantry Commander Willoughby received post rank, and was appointed to the *Néréide*, Captain Corbett being given the command of the *Caroline*, renamed the *Bourbonaise*.

The French frigates, *Venus* and *Manche*, and the 14-gun corvette *Créole*, under Commodore Hamelin, also committed depredations on British commerce in the Bay of Bengal and to the eastward. They succeeded in capturing the brig *Orient*, and later the Hon. Company's Indiamen *Charlton*, *United Kingdom*, and *Windham*, the last of which made a determined and prolonged resistance. Captain Stewart and his crew were taken on board the *Venus*, which, on the way to Port Louis, lost all three topmasts in a hurricane, and when on the point of foundering, with seven feet of water in the hold, Commodore Hamelin requested Captain Stewart to save the ship. This that skilful officer actually succeeded in doing when all hope had been abandoned by her French officers and crew, who had retired below to await their fate. The *Windham* was recaptured by the 36-gun frigate *Magicienne*, and Captain Stewart, who was sent to the Cape, again assumed command of his ship. The fourth French frigate, the *Bellone*, captured the 18-gun sloop *Victor*, Commander Stopford, and a few weeks later, she took the Portuguese frigate *Minerve*, the crew of which behaved with great cowardice.

In the course of the year 1809, a squadron of fourteen ships and vessels, from Goree, effected the capture of Senegal, and in the West Indies, an expedition on a large scale was despatched against Martinique. Sir Alexander Cochrane, with six sail-of-the-line, six frigates, and fourteen smaller ships, having in charge a fleet of transports, conveying 10,000 troops, under General Beckwith, arrived off the island, and on the 30th January, the soldiers were disembarked. The French troops being in greatly inferior force, the capital, Fort Royal, and the other fortified ports were easily reduced during the following month, and the whole island passed under the British flag. The Governor-General, Admiral Villaret-Joyeuse, Lord Howe's opponent on the

A BOARDING PARTY.

"glorious First of June," was tried by court-martial in Paris for not making a more effective resistance, and, with some of his officers, was stripped of his rank and honours. In the French settlement of Cayenne, Captain Yeo, of the 20-gun ship *Confiance*, acting in conjunction with about 500 Portuguese troops from Brazil, was equally successful. In the operations Captain Yeo, on this side of the Globe, like Captain Willoughby on the other, displayed the signal gallantry for which he had acquired a high character in the Navy, and both these officers were subsequently knighted.

Throughout the whole of 1810, owing to the vigilance of the British blockading squadron, few French ships were able to quit their ports. During the year Sweden entered into an alliance against England, but Sir James Saumarez effectually prevented either her navy or that of Russia from committing any mischief. England experienced a great loss by the death, on the 7th March, of Lord Collingwood, commanding the Mediterranean fleet, who was on his way home for the benefit of his health. Lord Collingwood was one of the best officers in the Navy, in this golden age of its greatness, and in every walk of life, both public and private, his worth was equally marked, and his character noble. He actually served afloat forty-four out of the fifty years his name appeared on the Navy List, and was rarely able to spend the briefest time on shore with his wife and family, for whom he entertained an intense affection. The true nobility of his character is apparent in the letters published, twenty years after his death, in his memoirs, written by his son-in-law, Mr. Newnham Collingwood. Brave as a lion in action, and the idol of all ranks of the service he adorned by his professional talents, he was modest to a fault, temperate in his habits, and was never heard to make use of an oath, a rare virtue at a time when swearing was common in all stations of life, from the throne to the cottage. Truly, take him for all in all, perhaps Collingwood was the noblest character the Navy has produced.

A British squadron and some troops, under General Oswald, took the island of Santa Maura, in the Ionian group, so that only Corfu remained in the possession of the French. The Navy had six killed, and 32 wounded, including Captains Eyre and Stephens, of the *Magnificent* and *Imogene*, and three other officers; and the troops lost 16 and 87 respectively. As in previous years, numberless were the gallant deeds performed in 1810, by British officers and seamen, in all parts of the globe, cutting out the enemy's vessels from under the protection of coast batteries, or capturing them at sea, but the exigencies of space prevent our affording them even the barest mention. Suffice it to say that, though owing to the French Marine having well-nigh disappeared from the sea, frigate actions were not so frequent or important as in earlier years of the war, yet the daring spirit that has always animated the Navy had in no way diminished, though its scope had become lessened by the very success that rewarded its efforts.

In the Gulf of Trieste the boats of the *Amphion* and *Cerberus*, commanded by Lieutenant Slaughter, second of the former, proceeded to bring out several vessels which the frigates had chased into the harbour of Grox. At dawn of day the party landed to the right of the town, and encountered a body of French troops, whom they drove back, capturing an officer and 39 men of the 81st Regiment. Entering the town, they took possession of the boats, twenty-five in number, and a detachment of men from the *Active*, just then landed, compelled another body of 24 French regular soldiers to lay down their arms. In effecting this service, the British experienced a loss of 10 killed, eight by the bayonet, showing the hand-to-hand nature of the conflict, and eight wounded. The boats of the *Thames* and *Pilot* also brought off a convoy of transport vessels with supplies for Murat's army, which ran ashore at Amanthea to prevent their being taken. A young officer, Midshipman Marshall, afterwards the author of the "Royal Naval Biography," a well-known and valuable work, greatly distinguished himself, when in command of two boats, in boarding, off the Spanish coast, a privateer of four guns and 59 men. His commanding officer, Lieutenant Davis, having been killed, this young officer, with only 26 seamen and marines, sprang on board the privateer, and carried her after a sharp encounter, his own loss being four killed and six wounded.

On one occasion a British force met with a repulse with serious loss. The boats of the seventy-fours *Kent* and *Ajax*, of the frigate *Cambrian*, and of the sloops *Sparrowhawk* and *Minstrel*, landed a party of 350 seamen and 250 marines, under Captain Fane of the *Cambrian*, in order to capture a convoy lying in the mole of Palamos, under the protection of some batteries. But they encountered severe opposition, and, retiring through the town instead of to the beach, where the ships would have covered their embarkation, they were subjected to a heavy fire from the walls and houses, when two officers and 31 men were killed, 15 officers and 74 men wounded, and two officers and 84 seamen and marines taken prisoners.

In the Indian seas during the year 1810, British commerce suffered heavily from the depredations of French privateers and ships-of-war, rendezvousing at Mauritius. On the 31st July three outward Indiamen, *Ceylon*, *Windham*, and *Astell*, were overhauled in the Mozambique Channel by the French frigates *Bellone* and *Minerve*, and corvette *Victor*, formerly the *Jena*, captured in October, 1808, but recaptured from us. The Indiamen, mounting 26 guns, made a gallant and protracted resistance against superior force, but ultimately the *Ceylon* and *Windham* were compelled to strike their flags, though the *Astell* effected her escape. The *Ceylon* had six killed and 21 wounded, among the latter being her captain and chief officer, and the lieutenant-colonel commanding a detachment of the 24th Regiment on board the ship. The *Windham* also had six killed and 18 wounded, including three of her officers, and the *Astell* lost eight killed and 37 wounded, among whom was her captain. The French aggregate loss was 22 killed and 38 wounded. The resistance made was most honourable to all concerned, and the East India Company suitably rewarded the officers and ships' companies.

Meantime a British naval force had arrived off Mauritius from the Cape, consisting of the 36-gun frigates *Iphigenia*, Captain Lambert, *Magicienne*, Captain Lucius Curtis, and *Néréide*, Captain Willoughby, and sloop-of-war *Otter*. Captain Willoughby, whose name has already been mentioned as an officer of great enterprise and gallantry, desired to cut out a large merchant-ship he discerned off Jacolet, on the island, and proceeded with his boats, carrying 50 men, to effect the capture. Landing he took a battery and spiked the guns, and then swimming and wading across a stream, stormed a battery on a hill. He now got possession of the ship, but, finding she was an American, released her, and returned to the *Néréide*. Soon after this event Commodore Rowley arrived to take command of the squadron, with the 38-gun frigates *Boadicea* and *Sirius*.

The first enterprise they undertook was the capture of the island of Bourbon, in which some troops under Colonel Keating participated, the total loss being 22 killed and drowned, and 73 wounded, chiefly among the soldiers. They next attacked the Isle de la Passe, about four miles off Grand Port, in Mauritius, which was gallantly captured by 71 officers and men of the *Sirius* and *Iphigenia*, under the command of Lieutenant Norman. While scaling the works that brave young officer was shot through the heart, but Lieutenants Chad and Watling, who commanded detachments, and were acting independently, stormed the works, with the loss of seven killed and 18 wounded.

Captain Willoughby landed with a strong party near Grand Port, and made a march of 22 miles along the enemy's territory, beating off their attacks, and captured a fort. This officer displayed equal daring in action and consideration towards the inhabitants he encountered. While thus engaged, a French squadron—the *Bellone*,

Victor, and *Minerve*, with their prizes, the *Windham* and *Ceylon*, appeared off Isle de la Passe, and were inveigled there by Captain Willoughby, who had secured the French private signals. When the *Victor* arrived within pistol-shot of the *Néréide*, Captain Willoughby, who commanded both that ship and the island, opened fire with good effect on the enemy's vessels which, on discovering their mistake, stood away and anchored at Grand Port. Captain Pym, of the *Sirius*, who had recaptured the Indiaman, *Windham*, with the *Iphigenia* and *Magicienne*, arrived off Isle de la Passe to the assistance of Captain Willoughby, and the squadron at 5 P.M. attacked the enemy's ships in Grand Port. Unfortunately the *Sirius* and *Magicienne* grounded, but the *Néréide* gallantly engaged the *Bellone*, of much superior force, when the French commodore was wounded, and Captain Willoughby was also severely wounded by a splinter, which knocked out his left eye. The *Néréide*, owing to her cable being cut away, swung stern on to the *Bellone*, which kept up so destructive a fire that nearly all her crew and the soldiers on board were killed or disabled, among the latter being the first lieutenant (mortally), the second lieutenant (dangerously), and one marine and three military officers. As nearly all her quarter-deck and many of her main-deck guns were disabled, and the ship was almost reduced to the condition of a wreck, Captain Willoughby surrendered shortly before midnight.

Of 281 of all ranks on board at the time of the action, including 69 officers and men of the 33rd and 69th Regiments and Madras Artillery, she had four officers and 88 men killed, and her captain, six officers and 130 wounded, so that it cannot be said that she was not defended to the last extremity. The *Iphigenia* had five killed and 13 wounded, including her first lieutenant, and the *Magicienne*, eight and 20 respectively. The French ships had 37 killed, including a lieutenant of the *Bellone*, and one of the *Victor*, and 112 wounded. As the *Magicienne* could not be got off, she was set on fire, and blew up with her colours flying; and on the following day, every effort to float the *Sirius* having failed, she also was destroyed, to prevent her falling into the hands of the enemy, who had erected on shore a fresh battery, from which they commenced cannonading her.

Meantime the *Iphigenia*, under the command of Captain Lambert, an officer of great enterprise and skill, had worked herself out of a position of much difficulty and danger, when she sighted a French squadron from Port Louis, coming to attack her, consisting of the frigates *Vénus*, *Astrée*, and *Manche*. Commodore Hamelin demanded her surrender and that of the Isle de la Passe, and as the Governor of Grand Port threatened that the *Bellone* would also attack her, Captain Lambert reluctantly yielded to superior force. Thus by this disastrous affair the British Navy lost four frigates, and the French gained a temporary ascendency in these waters.

On the 11th September, 1810, a fortnight after these events, the *Africaine*, 48, Captain Corbett, arrived from England, off Mauritius, on her way to Madras, and in trying to cut out an armed schooner, which had run ashore, her boats had two men killed and 16 wounded. The *Africaine* then bore up for Bourbon (now known as Réunion), which was at that time in our possession, and off the island sighted the frigates *Iphigenia* and *Astrée*.

Soon after, the 38-gun frigate *Boadicea*, Commodore Rowley, with the 16-gun sloop *Otter*, Commander Tomkinson, and gun-brig *Staunch*, Lieutenant Street, proceeded in chase of the French frigates, but the *Africaine* first ranged up within musket-shot of the *Astrée*, which she brought to action shortly after two in the morning. The second broadside mortally wounded Captain Corbett, when the command devolved on Lieutenant Tullidge, who, acting under the last instructions of his dying commander, brought the French frigate to close action. The *Astrée* ranged ahead, but the *Africaine*, making sail, closed with the *Iphigenia*, when a sudden fall of wind left her exposed within half pistol-shot of these ships, one of which, being on her starboard bow, raked her with terrible effect. Lieutenant Tullidge gallantly continued the action, though severely wounded in four places, with his second in command, Lieutenant Forder, mortally wounded, and the master killed by a round-shot. At length—the *Boadicea* being becalmed some miles astern, and the ship reduced to the condition of a wreck, with her masts in such a condition that, together with the bowsprit, they all went over the side an hour or two later, and her guns nearly all either disabled, or their crews decimated by the enemy's fire—at five the colours of the *Africaine* were hauled down. Of 295 seamen, marines, and soldiers on board her when she commenced the action, she had lost two officers (exclusive of the captain) and 47 men killed, and eight officers and 106 wounded. The *Astrée*, with 44 guns and 360 men, had only three casualties, and the *Iphigenia*, carrying 42 guns and 258 hands, had nine killed and 33 wounded.

A breeze soon after sprang up, and the *Boadicea*, with the *Otter* and *Staunch*, came up with the French frigates, which abandoned their prize, and made sail, the *Astrée* towing the *Iphigenia*. Rowley took the *Africaine* in tow, and made his way to the bay of St. Paul, where she left the dismasted frigate. Lieutenant Tullidge was acquitted of all blame by the verdict of a court-martial for the loss of his ship, and received promotion.

The next action fought in these waters took place on the 17th September, when the *Ceylon*, Captain Charles Gordon (formerly an Indiaman), of 40 guns and 295 men, including 100 soldiers of the 69th and 86th Regiments, with Major-general Abercrombie and his staff, whom she had taken on board at Madras, engaged the *Venus*, a heavy frigate, carrying 44 guns and 380 men, and the corvette *Victor* of 16 guns and 120 men.

The action with the *Vénus* began soon after midnight, and notwithstanding the disparity of force, Captain Gordon made a gallant and protracted resistance. By three o'clock the *Ceylon* had lost all her topmasts, and was much cut up aloft, but she continued for a further hour and a half, when the *Victor*, having taken up a position athwart her bows, she showed a light as a signal that she had surrendered. In the action she had lost 10 killed, and Captain Gordon, four officers, and 28 soldiers and seamen wounded. The *Vénus* also lost her topmasts and mizenmast, but her casualties were unknown. Commodore Rowley, lying at St. Paul's, discovered the French ships with the prize about three leagues in the offing, and, accompanied by the *Otter* and *Staunch*, got under way and proceeded in chase. The *Victor* now cast off the *Ceylon*, which again hoisted the British flag, and the *Boadicea*, soon after four in the afternoon, got alongside the *Vénus*, and after an action lasting only ten minutes, during which she lost nine killed and 15 wounded, the French frigate struck her colours. The *Victor* got away, and Commodore Rowley returned to St. Paul's Bay with his prize, which was renamed the *Néréide*, in commemoration of the gallantry displayed at Grand Port by Captain Willoughby's ship.

The British and Indian Governments had determined to undertake the conquest of Mauritius, which had so long afforded a rendezvous to French cruisers in the Indian seas, whence they preyed on English commerce, and on the 29th November, 1810, a fleet, consisting of the *Illustrious*, 74, twelve frigates, four sloops, besides small vessels, with about fifty transports, conveying some 10,000 troops, arrived from India and the Cape at Grande Baie, about 12 miles from Port Louis, the capital. The same day the troops were landed, and after a slight resistance, all opposition on the part of the French was overcome, and on the 3rd December, the island passed under the dominion of England, and has ever since remained an integral part of our Colonial Empire. In these operations the British loss was 28 killed, 94 wounded, and 45 missing. In Port

Louis harbour were found the frigates *Bellone*, *Minerve*, *Manche*, *Astrée*, and *Iphigenia*, the corvette *Victor*, two brigs, and the late English Indiamen *Charlton*, *Ceylon*, and *United Kingdom*, and twenty-four French merchantmen. The *Iphigenia* was restored to her position on the Navy list, and the *Bellone* and *Astrée* were purchased into the service under the names *Junon* and *Pomone*.

In February of this year, in the East Indies, the Dutch settlement of Amboyna, in the Moluccas,* was attacked by a squadron under the command of Captain Tucker, consisting of his ship, the 38-gun frigate *Dover*, the *Cornwallis*, 44, Captain Montagu, and *Samarang*, 16, Commander Spencer. A detachment of 400 seamen and soldiers was landed, under the command of Major Court, of the Hon. Company's service, and assisted by the fire of the ships, the enemy's works were captured after some sharp fighting, and the whole island surrendered. Celebes and other islands also submitted, but Captain Cole, of the *Caroline*, 36, had a heavy task in capturing the strongly-fortified settlement of Banda Neira, in the island of Banda. In company with him was the 38-gun frigate *Piemontaise*, Captain Foote, and the 18-gun brig *Barracouta*, Commander Kenah, the frigates having on board about 100 officers and men of the Madras European Regiment, which had done such good service at Amboyna. The town of Banda Neira was defended with several batteries, mounting in all 138 guns, and had a garrison of 700 regular troops and about 800 militia; but, nothing daunted, Captain Cole, on arriving off the port, embarked in his boats 140 seamen and marines and 40 soldiers, and landing at daylight on the 9th July, amid a storm of wind and rain, advanced and took the first battery. Proceeding thence, with Captain Kenah and Lieutenant Carew, he attacked the castle of Belgica. Favoured by the storm and darkness, the gallant fellows planted their scaling-ladders and carried the formidable fortress with a rush, a feat of arms that ranks with Captain Brisbane's brilliant exploit at Curaçoa. Fort Nassau now surrendered, and the Union Jack was soon hoisted on the whole of the Banda Islands. In the West Indies, also, a combined naval and military expedition effected the capture of Guadaloupe, but the Army are entitled to most of the credit here, as the sister service was scarcely engaged. The Dutch islands were also captured, thus completing the reduction of the colonies of those powers in the West Indies.

In the year 1811, the French Government, notwithstanding their losses at Trafalgar, by great exertions had succeeded in collecting a fleet of fifteen sail-of-the-line at

---

* The Molucca Islands, as well as the Banda group, had been captured in 1796 by Admiral Rainier's squadron, but were surrendered at the peace.

Flushing, and sixteen at Toulon. Besides these there were between twelve and fifteen ships under construction at Antwerp and Flushing, and a large number at Lorient, Rochefort, and Toulon; and eleven sail lay ready for sea in these ports, and seven in the Texel. Blockading the Scheldt and Texel were British squadrons, that in the Mediterranean, during the latter half of the year, being under Sir Edward Pellew, on his return from his command in the East Indies; but though he had only twelve ships under his command, his French rival made no attempt to meet him in battle on the open sea.

Some skirmishes took place between single ships off Toulon, and in the Channel the Boulogne flotilla again showed some signs of vitality. The 16-gun brig *Hawke*, Commander Bourchier, performed excellent service near Barfleur, where her boats, under Lieutenant Price, cut out a brig mounting 10 guns, together with three transports. The *Hotspur*, 36, Captain Percy, succeeded in sinking one brig and driving on shore two others, but herself taking the ground, suffered severely from the fire of a battery and some field-guns. The 10-gun brigs *Rinaldo*, Commander Anderson, and *Redpole*, Commander Macdonald, also engaged near Boulogne a "prame," or ship-rigged gun-vessel, carrying 12 long 24-pounders, and a brig. On the 20th September, in the presence of the Emperor Napoleon, a division of prames, under Admiral Baste, stood out of Boulogne and engaged the 38-gun frigate *Naiad*, Captain Carteret, but after a warm cannonade, returned to port without having silenced the British frigate. On the following day seven prames and ten brigs stood out again, and an engagement took place between them and the *Naiad*, *Redpole*, *Rinaldo*, and 18-gun brig *Castilian*. Captain Carteret engaged Rear-admiral Baste, and on one of the prames coming to the latter's assistance, boarded and captured her after an obstinate resistance, the French loss being between 30 and 40. The three British brigs participated in the action, in which the *Redpole* lost her first lieutenant, but the enemy succeeded in regaining the protection of their batteries, and altogether the French Emperor could not have been very well pleased with the results of the action.

In the previous month, ten boats of the *Quebec*, and brigs *Raven*, *Exertion*, *Redbreast*, and some armed cutters, with 117 officers and men, under the command of Lieutenant Blyth, first of the *Quebec*, attempted to cut out four gun-boats lying at anchor off the island of Nordeney, on the Dutch coast. Lieutenant Blyth carried by boarding the nearest brig, but as he was turning the fire of her guns on the others, an explosion of loose powder took place, by which 19 officers and men were killed or wounded, Lieutenant Blyth being blown into the sea, though he regained the deck. Nevertheless, the three remaining gun-boats were secured, the British loss in the attack being two killed and nine wounded, including four officers, one mortally. Lieutenant Blyth, who had been wounded, received promotion for his persevering gallantry.

Captain Maurice, who had defended the Diamond Rock some six years before, earned much distinction by the distinguished gallantry with which, while in command of the small island of Anholt, in the Cattegat, he repulsed the attack of over 1,500 Danish troops, and a flotilla of twelve gun-boats. His garrison consisted of 380 marines, and he succeeded in bringing about the surrender of 520 officers and men, with the loss of 32 killed and wounded. On this occasion the *Tartar*, 32, Captain Baker, and 16-gun brig *Sheldrake*, Commander Stewart, chased the flotilla, which was seeking to return to Jutland and Sweden, and the former captured two gun-boats, and the brig a third, carrying 64 men, and a large 6-gun lugger, having on board an officer and 60 men.

The year 1811 closed with the loss of three ships of the British fleet in the Baltic, with a great sacrifice of life. The *St. George*, 98, Captain Guion, bearing the flag of Rear-admiral Reynolds, was convoying a fleet of one hundred and twenty merchantmen, bound for England, when, on the 15th of November, while lying at anchor off the island of Zealand, she encountered a violent tempest, in which about thirty merchantmen were lost, and the *St. George* was driven ashore, but got off. Proceeding to Wingo Sound, under jury-masts, she sailed again from thence on 17th December, with the fleet under her convoy, accompanied by the *Defence*, 74, Captain Atkins, and *Cressy*, Captain Pater. Again she encountered a severe gale, which increased almost to a hurricane, and the *St. George* and *Defence* on the 24th, after five days' battling with the storm, were driven on the coast of Jutland, when the whole of their crews perished, with the exception of six from the flagship and twelve from the seventy-four. On the following day, the *Hero*, 74, Captain Newman, was lost off the Texel sands with all hands, except 12 men who were washed ashore. By these accumulated misfortunes the Navy sustained the loss of 2,000 gallant officers and men, and the catastrophe was the severest that had befallen the country since the foundering, a century before, of Sir Cloudesley Shovel's flagship and her consorts, off the Scilly Isles.

The most important naval action of the year was that between a squadron of British frigates and another of French and Venetians, off Lissa, in the Adriatic. On the 13th March, Commodore Dubourdieu arrived off the port, with three 40-gun French frigates, the *Favourite*, *Danae*, and *Flora*, and the Venetian ships *Corona*, 40, *Bellona* and *Carolina*, of 32 guns, the brig *Mercure*, and four smaller vessels. Here they fell in with Captain Hoste's squadron, consisting of his ship, the *Amphion*, 32, *Active*, 38, Captain James Alexander Gordon, and *Cerberus*, 32, Captain Whitby (which had been engaged with the enemy in the Gulf of Trieste, in the previous year, as already related), together with the 22-gun ship *Volage*, Captain Phipps Hornby. The Franco-Venetian squadron bore down to the attack, on the following morning, in two divisions, when the British ships, notwithstanding the disparity of force, stood towards the enemy. At the last moment, before entering into action, Captain Hoste hoisted the signal, "Remember Nelson," which, as may be imagined, was received by the crews of the squadron under his command with loud hurrahs, and acted as the inspiring principle in the battle on which they had entered.

The first ship to open fire, at 9 A.M., was the *Amphion*, leading the line, with the *Active*, *Volage*, and *Cerberus* in close order astern. The *Favourite*, on receiving the British fire, bore up with the object of boarding the *Amphion*, but a well-directed discharge from a howitzer loaded with 750 musket-balls, directed on the enemy's crowded forecastle, committed fearful havoc, among those slain being the French commodore. The *Danae*, *Corona*, and *Carolina*, forming the lee division, engaged the *Volage* and *Cerberus*, but a fortunate turn was given to the fighting by the *Favourite*, when putting her helm up in order to wear and get to leeward of the English, running aground, an object for which Captain Hoste had been manœuvring. The British squadron by this time had wore ship, and was standing off the shore, and soon the *Flora* and *Bellona* had taken up a position on either quarter of the *Amphion*, on which ship they opened a heavy fire. The *Danae* at the same time was engaged with the little *Volage*, which bravely resisted until the carronades with which she was armed, one after the other, carried away their breechings and capsized, and she had only the six-pounders on her forecastle to continue the action. The other van-ship, the *Cerberus*, also found more than her match in the *Corona*, assisted at long range by the *Carolina*, but on the approach of the *Active*, these ships made all sail. Meanwhile the *Amphion* was closely engaged with her two adversaries, and taking up a position on the starboard bow of the *Flora*, compelled her to strike her colours. Captain Hoste then bore up to close the Venetian ship *Bellona*, which was raking him from the stern, and coming up on the starboard tack, poured a couple of broadsides into his adversary's weather-bow, when, soon after noon, the action having lasted three hours, the *Bellona* surrendered.

Captain Hoste threw out a signal for a general chase, but the only ship that was in a condition to obey the order was the *Active*, which made sail after the *Corona*, which she overhauled and brought to action shortly before two. At the end of half an hour the Venetian frigate struck her flag, but the *Danae* and *Carolina* managed to escape and found safety under the guns of some batteries, as did also the *Flora*, contrary to the rules of war, she having surrendered.

The *Amphion* in this action, so honourable to the ships engaged, lost out of her crew of 251 men and boys, two midshipmen, the boatswain and 12 men killed, and Captain Hoste, seven officers and 38 men wounded. The *Active*, which suffered least, had four killed and 24 wounded out of her complement of 300 all told. The *Cerberus*, which had on board only 160 men, lost her purser, one midshipman and 11 men killed, and 41 wounded, including one lieutenant. The *Volage*, described as having her port side "completely riddled," had one midshipman and 12 men killed, and an officer and three seamen and marines wounded. The total British loss out of 880 men was, therefore, 45 killed and 145 wounded. That of the enemy was not accurately ascertained, but the *Favourite* was known to have lost the commodore, captain, first lieutenant, and other officers, and her casualties were said to number quite 200. The *Corona*, which was even more shattered, also sustained a loss of 200 killed and wounded; and the *Bellona* had 70 killed, and about the same number badly wounded. The hulls of this ship and the *Flora*—which also suffered heavily, among the severely wounded being her captain—were much shattered by shot, and bore unmistakable evidence of the accurate gunnery practice of the British seamen.

The crew of the *Favourite* blew up their ship, and the *Corona*, when in tow of the *Active*, caught fire and nearly experienced the same fate. In helping to extinguish the flames, five seamen of the *Active* were drowned, and one of her officers and three of the crew of the *Cerberus* were severely burnt. In every respect the victory was most honourable to British arms, as our men had opposed to them a force in guns fully one-third and in men nearly two-thirds greater than their own. The *Corona*, which as well as the *Favourite, Danae,* and *Flora*, was larger than the *Active*, the biggest ship in the British squadron, was added to the Navy under the name of the *Dædalus*, and the *Bellona* became a troopship, and was called the *Dover*. All the four captains received gold medals, and the first lieutenants were promoted.

Off the coast of Istria the 38-gun frigates *Belle Poule* and *Alceste* landed a strong body of men and attacked a battery, under which an 18-gun brig-of-war with supplies for the French frigates *Flore* and *Danae*, had taken shelter, and not only silenced the enemy's works but sunk the brig. In the Bay of Sagone, in the island of Corsica, the *Pomone*, 38, *Unite*, 36, and *Scout*, 18, attacked two armed store-ships as they lay at anchor, and after a smart action with a strong battery protecting them, set fire to both the ships which blew up. Off the same island the 16-gun brig *Alacrity*, with a crew of 100 men and boys, was captured after a protracted resistance by the French brig *Abeille*, of about the same force. It should be stated, however, in extenuation of the defeat, that Commander Palmer had sent away a portion of his crew in a prize, that his only lieutenant was killed, and all the other officers wounded. But his conduct on going below with only a slight wound in the head was as indefensible as it was rare, and it was fortunate for this officer that he died of lockjaw, and thus escaped trial for the loss of his ship.

Excellent service was performed during the year, on the coast of Italy, by the boats of the frigates *Active*, *Thames*, Captain Charles Napier, *Unite*, Captain Chamberlayne, *Impérieuse*, 38, Captain Duncan, and *Cephalus*, 18, Commander Clifford. On one occasion Lieutenant Travers, first of the *Impérieuse*, assisted by Lieutenant Pipon, of the Marines, particularly distinguished himself. Before the close of the year the 38-gun frigates *Active* and *Alceste*, the latter commanded by Captain Murray Maxwell, chased, not far from Lissa, the French 40-gun frigates *Pauline* and *Pomone* and the storeship *Persanne*, of 26 guns. A lucky shot from the *Pauline* carried away the main-topmast of the *Alceste*, on which her crew raised a cheer of "Vive l'Empereur!" Meanwhile Captain Gordon, in the *Active*, brought the *Pomone* to close action. Soon after, the *Alceste* and *Pauline* became closely engaged, but the latter, bearing the French commodore's broad pennant, soon made sail and escaped, leaving the *Pomone* to her fate. On the *Alceste* coming up, the latter, having lost her main and mizen masts, struck her flag. The *Alceste*, of 218 men, had one midshipman and six men killed, and a lieutenant and 12 wounded. The *Active* lost a midshipman and seven killed and 26 wounded, including her gallant captain, whose leg was carried off by a cannon-shot, and Dashwood, the first lieutenant, lost his arm. The ship was brought out of action by Lieutenant Haye, who was also wounded. The *Pomone* suffered greatly by the accuracy of her opponent's fire. Besides losing her main and mizen masts during the action, her foremast went over the side shortly after, and her hull was so shattered that she had five feet of water in the hold. Fifty of her crew, out of 332, were killed or wounded, including her commander, who was struck in the mouth by a grapeshot. The *Pauline* escaped to Ancona, though in a damaged condition, but the *Persanne* was overhauled by the *Unite* and struck her colours. The first and second lieutenants of the *Active*, and Lieutenant Wilson, first of the *Alceste*, were promoted, according to custom.

In Eastern waters two important events took place—an action off the island of Madagascar and the capture of the island of Java. The French Government despatched from Brest three 40-gun frigates, *Renommée*, *Clorinde*, and *Néréide*, under Commodore Roquebert, with munitions of war for Mauritius, but on their arrival off Isle de la Passe, on the 7th May, learnt for the first time of the loss of the important colony which was known to them as the Isle of France. The same morning the *Phœbe*, 44, and *Galatea*, 42, Captains Hillyar and Losack, and the 18-gun brig *Racehorse*, Commander de Rippe, hove in sight, when the French ships steered for Madagascar, where they surprised the settlement of Tamatave, taken from the French in the preceding February. On the following day, the 20th May, the same British ships, reinforced by the *Astræa*, Captain Schomberg, sighted the French squadron, and brought them to action. While manœuvring, the breeze fell to a dead calm, and the *Renommée* and *Clorinde* secured a raking position on the quarter of the *Galatea*, which was greatly shattered by their fire, to which she could only reply by her stern guns. At length the seamen got sweeps out, and brought the ship's broadside to bear upon her two antagonists, but at 8 P.M. ceased firing and joined the commodore's ship, *Astræa*, with nearly four feet of water in her hold and her fore and mizen topmasts over the side. Meanwhile the *Phœbe* closed the *Néréide* and raked her with telling effect until her consorts came to her assistance, and about 8.25, in company with the *Astræa* and *Racehorse*, she bore up to renew the engagement, which the French commodore appeared equally willing to continue. The two commodores were now closely engaged, but at the end of about twenty-five minutes, the *Rénommée* hauled down her colours, having made a gallant resistance.

The French acknowledged to a loss, out of 470 seamen and soldiers, of 93 killed and wounded, among the former being Commodore Roquebert, and among the latter, Colonel Barrois, commanding the troops, and the *Rénommée's* first lieutenant. The *Néréide* also lost her captain and 24 men killed, and 32 wounded. The British official account places the casualties of the former frigate at 145, and of the *Néréide* at 130. The *Clorinde* succeeded in making her escape, and, steering for France, reached Brest in safety, but her captain was tried by court-martial for deserting his commodore, dismissed the service, and imprisoned for five years. The squadrons were well-matched, their broadside weight of metal being almost identical, and the brig *Racehorse* rendered little or no assistance, while the French frigates were of considerably greater tonnage, and carried larger crews.

The *Astræa* had lost in the action, out of 271 men and boys, two killed and 16 wounded, including her first lieutenant; the *Phœbe* had seven killed and 24 wounded, and lost her fore-topmast; and the *Galatea*, which was greatly shattered, had 16 killed, including a marine officer, and 46 wounded, among whom were her captain and three other officers.

Commodore Schomberg, with the *Phœbe* and *Astræa*, made his way to Tamatave, where the *Néréide* was found at anchor, and the officer in command, on being summoned, surrendered the ship and port. The two captured frigates were added to the Navy, the *Rénommée* under the name of the *Java*, and the *Néréide* under that of the *Madagascar*, and the first lieutenants of the *Astræa* and *Phœbe* were promoted.

During the year 1811 the Dutch settlements in the island of Java passed under the British flag. A powerful fleet of four sail-of-the-line, fourteen frigates and seven sloops, under the command of Rear-admiral Hon. Robert Stopford, with a squadron of ships of the Indian Navy, under Commodore Hayes, acted in conjunction with the land forces, numbering some 12,000 men, under command of Sir Samuel Achmuty. The operations were mostly of a military character, but a naval brigade of seamen and marines was engaged on shore and assisted at the storm of the great entrenched camp of Cornelis, about nine miles from the city of Batavia, where the Dutch lost 1,000 slain and 5,000 taken prisoners. The island of Java, notwithstanding the great sacrifices made in its acquisition, was surrendered to Holland at the termination of hostilities.

In the latter part of the preceding year, Captain Farquahar, commanding the *Desirée*, 36, with a squadron of gun-boats, co-operated with a Russian force in an attack on the batteries defending Cuxhaven, at the mouth of the Elbe, then in possession of the French, and, in December, assisted the Crown Prince of Sweden's army at the reduction of Gluckstadt, which finally surrendered.

In January, 1812, the French 40-gun frigates *Arienne* and *Andromaque*, and the 16-gun brig *Mamelouck*, sailed from Nantes on a cruise, and committed great depredations on British commerce. The *Northumberland*, 74, Captain Hon. Henry Hotham, was detached to capture them on their return to Lorient, and sighted the frigates off Isle Groix, close to that port, on the 19th May, when she engaged them as they lay grounded, and also a battery on shore. In this affair she lost five killed and 28 wounded, including a lieutenant, but she succeeded in riddling the French ships as they lay with their copper exposed to view. During the night both the frigates blew up, and on the following day, the brig also was destroyed by an explosion, so that the service entrusted to Captain Hotham, which was effected within sight of a French two-decker in the harbour of Lorient, was successfully executed.

The British squadron in Danish waters was frequently engaged with the enemy, mostly to the advantage of the former. It would be impossible to detail, within the limits at our disposal, the whole of these actions and others with French ships-of-war and privateers, for particulars of which we would refer the enquirer to the pages of the accurate and painstaking James.

In the Adriatic, near Venice, the 74-gun ship *Victorious*, Captain Talbot, brought to action the French ship-of-the-line *Rivoli*, of like force. A furious engagement ensued, when the *Victorious* reduced her adversary to such a condition that only two quarter-deck guns could return her fire. Before the *Rivoli* hauled down her colours, her mizenmast was shot away, and her other masts went over the side soon after the termination of the action, in which she had lost, out of 810 on board, no less than 400 killed and wounded, including the greater number of her officers. The ships were well matched as to size, weight of metal, both of which were slightly to the advantage of the *Rivoli*; while as regards crew the British seventy-four commenced the action with only 506 men, out of which she lost 27 killed, including a marine officer, and 99 wounded, among them Captain Talbot and five officers, one mortally. On the same occasion the 18-gun brig *Weasel*, Commander Andrew, engaged for forty minutes the French 16-gun brig *Mercure*, which blew up, and chased, though ineffectually, two other brigs. Before the *Rivoli* struck, the *Weasel* poured into her a couple of broadsides, which, however, conduced but little to her surrender. The *Rivoli*, quite a new ship, was added to the Navy, and Captain Talbot was knighted; and Mr. Peake, his first lieutenant, and Commander Andrew both received promotion.

The Adriatic was the scene of many meritorious attacks by boats on the forts and batteries on the Italian coast, then under the rule of Murat. Also, on the northern coast near Trieste, and among the islands in the Adriatic, the occasions were frequent in which British seaman displayed their daring in action with the enemy. A spirited affair took place at Languelia, where the boats of the seventy-fours, *America* and *Leviathan*, and of the 18-gun brig *Eclair*, brought out sixteen settees, while the marines carried the battery adjoining the town. In this affair the British loss was 16 killed and drowned (a shot having sunk a boat), and 20 wounded.

Captain Sir James Yeo—who had so often performed acts of distinguished valour, and afterwards added to his reputation on the Canadian lakes—when in command of the *Southampton*, of 38 guns, fought a sanguinary action with the *Amethyste*, carrying 44 guns and 700 men of different nations, in the service of one of the parties struggling for mastery in the island of St. Domingo. Sir James Yeo sent a demand to Captain Gaspard that he should accompany him to Jamaica, for the British Commander-in-chief to determine as to the validity of his papers, and on receiving a refusal, opened fire. The action, which took place on the 3rd February, 1812, had not continued for more than half an hour, before the superiority of the British fire became manifest, and the *Amethyste's* main and mizen masts went over the side, while her hull was riddled with shot. Captain Gaspard made repeated attempts to board, which were frustrated by the manœuvres of the British frigate, and ultimately hauled down his flag when his three masts and bowsprit had been shot away. The loss of the *Southampton* was only nominal, and that of her antagonist no less than 105 killed and 120 wounded.

An action worthy special mention was that between the *Amelia*, Captain the Hon. Paul Irby, of 48 guns and 349 men and boys, and the *Arethuse*, of 44 guns and a complement of 340, a sister ship of the *Renommée*, afterwards called the *Java*, which was captured by the Americans. The *Arethuse*, with the frigate *Rubis*, sailed from Mauritius on a cruise in November, 1812, and was brought to action on the evening of the 7th February succeeding. Soon after the engagement commenced, the two frigates fell on board each other, and kept up a close and deadly fire both from great guns and small arms. Once the ships separated, but only again to be locked alongside, with the muzzles of the guns actually touching. The crews snatched the sponges out of each other's hands through the port-holes, and cut at one another with their cutlasses. So deadly was the fire from the *Arethuse's* decks and tops that the quarter-deck of the British frigate was cleared, and the third lieutenant, as senior officer uninjured, took command of her. At length, the breeze having died away, the ships parted, and about 11.20, three hours and a half after the action commenced, entirely ceased firing. The battle may be regarded as drawn, one of the few in which a British frigate of greater force than her French antagonist was unsuccessful in bringing about her surrender. The *Amelia* lost no less than 51 killed and mortally wounded, including four lieutenants —one an officer, late commander of the gun-brig *Daring*—a marine officer, a midshipman, and purser; and 90 wounded, among whom were Captain Irby and 10 other officers.

The *Arethuse* had 31 killed, among them 11 officers, and 74 wounded, including nearly the whole of those remaining. Captains Irby and Bouvet, who, each in their own service, were regarded as among its best officers, are equally entitled to great credit for the obstinate valour with which they carried on this sanguinary duel, but it should be admitted, in extenuation of the failure of the *Amelia's* crew to capture the enemy, that a large portion of them were in a debilitated state from sickness, and the number included about 40 boys.

In February, 1814, near Toulon, the British fleet, under Sir Edward Pellew, nearly succeeded in cutting off a French squadron of six ships, when endeavouring to re-enter the roads. The leading ships, the *Boyne*, Captain Boulton, 98, a sister ship of the *Victory*, was closely engaged with the *Romulus*, 74, which, however, managed to make good her escape, and the *Boyne* suffered also from the fire of the shore batteries. Her loss was 42 killed and wounded, but the *Romulus* had 70 casualties. During the months of March and April, all the French possessions and islands in the Adriatic surrendered to the allies, and Spezzia and Genoa to a small squadron under Sir Josias Rowley.

In Januray, 1814, the *Venerable*, 74, flagship of Admiral Durham, captured the 40-gun frigates, *Iphigénie* and *Alcmène*. The latter, finding herself overhauled, and expecting the assistance of her consort, ran on board the seventy-four, with the object of boarding, but paid dearly for this act of temerity, and was boarded in turn, and captured, after a gallant resistance, during which she had 32 killed and 50 wounded, including Captain Villeneuve. The *Iphigénie*, which was chased by the *Cyane* between the 16th and 20th January, also struck to the seventy-four. Both frigates were added to the Navy.

Off the Cape de Verde Islands, on the 23rd January, the British 36-gun frigates, *Creole*, Captain Mackenzie, and *Astræa*, Captain Eveleigh, fought a desperate and protracted action with the French 40-gun frigates *Etoile* and *Sultane*, which had sailed from Nantes in the preceding October. The *Creole* engaged the *Sultane*, but at the end of two hours nearly all her running rigging was shot away, and her masts badly wounded, and she abandoned the contest and steered for the island of St. Jago. The *Astræa*, after exchanging a couple of broadsides with the *Sultane*, closely engaged the *Etoile*, but was so terribly cut up, both in her hull and rigging, that after receiving a raking broadside from the *Sultane*, now free to engage her, she stood away and joined her consort at St. Jago. During the action the *Astræa* had her mizzenmast and the whole of her braces shot away, and out of a complement of 284 men and boys, lost her commander and eight men killed, and 37 wounded. The *Creole* had an officer and nine seamen and marines killed, and 28 wounded. The French frigates suffered no less both in men and *matériel*. The rival ships were equally matched, and fought with a like determination a drawn battle honourable to both sides.

The *Etoile* was sighted and chased on the 27th March, near Alderney, by the *Hebrus*, 36, Captain Palmer, and after a running fight, maintained with obstinate courage for two hours and a quarter, struck her colours. Her hull was much shattered, and she had four feet of water in her hold, while she had lost, out of 327 men on board, 40 killed and 73 wounded. The victory was very creditable to the *Hebrus*, which had a midshipman and 12 men killed, and 25 wounded, out of her complement of 284. At the same time the *Hannibal*, 74, which was in company with the *Hebrus*, overtook the *Sultane*, which hauled down her colours. Both these frigates were added to the Navy, the *Etoile* being re-named the *Topaze*, and the first lieutenant of the *Hebrus*, Mr. Jackson, received promotion. Shortly before this the 40-gun frigate *Ceres* was chased by the British frigates *Niger* and *Tagus*, and, after a running fight, surrendered to the latter, the *Niger* being in close company. The *Ceres* also was added to the Navy. Her consort, the *Clorinde*, mounting 44 guns, with a crew of 344 men, gallantly engaged the *Eurotas*, Captain Phillimore, of 46 guns and 329 men, having a considerable superiority in weight of metal, the respective broadsides being: —*Eurotas*, 601 pounds, *Clorinde*, 463. At 5 P.M. on the 25th February, the *Eurotas* commenced the action by passing under the stern of the *Clorinde*, and raking her, she ranged up on the quarter of the French frigate. A furious action now ensued, the *Eurotas* losing her mizzenmast at the end of twenty minutes, and the *Clorinde* her fore-topmast. The *Eurotas* tried to lay her adversary on board, but, failing in this, raked her, and getting alongside, continued closely engaged. At 6.20 the British frigate lost her mainmast, and the *Clorinde* her mizzenmast, and shortly before seven the former had her foremast shot away, and the latter her mainmast. Thus their position was nearly equalised, but the *Clorinde* had the means of carrying sail on her foremast, and, setting her foresail and fore-staysail, stood out of gunshot.

Nothing daunted by their helpless, dismasted condition, the gallant crew of the *Eurotas*, by working all night, rigged jurymasts, and at daylight made sail in chase of the enemy, which was still engaged in clearing away the wreck. But they were robbed of the anticipated fruits of their exertions, as, about noon, the British ships *Dryad*, 36, and *Achates*, 16, hove in sight, and the *Clorinde*, seeing the hopelessness of resistance, surrendered to the latter, the *Eurotas* being then only four or five miles off to windward. Out of her complement, the *Eurotas* had 21 killed, including three midshipmen, and 39 wounded, among them being her commander (very severely), and two other officers. The *Clorinde* lost 20 killed and 40 wounded. She was added to the Navy, and received the name of *Aurora*, there being already another captured French frigate of the name in the service. Lieutenant Robert Smith, who fought the *Eurotas* after Captain Phillimore was incapacitated, was promoted to the rank of commander.

The 56-gun frigate *Majestic*, Captain John Hayes, which was on the look-out for the American frigate *President*, carrying 52 guns, sighted two French 40-gun frigates, the *Atalante* and *Terpsichore*, and gave chase. With rare pusillanimity for a French naval officer, the commodore abandoned his consort, and the *Terpsichore*, after a running fight of nearly two hours, struck her colours to the *Majestic*, then within musket-shot range.

After Wellington's invasion of France, when Marshal Beresford advanced on Bordeaux, a squadron, under Admiral Penrose, assisted him in the Gironde, by taking some batteries, and causing the French to destroy the *Regulus*, 74, and other ships.

The entry of the allies into Paris on the 31st March, 1814, and the signature of the treaty of peace by which Louis XVIII. returned to the throne of his ancestors, put an end to further hostilities. Thus ended this long and exhausting war, which, with only a brief cessation in 1802, had desolated Europe since 1792. True, it broke out again in the following year, when Napoleon, quitting Elba, landed in France, and astonished the world by his last desperate struggle for power, but the "Hundred Days" was not distinguished by any naval operations, and only two incidents took place, the capture of the French 40-gun frigate, *Melpomene*, by the *Rivoli*, Captain Dickson, after a running fight, and the action between the 16-gun brig *Pilot* and the corvette *Légère*, 22, which escaped, though with the loss of 22 killed and 79 wounded, out of a crew of 170 men. On the 15th July, Napoleon, finding he had no hope of eluding the British cruisers watching the coasts of France, surrendered himself to Captain Frederick Maitland, of the *Bellerophon*, 74, then lying in the Basque Roads. The fallen Emperor was conveyed to Plymouth, and on the 8th August, sailed in the *Northumberland*, 74, bearing the flag of Rear-Admiral Sir George Cockburn, to St. Helena, where he was landed on the 16th October.

The negotiations for peace, suspended by the Waterloo campaign, were now resumed, and peace was finally signed on the 20th November, by the eighth article of which France received back all the conquests made by England during the long war, with the exception of St. Lucia and Tobago, in the West Indies, and the island of Mauritius and the Seychelles group, in the Eastern seas.

CHAPTER IV.

The War with the United States—The *President* and *Little Belt*—*President* and *Belvidera*—The *Guerrière* and *Constitution*—The *Frolic* and *Wasp*—The *Macedonian* and *United States*—The *Java* and *Constitution*—The *Peacock* and *Hornet*—Capture of the *Chesapeake* by the *Shannon*—Loss of the *Dominica* and *Boxer*—Capture of the *Argus*—Boat Attacks in Chesapeake Bay—The Fighting on the Canadian Lakes in 1813—Capture of the *Essex*—The *Epervier* and *Peacock*—Loss of the *Reindeer* and *Avon*—The Expedition to Washington—Captain Gordon at Alexandria—The Attack on Baltimore—The Fighting on the Canadian Lakes in 1814—The Operations near Mobile and on Lake Borgne—Capture of the *President*—Loss of the *Cyane*, *Levant*, *Penguin* and *Nautilus*.

IN 1812 this country became embroiled in a war with the United States. We will not seek to apportion the blame for this unfortunate calamity, which resulted in serious losses of ships and men to this country, and also in much sanguinary fighting ashore. The war arose, ostensibly at least, from our exercising rights we claimed to search American ships-of-war for deserters. The United States Navy department had been making preparations for the inevitable conflict, and on the 21st June, 1812, within three days of the declaration of war by the Government of Washington, Commodore Rodgers put to sea with a squadron of three frigates and two sloops. The former, though rated as frigates, were in fact "line-of-battle ships in disguise," as they carried 56 heavy guns, those on the main-deck being 24-pounders, and the rest 18-pounders and 42-pounder carronades.

In May of the preceding year, war nearly resulted from a collision which took place between the British sloop, *Little Belt*, Captain Bingham, of 20 guns and 121 men, and the *President*, one of these so-called 44-gun frigates, commanded by Commodore Rodgers. Both sides denied that they fired first, but at the end of half an hour the *Little Belt* ceased firing, having lost 11 killed and 21 wounded. Explanations were offered by the American Government, which were accepted by the English Ministry, but the event only deepened the ill-feeling between the two countries, which found vent in war in the following year.

Commodore Rodgers put to sea with the *President* and *United States*, the latter, of the same force, commanded by Commodore Decatur, the *Congress*, 50, Captain Smith, 18-gun sloop *Hornet*, Captain Lawrence, and the 16-gun brig *Argus*, Captain Sinclair. The squadron sighted and chased the *Belvidera*, 42, Captain Byron, and the *President*, on approaching him, opened fire, and a running action commenced, which lasted two hours, the British frigate returning the fire of her adversary from her quarter-deck and cabin stern-chase carronades. The *President* continued to gain until Captain Byron cut away his anchors, threw overboard most of his boats and started his water, and by the evening she had left her pursuers—for the *Congress* also opened fire on her—far astern, and succeeded in reaching Halifax. The *Belvidera*, out of 230 men, had two killed and 22 wounded; and the *President* had six casualties by her enemy's fire, but by the bursting of one of her guns, 16 were killed and wounded, including among the former two midshipmen, and among the latter Commodore Rodgers.

The next action was between the *Constitution*, Captain Hull, of 56 guns and 460 men, and the *Guerrière*, of 48 guns and 244 men, the broadside weight of metal being 517 and 768 pounds respectively, a disproportion so great that success could scarcely have been anticipated by the gallant Captain Dacres, commanding the British frigate. The *Constitution* had been chased by a small squadron, but had managed to escape, and, a few days later, fell in with the *Guerrière*, which was on her way to Halifax to refit. It was 4.50 P.M. when the engagement commenced by the *Guerrière* firing a broadside, but it was nearly three-quarters of an hour before the ships came to close action. It soon became apparent that the fire of the American frigate was superior to that of her adversary, not only in weight of metal but in accuracy. At six o'clock the *Guerrière's* mainmast was shot away by the board, and, falling over the counter, brought the ship up in the wind. Putting her helm up, the *Constitution* took up a position on the port bow of the British frigate, and a destructive fire was kept up both from great guns and small arms, to which a reply could only be made from her bow guns. The ships now fell foul of each other, and after a hot interchange of musketry fire — by which Captain Dacres and the master were severely wounded, and on the other side, the first lieutenant, the master and a marine officer were placed *hors de combat*—the ships broke away from each other, and the *Guerrière* was enabled to bring some guns to bear on her formidable antagonist. But matters only went from bad to worse, as the foremast went over the side and was quickly followed by the mizzenmast, so that the British frigate lay like a helpless log in the trough of the sea, rolling her main-deck guns under water. The *Constitution* ranged ahead to repair damages, which gave the British seamen a little time to clear away the wreck; but they could set no sail, and when the *Constitution*, having rove new braces, took up her station on their starboard quarter, the alternatives were either to surrender or be blown out of the water without power of resistance. Captain Dacres, who had refused to leave the deck, recognising the futility of resistance, fired a gun to leeward, and hauled down the Union Jack from the stump of the mizzenmast.

Of 244 men and 19 boys at quarters, the *Guerrière* lost 15 killed, including her second lieutenant, and 63 wounded, among whom were, besides her captain, her first lieutenant, master, two master's mates, and one midshipman. The *Constitution* had a lieutenant of marines and six men killed, and seven wounded, including the officers already named. That Captain Dacres had fought his ship to the last extremity was proved by the fact that, on the following day, she was found to be in a sinking condition, and was accordingly abandoned and blown up by her captors. Captain Hull and his brave men were entitled to credit for capturing a ship quite one-third less in strength, but it should be borne in mind that a considerable proportion of the crew of the *Constitution*, as of the other so-called Yankee frigates that beat our smaller ships, hailed from these islands and were deserters from the British flag.* Captain Dacres was tried by a court-martial, which honourably acquitted him of all blame, and agreed that "the surrender of the *Guerrière* was proper in order to preserve the lives of her valuable remaining crew."

The next encounter was between the 18-gun brig *Frolic*, Commander Whinyates, with a crew of 92 men and 18 boys, and the *Wasp*, Captain Jones, of like force, with 135 men, but, as in the case of the *Guerrière*, the *Frolic* was on her return to port to refit, having been five years in the West Indies, with the additional drawback of a sickly crew. The brig had carried away her mainyard and sprung her topmasts, besides receiving other damages, in a gale of wind, and was engaged repairing them when the *Wasp*, only five days out of port, hove in sight. The ships quickly engaged, the sea being so rough that the muzzles of their guns were frequently under water. Within a few minutes the *Frolic* shot away the *Wasp's* main-topmast, but the latter directed her aim at her adversary's hull with great effect, and by a lucky shot, carried away her gaff-head braces, thus making her boom-mainsail useless. As her mainyard had not been replaced, and she had consequently no square-sails set, the British brig at once became powerless to manoeuvre. The *Wasp* soon took up a position on her port bow,

* "It appeared in evidence on the court-martial," says Captain Brenton, "that there were many Englishmen on board the *Constitution*, and these were leading men, or captains of guns. The officers of the *Guerrière* knew some of them personally, and one man in particular, who had been captain of the forecastle in the *Eurydice*, a British frigate then recently come from England. Another was in the *Achille* at Trafalgar, and the third lieutenant of the *Constitution*, whose name was Reed, was an Irishman. It was said, and we have no reason to doubt the fact, that there were 200 British seamen on board the *Constitution* when she began the action."

and raked her without possibility of reply or cessation. Broadside after broadside was thus poured in, and then Captain Jones ran aboard of his defenceless antagonist, and sweeping her decks with musketry, boarded, and hauled down her colours, which had been lashed to the main rigging. At this time there remained on deck Captain Whinyates and his second lieutenant, both severely wounded, and about 17 men. The loss of the *Frolic* was 15 killed and 47 wounded, including, besides her commander, two lieutenants, one mortally, and her master, also mortally wounded, the casualties being more than half her entire crew of men and boys. She was also greatly shattered in her hull, and both her masts went over the side a few minutes after her surrender. The *Wasp* had eight killed and about the same number wounded, out of her crew of 135 full-grown men. The *Frolic*, however, did not long remain an American trophy, as the *Poictiers*, 74, Captain Beresford, hove in sight, and captured both ships.

The next action was between the American frigate *United States*, Commodore Decatur, of 55 guns and 474 men, and the *Macedonian*, Captain Carden, carrying 48 guns, and having a crew of only 254 men, not taking into account the boys in either ship. The relative broadside weight of metal was 864 and 528 pounds, and the tonnage 1,533 and 1,081, so that, as in the case of the *Guerrière* and *Constitution*, the disparity of force in favour of the American ship was one-third. About 9.20 the *Macedonian*, which was the better sailer of the two, took up a position on her adversary's port quarter, and exchanged a broadside with her, by which the British frigate lost her mizzen-topmast. A running fight now ensued, and the *United States*, by her diagonal fire, soon dismounted every carronade on the *Macedonian's* quarter-deck and forecastle, and inflicted great loss on her crew. The two ships now came to close action, and the superiority of the enemy's fire quickly made itself manifest. Soon after eleven the *Macedonian's* mizzenmast was shot away, falling over her starboard or engaged quarter, and was followed by her fore and main topmasts and mainyard; her rigging and running gear was also cut to pieces, her boats destroyed, many guns on the main-deck were disabled, and her hull pierced by over 100 shot. Owing to the absence of sail to steady her, the British frigate rolled her main-deck guns under water, but the indomitable spirit of British seamen animated every breast, and when, as a last resort, Captain Carden put his helm a-weather, with the object of boarding, "every man," says the gallant Lieutenant Hope, who was twice severely wounded, "was on deck, several who had lost an arm, and the universal cry was, 'Let us conquer or die.'" But a shot carried away the ship's fore-brace, and she flew up into the wind. The *United States*, having refilled her cartridges, took up a position

H.M.S. THRUSH.
1st CLASS GUNBOAT.

across the British frigate's stern, and, having no means of making further resistance, she struck her colours soon after noon.

The *Macedonian* lost, in this unequal conflict, 36 killed, including her boatswain and a master's mate, and two lieutenants, three other officers, and 63 men wounded. The *United States* had only five killed and seven wounded, including a lieutenant mortally, and so excellent were her fittings that, says an officer, " not an accident occurred nor was a rope-yarn of our gun-tackle strained." As in the case of the *President*, a large proportion of her crew were British seamen, and on Captain Carden observing the words, " Victory " and " Nelson," painted over her gun-ports, he asked Commodore Decatur the reason, when that officer replied, " The men belonging to these guns served many years with Lord Nelson, and in the *Victory*. The crew of the gun named ' Nelson ' were bargemen to that great chief." The *Macedonian* was a new ship, having only been built in 1810, and was purchased into the American Navy, under her own name.* Captain Carden and his officers and men were acquitted of all blame by a court-martial, which complimented them on their distinguished gallantry "with an enemy of very superior force."

The last action fought this year was on the 29th December, when the *Constitution*, now commanded by Captain Bainbridge, encountered the *Java*, Captain Lambert (late the French *Renommée*), of 46 guns and 300 men and boys, including a great many landsmen and others, recruited by press-gangs and from prisons, besides 86 supernumeraries. Among her passengers were General Hislop and staff, who were proceeding to Bombay.

On sighting the *Constitution*, the *Java* bore up to meet her antagonist, and at 2.10 the action began by a broadside from the American frigate, to which the *Java* replied with good effect. The *Constitution* preferred to play at long bowls, and manœuvred with that object for some time, but, at length, finding the *Java's* shot very effective, Commodore Bainbridge " determined," as he says, " to close with the enemy, notwithstanding his raking." She accordingly luffed up, and on arriving abreast of the *Java*, closely engaged her. Again the *Constitution* wore, followed by the British frigate, and a second time they came up abreast of each other, when the superior fire of the Yankee frigate told heavily, and in ten minutes' time the rigging of her antagonist was cut to pieces. As a last resort, Captain Lambert determined to board, but on bearing up with that object,

---

* The writer of this work may mention that, in 1854, he saw this frigate in the Canton river, bearing the American flag.

his foremast went over the side, and the ship soon lay at the mercy of the *Constitution*, which, wearing across the *Java's* bows, raked her with terrible effect, and carried away her main-topmast, which, as well as the wreck of the foremast, masked all her starboard guns. Again running round the *Java*, she luffed up and raked her on the starboard quarter, and, wearing round on the port tack, resumed her position and plied her with deadly effect. At this time, 3.30, the gallant Captain Lambert fell mortally wounded, when the command devolved on Lieutenant Henry Ducie Chads, who continued on deck though severely wounded. Within half an hour the ship's mizzenmast was shot away, and the *Java* remained in an almost defenceless state, exposed to a furious discharge of musketry, besides repeated broadsides, to which she could make but a feeble and intermittent response.

The *Constitution*, at 4.25, ranged ahead to repair damages, when the crew of her sorely-stricken antagonist, mistaking her purpose, cheered her and called to her to come back. Their jubilations were premature, for the American frigate, at ten minutes past four, having repaired her slight damages, and replenished her cartridges, wore and stood for the hulk, as she now was, the *Java's* mainmast having gone over the side, so that she had not a stick standing, the bowsprit having also been shot away. The gallant crew, notwithstanding their hopeless condition, had reloaded their guns, and tried to make sail on the stump of the foremast, but upon the *Constitution* taking up a position close athwart her bows, the hopelessness of further resistance became apparent, and at 5.45 the colours were lowered, and the *Java* became the prize of the Yankee frigate.

Of her total crew, including supernumeraries, of 354 men and 23 boys, the *Java* lost three masters' mates, two midshipmen, and 17 hands killed and 102 wounded, including her captain (mortally), first lieutenant, master, a marine officer, four midshipmen and the boatswain. The frigate was so shattered by shot that she could not float, and was set on fire and destroyed. A court-martial convened to try the survivors very properly relieved them from all blame in the action with a ship of so much greater force, and Admiral Graham Moore, the president, complimented Lieutenant Chads on his gallantry when returning him his sword.

In the first action fought in the year 1813, between English and American ships-of-war, the superiority in strength, as in previous contests, was with the latter. On the 24th February, when cruising off Demerara, the brig *Peacock*, Commander Peake, of 18 guns and 110 men, sighted the Yankee sloop, *Hornet*, Commander Lawrence, of 20 guns and 162 men. The first shot was fired at 5.25, when the ships passed each other on opposite tacks, at half pistol-shot range, and after receiving her second broadside, the *Hornet* closed on her adversary's starboard quarter, and poured in so heavy a fire that, in twenty-five minutes from commencing the action, the *Peacock* struck her colours. By the accurate fire of the *Hornet*, her hull and spars were much shattered, the mainmast went over the side, and she had six feet of water in her hold. All efforts to save her were unavailing, and she went down in a few minutes at her anchorage, carrying with her nine of her own seamen, and three of the prize crew, the remainder just managing to escape by jumping into a boat on her deck.

Out of 110 men and 12 boys, the *Peacock* lost her young commander, a most gallant officer, and four men killed, and her master, a midshipman and 31 wounded. The *Hornet*, as in the case of the *Constitution*, escaped with slight loss, proving that the gunnery of the British seamen was as ineffective as that of the enemy was efficient.

Then came a welcome break in the monotonous and painful record of defeat, and we have the pleasure of describing a victory, one of the most honourable and brilliant achieved by any ship in the British Navy in its long and glorious history. The very name of the *Shannon*, and of her gallant captain, Philip Bowes Vere Broke, will bring a glow of pride to the heart of every patriotic Englishman as showing that, where the national aptitude for gunnery was encouraged by diligent practice, the British sailor was as capable as ever of giving a good account of an enemy, no matter of what nationality. Since the 14th September, 1806, when Captain Broke joined the *Shannon*, he had systematically trained his men in the use, not only of the great guns, but of small arms, as well as of the cutlass and boarding pike, and when in August, 1811, he sailed for the American coast, there was good reason to believe that the prophecy of an enthusiastic admirer, which appeared in the *Naval Chronicle*, eight months before the action was fought, would prove true.

> "And as the war they did provoke,
> We'll pay them with our cannon;
> The first to do it will be Broke,
> In the gallant ship, the *Shannon*."

The *Shannon*, accompanied by the *Tenedos*, Captain Hyde Parker, sailed from Halifax on the 21st March, 1813, and reconnoitred Boston harbour, where they saw the *President* and *Congress* ready for sea, which, however, succeeded in eluding the vigilance of the British frigates on the 1st May, and escaped. The *Constitution* and *Chesapeake* were also there, and as the latter—now under the command of Captain Lawrence, late commanding the *Hornet* in her successful encounter with the *Peacock*—would be ready for sea in a week or two, Captain Broke sent away the *Tenedos* on the 25th May, with orders not to rejoin him before the 14th June, by which time he hoped to have completed the task he had set himself of capturing one or other of the Yankee frigates then refitting in Boston harbour. Captain Broke had sent in several verbal messages, challenging the captains of the *Constitution* and *Chesapeake* to a duel, and early in the morning of the 1st June, addressed a communication to Captain Lawrence, formally inviting him to single combat,* and stood in close to Boston lighthouse, with colours flying, and lay to.

Soon after noon Captain Broke went to the masthead to reconnoitre, and observed the *Chesapeake* fire a gun and get under weigh, and presently she came down gallantly with a fair wind, accompanied by numerous pleasure-boats, and a schooner in which were Commodores Hull and Bainbridge and several other naval officers. The two frigates, fit representatives of the nations unhappily at war, were not unequally matched, and what disparity of force existed, was decidedly in favour of the Yankee champion. The *Shannon* had 50 guns,† throwing a broadside of 538 pounds, with a crew of 306 men, (excluding boys), and the *Chesapeake* carried a similar number of guns, of which the broadside weight of metal was 590 pounds, with a picked crew of 376 men. As regards tonnage, the British frigate was 1,066 tons, and the American, 1,135.

The two ships stood out to sea, and at 5.10, Boston lighthouse being then distant about 18 miles, the *Shannon*, flying the Union Jack at the fore and a blue ensign at the mizzen-peak, lay to, and awaited her adversary, which, with three flags flying, stood straight for her starboard quarter. Captain Broke had ordered William Mindham, captain

---

* The letter begins :—" As the *Chesapeake* appears now ready for sea, I request you will do me the favour to meet the *Shannon* with her, ship to ship, to try the fortune of our respective flags." The *Shannon's* force he thus described. "The *Shannon* mounts 24 guns upon her broadside and one light boat-gun, 18-pounders upon her main deck, and 32-pound carronades on her quarter-deck and forecastle, and is manned with a complement of 300 men and boys (a large proportion of the latter), besides 30 seamen, boys, and passengers, who were taken out of re-captured vessels lately." After fixing the place of meeting, and providing against all interruption, Captain Broke concludes thus :—" I entreat you, sir, not to imagine that I am urged by mere personal vanity to the wish of meeting the *Chesapeake*, or that I depend only upon your personal ambition for your acceding to this invitation. We have both nobler motives. You will feel it as a compliment if I say, that the result of our meeting may be the most grateful service I can render to my country, and I doubt not that you, equally confident of success, will feel convinced that it is only by repeated triumphs in even combats that your little navy can now hope to console your country for the loss of that trade it can no longer protect. Favour me with a speedy reply. We are short of provisions and water, and cannot stay long here."

† One of these guns was a 12-pounder boat carronade, and another a brass long 6-pounder, both mounted on the quarter. In addition there were two 12-pounder carronades on the quarter-deck stern ports, used as stern-chasers The guns were loaded alternately with two round-shot and 150 musket balls, and one round and one double-headed shot.

of the fourteenth, or aftermost, main-deck gun, to fire when it bore on the *Chesapeake's* second main-deck port from forward. At 5.50 this was done, and the other guns were discharged in succession, the *Chesapeake* replying as fast as she could bring her guns to bear. Owing to her jib-sheet being shot away six minutes after the action commenced, the American frigate came up to the wind, which was very light at the time, thus exposing her stern and quarter to the *Shannon's* fire, and full use the British gunners made of their advantage. Four minutes later the *Shannon's* jib-stay was shot away, and she went off the wind, when the *Chesapeake* fell on board her with her quarter touching the British frigate's starboard main-chains. She forged slightly ahead, but was stopped by the *Shannon's* anchor hooking her quarter-port. On observing this, Captain Broke ran forward, and, observing the *Chesapeake's* men leaving their guns on the quarter-deck, he called away the main-deck boarders, and ordered the two ships to be lashed together. This was accomplished with devoted gallantry by the boatswain, Stevens, a veteran who had fought under Rodney in his action of the 12th April, 1782, who, while engaged outside the ship's bulwarks, had his left arm hacked off by repeated cutlass blows, and was mortally wounded by musket-balls. So also was the midshipman on the forecastle, Mr. Samwell. Captain Broke, with all the forecastle men he could muster, some 20 in number, at exactly two minutes past six, stepped from his ship's rail, just abaft the fore-channels, on the muzzle of the *Chesapeake's* aftermost carronade, and bounding over the bulwark, stood on her quarter-deck, where he was quickly followed by his gallant forecastle men. Some American seamen, between 20 and 30, clustered on the gangways, were quickly driven forward, where they laid down their arms or fled over the bows.

Meanwhile Lieutenant Watt, first of the *Shannon*, boarded with a division, and Lieutenant Falkiner quickly followed with another party and rushed forward, and while some kept down the men who were ascending from below, others directed their fire against the small-arm men in the main and mizzen tops of the *Chesapeake*. These, however, were dealt with in a more effective fashion, and one that makes this action unique in more ways than one. Mr. William Smith, midshipman of the *Shannon's* foretop, running along the fore-yard, which was braced up to the American's mainyard, now nearly squared, quickly boarded her top and killed or drove below the topmen. Mr. Cosnahan, midshipman of the maintop, meanwhile, by his accurate fire, caused the cessation of that from the *Chesapeake's* mizzen-top.

Captain Broke, having given orders to a sentry to keep guard over the American who had submitted on the forecastle, was moving aft when the marine called out to him. Turning round he found himself confronted with three of the enemy, who, finding themselves in superior force, had armed themselves afresh to renew the conflict. Captain Broke parried the pike of one and wounded him in the face, but at the same moment, received a blow from the butt end of a musket, which laid bare his skull, while the third man followed up the attack by cutting him down with his cutlass. But the last was in the next minute himself cut down by Mindham, the gun captain. This act of treachery, by which one of his men was killed and a few were wounded, met with severe punishment, as all concerned in the attack were killed, and it was with the utmost difficulty Captain Broke could save from the fury of his men a young midshipman, who had just then slid down by a rope from the *Chesapeake's* foretop, and claimed his protection. Now the British colours were hoisted over those of the Yankee frigate, but in the hurry, at first our ensign was below instead of above the "stars and stripes," on which the crew of the *Shannon* reopened their fire, and a grape-shot killed the gallant Lieutenant Watt, who had before been wounded, and four or five of his shipmates. The Americans below began to fire, upon which they were summoned either to surrender or suffer the consequences, on which they called out, "We surrender." Thus was finished this celebrated action, just 15 minutes after the first shot was fired, and four after Captain Broke boarded at the head of his score of gallant followers.

Of several shot that had struck the *Shannon*, only five passed through her, the greater number remaining lodged in her side; her bowsprit and mizzenmast were badly injured, and her standing rigging on the starboard side was almost cut to pieces. Of her crew of 306 men (including eight recaptured seamen and 22 Irish labourers taken two days before) and 24 boys, the British frigate lost her first lieutenant, purser, captain's clerk, 20 men and one boy, killed, and 59 wounded, including Mr. Samwell, midshipman, and Mr. Stevens, boatswain (both mortally).* According to the American official account,

---

* The late Commander Raymond, a midshipman of the *Shannon*, who boarded with the fourth division, and was wounded, made some corrections upon his copy of *The Naval History of the United States*. Referring to some depreciatory remarks in the American account of the action, he stigmatises as "false" the insinuation that the *Chesapeake's* crew was disorganised and made up with mercenaries. He says, "This is false: she had 440 as good men as ever went on board and not a boy among them, all Americans." Again, he denies that the Americans came up from below without arms. "They were all armed, but they fled from their quarters on perceiving we were on deck." He also corrects the American estimate of losses. We had, he says, 25 (not 23) killed and 56 wounded, the *Chesapeake* 84 (not 48) killed and 116 (not 98) wounded. James says that, three days after the action, 115 of the crew of the American frigate reported themselves as wounded to the surgeon of the *Shannon*, who wrote estimating their total loss at between 160 and 170 killed and wounded. The American court-martial attributed the loss of the *Chesapeake* to the following causes:—"The almost unexampled early fall of Captain Lawrence and all the principal officers, the bugleman's desertion

the *Chesapeake*, out of a crew acknowledged to number 381 men and five boys, lost 47 killed, among whom were the fourth lieutenant, her master, a marine officer, and three midshipmen, and 99 wounded, including her captain and first lieutenant (both mortally), her second and third lieutenants, chaplain, five midshipmen, and boatswain (mortally). The *Chesapeake* suffered severely below and aloft. All her three lower masts were badly wounded, and her rigging was much cut up. Three guns were disabled and one dismounted, and her hull, especially the port quarter, was a good deal damaged.

Lieutenant Provo Wallis,* second of the *Shannon*, took the ship out of action, and Lieutenant Falkiner, next in seniority, assumed command of the *Chesapeake*, which arrived at Halifax in company with her captor on the 6th of June. It was a Sunday, and as the *Shannon* with her prize passed along the wharf of the town, the people cheered her vociferously. Captain Lawrence had died of his wounds two days before, and Lieutenant Ludlow expired a few days after, and both officers were buried with military honours at Halifax. Captain Broke, who was in a state of much suffering from his wounds, was removed to the house of a naval friend. He received a baronetcy for the service he had rendered to his country, the importance of which it is almost impossible to exaggerate. Both Lieutenants Wallis and Falkiner were promoted, and Messieurs Smith and Cosnahan received lieutenancies. The *Chesapeake* was added to the Navy under her own name.

Though a defeat, few more gallant actions were fought than that between the British schooner *Dominica*, of 5 guns and 66 men and boys, and the Franco-American privateer *Decatur*, of seven guns and 120 men. The *Decatur*, after several unsuccessful attempts, ran on board her adversary, when a desperate hand-to-hand conflict ensued on the schooner's deck. The young officer in command, Lieutenant Barrette, though wounded by two musket-balls, refused to surrender, and was killed fighting, with two midshipmen and 13 men and boys, and 47 were wounded, including every other officer, except the surgeon and one midshipman. Thus the little schooner became a prize to the privateer.

---

from his quarters, and inability to sound his horn, for the Court are of opinion if the horn had been sounded when first ordered, the men being then at their quarters, the boarders would have promptly repaired to the spar-deck, probably have prevented the enemy from boarding, certainly have repelled them, and might have returned the boarding with success; and the failure of the boarders on both decks to rally on the spar-deck after the enemy had boarded, which might have been done successfully, it is believed, from the cautious manner in which the enemy came on board." So far from being "cautious," it was a most daring act of Captain Broke to board a ship of superior force with only 20 men.

* Admiral of the Fleet Sir Provo Wallis, G.C.B., who, in April, 1891, attained his hundredth year, died on the 13th February following.

The 14-gun brig *Boxer*, Commander Blyth, having 66 men and boys on board, was also captured by the *Enterprise*, of 16 guns and 120 men, after a smart action, carried on at half pistol-shot range. The *Boxer* had her commander and three men killed, and 17 wounded, and the *Enterprise* also lost her captain, and had 13 other casualties. Both these gallant officers were buried at Portland, whither the *Enterprise* took her prize.

This success was, however, counterbalanced by a loss the Americans sustained in the capture of the *Argus* by the *Pelican*, Commander Maples. Both were brigs, but the former, though she had 21 more men, was slightly inferior to the British brig in weight of metal, the broadsides being respectively 228 and 262 pounds. The *Pelican* proceeded to sea from Cork to engage the *Argus*, which had been committing depredations on British commerce in St. George's Channel, and she soon encountered and engaged the latter. In the action the *Argus* lost her captain, and the *Pelican*, which early established her superiority of fire, having cut up her antagonist's rigging, and repeatedly raked her, ran the American brig on board, and captured her, but not without the loss of a gallant officer, Mr. Young, who led the boarding party. Her loss was slight, only one man being killed and five wounded, but the *Argus*, out of 122 men and three boys, had six seamen killed and 18 wounded, including her commander and two midshipmen (mortally), and her first lieutenant (severely).

Some boat attacks occurred in Chesapeake Bay, in which severe fighting took place. The *Lottery*, schooner, was cut out by the boats of the British frigates *Belvidera* and *Statira*, and the boats of the 74-gun ships *San Domingo* and *Marlborough*, numbering 105 officers and men, which also, in the most gallant manner, boarded and carried with slight loss four privateer schooners, having an aggregate of 31 guns and 22 men. Rear-Admiral George Cockburn did some good service at the head of Chesapeake Bay, in which his first lieutenant, Mr. (afterwards Sir) George Westphal, who was wounded at Trafalgar when a midshipman of the *Victory*, distinguished himself. An attack on Crancy Island, near Norfolk, ended in a disastrous repulse, with considerable loss of life among the 500 soldiers and 200 seamen embarked in the boat with which the attempt was made. But shortly after, some 2,000 men, under General Beckwith, were landed, and captured the town of Hampton, about 18 miles from Norfolk, with trifling loss. In Delaware Bay, also, the British frigate *Junon* and sloop *Martin* beat off a flotilla of eight gunboats and two block-ships.

Severe fighting took place during the war on Lake Ontario, where the British had a 20-gun ship, the *Royal George*, a brig of 14 guns and a few smaller vessels, all manned by Canadians and commanded by a provincial officer named Earle. The Americans at Sacketts' Harbour appeared before Kingston, the principal British port, with a squadron, and gained command of the lake, as they did also of Lake Erie, where they took Detroit. But a different state of affairs arose when Sir James Yeo, of the British Navy, an officer of great experience and enterprise, arrived with about 500 officers and seamen from England to regain command of the Lakes. Captain Yeo, on arriving at Kingston, fitted out and put to sea with a brig and a schooner and some gun-boats, and appeared before Sacketts' Harbour; but the attack failed, owing to the conduct of his colleague in command of the troops, Sir George Prevost, an officer who displayed equal pusillanimity and incompetence. In the following June, Sir James Yeo, when acting alone, compelled the Americans to abandon their fortified camp, and inflicted other losses on them. Commodore Chauncey, commanding the American squadron, got ready for sea the *General Pike*, superior in weight of metal to the whole British squadron, but nevertheless Sir James Yeo did not hesitate to meet him, and captured two schooners without losing a man. Other desultory operations ensued, to the advantage of neither side.

In May, 1813, Captain Barclay assumed command of the Erie flotilla, consisting of six vessels, carrying 63 guns, but the crews were notoriously inefficient, only some 50 British seamen being among them. In September he sailed from Amherstburgh with his squadron, to risk an engagement with the enemy, whose aggregate broadside weight of metal was 928 pounds to his 459. Commodore Perry had almost an equal superiority in men, and the result was that the British squadron suffered a disastrous defeat. Captain Barclay, commanding the *Detroit*, was severely wounded, his first lieutenant, Garland, was killed, and eight out of the 10 British seamen were *hors de combat* when the ship's flag was struck. The *Queen Charlotte* was also compelled to surrender, after losing her captain and having her first lieutenant severely wounded, and soon after the *Niagara* struck. The British loss was three officers and 38 men killed, and nine officers and 85 wounded, out of 345 engaged. Commodore Perry acknowledged to losing 27 killed and 96 wounded, out of 580 men, and one of the brigs, the *Lawrence*, actually struck to the *Detroit*, but rehoisted her flag. Captain Barclay was tried by court-martial for the loss of the Erie flotilla, but was honourably acquitted of all blame, the court being of opinion that the defeat was due to "the very defective means" he possessed of equipping the flotilla, the very great superiority of the enemy, and "the unfortunate early fall of he superior officers in the action." In Lake Champlain there was some slight fighting, in which two American sloops were captured, and some British troops and seamen destroyed all the public buildings and stores at the port of Plattsburg.

The American frigate *Essex*, 46, Captain Porter, committed great depredations on British commerce in the Pacific, capturing twelve whaling ships, and in company with one of the prizes, named the *Essex Junior*, continued her cruise, until at Valparaiso, in March, 1814, she was brought to action by the *Phœbe*, 44, Captain Hillyar, and *Cherub*, 26, Commander Tucker, when making an attempt to escape. Captain Porter made a gallant resistance against superior force, and out of 260 men, the remainder of his crew being absent in prizes, lost 24 killed and 45 wounded, though he reported his loss greatly in excess of that number. The loss of the two British ships was only five killed and 10 wounded, and their damages were trifling. Nearly all the twelve prizes, including the *Essex Junior*, were recaptured by British cruisers while making their way to the United States, and the *Essex* was added to the Navy.

The fine 22-gun ship *Frolic* surrendered to the British 32-gun frigate *Orpheus* without firing a shot, and the brig *Epervier*, of 18 guns, also captured without opposition the American privateer brig *Alfred*, of 16 guns and 108 men, though it is right to add that the frigate *Junon* was in sight ten miles to leeward. A different result attended the duel between the *Epervier* and the ship-of-war *Peacock*, of 22 guns and 135 men. The *Epervier* was in a notoriously ineffective state, and Commander Wales had represented to the authorities at Halifax that her crew were disaffected, but without success. Commander Wales did not avoid an action, though he must have entered into it with distrust. The enemy's broadside of bar-shot speedily cut his rigging to pieces, while his own carronades capsized and carried away their breeching-bolts. As a last resort, the gallant captain of the British brig called upon his men to follow him in an attempt to board the *Peacock*, but this they declined, and after the engagement had lasted an hour he struck his colours, the brig then having nearly five feet of water in the hold. Out of 101 men and 16 boys, she had eight killed and mortally wounded, and 15 wounded, including the first lieutenant, Mr. Hackett.

A like fate befell her sister ship, the *Reindeer*, of 18 guns and 98 men, in her engagement with the *Wasp*, mounting 22 guns and having 173 men, also a sister ship of the *Peacock*.

Notwithstanding the disparity of force, the respective broadside weight in pounds being 539 and 385, Commander Manners eagerly engaged, and a close and furious action ensued. Disabled by the heavy fire, the *Reindeer* fell bow-on to the port quarter of the *Wasp*, and the gallant Manners, though twice severely wounded, and bleeding profusely, called out to his men, " Follow me, my boys; we must board." He was in the act of showing his men the way when two balls fired from the *Wasp's* maintop penetrated his skull, and came out under his chin. Convulsively clasping his forehead with one hand and his sword with the other, the hero fell dead, ejaculating, " Oh, God! " Soon after this the *Reindeer's* fire almost entirely ceased, when the Americans boarded the brig, of which they received possession from the captain's clerk, the senior surviving officer on deck. Out of 98 men and 20 boys, she had her commander, purser, and 23 hands killed, and 42 wounded, including her only lieutenant, and three other officers. The *Wasp's* crew did not escape scot-free, losing two midshipmen and nine seamen killed and 15 wounded. The *Reindeer* was almost cut to pieces below and aloft, and that she was not surrendered until every hope of successful resistance had passed, was proved by her captors having to set fire to and destroy her, as she could not float.

After refitting at Lorient, the *Wasp* again put to sea and encountered the 18-gun brig *Avon*, Commander Hon. A. Arbuthnot. The action commenced at 9.30 P.M., but so effective was the fire of the American ship-of-war that the *Avon* was rendered helpless by the loss of her mainmast by the board, when the boom mainsail covered the guns, many of which had upset from the usual defects in their fittings. Shortly before eleven Commander Arbuthnot surrendered, but as Captain Blakeley was about to take possession of his prize, the 18-gun brig *Castilian* hove in sight, and he made sail to escape. The *Castilian* took on board the crew of the *Avon*, which was in a sinking state, and indeed, she foundered just as the last boat pushed off from her side. Out of her crew of 104 men and 13 boys, the *Avon* lost her first lieutenant and nine men killed and 32 wounded, including her commander, second lieutenant and one midshipman. The brave officers and men of the *Wasp* were not destined to receive the plaudits of their countrymen, as she never reached an American port, and is supposed to have foundered off Madeira.

Rear-Admiral Cockburn conducted attacks in Chesapeake Bay against Commodore Barney, an enterprising Irish officer in the service of the States. In August, 1814, a squadron arrived from the Gironde with a portion of Wellington's army, no longer required in France in consequence of the peace by which Napoleon was banished to Elba. Admiral Cockburn suggested to General Ross the possibility of an attack on Washington, and the whole expedition proceeded up the Patuxent, by Bladensburg, while Captain Alexander Gordon, of the 38-gun frigate *Seahorse*, co-operated with a squadron up the Potomac, the direct route by water to the capital, and Sir Peter Parker in his ship, the *Menelaus*, created a diversion up Chesapeake Bay.

The advance up the Patuxent was begun by a successful attack by the boats of the fleet on Commodore Barney's flotilla, which secured the right flank of the army. General Ross made a rapid advance of 40 miles in three days, and encamped at the town of Upper Marlborough, 16 miles from Washington. Thence the British army advanced on Bladensburg, 12 miles from their camp, and on the 24th August was fought the action which received its name from that place, when General Ross, with 4,000 men, defeated General Winder, who had under his command, according to the American account, 7,000 soldiers and 600 seamen, with 23 guns. The American army, in the presence of President Madison, was driven from its position on the heights, leaving 10 guns on the field, and retreated on Washington. The British loss was 65 killed and 191 wounded, including a few casualties in the Naval Brigade, who were accompanied by Rear-Admiral Cockburn. During that and the following day, the capital, President's house, and other public buildings were set on fire, a proceeding which reflects little credit on those responsible. The bridge over the Potomac was destroyed, with an immense quantity of military stores and arms, but private property was respected and the citizens were unmolested. The same night the British army evacuated Washington, and re-embarked on board the fleet.

Meantime, Captain Gordon, with the *Seahorse*, *Euryalus*, 36, Captain Charles Napier, three bomb-vessels and a rocket-ship, ascended the intricate channel of the Potomac, leading to the capital, no less than five days being consumed in warping his squadron a distance of 50 miles, to Fort Washington, about 14 miles below the city. He shelled the works on the 27th August, and on the following morning they were evacuated by the garrison. As a result of this success the town of Alexandria capitulated. On the 31st, Captain Gordon received Admiral Cockburn's orders to retire, and the same day he sailed with twenty-one prizes, and, the winds being contrary, had to resort to warping his ships down the channel, and met with a determined resistance by Commodore Rodgers, who had under his command detachments of seamen from the new 44-gun frigate *Guerrière* and the *Constellation*, as well as from Commodore Barney's flotilla. Fireships were ineffectually employed and the batteries erected on the river bank were silenced, and on the 9th September, twenty-three days after leaving the anchorage, the squadron was once more there in safety. The enterprise so gallantly executed only cost the British ships one lieutenant and six men killed and 35 wounded, including Captains Napier and Bartholomew, of the rocket-ship.

Sir Peter Parker did not escape equally well in the service on which he was detached up Chesapeake Bay. Landing with 130 seamen and marines, he fell into an ambush and was slain, together with a midshipman and 12 men, 27 men being also wounded. Failure again marked the attack on Baltimore by a body of 3,270 men, including 600 seamen, and the frigates and sloops, under the naval Commander-in-Chief, Vice-Admiral Sir Alexander Cochrane, which proceeded up the Patapsco. During the advance General Ross was mortally wounded and died the same day, when the command of the troops devolved on Colonel Brooke, of the 44th Regiment. The American army was drawn up five miles from the city, and was driven from its positions at the bayonet's point. The British loss was 46 killed and 300 wounded, the Navy losing an officer and six men in the former category and 45 in the latter. Arrangements were now made for storming the entrenchments, where General Stricker had taken up a position with a strong force, and during the night of the 13th a division of nine boats, detached up the Ferry branch of the Patapsco, under Captain Napier, acting in co-operation, opened a heavy fire. But further operations were abandoned the same night, as, owing to the entrance to the harbour of Baltimore being obstructed by a barrier of sunken vessels, the large ships could not co-operate in the attack on the city and entrenched camp, and heavy rains began to fall. Before daylight the British troops commenced to retreat, and the frigate and smaller vessels rejoined the squadron at anchor off North Point. Boat expeditions were successfully executed up the Connecticut River by Captain Coote, of the 14-gun sloop *Borer*, having under his orders six boats, with 136 men, when twenty-seven vessels were destroyed; and by Lieutenant Garland, of the *Superb*, 74, who also destroyed a large number at Wareham. An expedition with the same object up the Penobscot was conducted by Captain Barrie, of the 74-ship *Dragon*, in which a body of troops assisted, and the *Adams*, corvette, of 20 guns, was destroyed, and the enemy were defeated.

The fighting on the Canadian Lakes was of a most desperate character during the year 1814. In May Sir James Yeo proceeded from Kingston with a squadron of seven vessels and eleven gun-boats, together with 1,080 troops, under General Drummond, against Oswego, situated on the river of the same name near its confluence with Lake Ontario. The operations were successful, and Oswego was taken, with the loss of 18 killed and 64 wounded. But an attempt to cut out some boats, waiting at Sandy Creek to reach Sackett's Harbour, resulted in a sanguinary repulse. On this occasion Captains Popham and Spilsbury, with 180 seamen and marines, were overpowered and made prisoners by a large body of militia and Indians, after losing 18 killed and 50 wounded.

After the defeat of Captain Barclay's squadron in the preceding year, Lake Erie remained under the control of the American flotilla. Lieutenant Worsley had, however, a success on Lake Huron, where he cut out the schooners *Tigress* and *Scorpion*, and Captain Dobbs, of the *Charwell*, with 75 men from his ship and the *Netley*, carried by boarding the two American schooners, *Somers* and *Ohio*. Both these exploits were worthy of the reputation of the noble service to which these gallant officers belonged.

Sir George Prevost, who had before displayed great incapacity, though in superior force, again met with a disastrous repulse at Plattsburg, on Lake Champlain. Acting in co-operation was a Captain Downie, formerly first lieutenant of the *Seahorse*, an officer of signal bravery, who was induced, at the urgent solicitation of the general, to attack the superior American squadron with his ships, the *Confiance*, of 26 guns, and the brig *Linnet*, 16, cutters *Chubb*, of 10 guns, and *Finch* of six, with 10 gunboats, carrying between them 13 guns and 224 men and boys, of whom only 30 were British seamen. His aggregate was 38 broadside guns and 537 men, and that of the Americans 52 guns and 950 men, almost entirely drawn from the regular ships-of-war then laid up in port. The result might have been foreseen, and after a desperate resistance, in which Captain Downie was killed, the *Confiance*, which had begun the action in a state of unpreparedness, her guns having only just been mounted, was forced to strike her colours. The *Linnet* also surrendered, having for ten minutes withstood the united fire of the American squadron, as did also the two cutters, and the gunboats alone effected their escape. The *Confiance* lost 41 killed and about 60 wounded. The *Linnet* had two officers and eight men killed and 14 wounded, including a midshipman, and the *Chubb* had six killed and 16 wounded. The American flagship, *Saratoga*, which was at one time on the point of surrendering, had 28 killed and 29 wounded, and the total American loss was 52 and 58 respectively.

Not less sanguinary was the repulse inflicted by the American privateer, *General Armstrong*, of seven guns and 90 men, on the boats of the *Plantagenet*, 74, and 38-gun frigate *Rota*. These ships discovered the privateer at anchor in Fayal roads, and Captain Lloyd despatched four boats from the seventy-four and three from the *Rota*, containing 180 seamen and marines, to cut her out. But they were received with so deadly a fire that two boats were sunk, and the first and second lieutenants of the *Rota*, a midshipman and 31 men were killed, and 86 were wounded, including five officers.

The Navy was not engaged in the disastrous attack on New Orleans on the 8th

January, 1815, when the British army was repulsed by the Americans, under General Jackson, and the commander-in-chief, Sir Edward Pakenham, was slain, and nearly 2,000 were killed, wounded, and made prisoners. But they suffered in the fighting off the coast of Florida, near Mobile, in the preceding September. The 20-gun ships *Hermes* and *Carron* and the 18-gun sloops *Sophie* and *Childers*, made an attack on Fort Bowyer, about six miles to the eastward of Mobile Point, but unfortunately the *Hermes* was carried by the current until she grounded with her head to the fort, which swept her decks with so destructive a fire, to which she could make no return, that the ship had to be abandoned after losing 25 killed and 24 wounded. The *Sophie*, the only other vessel effectively engaged, had 22 casualties.

Shortly before the failure at New Orleans, Admiral Cochrane made an attack on five gunboats and two other vessels, mounting an aggregate of 39 guns, and having on board 204 men, which had taken post in the bayou Catalan, at the head of Lake Borgue. On the night of the 12th December, forty-two armed launches, carrying 980 seamen and marines, under the orders of Captain Lockyer, proceeded to carry out the enterprise. The boats had a long pull before them of some forty miles from the anchorage at Cat Island against a strong current, and on attacking met with a desperate resistance, every preparation having been made to give our men a warm reception. Captain Lockyer succeeded in capturing the American commodore's ship, and turning her guns on the other gunboats, they were all boarded and secured; but the success was not achieved without heavy loss, mostly occasioned by the fire opened on the boats while pulling against the stream. Three midshipmen and 14 men were killed and 77 wounded, including Captain Lockyer, four lieutenants (one mortally), a marine officer, three master's mates, and seven midshipmen (one mortally). Commanders Lockyer, Montresor, and Roberts were posted for their gallantry, and some of the lieutenants and midshipmen were promoted. In January some boats ascended the St. Mary's River, in Florida, and captured an Indiaman, made prize by a privateer and a gunboat; but towards the end of February, when eleven boats, with 186 men, ascended the river a distance of 120 miles, they met with a repulse and returned to Cumberland Island, where Admiral Cockburn had established his headquarters, with a loss of four killed and 25 wounded.

On the 25th of the month the admiral received intimation of the conclusion of peace between England and the United States, signed at Ghent, in Belgium, on the 24th December preceding, and ratified by the President at Washington on the 18th February. But before this event, the boats of the *Endymion*, under Lieutenant Hawkins, sustained a sanguinary repulse in an attack made during a calm on a privateer brig, carrying 18 guns and 120 men, which she encountered off Nantucket. The launch was captured, and Lieutenant Hawkins, one midshipman and 26 men were killed, and two officers and 35 men wounded. The British frigate had her revenge shortly after, when she brought to action the *President*, Commodore Decatur, of 58 guns and 465 men. The latter escaped from New York, where she was blockaded by a British squadron, consisting of the *Majestic*, 74, and the frigates *Endymion*, *Tenedos*, and *Pomone*. She was chased and brought to action by the *Endymion*, carrying 48 guns and 319 men, but making sail, managed to get away until the *Pomone* engaged her, when she surrendered to this ship and the *Tenedos*, which came up. The *Endymion*, which lost eleven killed and 14 wounded, was much cut up aloft, but quickly repaired her damages and was in a condition to renew the action. The skilful gunnery of her well-trained crew, under Captain Henry Hope, was displayed in the shattered condition of the *President's* hull and her heavy loss, three lieutenants and 32 men being killed, and her commander, three officers and 66 men wounded. Captain Hayes was amply justified in his assertion that "When the effect produced by the well-directed fire of the *Endymion* is witnessed, it cannot be doubted that Captain Hope would have succeeded either in capturing or sinking her had none of the squadron been in sight." While on their way to Bermuda, the two ships encountered a violent gale, in which the *Endymion* carried away her bowsprit and fore and mainmasts, and the *President* all three masts, and they were only saved from foundering by throwing overboard the greater portion of their guns.

After the declaration of peace, but before it was generally known, the British schooner *St. Lawrence*, of 13 guns and 51 men and boys, was captured after a desperate resistance by the privateer brig *Chasseur*, of 14 guns and a crew of 115 men. The schooner in this action lost six killed and 18 wounded out of her small complement. The 44-gun frigate *Constitution*, Captain Stewart,* when about sixty leagues off Madeira, engaged the British ships *Cyane*, 22, Captain Falcon, and *Levant*, 20, Captain Hon. George Douglas. But the conflict between the long 24-pounders of the American frigate and the carronades of these small ships was too unequal to admit of successful resistance and both were constrained to haul down their colours after a creditable display of gallantry. The *Cyane* was almost unrigged, and out of 145 men and 26 boys, had 12 killed and 29 wounded, and the *Levant*, which had also greatly suffered, lost 22, of whom six were killed. Shortly after, the *Levant* was recaptured by a British squadron in the har-

* Captain Stewart was grandfather, on the mother's side, of Mr. Charles Stewart Parnell, the late Irish leader.

bour of Porto Praya, in the Cape de Verde Islands, and the *Constitution* escaped capture on the same occasion by the signal made by Sir George Collier, of the *Leander*, 50, being misunderstood, or, as James says, by the blundering of the British commodore.

A few days after the *President* escaped from New York, the *Peacock* and *Hornet* also succeeded in getting to sea from the same port, and on the 23rd March, three days after hearing of the conclusion of peace, Captain Biddle, commanding the *Hornet*, then off Tristan d'Acunha Island, fell in with the brig *Penguin*, Captain Dickinson, of 16 carronades and two small 6-pounders and a crew of 105 men and 17 boys. Captain Dickinson had served at Lissa, as first lieutenant of the *Cerberus*, and though his enemy had 20 guns, two of them long 18-pounders, and 165 men, and had captured the *Peacock*, of the same force as his brig, he did not hesitate to engage her. The action raged within pistol-shot range, and soon the *Penguin* had her rigging cut to pieces by the bar-shot of her antagonist. As a last resort, Captain Dickinson bore up with the intention of boarding, but fell mortally wounded. Lieutenant McDonald, who succeeded to the command, resolved on the same desperate expedient, but when he ran the enemy on board, the lift of the sea carried away his bowsprit and foremast, which fell on the foremost and waist guns, disabling them, and as he could not bring a fresh broadside to bear, he hailed to say that the *Penguin* had surrendered. In this action the brig lost, besides her commander, the boatswain and eight men killed and mortally wounded, and four officers (very severely) and 24 men wounded. The *Hornet* was chased, on the 28th April, by the *Cornwallis*, 74, and only escaped capture by throwing overboard her guns, anchors, and spare spars, and had to return home in consequence.

The last event of this war, which on the whole was disastrous, and save for the gallantry of our men, not altogether creditable to the British Navy, was the capture, on the 30th June, in the Straits of Sunda, of the 14-gun brig *Nautilus*, a cruiser belonging to the East India Company, by the Yankee sloop *Peacock*, of like force with the *Hornet*. Captain Warrington, when he hailed Lieutenant Boyce, commanding the *Nautilus*, to surrender, was informed that peace had been proclaimed between the two nations, but nevertheless peremptorily ordered that officer to "haul down his colours instantly." Lieutenant Boyce, imbued with a proper sense of his country's honour, refused to do so, on which Captain Warrington, in a cowardly spirit seldom found among men of his cloth, fired into the little brig, which he could almost have hoisted inboard. In the short action that ensued, Lieutenant Boyce was wounded by a grape-shot, which entered near the hip and passed out under the backbone, and by a round shot which shattered his right leg at the knee. Six men were killed, and the first lieutenant (mortally) and seven men wounded, when the gallant young commander, who had vindicated the honour of his flag, ordered the colours to be hauled down.* The *Nautilus* was subsequently surrendered to the East India Company, with an apology by the American Government.

On the conclusion of the general peace in 1815, our Naval forces were reduced to the level at which they stood in 1793, when war with the French Republic was first declared,† that is, to 33,000 seamen and marines. The highest number voted by Parliament was in 1812, when it stood at 145,000; next year it was 5,000 less, but in the latter half of 1814 the number was further reduced to 90,000. Now the country entered upon a period of protracted European peace, which, with the exception of the expeditions to Algiers and Acre, was unbroken, so far as the Navy was concerned, until the Russian War, forty years after the events we have been describing.

* Lieutenant Boyce, whose leg was amputated close to the thigh, survived his grievous wounds to the age of ninety, and was well known to the author of this work. He possessed the rare accomplishment for a naval officer of being an excellent classical scholar, and to the day of his death always carried a well-thumbed copy of Horace in his pocket.

† From May, 1803, when war was a second time declared, to July, 1815, the French Navy had lost twenty-six ships-of-the-line taken by our fleet, and nine destroyed, and fifty-five frigates taken and destroyed. The Spaniards had lost ten ships-of-the-line and six frigates captured, besides one of each class destroyed. From the Danes we took eighteen of the former and nine of the latter, and three Dutch ships-of-the-line were destroyed and five frigates taken.

CHAPTER V.

Biographical Notices of some distinguished Admirals and Captains of the Revolutionary War—Captain John Harvey—His Gallantry and Death in the Action between the *Brunswick* and *Vengeur*—Captain Robert Faulknor—His glorious Death on board the *Blanche*—Captain Richard Bowen—His Career and Death at Teneriffe—Some Account of Sir Andrew Douglas—A brief Notice of Earl Howe—Also of Lord Graves and of Lord Duncan; of Captain Hood, who fell when in Command of the *Mars*; and of Captains John Cooke and George Duff, who were slain at Trafalgar.

SOME details of the life and services of famous officers* during the most glorious period of our Naval History, will be of interest to our readers, and indeed no record would be complete without particulars by which these heroes are presented "in their habit, as they lived."

Among the most gallant and meritorious of these, although they did not live to attain the rank of admiral, having perished in their country's service, were Captains John Harvey, Robert Faulknor, and Richard Bowen. The first named of these officers was born in 1740, in the county of Kent, and went to sea at the age of fifteen, with the famous Captain (afterwards Sir Piercy) Brett, in the *Falmouth*, of 50 guns. When only seventeen years of age he displayed high professional knowledge. The pilot, mistaking the North Foreland light for that on the coast of Suffolk, was actually steering for the Goodwin Sands, when the young officer pointed out his mistake. The pilot persisted, and had not Captain Brett coincided with Mr. Harvey, the ship would have been lost, as it was blowing "great guns" at the time.

When commanding the *Panther*, Captain Harvey served under the orders of Admiral Rodney at the relief of Gibraltar, early in 1780, and in the month of June he was in chief naval command at the Rock. On the night of the 6th the Spaniards made a determined and well-concerted effort to destroy the British ships in the Bay and off the new mole. Several fireships, with a large number of boats, were sent in with this object, while the Spanish ships lay at the entrance of the bay to intercept any that attempted to escape. Captain Harvey got the boats of the squadron out and towed the fireships ashore, though three of them, all in flames, were linked together with chains.

* A more detailed account of the biography of the officers named on the following pages, will be found in the concluding volumes of Campbell's great work, "Naval History of Great Britain."

The *Panther* was in great danger, as some of these instruments of destruction were in such close proximity as to melt the pitch on her sides.

After her return to England, the *Panther* accompanied Sir Samuel Hood to reinforce Sir George Rodney in the West Indies, and was present at the capture of St. Eustatia, and with two other ships went in pursuit of a richly laden Dutch convoy, that had sailed only twenty-four hours before. The convoy was overtaken and captured, together with a 60-gun ship. In Lord Howe's relief of Gibraltar, in 1782, Captain Harvey commanded the *Sampson*, 64. Lord Howe discovered the merits of our hero, and offered him the command of his flagship, the *Victory*, but the peace, signed in the following year, prevented his joining that ship. On the outbreak of the Revolutionary War, his lordship, mindful of the gallant officer, appointed him to the command of the *Brunswick*, of 74 guns and 650 men. Lord Howe's secretary wrote to Captain Harvey on this occasion :—" As his lordship has an idea occasion might arise wherein it might be more convenient for him to shift his flag into a two-decked ship, in that case he would prefer the *Brunswick*, and therefore wishes to have a captain in her with whom he is acquainted, and has authorized me to ask you whether it would be agreeable to you to be appointed to her, in case he can get it done."

In the partial action on the 29th May, 1794, the *Brunswick* being to leeward of the line, Captain Harvey found it impossible to take his proper station next the *Queen Charlotte*, but resolving, as he said, "to have a berth somewhere," he hailed the captain of the *Culloden* to shorten sail, and pushed in between her and the *Montagne*, about the seventh ship from the rear, and in that station received the fire of the French line as the fleet passed each other. Perceiving his friend, Captain Bazeley, of the *Alfred*, hard pressed by an 80-gun ship, Captain Harvey bore down to his assistance, and obliged the Frenchman to sheer off.

But the most striking event in his life, as well as his glorious death, took place on the ever-memorable First of June. The *Brunswick* had kept close to the *Queen Charlotte* all night, and when the signal was made for each ship to bear down and engage her opponent, he put up the helm of his ship at the same time as the flagship, and both ran down together for the centre of the enemy's line. In obedience to signal the fleet made more sail, which brought the *Brunswick* slightly ahead of the *Queen Charlotte*, thus covering her from the fire of the enemy's centre and rear. In consequence she suffered severely, and before firing a shot, her cock-pit was full of wounded.

When Lord Howe, rounding under the stern of the French flagship, *Montagne*, raked the *Jacobin* ahead with his starboard guns, Captain Harvey, being unable to carry out his intention to pass between the latter and the *Patriote*, bore up for an opening between her and the *Vengeur*, the fourth ship from the *Montagne*. This he effected, and soon the two were locked in the deadly embrace of battle, the starboard anchor of the *Brunswick* hooking on the fore-chains of the French seventy-four. So closely were they grappled that the *Brunswick's* seamen, unable to haul up eight of her starboard ports from the third abaft, blew them away, and thus furiously engaged, the combatants went off before the wind. Captain Harvey displayed the true spirit of a British seaman, and when it was suggested to him that they should cut the ship clear of the Frenchman, he replied, "We have got her now, and we will keep her." But a fresh danger menaced the *Brunswick*. The *Achille* was seen bearing down on her port quarter, with her rigging and decks full of men ready to board. Captain Harvey immediately turned over the crews of the five after starboard guns on the lower deck to the port side, and when the enemy came within musket-shot range, the guns were loaded with a double-headed shot in addition to the ordinary projectile, and were fired with fatal effect. Quickly reloading, five or six broadsides were poured into the seventy-four, the forward starboard guns being still engaged with the *Vengeur*. The effect was soon visible, and first the foremast and then the other masts went over the side, thus disabling her second antagonist. Now the tables were turned, and the *Ramillies*, commanded by Captain Henry Harvey, brother of the *Brunswick's* captain, was seen standing to her aid. The crew of the *Ramillies* made signals to the *Brunswick* to cut the *Vengeur* adrift, that they might fire into her, and when this was done, they gave the shattered Frenchman a couple of telling broadsides, and then stood on towards a disengaged foe.

The *Brunswick* had now taken up a position athwart the hawse of the *Vengeur*, and shot away her fore and main-masts, which dragged overboard the mizen-mast, thus leaving her a helpless hulk. Her rudder had been split and her sternpost and counter so shattered that the water poured into the ship, whose gallant crew having done all that honour demanded, displayed a Union Jack in token of surrender. The *Brunswick* could afford no relief to the sinking ship as all her boats had been shot away, and when the *Vengeur* went down she carried with her to a watery grave some 600 men. The *Brunswick* was also in evil plight. All her lower masts, bowsprit, and spars were shot through, and her mizen and foretop gallant-masts were gone, while her running and standing rigging were shot away, and her sails cut to pieces. The hull was also greatly damaged, and 23 guns were dismounted. She had been three times on fire, and her loss consisted of 47 killed, and Captain Harvey and 117 officers and men wounded, mostly severely from the langridge shot and grape with which the *Vengeur's* guns were charged.

As she could take no further effective part in the action, the *Brunswick* bore up for port, and favoured by fine weather, succeeded in making Spithead in eleven days. On arriving here the gallant captain of the *Brunswick* was conveyed on shore.

Captain Harvey had been wounded early in the action by a musket ball, which carried away part of his right hand, but he concealed the injury from his men and bound the wound up with a handkerchief. Some time after this he received a violent contusion in the groin, and though struck to the deck almost lifeless, he brought his strong will to his aid and continued to fight his ship. Shortly after repulsing the attack of the *Achille*, Captain Harvey was struck by a double-headed shot, which splintered his right elbow. Still he remained on deck until the loss of blood made him faint, and he could do no more. But he refused the assistance of anyone to take him below, and with a self-abnegation almost unparalleled, said, " I will not permit a man to leave his quarters on my account. I have still my legs to carry me below." As he quitted the scene of carnage and destruction, he called out, as well as his failing strength would allow, "Persevere, my lads, in your duty, and remember my last words, the colours of the *Brunswick* shall never be struck." When he reached the cockpit he evinced a fortitude that only the most heroic souls possess. His sympathies were aroused for the poor, writhing wretches around him, and it was of the sufferings of his brave men that he spoke, though his own were great indeed. That evening his arm was amputated above the elbow, and he lingered in great pain till the 30th June, the noblest victim of that memorable victory inscribed in our annals as "The Glorious First of June."

The remains of Captain Harvey were interred at Eastry, in Kent, where the following inscription was placed to his memory:—"In a vault near this place are deposited the remains of Captain John Harvey, late commander of his Majesty's ship *Brunswick*, who, after gloriously supporting the honour of the British Navy on the memorable 1st of June, 1794, under Earl Howe, died at Portsmouth, on the 30th of the same month, in consequence of the wounds he received in the engagement, aged 53." The inscription goes on to record that the House of Commons, to perpetuate his most gallant conduct on the day of the victory, unanimously voted a monument to his memory in Westminster Abbey. Captain Harvey's untimely death only prevented his being mentioned in the flag promotions which took place on that occasion.

A man in every way of the same stamp was Captain Robert Faulknor. For generations his family had been distinguished in the annals of their country. His great-grandfather saw much service in the latter part of the seventeenth and early in the eighteenth century, and died lieutenant-governor of Greenwich Hospital in 1724. His grandfather also served with distinction in the *Victory*, *Royal Sovereign*, and *Britannia*, under many celebrated admirals, and was captain of the *Victory* when she carried the flag of the ill-fated Admiral Sir John Balchen on her last cruise. With him and nigh 1,000 officers and men, he perished when the three-decker, considered the finest ship in the world, was lost on the ridge of rocks called the Caskets, off Alderney, on the night of the 4th October, 1744.

Captain Faulknor's father was even more celebrated than his ancestors, and gained a name for valour equal to that of his son, though he did not meet the same tragic end. When only fifteen years of age, young Robert Faulknor served under Admiral Vernon's command at the capture of Carthagena, in 1741, and received a serious wound from the effects of which he never recovered. He also served under Admiral Byng, in his unfortunate action off Minorca, and in 1761, when in command of the *Bellona*, of 74 guns and 558 men, fought one of the most stubbornly-contested actions of the war with the *Courageux* of like force, and carrying 700 men.

Captain Faulknor sailed from Lisbon in company with the *Brilliant*, 36, Captain Logie, and, on the 14th August, sighted three sail, which proved to be the *Courageux* and 36-gun frigates *Malicieuse* and *Ermine*. "These," says Commodore Johnstone, who commanded at Lisbon, in a letter to Lord Howe, giving a quaint account of the engagement, "were returning full of wealth and full of pride from a successful voyage round the French West India Islands, in which they had made many prizes, having now eight ransomers on board. The seventy-four was commanded by Monsieur Lambert, who was esteemed the best officer in France, and had been entrusted with discretionary power, under promise of what he was to perform. The glory of this scheme departed on the issue of the battle. The French ships (intending for Vigo) bore down to make the British distinctly, which the close of the evening left them uncertain, but rather inclined to believe both of the line-of-battle. The French fled, the British pursued during a serene night, a pleasing gale, and every circumstance that could keep the imagination employed. The beams of Aurora discovered the force of the *Brilliant*. The French commodore immediately shortened sail, and made the signal for the frigates to attack her. At six the combat began between those three, when Mons.

Lambert, like a fair gamester, hauled for the *Bellona*, so that their bows pointed to each other. At the distance of two cables' lengths the enemy began to fire. Captain Faulknor received his second broadside before he permitted a gun to be discharged; this enabled him to lock the yards when he gave orders to begin. The execution (as I have it from the French) was incredible. They received two broadsides in that situation, when the *Bellona* backed astern, in order to run on the other side. In performing this, her mizen-mast went away, and fell directly over the stern, several were bruised, some killed, and all the men on the top got in at the gun ramparts. The driver boom broke the fall; this rather served to assist Captain Faulknor's scheme of wearing quickly under the *Courageux's* stern, and ranging on the other side. It was performed to a miracle, every gun told on the quarter as they passed, till the *Bellona* was placed on the *Courageux's* bow, whose jib-boom was entangled in the other's fore shrouds. Here the guns were as quickly traversed, and as keenly plied. Taken in all directions, beat and buffeted on every quarter, her captain killed, her mizen-mast gone, her main-mast wagging, her tiller rope cut, her quarters laid open, 240 of her crew carnaged, 130 wounded, courage submitted to superior powers; the main-mast fell with the flag. The action lasted fifty-five minutes. The prize was conducted into Lisbon, under the eyes of the king and court, as well as those of every nation in Europe.

"The opposite shores were covered from St. Julien's to the town with thousands of people. What is strange the *Bellona* had only a few shots which pierced her hull, though shattered and torn in the sails and rigging. She lost but five men and 20 wounded, mostly by musket balls, and the tumbling of her masts. It is natural to inquire into the reason of this disproportion, and it is imputed with truth to superior management; for the ship was more shattered than the *Formidable*. She appears to have been appointed in every respect superior to any of the French captures which have fallen under my notice—short guns, smooth cylinders, good powder, and grape well prepared, clear of cabins and other obstructions, the officers regarded as the best in France, the captain confident in his strength and daily wishing for an opportunity to redeem the credit of his country; but the fact is he was fairly outworked. I can only compare the conduct of the *Bellona* to a dexterous gladiator, who not only plants his own blows with surety, but guards against the strokes of his antagonist. Fortune had little to say in the action, because it appeared that everything that happened was told and foreseen. Each design was carried into execution, no confusion, no balk, no powder blown up, no cannon fired in vain. The people, it is true, had been twice in action, all the officers

2nd CLASS PETTY OFFICER.

were of a superior class. The first lieutenant, Mr. Male, is not to be equalled for modesty or merit, nor can the master be compared with any of his corps.

"Captain Faulknor's speech* in the note below to the people will explain what I mean by saying everything was foreseen. Every action corresponded with the speech, which is the circumstance I admire the most. It appears wonderful to some that so many men should be killed in so short a space. But on viewing the ship, that reason is called to account how any could escape. The force of a man-of-war when well applied was never more evident. Your lordship will easily conceive this who knows the slaughter committed in the *Hero* about the same time.

"There is an anecdote of Faulknor which I think not unworthy of being related even to your lordship. It is true, and it is natural, and I think favours more of presence of mind than some I have met with in noted histories:—

"When the *Bellona's* mizen-mast went away, a fellow, looking afraid, cried out, 'Oh, Lord! we have lost our mizen-mast.' Faulknor immediately replied, 'What has a two-decked ship to do with a mizen-mast in time of action? See and knock away his mizen-mast.' Not to interrupt the thread of the principal action, I seemed to have forgot poor Logie in the *Brilliant*. We left him engaged with two. He never perfectly closed with either, but pursued his excellent plan of employing both, to prevent any from interfering with the gladiators, who were fitted. He succeeded, and they left him. They are since got into Vigo. The circumstance which amazes foreigners most in this affair, is the pursuing a superior force with so much money on board. It shows so much despite, so much confidence, and the issue appears so complete a proof that even the French, on this occasion, yield with the tongue what they lost with the sword. When the second captain came on board he told Faulknor he had got a rich prize. 'By Jove,' says Bob, 'I gave you a chance for a better. There is £100,000 in the hold you might have divided without agency.' The man stood amazed, as he declared himself. During the

---

* "Gentlemen—I have been bred a seaman from my youth, and consequently am no orator, but I promise to carry you all near enough, and then you may speak for yourselves. Nevertheless, I think it necessary to acquaint you with the plan I propose to pursue in taking the ship, that you may be the better prepared to execute my orders with quickness and facility. French men-of-war have been taken with their guns lashed on the opposite side. They know little of this business, put them to management, and they run into confusion; for this reason I propose to run you close on the enemy's larboard quarter, when we will exchange two broadsides and then back astern and range upon the other quarter; and so tell your guns as you pass. I recommend at all times to point chiefly at the quarters, with your guns slanting fore and aft; this is the principal part of a ship. If you kill the officers, break the rudder, and snap the braces, she is yours of course, but for this reason I desire you may only fire one round shot, and grape above, and two round shot only below; take care and send them home with exactness. This is a rich ship, they will render you in return their weight in gold."

action Captain Faulknor was induced from the heat to throw off his coat; nor would he listen to his officers, who fearing it might prove a mark to the enemy, earnestly requested him to put it on; but he peremptorily refused—'Never mind such thoughts, I must take my chance for that.'" The ships steered for Lisbon, where the French commodore died of wounds he had received in the neck. The first lieutenant of the *Bellona* was promoted, and the *Courageux* was added to the Navy, in which she saw much service until her loss on the coast off Gibraltar in 1797.

Our hero had also two uncles in the Navy; one, named Samuel, repeatedly distinguished himself, and a second, Admiral Jonathan Faulknor, was second captain of the *Victory*, Keppel's flagship, in his indecisive action with the French fleet, and received the encomiums of his superiors.

Young Robert Faulknor, who lost his father in 1769, when only seven years of age, entered the Navy in 1771, on board the *Isis*, 50, Captain the Hon. W. H. Cornwallis, and was engaged on the coast of America against the revolted colonies. He accompanied Captain Cornwallis into the *Bristol*, and a passage in a letter addressed by that officer to the boy's mother, will show the estimation in which he held his "dear little friend," as he called him. "He has behaved extremely well in all things, and bids fair to be as great a credit to the service as his father was." The same year the young midshipman followed his patron into the *Ruby*, *Medea*, and *Lion*, 64, in which he sailed for the West Indies.

In December, 1780, Mr. Faulknor received a lieutenant's commission, and served in the *Princess Royal*, 98, flagship of Admiral Rowley, who spoke of him as "a young man of great merit." In April, 1782, Lieutenant Faulknor was appointed to the *Britannia*, 98, Vice-Admiral Barrington's flagship, which sailed with a squadron to intercept a French convoy bound for the East Indies. The *Pegase*, 74, and *L'Actionnaire*, 64, with twelve merchantmen, were taken, and the *Britannia* participated in Lord Howe's relief of Gibraltar. He served much afloat during the peace, and on the 2nd April, 1791, was promoted to the rank of commander, and commissioned the *Pluto*, fireship, of 14 guns, and in June, 1793, soon after the outbreak of war with France, was transferred to the *Zebra*, 16, which formed one of the fleet sent under command of Sir John Jervis to the West Indies. Here Commander Faulknor made a great reputation for daring and professional skill.

At the attack on Martinique, his small ship, with the *Asia*, 64, Captain Brown, was ordered to run in close and cover the boats of the fleet, under the command of

Commodore Thompson, supported by Captains Riou and Nugent; a detachment from the army advancing at the same time along the side of the hill, under Fort Bourbon, towards the bridge over the canal, at the back of Fort Royal. Sir John Jervis says in his despatches:—"This combination succeeded in every part except the entrance of the *Asia*, which failed for the want of precision of the French officer who had undertaken to pilot the *Asia*. Captain Faulknor observing that ship baffled in her attempts, and the *Zebra* having been under a shower of grape-shot for a great length of time (which he, his officers, and ship's company, stood with a firmness not to be described), he determined to undertake the service alone, and he executed it with matchless intrepidity and conduct. Running the *Zebra* close to the wall of the fort, and leaping overboard at the head of his ship's company, he assailed and took this important post before the boats could get on shore; although they rowed with all the force and animation which characterize English seamen in the face of an enemy. No language of mine can express the merit of Captain Faulknor on this occasion; but as every officer and man in the army and squadron bears testimony to it, this incomparable action cannot fail of being recorded in the page of history." Sir Charles Grey also highly commended Captain Faulknor. "The Navy acquitted themselves with their usual gallantry (particularly Captain Faulknor, whose conduct justly gained him the admiration of the whole army), carrying the fort by escalade about 12 o'clock of the 20th inst., under the able conduct of Commodore Thompson, whose judicious disposition of the guns and flat boats, assisted by that spirited and active officer Captain Rogers, contributed materially to our success."

The following extracts from some of his letters to his mother, whom he addresses as "Honoured Madam," according to the quaint custom of the time, cannot fail to be of interest. The first is dated from Martinique harbour, March 25th, 1794, on board the *Undaunted*, the *Bienvenue's* prize, into which he had been posted by Sir John Jervis:—"On the 20th of this month I was made post-captain into the *Undaunted*, a French frigate of 28 guns, captured in Fort Royal harbour, the magazine and arsenal of all the French West India Islands. The whole island has surrendered to the British arms. The *Zebra* has been employed during the whole siege, and I have served alternately on board and on shore. At the storming of Fort Royal a circumstance so fortunate happened to myself that I cannot help relating it:—I had a ship's cartouche box, which is made of thick wood, buckled round my body, with pistol cartridges in it for the pistol I carried at my side. As the *Zebra* came close to the fort a grape-shot struck, or rather grazed my right-hand knuckles and shattered the cartouche in the centre of my body; had it not miraculously been there I must have been killed on the spot. Thanks to Almighty God for His kind preservation of me in the day of battle! This important island being secured, the fleet and army will next proceed to St. Lucia, and then to Guadaloupe, where we expect to find but little resistance. The admiral told me to-day, I was immediately to go into the *Rose;* a removal which will be very pleasant to me, as she is an excellent English frigate, quite manned, and in good order. She becomes vacant by Captain Salisbury being appointed Commissioner of the dockyard at Martinique. Adieu, my dearest mother! may this find you well and happy, sincerely prays your most affectionate and dutiful son."

"POSTSCRIPT.—The admiral has appointed me to the *Rose*, paying me such compliments that it is impossible for me to relate them. The sword and colours of Fort Royal were delivered to me by the Governor of the fort, and I take some credit to myself that after the *Zebra* had stood an heavy fire, and when we had the power to retaliate, for we were mounted upon the walls, I would not allow a man to be hurt, on their being panic-struck and calling for mercy. It would take a volume to relate the events which have happened to me since I left England. The *Zebra*, when she came out of action, was cheered by the admiral's ship, and the admiral himself publicly embraced me on the quarter-deck, and directed the band to play 'See the Conquering Hero comes!' Such compliments are without example in the Navy: I never could have deserved them."

Captain Faulknor's next letter was dated from on board the *Blanche*, Barrington Bay, St. Lucia, April 4th:—"Since my last of the 25th March, from Martinique, the fleet and troops have proceeded to this island, and found it an easy capture, after sustaining the fire from the different batteries, and intending to storm the strong fort of Morne Fortunée, in which I was to have commanded a party of my own seamen of the *Rose*, which ship I had till the island was taken, when the admiral was good enough to remove me to a frigate of 32 guns, the *Blanche*, where I mean to stop, not wishing to have a larger ship. The *Rose* was the first ship into Barrington Bay, so named by Sir John Jervis, it being the famous place where that good admiral made so gallant a defence in the late war. I think he will receive pleasure to hear of this event, and had I a moment's time I should not fail to write to him. We next proceed to Guadaloupe, where we shall probably meet with some opposition." In the subsequent conquest of this island Captain Faulknor continued to distinguish himself, and at the storming of the principal fort, which was attended with a good deal of loss, he commanded a detachment of seamen. In a subsequent letter from Halifax, Captain Faulknor gives the following account of his success:—"After a pleasant passage of eleven days, I arrived safe at the port on the 16th instant, with his Royal Highness Prince Edward.* I was ordered to take my old ship the *Zebra* under my command, and to cruise after the two ships are refitted, along the whole coast of America until the end of October. A large force of one hundred and fifty ships have sailed from America to France, guarded by three sail-of-the-line and six frigates. One frigate and a sloop are left in the Chesapeake to block up the *Dædalus*, a British frigate which has been kept in port these last five months, by superior force. The *Blanche*, I trust, will be ready for sea in a few days, and I mean without a moment's delay to proceed to her relief. The public papers and the different letters I have written will inform you of the singular success of our arms in the West Indies. The exertions in the different operations were a continual competition, and each officer and man in the army and navy was zealous to excel the other; the sailors became good soldiers. Among others, it fell to my lot to serve alternately on board and on shore, but chiefly the latter, and although I had but a small share in the business, yet the escapes I have had have been great. I commanded a detachment of seamen at the storming of the strong fort of Fleur d'Epée, at Guadaloupe, and which was thought impracticable to be taken by assault. The grenadiers, light infantry, and seamen were sent on this service. The side of the mountain which the seamen had to get up, was almost perpendicular, and defended by nature and art. All difficulties were overcome, but by the time we got upon the ramparts we were so blown and our strength so exhausted, that the strongest amongst us were unmanned.

"I was attacked by two Frenchmen, one of whom made a thrust at me with his bayonet, which went through my coat without wounding me; and the other made a blow at me, which I parried, and he eluded mine in return, but immediately sprang upon me, clasping his arms round my neck, and fixing his teeth in the breast of my shirt, wrenched the sword from my hand, and tripped me up, falling with great violence to the ground, with this French officer upon me. In this situation two of my seamen flew to my relief and saved my life, and at the moment when the man upon me had his hand lifted up to stab me. An escape so providential, and an event so critical, call for my warmest thanks to the Almighty. The conquest of this fort determined the fate of Guadaloupe: the troops who had intended before to make a vigorous opposition, now ran before us, and we had little to do afterwards

* Afterwards Duke of Kent, father of Her Majesty the Queen.

but to march through the island, a march of great severity in a climate so unhealthy. Thus ended the conquest of the French West Indies before the rainy season had set in, which alone might have frustrated all our hopes."

In a letter, dated December 31, 1794, Captain Faulknor informs Admiral Caldwell that he had chased an armed schooner on shore, laden with gunpowder, near Fort Louis, Guadaloupe, which he afterwards got off and sent to St. John's, Antigua. He also, the day before, chased a national corvette into the bay of Deseada, where she was moored close under a battery, on which he anchored, engaged and silenced the battery, and brought the schooner out. The *Blanche* suffered slightly in her hull, masts, and rigging, and a midshipman and one man were killed and five wounded. The enemy, both in the battery and on board the schooner, suffered considerably.

Within a few days of this our hero ended his glorious career in the desperate engagement which took place off Point à Petre, between the *Blanche*, which had two master's mates and 12 men away in prizes, and the *Pique*, frigate, of 38 guns, besides a number of brass swivels on her gunwale. In this engagement, fought on the 5th January, 1795, Captain Faulknor was shot through the heart from the bowsprit of the *Pique*, having previously lashed it to the capstan with his own hands.

Mr. Watkins, first lieutenant, gallantly fought the ship after Captain Faulknor was killed. Some further account of the action is given in an abstract from an official letter from Vice-Admiral Caldwell to Mr. Stephens, dated off Martinique, 11th January, 1795. " For the information of my Lords Commissioners of the Admiralty, I enclose two copies of letters received from Lieutenant Watkins, of the *Blanche*, with minutes of Mr. Milne,[*] her second lieutenant, who came to me express, giving an account of their taking the French frigate *La Pique*, of 38 guns and 360 men, after an action of five hours, as brilliant and decided as ever happened; nor can too much praise and commendation be given to all the officers and ship's company. Their lordships will see by the minutes the judicious manner in which the *Blanche* laid the enemy on board, and twice lashed her bowsprit to the *Blanche's* capstan; and when the former's main and mizenmasts fell, she payed off before the wind and towed the enemy, when the stern-posts, not being large enough, they blew the upper transom beam away to admit the gun to run out, and fired into her bows for three hours, the marines under Lieutenant Richardson keeping up so well-directed and constant a fire, that not a man could appear upon her

[*] This officer was promoted to the rank of post-captain, and commanded the *Pique*, when she was lost on the coast of France, after an action with the *Seine*, frigate. Her crew were saved, and Captain Milne was appointed to the *Seine* in 1798.

forecastle until she struck, when the second lieutenant and ten men swam on board, and took possession of her. Captain Faulknor was unfortunately killed after two hours' action, by which his Majesty has lost an officer as truly meritorious as the Navy of England ever had."

The death of Captain Faulknor made a considerable impression on the public mind, and the gallantry he displayed was long the theme of praise by his countrymen. On the 6th May, an interlude, called "The Death of Captain Faulknor," was performed at Covent Garden Theatre. It was also selected by an eminent artist as a subject well adapted to his genius, and the treatment was worthy of this glorious event. But the sense which the nation at large entertained of the heroism of Captain Faulknor is best shown by the speeches in the House of Commons on Tuesday, April 4th, when a public monument was voted to his memory. This was executed by Rossi and placed in St. Paul's, with the following inscription: "This monument was voted by his country to Captain Robert Faulknor, commander of his Majesty's ship *Blanche*, whose ancestors had, without cessation, served with glory in the British Navy for nearly two centuries, and who himself fell on the 5th January, 1795, when engaging *La Pique*, of superior force, which was afterwards captured by the *Blanche*."

A third post-captain in the Navy, not less distinguished and gallant than either Harvey or Faulknor, and we could give him no higher praise, was Captain Richard Bowen, of whom Nelson wrote at the time of his glorious death, "A more enterprising, able, and gallant officer does not grace his Majesty's Naval service."

Richard Bowen was born in Devonshire, the county of Drake, and so many other naval worthies, in the year 1761, and went to sea when thirteen years of age with his father, who commanded a trading ship. In 1778, when serving in the West Indies with his elder brother, the master of a merchantman, he volunteered to serve under Captain Calder, then commanding the *Emerald* frigate. On her return to England in the following year, young Bowen served in the *Lightning* fireship, under Captain Calder, who, on his promotion, recommended him to the notice of Captain Jervis (afterwards Earl St. Vincent), with whom he served in the *Foudroyant*. Captain Jervis quickly appreciated the merits of the young officer, who commanded one of the ship's boats when it was employed with others towing the *Perseverance*, of Admiral Darby's squadron, to attack the *Lively* (formerly of the British Navy), of 26 guns and 205 men, which was captured.

In April of the following year, 1782, the *Foudroyant*, one of the Channel squadron, under the command of Admiral Barrington, chased two ships-of-the-line, and about one o'clock on the morning of the 21st April, brought the sternmost to close action. In less than an hour Captain Jervis, by superior seamanship and gunnery, effected the capture of the ship, the *Pegase*, of 74 guns and 750 men. The enemy on this occasion suffered considerably, losing 80 men, among the wounded being the commander. During the action Bowen again attracted the notice of Captain Jervis, who promoted him to be junior acting lieutenant of his ship. While the *Foudroyant* was refitting, Bowen, whose spirit eagerly sought the excitement of active service, went afloat as third lieutenant in the *Artois*, frigate, of which his elder brother was the master. The conclusion of peace robbed him of further chance of earning distinction, and he served for some years chiefly in the West Indies, but without having his acting rank confirmed, though his patron, Sir John Jervis, used his utmost endeavours on his behalf.

Not until 1790 did Bowen receive his promotion to the rank of lieutenant, and in March of the following year we find him appointed to the charge of the *Atlantic*, and two other transports, which were sent with supplies to the newly founded colony of New South Wales. Thence he sailed past New Caledonia, and by way of Malacca, to Calcutta, where he arrived in January, 1792, and having procured a further supply of provisions, returned to Port Jackson on the 19th June. Lieutenant Bowen, taking on board Governor Phillips, sailed for England, on the way touching for the second time at Norfolk Island, and arrived at Spithead on the 10th May, 1793, having completed the voyage round the world.

War having been declared with France, Bowen embarked with Sir John Jervis as fourth lieutenant of the *Boyne*, 98, carrying his flag. He proceeded to the West Indies, and rivalled in glory the officer whose exploits in the *Zebra* we have already detailed. Admiral Jervis placed him in command of the guard boats at the siege of Fort Royal, in Martinique, and entrusted to him the duty of boarding the *Bienvenue*, a French frigate, which lay in the careening ground, under the walls of Fort Royal. Having made his arrangements, Lieutenant Bowen, on the 17th February, led the attack in the *Boyne's* barge, and before the enemy could bring a gun to bear, he boarded her under a heavy fire from the fort, and carried the ship, killing or driving overboard all except 20 of the crew, who became his prisoners, but as the wind blew straight into the harbour, he could not bring the *Bienvenue* off. "The success of this gallant action," wrote Captain Faulknor, "determined the general and me to attempt the fort and town of Fort Royal by assault."

On the 20th March, when this officer was appointed to the command of the *Bienvenue*, Lieutenant Bowen succeeded him in the *Zebra*, with the rank of commander, and was employed at the reduction of St. Lucia, Guadaloupe, and other islands.

In the following April Commander Bowen received post rank, and was appointed first to the *Veteran*, and then to the 32-gun frigate *Terpsichore*. In this ship he effected the release of the *Dædalus*, which was blockaded in the Chesapeake by two large French frigates, which, however, declined to engage the English ships on equal terms. Thence he returned to Guadaloupe, which the French succeeded in recovering, and he was of great service at the evacuation of Fort Matilda, in bringing off the garrison, when he received a sword wound in the face, which necessitated his return to England. Rear-Admiral Thompson and Sir John Vaughan, commanding the forces in the West India Islands, bore testimony to the services rendered by Captain Bowen, and the latter officer states, on the authority of General Prescott, commanding the troops at Fort Matilda, that when the fort became untenable, "by his able disposition of the boats everything was managed with the most perfect order and regularity."

Sir John Jervis was appointed to the command of the Mediterranean fleet in December, 1795, when Captain Bowen joined him in the *Terpsichore*, and was appointed to the command of a squadron of small vessels employed to protect the trade of Gibraltar and the supplies for the garrison. In introducing him to General O'Hara, commanding the troops at the fortress, the admiral described the captain of the *Terpsichore* as possessing "the most inexhaustible spirit of enterprise and skilful seamanship that can be comprised in any human character."

In October, 1796, when Admiral Man's squadron was chased into Gibraltar by a Spanish fleet, Captain Bowen was despatched to give information to Sir John Jervis, and when off Carthagena, on the 13th of the month, he sighted a Spanish frigate of superior force, which proved to be the *Mahonesa*, carrying 34 guns and a crew of 275 men. Though his ship's company was considerably reduced by sickness, and the Spanish fleet was known to be cruising in the neighbourhood, Captain Bowen determined to engage the enemy. He says in his official letter to the commander-in-chief: "On the morning of the 13th instant at day-light, we discovered a frigate to windward standing towards us. About eight I could perceive her making preparation for battle, and was then apparently in chase of us. Our situation altogether was such as to prevent me being over-desirous of engaging her; out of our small complement of men we had 20 in the hospital, and we had more than that number still on board on our sick and convalescent lists, all of whom were either dangerously ill or extremely weak. We were scarcely out of sight of the spot where we knew the Spanish fleet had been cruising only two days before, and in fact we had stood on to look for them, with a view of ascertaining their movements; a small Spanish vessel which we conjectured to be a sort of tender was passing us, steering towards Carthagena, so that I could hardly flatter myself with being able to bring the frigate off, in the event of a victory, or of even escaping myself if disabled. On the other hand, it appeared that nothing but a flight and superior sailing could enable me to avoid an action, and to do that from a frigate apparently not much superior to us except in point of bulk, would have been committing the character of one of his Majesty's ships more than I could bring myself to resolve on. I therefore continued standing on without any alteration of course. Having with infinite satisfaction and comfort to myself, commanded the *Terpsichore's* crew for two years and a half, through a pretty considerable variety of services, I well knew the veteran stuff I still had left in health to depend upon for upholding the character of British seamen, and I felt my mind at ease as to the termination of any action with the frigate in sight only. At half-past nine she came within hail, and hauled her wind on our weather beam, and as I conceived she only waited to place herself to advantage, and to point her guns with exactness, and being myself unwilling to lose the position we were well in, I ordered one gun to be fired as a trier of her intention. It was so instantaneously returned and followed up by her whole broadside, that I am confident they must have done it at the sight of our flash; the action of course went on, and we soon discovered that her people would not or could not resist our fire. At the end of about an hour and forty minutes, during which time we had twice wore, and employed about twenty of the last minutes in chase, she surrendered. At this period she appeared almost entirely disabled, and we had drawn close up alongside with every gun well charged and well pointed. It was, nevertheless, with considerable difficulty that I prevailed on the Spanish commander to decline the receiving of such a broadside by submitting; and from everything I have since heard, the personal conduct, courage, and zeal of that officer, whose name is Don Thomas Ayalde, was such during the action, notwithstanding the event of it, as reflects on him the greatest honour, and irresistibly impressed on my mind the highest admiration of his character. After (from the effects of our fire) his booms had tumbled down, and rendered his waist guns unserviceable, all the standing rigging of his lower masts shot away, and I believe every running rope cut through, and a great number of his people killed and wounded, he still persevered, though he could rally but few of his men to defend his ship, almost longer than defence was justifiable. Had there been the smallest motion in the sea every mast must have inevitably gone by the board.

"Our loss (which will appear by enclosed list) has been much less than could have been expected; but our masts, sails, and rigging were found to be pretty much cut up. The spirited exertion of every man, officer, and boy belonging to the ship I command, as well in the action as in securing the two disabled ships and bringing them off instantly from a critical situation, by taking the prize in tow, and by their incessant labour ever since, will, I trust, when their small number is considered, place them in a light superior to any praise I could bestow. I am unwilling to speak of the particular conduct of any of the officers, but the talents displayed by the first lieutenant, Devonshire, who was but just out of the sick list, during the action, added to the uncommon fatigue in taking charge of the prize, and the very able manner he conducted and prepared to defend her, entitle him to this distinction, and prove him highly deserving of the recommendation you gave him with his appointment in the West Indies; and although I had rather any other person should observe the conduct of a brother of mine in action, and speak of it afterwards, yet I feel it my duty, as captain of the ship, to state that I thought Mr. Bowen's (the second lieutenant's) conduct was particularly animating to the ship's company, and useful from the number of guns he saw well pointed in the course of the action, and from the absence of the first lieutenant on board the prize, the labouring oar of this ship has fallen upon him, and in my mind, the task we have had since the action has been infinitely more arduous than that of the action itself."

Lloyd's committee voted Captain Bowen a piece of plate of the value of one hundred guineas, and the Admiralty promoted Lieutenant Devonshire. Having refitted his ship Captain Bowen sailed on a cruise and captured several small prizes, and a fine ship from Monte Video, which he took at the mouth of Cadiz harbour. Soon again he had an opportunity of displaying his gallantry and skill.

On the night of the 13th December, in this year, he chased and brought to action the French frigate *Vestale*, of 36 guns and 270 men. The action was fought yard-arm to yard-arm, and was obstinately contested for two hours, when the enemy surrendered, having lost her captain and 40 men killed, and her second captain and about 50 wounded. Within a few minutes after the conclusion of the action, the masts and bowsprit of the *Vestale* went over the side. The *Terpsichore* had only four killed and 19 wounded, including Lieutenant George Bowen, the captain's younger brother, who received his well-earned promotion, and midshipman Fane. There being no lieutenant besides Mr. Bowen on board the *Terpsichore*, the master was sent with a few men as a prize crew to the *Vestale*, which, however, was forced to "bring to" close to the rocks and shoals between Cape Trafalgar and Cadiz. On the following day Captain Bowen was under the necessity of abandoning the prize, which during the night the French carried into Cadiz harbour, to the great mortification of her captors. Sir John Jervis wrote a consolatory letter to Captain Bowen, in which he said:—"I lament exceedingly that you and your brave crew were deprived of the substantial reward of your exertions; but you cannot fail to receive the tribute due to you from the Government and country at large. I was very much agitated with the danger you apprehended your brother was in when you wrote; I have, however, derived great consolation from the report of Captain Mansfield, that he was much recovered, and able to walk down to the Mole, before he sailed. The account you gave of Francis Fane is very grateful to my feelings, and I have sent your postscript to Lady Elizabeth, as the greatest treat I could give to a fond mother and an high-minded woman. I hope when the upper works of the *Terpsichore* are thoroughly repaired and well caulked, you will not find her so crazy as you apprehend." Captain Bowen was not present at the glorious victory achieved by his patron, Sir John Jervis, over the Spanish fleet on the 14th February, 1797, but on hearing of it, got under weigh for Gibraltar, to join the commander-in-chief. When returning to his station he fell in with the *Santissima Trinidada*, carrying 138 guns, which had only her foremast standing, and had the temerity to attack the huge four-decker.

Regarding the effects of his fire Sir John Jervis wrote to him on the 2nd April:— "The gallant attack you made deserved success; but it is not given to mortals to command it. An American gentleman, who called upon me at Lisbon, saw the second captain of the *Trinidada*, who was badly wounded by the *Terpsichore*, and told my informant that he had nine killed on the spot, and wounded a great number, several of whom he had reason to believe had since died of their wounds, and they described your fire as infernal."

In June the admiral detached Captain Bowen to look into Teneriffe, in the Canaries, and at midnight on the 18th, he cut out from under the batteries of Santa Cruz a ship from Manilla. He was also engaged, under Nelson, in the first bombardment of Cadiz, and was entrusted by that officer with the conduct of the second bombardment, on the 5th July. The enemy's gun-boats on this occasion did not venture out from under the walls, and, says Nelson, "No opportunity was offered to Bowen to make a dash." Lord St. Vincent had long meditated an attack on Teneriffe, and when it took place, "Terpsichore Bowen," as the commander-in-chief called our hero in his letters to Rear-Admiral Nelson, had the glorious but hazardous duty assigned him of leading the attack.

We have already given a detailed account of this disastrous enterprise, and will only add that Captain Bowen landed at the Molehead with 40 or 50 of his men, and stormed the battery, and was proceeding towards the town when he was met with a shower of grape from some field-pieces and was slain, together with his first lieutenant and many of his brave men. "The body of Captain Bowen," says Campbell, "covered with wounds, was discovered in the morning under those of his first lieutenant and his whole boat's crew, who had been his faithful companions in many hazardous and successful enterprises, and sealed their attachment to their lamented leader by participating in his glorious fate. His body was committed to the deep with the honours of war on the 27th July."

It is not too much to say that the Navy has produced no finer seaman that the captain of the *Terpsichore*, the "little devil," as the Spaniards called the ship. His devotion to duty, his dashing gallantry and professional skill were unsurpassed, and gave promise of the highest distinction, while his many amiable qualities endeared him to his crew. Notwithstanding that both St. Vincent and Nelson urged Lord Spencer, then First Lord of the Admiralty, to erect a national memorial in St. Paul's to the memory of Captain Bowen, nothing was done, on the plea that there was no precedent for thus honouring an officer who had fallen in an unsuccessful enterprise, and the only monument in the land was put up by his father in the church at Ilfracombe, his native place.

Sir Andrew Snape Douglas was a famous officer in his day, and commanded Lord Howe's flagship, the *Queen Charlotte*, in his great victory on the 1st June. He was born in 1761, went to sea when only ten years of age, in the *Arethusa*, commanded by his uncle, afterwards Sir Andrew Hammond, after whom he was named. He rendered important services during the American War of Independence. At the siege of Charlestown, in 1780, he commanded the *Sandwich*, floating battery, and after the surrender, though only in his nineteenth year, was made post-captain and commissioned the *Providence*, an American 32-gun frigate, an extraordinary instance of rapid promotion. The same year his uncle, then commanding the *Roebuck*, Admiral Arbuthnot's flagship, left for England, when this young officer succeeded to the command, and captured the *Confederacy*, 36, the *Protector*, 28, and several privateers. In July, 1781, when the *Roebuck* was ordered home, Captain Douglas was appointed to the *Chatham*, 54, and continued on active service on the American coast till the conclusion of the war. During a great portion of the time he was commodore of a squadron of frigates, and took and destroyed fifty sail belonging to the enemy, including several privateers, and the French 36-gun frigate, *Magicienne*.

In August, 1786, Captain Douglas was appointed to the command of the *Southampton*, 32, and served in the Mediterranean and in attendance on King George III. at Weymouth. His Majesty often embarked on board the frigate, and knighted her gallant commander. Captain Douglas commanded successively the seventy-four's, *Goliath* and *Alcide*, under Lords Howe and Hood, and in 1793, on the outbreak of war with France, was appointed to the *Phaeton*, 38, and was very successful in cruising for the protection of British commerce. On the 14th April, he captured the French galleon, *St. Jago*, which greatly enriched the officers and men of the *Phaeton*. He says, in a letter to his uncle: "Yesterday our squadron gave chase to two sail in the north-west. I came up with a large Spanish galleon with French colours, dropped a boat on board of her as I passed, leaving her to be taken possession of by Molloy, and stood in chase of the headmost, which I took two hours afterwards, a French privateer, coppered, the *General Dumourier*, of 22 guns, six-pounders, and 196 men, having on board 680 cases of silver, and each case containing 3,000 dollars. The galleon is from Lima, and had been taken by the French eleven days before. The two prizes are of immense value, exceeding Commodore Anson's. We have had a meeting in the admiral's cabin, and we consider ourselves fully entitled to all and everything found on board the *General Dumourier*, but we imagine we shall only receive the salvage of the galleon. I think it is one-half. The admiral sends the *Edgar* in with the prize. If this money had got to France, how it would have operated in their favour! The money in the privateer weighs fifty-five tons. We had it all put into the *Edgar*."

In the same year Captain Douglas captured the *Prompte*, 28, and a privateer, and was afterwards attached to the Channel fleet under the command of Lord Howe, who placed the whole of his frigates under his orders. On the 8th April, 1794, his lordship nominated him captain of his flagship, the *Queen Charlotte*, which he commanded in the memorable victory of the 1st June. During the battle a piece of grape-shot struck Sir Andrew Douglas above the right eye. Though suffering greatly from the wound, which eventually deprived him of his life, the gallant captain of the *Queen Charlotte* soon returned on deck, and resumed his duties, holding the tourniquet, which was applied to his head, in one hand. Lord Howe, who entertained the highest opinion of his flag-captain, always spoke with admiration of his devotion to duty on this occasion.

Sir Andrew also commanded the *Queen Charlotte* when she formed one of Lord Bridport's fleet in the action with the French on the 23rd June, 1795, off Lorient. He never left the deck during the previous night, and by taking advantage of any flaw of wind and trimming his ship's sails incessantly, had the satisfaction of being nearest the enemy's rear when day broke. He received the fire of five or six of their ships, and standing on, closely engaged the *Formidable*, which struck her colours after a gallant resistance. The *Queen Charlotte*, which had suffered considerably aloft, dropped astern to repair damages, and received the submission of the *Alexandre* (late the British *Alexander*) which had been brought to action by the *Irresistible*. These two ships and the *Tigre*, which surrendered to superior force, represented the results of this victory. Sir Andrew Douglas had never ceased to suffer from the effects of the wound received in Lord Howe's victory, and was compelled to resign the command of the *Queen Charlotte*, and after much suffering, he expired at his uncle's villa at Fulham on the 4th June, 1797.

The career of Earl Howe, scarcely less than that of Lord Nelson, his great successor at a later period, is a brief epitome of the Naval history of this country during a memorable epoch. The second son of Viscount Howe, he was born in 1725, and was educated at Eton, which he left at the age of fourteen, to serve in the *Severn*, 50, Captain Hon. Edward Legge, in Commodore Anson's famous voyage of circumnavigation. But the *Severn* got no farther than the coast of Patagonia, and being greatly injured by the continual storms she met, returned to England. In February, 1743, he served in the *Burford*, Captain Lushington, under Sir Charles Knowles, in the attack made on La Guayra, in South America. The *Burford* suffered severely in the action and lost her captain, one of whose legs was carried away at the thigh by a chain-shot. Young Howe was greatly attached to his commander, and when relating the circumstances of his death before a court-martial, was so greatly affected as to burst into tears. Captain Lushington continued giving his orders until the faintness from loss of blood necessitated his removal to the cockpit. The first lieutenant sent the young officer down for orders, when the dying commander directed him to return and request him to use his own judgment.

Soon after Mr. Howe was promoted to a lieutenantcy on board of a sloop-of-war, and had an opportunity of displaying his intrepidity. A French privateer had captured an English merchantman under the guns of the Dutch settlement of St. Eustatia, and as the governor refused to interfere, Mr. Howe requested and received permission to cut her out. Though his captain tried to dissuade him from so rash an adventure, as he conceived it, the young officer persisted, and succeeded in recovering the ship, which he restored to the owners. In 1745, he served under Admiral Vernon in the Downs, and in the following year was promoted and appointed to the command of the *Baltimore*, sloop-of-war, which served on the coast of Scotland during the rising. Here he gave a signal proof of his gallantry. The *Baltimore*, in company with another ship, fell in with two French frigates of superior force, when Commander Howe ran between them and brought one to close action. A desperate engagement ensued, in the course of which our hero was severely wounded by a musket ball in the head. He was insensible for some time, but at length showed signs of returning consciousness. On the wound being dressed he returned to the deck and was received with shouts of joy by his crew, who continued the action till the enemy sheered off. For his gallantry he was posted and appointed to the *Triton*, frigate, but afterwards exchanged into the *Ripon*, and sailed for the Guinea coast, and then steered for Jamaica, where he joined Admiral Knowles. By him he was appointed to his flagship, the *Cornwall*, 80, and on the conclusion of peace, in 1748, returned in her to England.

In March, 1750, Captain Howe commissioned the *Gloire*, 44, and took command of the squadron on the west coast of Africa, and on his return home, commanded the *Dunkirk*, 60, on the outbreak of war with France in 1755. He accompanied Admiral Boscawen's fleet to America, and overtook and engaged the *Alcide*, which, though of superior force, he compelled to surrender in half an hour. This was the first blow struck in a war which had such disastrous results for France. On board the *Alcide* were 900 men, including soldiers, who, together with the garrison of Louisburg, were made prisoners.

In 1758 Captain Howe succeeded to the peerage on the death of his brother, and a few years later was appointed to the Board of Admiralty. In 1770, on attaining flag-rank, he was appointed to the command in the Mediterranean, and in 1775 was elected member for Dartmouth. On the rupture with our colonies, Lord Howe was nominated to the command in North America, and hoisted his flag in the *Eagle*, 64. Every enterprise in which the fleet under his command participated was uniformly successful, and New York, Rhode Island, and Philadelphia fell to the arms of England, but the same cannot be said of the military operations, and after his return to England, our fleet temporarily lost command of the sea, and the surrender of Lord Cornwallis at York Town put a disastrous termination to the war.

In the spring of 1782 Lord Howe received an English peerage, and in the following October effected the relief of Gibraltar. It has been well said of this enterprise :— " That foreign nations acknowledge its glory, and every future age will confirm it. Not only the hopes, but the fears of his country accompanied Lord Howe. The former rested upon his consummate abilities and approved bravery, while the latter could not but look to the many obstacles he had to subdue, and the superior advantage of the fleet that was to oppose him. Nevertheless he fulfilled the grand objects of the expedition, the garrison of Gibraltar was effectually relieved, the hostile fleet baffled and dared in vain to battle, and the different squadrons detached to their important destinations, while the ardent and certain hopes of his country's foes were disappointed." On Lord Howe's return, the Corporation of London ordered Copley to paint a picture of the siege and relief of the great fortress, to perpetuate the gallantry of the army under General Elliot (now Lord Heathfield), and of the fleet under the command of Lord Howe.

In January, 1783, his lordship was appointed First Lord of the Admiralty, but finally retired in July 1788. Two years later he hoisted his flag on board the *Victory*, until the *Queen Charlotte* was ready, and on the outbreak of the Revolutionary War, at the especial request of the King, undertook the command of the fleet to which was entrusted the task of safeguarding his country's shores.

While cruising off Ushant Howe learned, on the 19th May, 1794, that the French fleet, under the command of Admiral Villaret-Joyeuse, had quitted Brest. There is no need to repeat the story of the action of the 29th May and the glorious and decisive victory of the first of June, when the armament that formed the hope of France on the sea was defeated and seven ships-of-the-line were captured. Portsmouth presented a scene of anxious and proud expectancy on the 13th June, when the British fleet was seen with its prizes in the offing. The artillery on shore fired a salute when the *Queen Charlotte* anchored, and again as the victorious admiral landed at the Sally Port, where he was received with acclamations by the populace, a military band playing " See the conquering Hero comes." King George and his consort, after whom the flagship was named, arrived at Portsmouth on the 26th, and, on the following day, paid a visit to Lord Howe on board the *Queen Charlotte* at Spithead. The King held a levee of the officers of the fleet, and presented the admiral with a magnificent sword, valued at 3,000 guineas, and a gold chain to which the medal presented for the victory was suspended. His Lordship received the freedom of the City of London in a gold box, and the Houses of Parliament voted their thanks to him and the officers and men of his fleet.

Lord Howe resigned the command of the Channel fleet in May, 1795, and before his death, on the 5th August, 1799, in his seventy-third year, rendered his country yet one more service by bringing the mutinous crews at Spithead to a sense of their duty. When the venerable seaman, whose silver hair told of a life passed among them, came down from London, at the earnest entreaty of the Ministry, to mediate between them and the mutineers, he was received with expressions of devotion by the crews, who knowing they could trust him, hearkened to his appeal. A grateful country erected a monument to Lord Howe in St. Paul's Cathedral, where were hung the colours he had taken from the enemy.

Lord Howe's second in command on the 1st of June, was Admiral (afterwards Lord) Graves. This officer went to sea at an early age, and served in the *Norfolk*, 80, under his father, at the unsuccessful attack on Carthagena, and again was present on board the *Romney*, 50, in the indecisive action in the Mediterranean, between Admiral Matthews and the combined French and Spanish fleets in February, 1744. More fortunate, he participated in Lord Anson's victory over the French squadron, under Admiral Jonquière, and the even more memorable action between Lord Hawke and L'Etendeur. On the latter occasion his ship, the *Monmouth*, commanded by Captain Harrison, took a conspicuous part and suffered to a proportionate extent.

That he was a very capable officer was proved by the confidence placed in him by Lord Anson, who appointed him to the command of the *Hazard*, sloop, in which he reconnoitred the French fleet, then supposed to be on its way to America, and so complete and detailed was the information he brought back to his patron, that he was made post captain as a mark of his approval.

Between 1755 and 1761, when he was appointed Governor of Newfoundland, Captain Graves held command of several ships, and acquired great credit for his skill and judgment in the operations that ended in the capture of St. John's, which had been taken by a French squadron and some troops under De Tiernay. Captain Graves was one of those useful officers for the possession of which the Navy has always been distinguished, who could be counted upon to perform missions outside the strict routine of his profession. He also served in Parliament as member of a Cornish borough. During the war with America and France, Captain Graves commanded the *Monmouth*, 64, and

Conqueror, 74, and on the 19th March, 1779, was raised to flag rank and returned to England. In the ensuing summer he sailed for America in the *London*, 98, with five other ships-of-the-line and a frigate, to reinforce Admiral Arbuthnot, and when the enemy put to sea from Rhode Island, on the 8th March, 1780, he gave chase and a slight encounter took place, which ended indecisively, owing to the disinclination to engage of the French admiral, his old antagonist, De Tiernay. Soon after Admiral Arbuthnot resigned to him the chief command, and his position became critical, owing to the superiority of the French fleet, now reinforced by the squadron of De Grasse from the West Indies. Sir Samuel Hood had indeed arrived at Sandy Hook on the 28th August from the West Indies with fourteen sail-of-the-line, but still the preponderance was greatly in favour of the French.

With Hood's squadron and his own, consisting of five ships-of-the-line and one of 50 guns, Admiral Graves, three days later, proceeded to sea, hoping to encounter the squadron of ten sail from Rhode Island, now under De Barras, before he had effected a junction with De Grasse. On arriving off Cape Henry, it was discovered that the combined fleet numbered twenty-four sail, five more than the British squadron, but the commanders did not hesitate to engage. The action that ensued was chiefly between the van of the rival fleets, which were abreast of each other, but De Grasse kept continually edging away, and the rest of his fleet was considerably to leeward of his van and centre, while seven in the rear did not fire a shot. The action ceased at sunset, and though Admiral Graves was under the necessity of destroying one of his ships, which had sustained much damage and was in other respects unseaworthy, De Grasse took no opportunity during the five succeeding days of accepting the gage of battle.

On the declaration of war with France, in 1793, Admiral Graves was appointed second in command under Lord Howe in the Channel fleet, and took part in the *Royal Sovereign* in the battle of the 1st of June. The admiral carried his ship into the thick of the fight, and conduced greatly to the success achieved, while the *Royal Sovereign* lost her fore and mizen-top-gallant masts and had 14 killed and 44 wounded, among the latter being the gallant admiral, who was severely wounded in the right arm. As has been mentioned, he received an Irish peerage for his services, and survived till 1801, when he expired in the seventy-sixth year of his age. Lord Graves cannot be considered a seaman of the first rank, but he was a most useful and meritorious officer.

A more renowned admiral was Lord Duncan, the victor of Camperdown. He was born in 1731, and went to sea at the age of fifteen on board the *Shoreham*, frigate, commanded by Captain Shuldham. Mr. Duncan next sailed under Commodore Keppel in the *Centurion*, and though so young, attracted the attention and friendship of that great man, on whose recommendation he was promoted to a lieutenancy and appointed to the *Norwich*, which formed one of the squadron despatched, in 1755, to America under the command of Commodore Keppel. A vacancy occurring in the *Centurion*, Mr. Duncan was removed into the ship by the commodore, who again took him with him into the *Torbay*, 74.

At the attack on the French settlement of Goree, Mr. Duncan was wounded, and on his return to England, was promoted to the rank of commander, on the 21st September, 1759, and in February, 1761, to that of post-captain, with the command of the *Valiant*, 74. When Admiral Keppel was appointed to command the expedition against Belleisle, he hoisted his flag in the *Valiant*, and on the successful completion of that duty, proceeded in the same ship in command of a division of the fleet, destined under Sir George Pocock to undertake the reduction of Havanna. Captain Duncan commanded the boats engaged in the disembarkation of the army, and was actively employed during the siege. On the surrender of the city he was sent to take possession of the Spanish ships, consisting of five 70-gun ships, and four of 60 guns, but as the Spanish commander-in-chief showed hesitation in giving them up, Captain Duncan put an end to the controversy by setting fire to the ships.

In 1778, on the outbreak of hostilities with France, Captain Duncan was first appointed to the command of the *Suffolk*, 74, and then to the *Monarch*, of the same force, and served under Sir Charles Hardy in the Channel fleet. The latter ship participated in the relief of Gibraltar by Sir George Rodney in 1780, and her captain displayed his dash by being among the foremost ships that engaged De Langara off Cape St. Vincent. Finding himself alongside a Spanish ship of equal force, while two others lay within musket-shot to leeward, he engaged all three, and after a brief but well-contested fight, compelled the *San Augustin*, 74, to strike her colours. The *Monarch* was too much damaged to enable her to take possession of his prize, and Captain Duncan left the task to another ship coming up astern. She was accordingly taken in tow, but owing to the heavy weather that ensued, was cast off, when the Spanish crew regained possession of her, and she was navigated to Cadiz.

An anecdote is told of the gallant captain of the *Monarch*, that, as he was pushing on ahead, under all sail, without support, he was hailed by one of the British captains, and replied that he "wished to be among them." Captain Duncan returned to England,

and early in 1782 was appointed to the *Blenheim*, 90, in which he served in the Channel fleet, under Lord Howe, and took part in the final relief of Gibraltar, when he led the port division of the centre, and earned the commendation of the commander-in-chief. On his return home Captain Duncan was transferred to the *Foudroyant*, 80, which had been throughout the war commanded by a kindred spirit, Sir John Jervis, the victor in the next war at St. Vincent.

Our hero was promoted to flag rank on the 14th September 1789, but though he often solicited employment, his application and merits remained alike unheeded until February 1795, when he was appointed to the North Sea command. Admiral Duncan first hoisted his flag in the *Prince George*, 98, but as she was thought too large for the shallow waters of the Dutch coast, he shifted into the *Venerable*, 74. This important command Admiral Duncan held for five years, during which he was enabled to render his country most important services. Notwithstanding the tempestuous seas and inclement weather, during the winter he kept afloat watching the Dutch fleet in the Texel, until at length his assiduity received its reward by his glorious victory off Camperdown. Not a month passed during that long period that the admiral did not show his flag off the shoals and sands of the "United Provinces," and he commanded in a high degree not only the confidence of his men, but of the crew of a Russian squadron placed under his command by the Empress Catherine, who rewarded him with the Order of Alexander Newski, which only came second in distinction to the Order of St. Andrew. A memorable instance of his popularity among the men under his command, and of the indomitable courage and high sense of duty that distinguished this fine seaman, was displayed at the time of the mutiny of the British fleet. As soon as he became aware that the evil spirit of disaffection had spread among the crews of his squadron, he visited every ship, and for a time shamed the men into abandoning an attitude of hostility. But while lying in Yarmouth Roads, awaiting the signal to put to sea, the crew of the *Montague*, 74, and *Nassau*, 64, refused to weigh anchor, and the admiral was compelled to proceed off the Texel with the *Venerable* and *Adamant* alone. In order to make up by stratagem for his weakness, the knowledge of which to the enemy would have had fatal results, Admiral Duncan made a variety of signals as if communicating with ships in the offing, thus effectually duping Admiral de Winter, as he afterwards confessed, into the belief that the channel of the Helder was blockaded by the whole squadron.

At this time the men of the *Venerable* displayed symptoms of mutiny, which were disclosed by some of the gunner's crew. The admiral ordered all hands to be turned up on deck, and addressed them in firm and reproachful terms, when six men, charged with being the ringleaders in the revolt, were brought before him. The time was critical, as too strong measures might be not less fatal than weakness. "My lads," he said, "I am not in the smallest degree apprehensive of any violent measure you may have in contemplation; and though I assure you I would much rather acquire your love than incur your fear, I will, with my own hand, put to death the first man who shall presume to display the slightest symptom of rebellious conduct." Turning round immediately to one of the mutineers; "Do you, sir," said he, "want to take the command of the ship out of my hands?" "Yes, sir," replied the fellow, with the greatest assurance. The admiral immediately raised his arm, with an intent to plunge his sword into the mutineer's breast, but was prevented by the chaplain and secretary, who seized his hand, from executing this summary act of justice. The blow being averted, the admiral called to the ship's company with some agitation: "Let those who will stand by me and my officers, pass over immediately to the starboard side of the ship, that we may see who are our friends and who are our opponents." In an instant the whole crew, excepting the six fomenters of the disturbance, ran over with one accord. The culprits were immediately seized, put in irons, and committed to the gun-room, from whence they were afterwards liberated, one by one, after having shown contrition, an act of clemency which endeared the admiral still more to his men.

From this painful episode we will turn to the great victory which has immortalised the name of Duncan. The enemy's fleet, consisting of fifteen sail-of-the-line, six frigates and five sloops, had long been in a state of readiness for war, and Duncan, who lay at the mouth of the Texel, in company with the *Adamant*, both ships being anchored with springs on their cables, awaited with calmness their advance upon him, when at length he was joined by the *Sans Pareil*, 84, and *Russell*, 74, and soon afterwards other ships arrived from England.

The *Venerable* kept the sea for a period of eighteen weeks and three days without going into port, notwithstanding the heavy weather which drove the ships, one after the other, back to our coasts to re-fit or re-victual, and the admiral, who had despatched orders to Yarmouth to purchase the necessities of which he was in need, bore up thither in company with his fleet. De Winter, meanwhile, put to sea, urged by the representations of his own Government, and desirous as a brave officer to measure swords with his opponent. The gallant admiral was well aware of the superiority of the British ships to those under his command, but he consoled himself with the reflection that he could, if he thought proper so to do, return to port without fighting the English, while his action would calm the minds of his countrymen. But Admiral Duncan, who had spared no personal effort, was too quick for him, and within four days had re-fitted and re-victualled his own ship, and in four more the whole of his fleet was ready to sail again, and actually put to sea. He had his reward, for at nine on the morning of the 11th October, the headmost of his ships signalled the enemy, and after a pursuit of three hours, succeeded in getting between them and the land, thus cutting off their return. We have already given an account of the memorable action that ensued, which raised the successful admiral to the pinnacle of fame as one of England's most skilful and gallant seamen. As after Trafalgar, a gale came on the day succeeding the action, and three of the captured ships were lost, but Admiral Duncan arrived at the Nore on the 17th with the remainder. The hull of the *Venerable* had been so much shattered by shot, and she had become so leaky, that it was found useless to re-fit her for further service, and she was dismantled.

The admiral (now Baron Camperdown and Viscount Duncan) hoisted his flag on the *Kent*, a new seventy-four, and as soon as the ships under his command were re-fitted, returned again to his station off the coast of Holland. So effective was the blockade he instituted that no vessels could escape to sea without almost the certainty of capture. Lord Duncan retained the North Sea command until the beginning of the year 1801, when he retired from active service, and three years later he expired, in the seventy-third year of his age. He is described as a man of tall and athletic frame, and one who personally knew him said, with the partiality, perhaps, of an admiring friend, that "it would be difficult to find in modern history another man in whom, with so much meekness, modesty, and unaffected dignity of mind, were united so much genuine spirit, so much of the skill and fire of professional genius, such vigorous and active wisdom, such alacrity and ability for great achievements, with such entire indifference for their success except so far as they might contribute to the good of his country."

Captain Alexander Hood came of a good fighting stock. His uncles were those famous seamen Lords Hood and Bridport, better known in their time as Sir Samuel and Sir Alexander Hood. Young Hood first shipped in the *Endeavour*, with the great circumnavigator Captain Cook, between the years 1772-75. In the early part of the American War he served under Lord Howe, and on the 14th March 1780, when just twenty-two years of age, was appointed to command the *Ranger*, cutter. He remained for some time in active employment on the American station, and thence was ordered to join Sir George Rodney in the West Indies. The *Ranger* was now rated as a sloop-of-war under the name of *Pigmy*, and Lieutenant Hood was raised to the rank of commander on the 17th May 1781, and on the 26th July following, was appointed post-captain on board the *Barfleur*, 98, flagship of his uncle, Sir Samuel Hood, commanding a division of Rodney's fleet. The latter admiral now sailed for England, leaving in command Sir Samuel, who in August steered for the coast of America to oppose the combined French fleet under De Grasse and Barras, who had concerted the attack on Lord Cornwallis, in conjunction with Washington's army, which ended so fatally for British interests at Yorktown on the 19th October.

The fleet returned to the West Indies in December, and early in June 1782, Admiral Hood sailed with twenty ships to relieve St. Kitts, besieged by an army of 8,000 men, the operations of which were covered by De Grasse with thirty-three ships. After participating in these events, Captain Hood was appointed, on the 4th February, to the command of the *Champion*, frigate, which was employed by Sir George Rodney, who had returned from England, and resumed command of the fleet, in watching with other frigates the movements of De Grasse's fleet in Port Royal harbour, nearly within sight of St. Lucia, where the British commander-in-chief lay with his'fleet.

After Rodney's great victory of the 12th April, the *Champion* formed part of the division which was detached under Sir Samuel Hood to pursue the flying enemy. On the 19th the British ships came up with a part of them as they were endeavouring to escape through the Mona Passage, and captured the 64-gun ships *Caton* and *Jason*, the *Aimable*, 32, and the *Ceres* of 18 guns (formerly a British ship) which struck to the *Champion*. Captain Hood was now appointed to the command of the *Aimable*, in which he sailed for England on the ratification of peace, and the frigate was paid off on the 29th July 1783.

Captain Hood passed seven years in quiet retirement until 1790, when he was appointed to the *Hebe*, and in July 1794, to the *Audacious*, 74. After serving in her a year he was compelled by the state of his health to resign the command, but on this being re-established, in January 1797, he commissioned the *Ville de Paris*, and in the following month, the *Mars*, which formed one of the Channel fleet. He had not been long in command when the opportunity for distinction for which Captain Hood had long

AT THE BREECHLOADING GUN.

yearned, was given to him. Unhappily for his country, he fell towards the close of the action, at the age of forty, universally esteemed, and regretted for his amiable qualities no less than for his personal gallantry and professional attainments.

Lieutenant Butterfield, who succeeded to the command, wrote to Lord Bridport, briefly announcing the capture of the *Hercule*, of 74 guns and 700 men, which had just left Lorient on her first cruise, with the object of joining the Brest fleet. He says:—
"The ship chased by H.M. ship *Mars* yesterday, per signal, endeavoured to escape through the Passage du Raz, but the tide proving contrary, and the wind easterly, obliged her to anchor at the mouth of that passage, which afforded Captain Hood the opportunity of attacking her by laying her so close alongside as to unhinge some of the lower deck ports, continuing a very bloody action for an hour and a half, when she surrendered. I lament being under the necessity of informing your lordship that his Majesty has, on this occasion, lost that truly brave man Captain Hood, who was wounded in the thigh late in the conflict, and expired just as the enemy had struck her colours. I cannot sufficiently commend the bravery and good conduct of the surviving officers and men, who merit my warmest thanks. Lieutenants Argles and Ford are the only officers wounded; Captain Hood and Captain White of the marines are killed. Lieutenant Argles, though badly wounded, never quitted the deck."

The success achieved on the 22nd April, 1797, was one of the most brilliant our Navy has won, as Captain Hood was denied the advantage of superior seamanship from the fact of the *Hercule* being anchored, and that on her own coast, and in a difficult and dangerous passage. Moreover, the engagement was fought after darkness had set in, and was decided by the superior gunnery and tenacity of the British crew. The ships fought at such close quarters that the lower-deck guns were actually fired within board, and the sides of both the combatants were much burnt and blackened. After receiving the wound from a musket ball, of which he expired, Captain Hood was carried below, and on recovering consciousness, expressed regret at being removed from his quarter-deck. The *Mars*, besides her captain and the commanding marine officer, had one midshipman and 28 men killed, and 60 officers and men wounded. The *Hercule* had no less than 250 casualties, and was carried into Plymouth, when she was added to the Navy and commissioned by Lieutenant Butterfield with the rank of commander.

Lord Bridport, in transmitting to the Secretary of the Admiralty Lieutenant Butterfield's letter, adds the following tribute to the memory of his gallant nephew:—

"No praise of mine can add one ray of brilliancy to the distinguished valour of Captain Alexander Hood, who carried his ship nobly into battle, and who died of the wounds he received in supporting the just cause of his country. It is impossible for me not to sincerely lament his loss, as he was an honour to the service, and universally beloved. He has fallen gloriously, as well as all who are so handsomely spoken of by Lieutenant Butterfield."

A brief notice is due to the memory of two gallant officers who died in command at the battle of Trafalgar. Captain John Cooke first saw service under Lord Howe, on board the *Eagle*, 64, during the American War of Independence. At the attack on Rhode Island young Cooke specially distinguished himself, and was one of the first to enter the fort. He attracted the notice of his lordship, who on one occasion observing his activity, clapped him on the back, exclaiming, "Young man, you will become a lieutenant before you are of sufficient age." And soon after his return to England he had his wish gratified, and was appointed to the *Worcester*, and accompanied Sir Edward Hughes to the East Indies. Lieutenant Cooke witnessed some of the hardest-fought actions that ever took place at sea, for Sir Edward Hughes found in de Suffren an adversary his equal both in skill and determination. In the last but one of the five actions that took place for the naval supremacy of the East, the captain of the *Worcester* was killed, and she had altogether 106 casualties. His health became affected by the climate, and he was sent to England invalided, and thus lost his promotion for some years, as Sir Edward Hughes, who had a high opinion of the young officer, had his name next on his list for a commission.

On the restoration of his health Mr. Cooke proceeded to the West Indies as first lieutenant of Lord Gardner's flagship, the *Europa*. But again a hard fortune robbed him of the promotion he might reasonably have anticipated. At the end of about three years he had a fall, the consequences of which were so serious that the surgeons sent him home. On his recovery he was appointed by Lord Bridport third lieutenant of his flagship, the *London*, 98, and on the outbreak of the French Revolutionary War his lordship again selected him, this time to be first lieutenant of his ship, the *Royal Sovereign*. At length before the close of the century he was made a commander, and appointed to the *Incendiary* fireship. Good luck now attended him, as owing to an accident which incapacitated the captain of the *Monarch*, he was temporarily appointed to command her, with the rank of captain, and through the interest of his staunch friend Lord Bridport, the appointment was confirmed. The *Monarch* sailed for Newfoundland as flagship of Sir James Wallace, but when she returned the same year to England, he was transferred to the command of the *Nymphe*, frigate, and proceeded to join the Channel fleet. In company with the *San Fiorenzo*, Captain Sir Henry Neale, she engaged and captured two French frigates then returning from landing troops on the Welsh coast. He was next appointed to the *Amethyst*, but at the conclusion of the treaty of Amiens lost his command. The peace that ensued was short-lived, and we find him in command of the *Bellerophon*, 74, in which, in October 1805, he joined the blockading squadron off Cadiz.

It had ever been Captain Cooke's dearest wish to serve under Lord Nelson, and to be in a general engagement under his command, he used to say, would be the greatest honour that could befall him. Now, at length, this desire of his heart was gratified, and by a singular fatality they were both destined to fall at the same moment, and almost in the same manner. His letters home at this time expressed the general wish that they might encounter the enemy, and the equally general expectation that if they were so fortunate, the French and Spanish fleets would receive, to use his words, "their final blow." Captain Cooke was often summoned on board the *Victory* to attend Lord Nelson during the three weeks immediately preceding the action. The *Bellerophon* formed one of the lee division, under the command of Lord Collingwood, which first got into action with the enemy.

After Lord Nelson made his last memorable signal, Captain Cooke went below and visited the guns' crews at their quarters on each deck, exhorting them to act up to the commander-in-chief's expectations, and on his return to the deck, cheers rang through the ship for their captain, and the men wrote in chalk on their guns, "*Bellerophon*: death or glory." "Captain Cooke," says Campbell, "had appointed his orders to be given by the sound of a bugle horn; but, unfortunately, just as the *Bellerophon* was bearing down, an unfortunate accident happened, which afterwards materially affected her. In the bustle of preparation, one of the midshipmen inadvertently trod upon a rope, which, communicating with the lock of a gun, let it off. The enemy immediately took this for a signal, and conceived that she was the flagship, a circumstance which, in a great measure, accounts for the *Bellerophon*'s being attacked by so many of the enemy's ships. In attempting to range alongside the *Monarca*, 74, which had been engaged by the *Tonnant*, the ship immediately ahead of her in the line, the *Bellerophon* fouled the *Aigle*, 74, and thus had an adversary on both sides. The *Montanez*, *Swiftsure* and *Bahama* also attacked her, and about one o'clock her main and mizen-topmasts fell over the side, causing her sails to catch fire from the discharge of her guns. The *Monarca* struck her colours to the *Bellerophon*, which continued closely engaged with the *Aigle*. The latter's mainmast and the foremast of the *Bellerophon* came into contact, and the former being a lofty ship, her men stationed aloft fired into the British 74 to great advantage.

The seamen on the poop of the *Bellerophon* fell so fast, that Captain Cooke called them down on the quarter-deck. The master's leg was taken off and another man was wounded as he was speaking to them, till, at last, only his first lieutenant and a midshipman were left on deck. The former officer, noticing that Captain Cooke was wearing his epaulets, observed that he was marked out by the men in the tops. His reply was, "It is now too late to take them off; I see my situation, but I will die like a man." His last orders to the lieutenant commanding were to go down and direct the quoins to be taken out of the guns to raise them, in order to force the decks of the *Aigle*. This had the desired effect, for she disengaged herself immediately, and went off, receiving under her counter three broadsides from the *Bellerophon*.

It was during the lieutenant's absence that Captain Cooke fell. He had discharged his pistols very frequently at the enemy, who often attempted to board, and had killed a French officer on his own quarter-deck. He was in the act of re-loading his pistols, when he received two musket balls in the breast. He immediately fell, and on the quartermaster going up, and asking him if he should take him down below, his answer was, "No, let me lie quietly one minute; tell Lieutenant Cumby never to strike," and so died Captain John Cooke, in the 43rd year of his age. The ship's company of the *Bellerophon* nobly followed their captain's example, and of their number 27 were killed and 127 wounded, exclusive of officers.

Captain George Duff, of the *Mars*, the same ship that Captain Hood commanded at the time of his glorious death, who also fell at Trafalgar, was from early youth the friend of Captain Cooke. He had a marked predilection for the sea, and when only nine, finding his father averse from indulging his propensity, he ran away and concealed himself on board a small merchant vessel, then lying in the harbour of his native town of Banff. The master sent him back to his father, who finding it vain to thwart the boy's inclination, agreed to his going into the Navy, and directed his tutor to educate him in the branches of mathematics most useful in the profession. According to the custom of those days, he was rated on the books of a ship-of-war, and in 1777, when thirteen years of age, joined his great-uncle, Commodore (afterwards

Admiral) Robert Duff, then flying his broad pennant on board the *Panther*, 64, at Gibraltar.

Young Duff was fortunate in seeing a great deal of active service, and before he was sixteen years of age had been present in thirteen engagements in the West Indies, Mediterranean, and on the coast of America. As a reward for his services he was at that early age promoted to the rank of lieutenant. He was present, says Campbell, at the taking of the Spanish Admiral Langara and his squadron of five sail-of-the-line, off Cadiz, in the beginning of 1780, and went from thence with Sir George Rodney's fleet to the West Indies. Mr. Duff was probably at that time a lieutenant in the *Montagu*, of 74 guns, for in October that year he served in her when she was blown out of St. Lucia in the great hurricane, totally dismasted, thrown upon her beam-ends, and in the greatest danger of being lost. Upon that occasion his exertions were said to have been very conspicuous, and by the falling of one of the masts he unfortunately received a contusion on his right leg, which was healed with difficulty, and was often troublesome to him during the rest of his life, particularly in tropical climates. The *Montagu*, having weathered the hurricane, was rigged with jury-masts, and got back with great difficulty to St. Lucia. She was there re-fitted, and Lieutenant Duff continued to serve in her in the various encounters which our fleet had with the French, till the glorious 12th April, 1782, when the Count de Grasse, their Commander-in-Chief, in the *Ville-de-Paris*, of 110 guns, the largest ship in the world, and four other ships of the line, were taken and brought to Jamaica by our victorious fleet.

In 1790 Lieutenant Duff was promoted to the rank of commander, and three years later, on the declaration of war with France, to that of captain. In this capacity he served in the *Duke*, 90, carrying the broad pennant of Commodore Murray, and was present at the attack on Martinique. At the close of the action, after silencing the battery to which she had been opposed, the ship was struck by lightning, her mainmast shivered to pieces, and her hull so damaged that it was necessary to send her home to be repaired. The further attack on Martinique having been deferred, the commodore returned to England in the *Duke*. He reported in the highest terms of Captain Duff, who was immediately appointed to the command of the *Ambuscade* frigate, of 32 guns, and two years afterwards, to the *Glenmore*, of 38 guns. In these ships he served in the North Sea and upon the coast of Ireland until 1801, when, upon a general promotion in the Navy, he was appointed to the *Vengeance*, of 74 guns, belonging to the Channel fleet. This ship, after being detached to the Baltic, to reinforce the fleet that attacked Copenhagen, joined the squadron under Rear-Admiral Campbell, which, after cruising for some time off Rochefort, was sent to Bantry Bay for the protection of that part of Ireland. Upon this station these ships continued until the signature of the preliminaries of peace, when they were ordered to Jamaica, to watch the movements of the armament sent from France to attempt the recovery of the French part of the island of St. Domingo from the natives.

When the ringleaders of the mutiny, which arose in the squadron while it lay in Bantry Bay, sounded the crew of the *Vengeance*, they found them so attached to their captain that they could not be induced to join. That ship, there is reason to believe, was the only one in which no mutinous spirit broke out; and upon the squadron coming to Portsmouth, previous to their sailing for the West Indies, her crew were indulged with leave to come on shore by turns, while all the others were confined to their ships.

Not long after this event, Captain Duff was appointed to the command of the *Mars*, of 74 guns, and immediately proceeded to join her off Ferrol. He cruised off that port, and successively off Rochefort and Brest, as one of the Channel fleet, until in May of the following year he was detached to Cadiz, under Vice-Admiral Collingwood, whose small squadron of four ships-of-the-line, afterwards increased to eight, continued to keep their station off that port, unawed by the arrival of the combined fleet. When Lord Nelson returned from England to resume the command off Cadiz, he made a disposition of his fleet into two divisions, one of which was to be led by himself, and the other by Vice-Admiral Collingwood.

Rear-Admiral Louis having been detached to the Mediterranean with five sail-of-the-line, Captain Duff had the honour, upon his departure, though there were senior captains in the fleet, to be appointed to command the advance or inshore squadron of four sail-of-the-line, by the recommendation, it is said, of Lord Collingwood, who selected the *Mars* as second to himself in his division. The squadron commanded by Captain Duff was stationed midway between the frigates, which cruised close to the harbour of Cadiz, and the fleet, which kept out of sight of the port. From the time the enemy's ships began to come out on the 19th October, he was constantly employed repeating signals from the frigates to the fleet. On the following day he followed, and kept sight of the enemy, and continued making signals with colours by day and blue lights at night, until the memorable morning of the 21st, when, it being certain that the enemy's fleet could not escape, the signal was made for his squadron to return and take their places in the order of battle. The signal was then hoisted for the *Mars* to lead the lee (or Lord Collingwood's) division of the fleet, and to break the enemy's line. Captain Duff, says Campbell, knowing that his ship sailed ill, ordered every stitch of canvas to be set, and while bearing down upon the enemy, went through his ship to see that everything was in readiness for action. He spoke to his officers and men, and among other directions for their conduct, strictly enjoined them not to waste their fire, as he would take care to lay them close enough to the enemy.

The *Mars*, notwithstanding every exertion, was passed by the *Royal Sovereign*, bearing Collingwood's flag, then the *Belleisle* shot ahead, and they were both in action a few minutes before the *Mars*, each ship breaking through a different part of the enemy's line. The wind, which had been light, then became more uncertain, and prevented the rest of the ships from closing immediately with the enemy; so that the few who were first engaged were surrounded, and had for some time to maintain the unequal conflict. The *Pluton* and *Fougueux* were on either side of the *Mars*, and the *Santa Anna*, of 112 guns, flagship of Admiral Alava, on her bow, and the *San Juan* was also within range of shot. The ship on her starboard quarter, the *Fougueux*, was soon disabled, and it was thought she had struck, but her colours had only been shot away. The captain of marines on the poop, seeing that the *Fougueux*, in dropping to leeward, was getting in a position which would enable her to rake the *Mars*, came down to the quarter-deck to inform Captain Duff. The want of wind rendered it impossible to alter the position of the *Mars*, nor could it with safety be attempted in regard to the enemy's other ships; Captain Duff, therefore, said to the captain of marines, "Do you think our guns would bear on her?" He answered, "I think not, but I cannot see for smoke." "Then," replied the Captain, "we must point our guns at the ships on which they can bear. I shall go and look; but the men below may see better, as there will be less smoke." Captain Duff went to the end of the quarter-deck to look over the side; and then told Mr. Arbuthnot to go below and order the guns to be pointed more aft, meaning against the *Fougueux*. He had scarcely turned round with these orders, when the *Fougueux* raked the *Mars*. A cannon shot killed Captain Duff, striking him on the breast, and carried off his head; his body fell in the gangway, where it was covered with a spare Union Jack, until after the action. Two seamen immediately behind him were killed by the same shot. About the same time that the gallant Duff fell in the *Mars*, Captain Cooke, the companion of his youth, was killed in the *Bellerophon*, and their commander-in-chief, the illustrious Nelson, was mortally wounded on board the *Victory*.

The *Mars* continued engaged during the whole of the action, frequently with fresh ships, but suffered from none so severely as she had done from the *Fougueux*, which (with her captain on board mortally wounded) continued to drift to leeward, until she was engaged by others of our ships, and finally captured by the *Téméraire*.

On board the *Mars*, besides Captain Duff, there were killed in the action, Mr. Alexander Duff, acting lieutenant, Messrs. Corbyn and Morgan, midshipmen, and 25 seamen and marines. The wounded amounted to 16 officers, 5 petty officers, and 60 seamen and marines; in all 98 killed and wounded. Among the latter was the gallant captain of marines, Norman, who afterwards died of his wounds.

Captain Duff was a man of noble presence, strong and well made, above six feet in height, and had a manly, benevolent countenance. During thirty years' service he had been less than five years unemployed. When the battle had ceased, and it was generally known in the *Mars* that their gallant captain was killed, there was scarcely a dry eye among the crew. Each one felt that he had lost his friend and benefactor, and all exclaimed: "We shall never again have such a commander." These three great seamen, Hood, Cooke, and Duff, who died at the post of duty, were only a sample of those who adorned the annals of the British Navy in the most palmy days of her history, and the names of dozens have been mentioned in these pages who deserved not less well of their country, but not being equally fortunate in the manner of their death, their names are not handed down to posterity surrounded with the same halo of glory.

CHAPTER VI.

A Brief Notice of Lord Nelson's Career—Also of some of the most celebrated Commanders of the British Navy during the War with France: Sir Thomas Troubridge—Captains Hardinge and Lydiard—Lord Gardner—Lord Collingwood—Lord Bridport—Lord Hood—Sir Samuel Hood—Lord Keith—Sir Sydney Smith—Earl Howe—Lord Duncan—Earl St. Vincent—Sir John Louis—Sir John Duckworth—Sir Charles Cotton—Some of Nelson's most famous Captains and other Officers.

WE will begin this chapter with a brief biographical notice of the most famous seaman in our Navy, or that of any other maritime power. It does not claim to be considered anything more than a *resumé* of facts of a personal nature, derived from the pages of Campbell's History, the *Naval Chronicle*, and Southey's Memoir. Nelson's life has been adequately treated in this famous biography, and we have already given detailed accounts of the battles of the Nile, Copenhagen, and Trafalgar, as well as of the actions in which he took a minor part, including St. Vincent, and the only failure of his life, that at Teneriffe.

Horatio Nelson was born on the 29th September 1758, at Burnham Thorpe, in the county of Norfolk, not far from which, at a small village called Cock Thorpe, was the birthplace of three naval heroes of an earlier age, Sir Christopher Myngs, Sir Cloudesley Shovel, and Sir John Narborough. The hero, like many other distinguished naval officers, including Sir Francis Drake, and Lords Hood and Bridport, was the son of a clergyman. His father was the Reverend Edmund Nelson, rector of Burnham Thorpe, and he was related to the noble families of Walpole, Cholmondeley and Townsend through his mother, one of the Sucklings, who had resided for three centuries at Woodton in Norfolk.

Young Nelson received his early education at Norwich High School, and at North Walsham, whence at the age of twelve he went to sea on board the *Raisonable*, 64, commanded by his uncle, Captain Maurice Suckling. The boy was left to find his own way by coach to the Medway, where the ship lay, and being of an affectionate nature, and weakly in health, suffered both in mind and body in this his initiation into life. At the end of the journey he was put down with the other passengers, and had to seek for his ship as best he could. After wandering about in the cold he was observed by an officer who happened to know his uncle, who took him home and gave him some refreshment, and then saw him to the ship, where he remained unnoticed by any one till his uncle came on board. The *Raisonable*, which had been commissioned on an apprehended rupture with Spain, was paid off, when his uncle sent him to sea in a ship trading to the West Indies, under the care of Mr. John Rathbone, who had formerly served with Captain Suckling in the *Dreadnought*.

On his return from the voyage in July 1772, young Nelson was received by his uncle in the *Triumph*, then lying at Chatham. He had imbibed a distaste for the Royal service, and it was with some difficulty he could reconcile himself to his altered lot. There was much nepotism in the service in those days, and Nelson had a saying, "Aft the most honour, but forward the better man," in this respect entertaining much the same opinion as was held by Benbow, who served his apprenticeship to the sea in the mercantile marine. Nelson early exhibited his nautical proficiency, and having, in the *Triumph's* decked long-boat, acquired a knowledge of the river from Chatham to the Tower of London, and also down the Swan Channel to the North Foreland, became a skilled pilot for these waters. In July 1773 he accompanied the Hon. Captain Phipps, afterwards Lord Mulgrave, on a voyage of discovery towards the North Pole. Two vessels were fitted out, the *Racehorse* and *Curcase*, bomb-ketches, and Nelson sailed with Captain Lutwidge in the latter, with the rating of coxswain. On this expedition occurred the famous incident of the pursuit of a polar bear by Nelson, who was armed with a musket. The lock of the weapon being injured it could not go off, but nothing daunted, the boy pursued the bear with the intention of attacking it with the butt end. On Captain Lutwidge demanding what could be his motive for this rash act, the young hero replied with perfect simplicity, "I wished, sir, to get the skin for my father." The ships penetrated as far as $81° 36'$ North lat., and visited Spitzbergen, and returned to England in October 1773.

Hearing that a squadron was about to sail for the East Indies, he succeeded in getting himself appointed to the *Seahorse*, 20, commanded by Captain Farmer, who six years later met his death in the *Quebec* when, in the course of an action with a French frigate of superior force, she blew up. In the *Seahorse* Nelson visited a great part of the East Indies, from Bengal to Bussorah in the Persian Gulf. But he suffered much in health, and was sent home by Sir Edward Hughes in the *Dolphin*, 20, Captain Pigot, to whose attention it was mainly due that his valuable life was preserved. Long after he wrote of this time of depression: "I felt impressed with an idea that I should never rise in my profession. My mind was staggered with a view of the difficulties which I had to surmount and the little interest I possessed. I could discover no means of reaching the object of my ambition. After a long and gloomy reverse, in which I almost wished myself overboard, a sudden glow of patriotism was kindled within me, and hope presented my king and country as patrons. Well then, I exclaimed, I will be a hero, and confiding in Providence I will brave every danger." From that moment a "radiant orb," according to his own description, was suspended before his mind's eye, which urged him onward to renown.

The *Dolphin* was paid off at Woolwich on the 24th September 1776, and only two days afterwards Nelson received an order from Sir James Douglas, then commanding at Portsmouth, to act as lieutenant of the *Worcester*, 64, Captain Mark Robinson, who two years later was engaged in Keppel's action, and on the 5th September 1781, commanded the *Shrewsbury*, in Admiral Graves' engagement with the French fleet off the Chesapeake, when she had 14 killed and 52 wounded, including her captain, who lost his leg. The *Worcester* was at sea with convoys until April 1777, and so great was the reputation Nelson, though only nineteen, had already earned, that Captain Robinson was heard to declare that he felt as easy in his mind during the night when Nelson was the officer of the watch as if the oldest lieutenant on board had charge of the ship.

On the 10th April Nelson passed his examination for a lieutenancy, and on the following day was appointed second lieutenant of the *Lowestoft*, 32, Captain Locker, which sailed for Jamaica. At his request he was given the command of a schooner, tender to the frigate, and speedily became an experienced pilot of the passages through the Keys, which are islands dotting the northern coast of Cuba, all of which he explored. An incident indicative of his high courage is recorded of him while serving in the *Lowestoft*. The ship had captured an American privateer, and the first lieutenant had endeavoured in vain to board her, owing to the heavy sea that was running. Captain Locker exclaimed, "Have I then no officer who can board the prize!" The master immediately ran to the gangway, on which Nelson stopped him, with the exclamation, "It is my turn now. If I come back it will be yours."

In 1778 Sir Peter Parker appointed Nelson third lieutenant of his flagship, the *Bristol*, and by rotation he became second lieutenant. On the 8th December in that year he was made a commander and placed in charge of the brig *Badger*, in which he protected the Mosquito shore and coast of Honduras from the depredations of American privateers. This he did so effectually as to elicit the grateful thanks of the settlers. He was also instrumental in saving the lives of the crew of the *Glasgow* frigate when she caught fire off Jamaica. Nelson received post rank on the 11th June, 1779, when in his twenty-first year, and was appointed to the command of the *Hinchinbroke*. When D'Estaing, who had arrived at Cuba from Martinique, was expected to attack Jamaica, Nelson was entrusted with the command of the batteries at Port Royal, the most important place in the island. In January 1780 he commanded the naval portion of an expedition, having Major Polson as his coadjutor, for the reduction of Fort Juan, in the St. John River, in Nicaragua. Quitting his ship, he superintended the transport of the troops in boats, 100 miles up a difficult river, and after storming an outpost of the enemy situated on an island, constructed batteries for the attack on Fort Juan. To his natural quickness of perception, skill, and ready resource may be ascribed the reduction of this fort, which mounted 20 guns and one mortar. But his health, always feeble, gave way under the strain, and on his arrival at Jamaica, to assume command of the *Janus*, 44, to which he had been appointed, Sir Peter Parker persuaded him to live on shore at his house. But he got gradually worse, and was compelled to return to England in the *Lion*, Captain Hon. W. Cornwallis, to whose care he owed the preservation of his life.

In August 1781 we find him appointed to the command of the *Albemarle*, 20, which was employed in the North Sea throughout the winter, and in the following April, he sailed with a convoy for Quebec, where he became acquainted with a gentleman, Mr. Davidson, who saved him from an imprudent marriage in which he displayed the weak point of his strong but impulsive nature. Nelson, we are told, was about to quit the station, and had taken leave of his friends, and gone down the river to rejoin his ship. Nevertheless, on the following morning, as Mr. Davidson was walking on the beach, he saw him coming back in his boat. "He could not," he said, "leave Quebec without offering himself and his fortune to the woman he loved." Davidson told him his utter ruin, situated as he was, must inevitably follow. "Then let it follow," was his reply; "for I am resolved to do it." His friend, however, was equally resolute that he should not; and, after some dispute, Nelson, with no very good grace, suffered himself to be led back to the boat. Shortly after this he became acquainted with Prince William, afterwards William IV., then serving as midshipman in the *Barfleur*, under Lord Hood. "I had the watch on deck," says his Royal Highness, "when Captain Nelson came in his barge alongside, who appeared to be the merest boy of a captain I ever beheld; and his dress was worthy of attention. He had on a full-laced uniform, his rank unpowdered hair was tied in a stiff Hessian tail of an extraordinary length; the old-fashioned flaps of his waistcoat added to the general quaintness of his figure, and produced an appearance which particularly attracted my notice; for I had never seen anything like it before, nor could I imagine who he was, nor what he came about. There was something irresistibly pleasing in his address and conversation, and an enthusiasm, when speaking on professional subjects, which showed that he was no common being." Lord Hood, who had been intimately acquainted with Captain Suckling, took the *Albemarle* with him to the West Indies, and treated Nelson with kindness. "He treats me," says Nelson, "as if I were his son, nor is my situation with Prince William less flattering. Lord Hood was so kind as to tell him, that, if he wished to ask questions relative to naval tactics, I could give him as much information as any officer in the fleet."

On one occasion, when cruising off Boston, the *Albemarle* was chased by three French ships-of-the-line and a frigate, and as they were overhauling him fast, Nelson, trusting to his experience in pilotage, ran his ship among the shoals off St. George's Bank, on which the enemy abandoned the chase, except the frigate, when the young captain laid his main-topsail to the mast, and awaited his adversary, though of very superior force, but she declined the challenge. In November 1782, Captain Nelson joined the fleet under Sir Samuel Hood and accompanied him to the West Indies, and soon after the declaration of peace, sailed for Portsmouth, when the *Albemarle* was paid off on the 31st July 1783.

During the autumn of this year Nelson went on a visit to France, whence he returned in the spring of the following year, when he commissioned the *Boreas*, 28, and sailed for the West Indies. While here Nelson learned that a French frigate was about to make a survey of the islands in the possession of this country, and following her to St. Eustatia, was invited by the Dutch governor to meet her officers at dinner. With great tact Nelson informed the French captain that he understood it was his intention to honour our settlements with a visit, and proposed to escort him in his Majesty's ship, and though the Frenchman protested that he was doing him too much honour and sought to evade the compliment, Nelson insisted on accompanying the frigate, and never lost sight of her until her commander, despairing of shaking off his polite friend, gave up the attempt. Nelson enforced the maritime laws that bore upon the position of the Americans as foreigners, which made him unpopular with all classes there, as tending to diminish the trade; but conscious that he was performing his duty he refused to be moved by popular clamour, and an Act of Parliament afterwards confirmed his views of the matter. On one occasion, when Nelson addressed Sir Henry Shirley, Governor of the Leeward Islands, on the question, that official replied that old generals were not accustomed to take advice from young gentlemen, on which Nelson replied, "Sir, I am as old as the Prime Minister of England,* and I think myself as capable of commanding one of his Majesty's ships as the Minister is of guiding the State." Resolved to do his duty, he ordered all American vessels to quit the islands in eight-and-forty hours, declaring that if they refused, or presumed to land their cargoes, he would seize them. The Americans resisted these orders, and the planters were, to a man, against him. The governor and presidents of the islands gave him no support; and the admiral, Sir Richard Hughes, desirous of obliging the planters, advised him to be guided by the wishes of the presidents of the council, and after a while, issued an order requiring the officers under his command to abstain from hindering the Americans from having free ingress and egress if the governor chose to allow them. General Shirley and others sent him letters little different from orders in their style. "These persons," says he, "I soon trimmed up and silenced. Sir Richard Hughes was a more delicate business. I must either disobey orders or disobey Acts of Parliament. I determined upon the former, trusting to the uprightness of my intentions, and believing that my country would not allow me to be ruined by protecting her commerce." Accordingly he wrote to the admiral, and, in respectful language, told him he should decline to obey his orders till he had an opportunity of seeing and talking to him. Sir Richard's first feeling was that of anger, and he was about to supersede Nelson, but, having mentioned the business to his captain, the latter told him he believed all the squadron thought he had issued illegal orders, and, therefore, did not know how far they were bound to obey them. Luckily, though the admiral wanted vigour of mind to do what was right, he was not obstinate in wrong, and he afterwards thanked Lord Nelson for having shown him his error.

At Nevis, says Campbell, the *Boreas* found four American vessels deeply laden, with the island colours flying, on which they were ordered to hoist their proper flag, and leave it in eight-and-forty hours. At first they denied their country and refused to obey, but upon being examined before the Admiralty Court Judge, they confessed that

* The great William Pitt, to whom Nelson alluded, was born on the 20th May, 1759, a year after our hero, and was Chancellor of the Exchequer when twenty-three, and Prime Minister before completing his twenty-fourth year.

they were Americans and that their vessels and cargoes were wholly American property. Upon this Nelson seized them. The governor, the custom-house, and the planters, were all against him; the admiral, though his flag was then in the roads, stood neutral, and subscriptions were raised to carry on the law-suits against him. Summonses were taken out against Nelson, and damages laid to the enormous amount of £40,000. The marshal was called upon to arrest him, and the merchants promised to indemnify him for so doing, but the judge did his duty, and threatened to send him to prison if he attempted to violate the protection of the court. The president of Nevis, Mr. Herbert, behaved with singular generosity on this occasion. Though no man had suffered more by the measures which Nelson thought it his duty to pursue, he offered to become his bail for £10,000 if he chose to suffer the arrest. His lawyer proved an able as well as an honest man; and the law was so plain, the case so clear, and Nelson maintained his cause so well, that the four ships with their cargoes were condemned. During this affair he sent a memorial to the king, in consequence of which orders were given to defend him at the expense of the Crown, and upon the representation which he made at the same time to the Secretary of State, the Register Act was framed. The Treasury upon this occasion transmitted thanks to Sir Richard Hughes and the officers under him, for their activity and zeal in protecting the commerce of Great Britain. "I feel much hurt," said Nelson, "that after the loss of health and fortune, another should be thanked for what I did, and against his orders. I either deserved to be sent out of the service, or at least to have had some notice taken of what I had done. They have thought it worthy of notice, and yet have neglected me."

On the 11th March, 1787, Captain Nelson married Frances Herbert Nesbit, widow of Doctor Nesbit, of the island of Nevis, and niece of Mr Herbert, president of that island, the bride being given away by the Duke of Clarence. Some part of his stay in the West Indies was employed in detecting public frauds, but the peculators were too powerful, and they succeeded not only in suspending inquiry, but in raising prejudices against Nelson at the Board of Admiralty, which prevailed for many years. He returned to England three months after his marriage, and the *Boreas* was kept till the end of November at the Nore, as a receiving ship. This unworthy treatment excited in Nelson the strongest indignation. During the whole four months he seldom or never quitted the ship. When orders were received to prepare the *Boreas* for being paid off, he expressed his joy to the senior officer of the *Medway*, "It will release me for ever from an ungrateful service, as it is my firm and unalterable determination never again to set my foot on board a king's ship. Immediately after my arrival in town I shall wait on the First Lord of the Admiralty and resign my commission." This officer, finding it in vain to reason with him against this resolution in his present state of feeling, used his influence with the First Lord of the Admiralty to save Nelson from taking a step so injurious to himself, little foreseeing how deeply the welfare and honour of England depended upon his decision. This friendly representation produced a letter from Lord Howe, intimating a wish to see him on his arrival in town, and so pleased was he with his conversation, and convinced by his explanations of the propriety of his conduct, that he presented him to the King, whose gracious reception removed his resentment.

The affair of the American captains was not yet over. Nelson had retired to his father's parsonage, where he amused himself with rural occupations and sports. It was his great ambition at this time to possess a pony, and while he was gone to purchase one at a neighbouring fair, two men entered the parsonage and inquired for him; they then asked for Mrs. Nelson, and presented her with a notification on the part of the American captains, who now laid their damages at £20,000. On Nelson's return in high glee with his pony, the paper was presented to him. His indignation and astonishment may well be imagined. "This affront," he exclaimed, "I did not deserve, but I will be trifled with no longer. I will write immediately to the Treasury, and if Government will not support me, I am resolved to leave the country." Accordingly he informed the Treasury, that if a satisfactory answer was not sent by return of post he should take refuge in France. The answer was that Captain Nelson was a very good officer, and need be under no apprehension, for he would assuredly be supported.

On the outbreak of war with France early in 1793, Nelson was appointed to the *Agamemnon*, 64, and joined Lord Hood in the Mediterranean. He always took a keen interest in the welfare of his midshipmen, and the following instructions he gave them indicates his views of their duties in the great war upon which they had entered:— "There are three things, young gentlemen, which you are constantly to bear in mind: first, you must always implicitly obey orders without attempting to form any opinion of your own respecting their propriety; secondly, you must consider every man your enemy who speaks ill of your king; and thirdly, you must hate a Frenchman as you do the devil."

During his career in the *Agamemnon*, if batteries were to be attacked, if ships were to be cut out of harbours, if the hazardous landing of troops was to be effected, or difficult passages to be explored, Horatio Nelson was ever foremost with his gallant crew, many of whom had been actually reared in the neighbourhood of Burnham Thorpe. It was well observed in the Mediterranean at this time, that before Captain Nelson quitted his old ship he had not only fairly worn her out,* but had also exhausted himself and ship's company. At Toulon, and at Bastia and Calvi, Lord Hood bore ample testimony to the skill and exertions of Nelson, who during the siege of Bastia, not only superintended the disembarkation of troops and stores, but after St. Fiorenzo had surrendered, and General Dundas and his successor, General d'Aubert, had declined to furnish soldiers, undertook the reduction of that place. Lord Hood obtained only a few artillerymen, and ordering on board those troops who, having embarked as marines, were borne on the ships' books as part of their respective complements, began the siege with 1,183 soldiers, artillerymen and marines, and 250 sailors. "We are but few," wrote Nelson, "but of the right sort, our general at St. Fiorenzo not giving us one of the five regiments he has there lying idle." They were landed on April 4th, under Colonel Vilette and Nelson, who had the title of brigadier, and the sailors dragged the guns up the heights, which he said would never have been accomplished by any but British seamen. The soldiers behaved with the same spirit. "Their zeal," said Nelson, "is, I believe, almost unexampled. There is not a man but considers himself personally interested in the event, and deserted by the general, it has, I am persuaded, made them equal to double their numbers." The siege continued nearly seven weeks, and on the 19th May, when a treaty of capitulation was begun, the troops made their first appearance on the hills, and on the following morning, General d'Aubert arrived with the whole army to take Bastia. "I am all astonishment," says Nelson, "when I reflect on what we have achieved; 1,000 regulars, 1,500 national guards, and a large body of Corsican troops laying down their arms to 1,000 soldiers and marines, and 200 seaman. I always was of opinion, have ever acted up to it, and never have had any reason to repent it, that one Englishman was equal to three Frenchmen. Had this been an English town, I am sure it would not have been taken."

The enemy were supposed to be far inferior in number when it was resolved to attack the place, and it was not till afterwards that Nelson received certain information of their great superiority. "My own honour," said he to Mrs. Nelson, "Lord Hood's honour,

---

* When the *Agamemnon* came into dock to be re-fitted at the beginning of October 1796, there was not a mast, yard, sail, nor any part of the rigging but was obliged to be removed, the whole being so cut to pieces with shot, while her hull had long been kept together by cables served round.

and the honour of the country, must all have been sacrificed had I mentioned what I knew. Therefore you will believe what must have been my feelings during the whole siege, when I had often proposals made to me to write to Lord Hood to raise it." And yet Nelson received no reward. The siege of Calvi was carried on by General Stuart, and Nelson had less responsibility here than at Bastia, but the service was not less hard. " We will fag ourselves to death," said he to Lord Hood, " before any blame shall be at our doors. I trust it will not be forgotten that twenty-five pieces of heavy ordnance have been dragged to different batteries and mounted, and all but three fought by seamen. During the four months he was thus employed on shore, the climate proved more destructive than the war. Nelson described himself as the reed among the oaks, bowing before the storm when they were laid low. " All the prevailing disorders have attacked me, but I have not strength for them to fasten upon. One plan I pursue, never to employ a doctor. Nature does all for me, and Providence protects me."

His services before Calvi were, by a strange omission, altogether overlooked, and his name did not appear in the list of wounded, though he had lost an eye. " One hundred and ten days," said he, " I have been actually engaged at sea and on shore against the enemy ; three actions against ships, two against Bastia in my own ship, four boat actions, and two villages taken, and twelve sail of vessels burnt. I do not know that any one has done more; I have had the comfort to be always applauded by my commanders-in-chief, but never to be rewarded, and what is more mortifying, for service in which I have been wounded others have been praised, who, at the time, were actually in bed, far from the scene of action. They have not done me justice, but never mind, I'll have a gazette of my own " ; and he kept his word.

Nelson bore a brilliant part in Admiral Hotham's action in the Mediterranean. During the first day, when there was no ship-of-the-line within several miles to support him, he engaged the *Ça Ira*, of 84 guns, which, having carried away her main and fore top-masts, was taken in tow by a frigate. This ship he engaged for two hours and a half, when 110 of her men were killed and wounded, and on the following day came up with her again in tow of the *Centaur*, 74, when a partial action ensued, till the French judged it more prudent to abandon both ships than risk the loss of more. Nelson was afterwards appointed by Admiral Hotham to co-operate with the Austrian general, at Vado Bay, on the coast of Genoa, where he continued till November, when Hotham was superseded by Sir John Jervis, who in May 1796, appointed Nelson to the *Captain*, 74, with the rank of commodore.

From April to October he was constantly employed in the blockade of Leghorn, the taking of Porto Ferrajo, with the island of Capri, and lastly in the evacuation of Bastia, whence, having conveyed the troops in safety to Porto Ferrajo, he joined the admiral at Fiorenzo Bay, and proceeded with him to Gibraltar. In December 1796, Commodore Nelson hoisted his broad pennant on board the *Minerva* frigate, Captain George Cockburn, and was despatched with that ship, and the *Blanche*, to Porto Ferrajo, to bring the naval stores left there to Gibraltar. On the passage thither, in the night of the 19th December, the commodore fell in with two superior Spanish frigates, and attacking the ship which carried the poop-light, he directed the *Blanche* to engage the other. At 12.40 p.m. Nelson brought his ship to close action, which continued without intermission until half-past one, when the *Sabina*,* of 40 guns and 286 men, commanded by Captain Don Jacobo Stuart, struck to the *Minerva*. Captain Preston, in the *Blanche*, silenced the ship he had engaged, but could not take possession, owing to three more ships heaving in sight. Commodore Nelson, in his letter to Sir John Jervis, characteristically assumes no credit to himself, but gives the whole to Captain Cockburn, his officers, and crew. "You are, sir, so thoroughly acquainted with the merits of Captain Cockburn, that it is needless for me to express them; but the discipline of the *Minerva* does the highest credit to her captain and lieutenants, and I wish fully to express the sense I have of their judgment and gallantry. Lieutenant Culverhouse, the first lieutenant, is an old officer of very distinguished merit; Lieutenants Hardy, Gage, and Noble deserve every praise which gallantry and zeal justly entitle them to, as does every other officer and man in the ship. You will observe, sir, I am sure with regret, among the wounded, Lieutenant James Noble, who quitted the *Captain* to serve with me, and whose merits, and repeated wounds received in fighting the enemies of our country, entitle him to every reward a grateful nation can bestow."

Nelson arrived at Gibraltar a few days after the Spanish fleet had passed through the straits from Carthagena, and impatient to join Sir John Jervis, remained only a single day at Gibraltar. On the 11th February he was chased by two Spanish line-of-battle ships, and fell in with their whole fleet off the mouth of the Straits, but fortunately effected his escape, and joining the admiral off Cape St. Vincent on the 13th February, shifted his pennant to his former ship, the *Captain*, 74, Captain Miller in command.

* The *Sabina* had 55 men killed and wounded, and lost her mizen-mast, and the *Minerva* had 7 men killed and 34 wounded, while all her masts and rigging were much cut by shot.

We will not repeat the wonderful record of the manner in which Commodore Nelson boarded and captured in succession two Spanish ships-of-the-line,* each of far greater force than his own ship, but will pass on to the later events in his career.

* Colonel Drinkwater, military secretary to Sir Gilbert Elliot, Governor of Corsica, who was on board the *Lively* repeating frigate, commanded by Lord Garlies, gives an interesting account of Nelson's achievements on this memorable day. "When Sir John Jervis, on the 14th February, had accomplished his bold intention of breaking the enemy's line, the Spanish admiral, who had been separated to windward with his main body, consisting of eighteen ships-of-the-line, from nine ships that were cut off to leeward, appeared to make a movement as with a view to join the latter. This design was completely frustrated by the timely opposition of Commodore Nelson, whose station in the rear of the British line afforded him an opportunity of observing this manœuvre ; his ship, the *Captain*, had no sooner passed the rear of the enemy's ships that were to windward, than he ordered her to wear and stood on the other tack towards the enemy. In executing this bold and decisive manœuvre, the commodore reached the sixth ship from the enemy's rear, which bore the Spanish admiral's flag, the *Santissima Trinidada*, of 138 guns, a ship of four decks, reported to be the largest in the world. Notwithstanding the inequality of force, the commodore instantly engaged this colossal opponent, and for a considerable time had to contend not only with her, but with her seconds ahead and astern, each of three decks. While he maintained this unequal combat, which was viewed with admiration, mixed with anxiety, his friends were flying to his support. The enemy's attention was soon directed to the *Culloden*, Captain Troubridge, and in a short time after by the *Blenheim* of 90 guns, Captain Frederick, who opportunely came to his assistance. The intrepid conduct of the commodore staggered the Spanish admiral, who already appeared to waver in pursuing his intention of joining the ships cut off by the British fleet, when the *Culloden's* timely arrival and Captain Troubridge's spirited support of the commodore together with the approach of the *Blenheim*, followed by Rear-Admiral Parker, with the *Prince George, Orion, Irresistible* and *Diadem* not far distant, determined the Spanish admiral to change his designs altogether, and to throw out the signal for his main body to haul their wind, and make sail on the larboard tack. Not a moment was lost in improving the advantage now apparently in favour of the British squadron. As the ships of Rear-Admiral Parker's division approached the enemy's ships in support of the *Captain* and her gallant seconds the *Blenheim* and *Culloden*, the cannonade became more animated and impressive. In this manner did commodore Nelson engage a Spanish three-decker, until he had nearly expended all the ammunition in his ship, which had suffered the loss of her fore-top-mast, and received such considerable damage in her sails and rigging that she was almost *hors de combat*. At this critical period the Spanish three-decker, having lost her mizen-mast, fell on board a Spanish two-decker, of 84 guns, that was her second ; this latter ship consequently now became the commodore's opponent, and a most vigorous fire was kept up for some time by both ships within pistol-shot. The commodore, from a sudden impulse, instantly resolved on a bold and decisive manœuvre, and the boarders were summoned and orders given to lay his ship on board the enemy. Ralph Willett Miller, the commodore's captain, so judiciously directed the course of his ship that he laid her aboard the starboard quarter of the Spanish 84, her sprit-sail-yard passing over the enemy's poop, and hooking in her mizen-shrouds, when the word to board being given, the officers and seamen destined for this perilous duty, headed by Lieutenant Berry, together with the detachment of the 69th regiment, commanded by Lieutenant Pearson, then doing duty as marines on board the *Captain*, passed with rapidity on board the enemy's ship, and in a short time the *San Nicholas* was in the possession of her intrepid assailants. The commodore's ardour would not permit him to remain an inactive spectator of this scene, and he thought his presence might animate his brave companions, and contribute to the success of this bold enterprise ; he therefore accompanied the party in this attack, passing from the fore-chains of his own ship into the enemy's quarter gallery, and thence through the cabin to the quarter-deck, where he arrived in time to receive the sword of the dying commander, who had been mortally wounded by the boarders. He had not been long employed in taking the necessary measures to secure the hard-earned conquest, when he found himself engaged in a more arduous task. The stern of the three-decker, his former opponent, was placed directly amidships of the weather beam of the prize *San Nicholas*, and from her poop and galleries the enemy sorely annoyed with musketry the British who had boarded the latter. The commodore was not long in resolving as to the conduct to be adopted upon this momentous occasion. Directing, therefore, an additional number of men to be sent from the *Captain* on board the *San Nicholas*, the undaunted commander, who no danger ever appalled, himself headed the assailants in the new attack, exclaiming, "Westminster Abbey, or glorious victory." Success in a few minutes, and with little loss, crowned the enterprise.

In 1797, Sir Horatio Nelson, as he now was, hoisted his flag as rear-admiral of the blue, and was directed to bring away the garrison of Porto Ferrajo. On the 27th May he shifted his flag from the *Captain* to the *Theseus*, and was appointed to the command of the inner squadron at the blockade of Cadiz. In the attack on the Spanish gunboats, July 3rd, 1797, he was in the barge, with only its usual complement of 10 men and the coxswain, accompanied by Captain Fremantle, when the commander of the Spanish gunboats, Don Miguel Tyrason, having 26 men, including two officers, made a desperate effort to capture Nelson. The conflict was long and doubtful, and his faithful coxswain, John Sykes, was wounded in defending the admiral, and saved his life by parrying blows that were aimed at him, and mortally wounded his assailants. Eighteen of the Spaniards were killed, and the commandant and the rest wounded, when the rear-admiral, with his gallant sailors, succeeded in carrying the barge. During the night of the 5th July, Sir Horatio Nelson directed a second bombardment of Cadiz, and on the 15th July was detached with a small squadron to make an attack on the town of Santa Cruz, in the island of Teneriffe. We have given particulars of this disastrous enterprise, in which Nelson lost his right arm by a cannon shot, and no less than 246 officers and men were killed, drowned, and wounded.

The admiral, whose life was only saved by Lieutenant Nisbet, his step-son, received his wound as the detachment was landing, in the act of pressing on with the usual ardour of British seamen. The shock caused him to fall into the boat, when Lieutenant Nisbet applied his neckerchief as a tourniquet to the shattered arm, and conveyed him to the *Theseus*, commanded by his friend Captain Miller. The same night at ten o'clock the admiral's arm was amputated on board the *Theseus*, and he immediately after began his official letter, and finished it by eleven. The next day he wrote to Lady Nelson; and in narrating the foregoing transactions, said, "I know it will add much to

---

Such indeed was the panic occasioned, that the British no sooner appeared on the quarter-deck of their new opponent than the commandant advanced, and asking for the British commanding officer, dropped on one knee and presented his sword, apologizing at the same time for the Spanish admiral not appearing, as he was dangerously wounded. For a moment Commodore Nelson could scarcely persuade himself of this second instance of good fortune; he therefore ordered the Spanish commandant who had the rank of a brigadier, to assemble the officers on the quarter-deck, and direct means to be taken instantly for communicating to the crew the surrender of the ship. All the officers immediately appeared, and the commodore had the surrender of the *San Josef* duly confirmed by each of them delivering their sword. The coxswain of the commodore's barge had attended close by his side throughout this perilous attempt. To him the commodore gave in charge the swords of the Spanish officers as he received them, and the undaunted tar, as they were delivered to him, tucked these honourable trophies under his arm, with all the coolness imaginable. It was at this moment also that a British sailor who had long fought under the commodore, came up in the fulness of his heart, and excusing the liberty he was taking, asked to shake him by the hand to congratulate him upon seeing him safe on the quarter-deck of a Spanish three-decker.

your pleasure, in finding that your son Josiah, under God's providence, was instrumental in saving my life." During the painful operation of amputating the arm, there was some blunder in taking up the arteries, owing to which he suffered great and constant pain, and was obliged to come to England for advice. It was the 13th December before the surgeons pronounced him fit for service. On Sir Horatio Nelson's first appearance at court his sovereign received him in the most gracious manner, and on expressing his sorrow for the loss he had sustained and his impaired state of health, Nelson replied: "May it please your Majesty, I can never think that a loss which the performance of my duty has occasioned, and so long as I have a foot to stand on I will combat for my king and country."

The ship that was intended for Sir Horatio's flag not being ready, the *Vanguard* was commissioned, and on the 1st April 1798, he sailed with a convoy from Spithead, but the wind veering to the westward, was forced to return to St. Helens. On the 9th he again sailed for Lisbon, and on the 29th April joined Earl St. Vincent off Cadiz. On the following day Nelson was detached with the *Vanguard*, *Orion*, and *Alexander*, 74's, the *Emerald* and *Terpsichore* frigates, and *La Bonne Citoyenne* sloop-of-war, and was afterwards joined by Captain Troubridge, of the *Culloden*, with ten sail-of-the-line. On the 1st August he gained his memorable victory of the Nile. The severe wound which Nelson received was supposed to have proceeded from a piece of iron, part of a langridge shot, and the skin of his forehead, being cut at right angles, hung down over his face. Captain Berry, who happened to be near, caught the admiral in his arms. It was Sir Horatio's first idea, and that of every one, that he was shot through the head. On being carried into the cockpit, where several of his gallant crew were stretched, with their shattered limbs and mangled wounds, the surgeon, with great anxiety, immediately came to attend on the admiral. "No," replied the hero, "I will take my turn with my brave fellows!" The agony of his wounds increasing, he became convinced that it was mortal; he sent for his chaplain, and begged of him to remember him to Lady Nelson, and having signed a commission appointing his friend Hardy, commander of the *Mutine* brig, to the rank of post-captain in the *Vanguard*, took an affectionate leave of Captain Louis, of the *Minotaur*, who had come on board by his desire, and then composedly resigned himself to death. When the surgeon examined the wound, it appeared that it was not mortal, and as soon as the painful operation of dressing was over, Nelson wrote the celebrated official letter that appeared in the Gazette. He came on deck just in time to behold the destruction of the *Orient*. The victorious admiral was created Baron Nelson of the Nile, and of Burnham Thorpe, with a pension of £2,000 for his own life and those of his two immediate successors. When this was moved in the House of Commons, General Walpole expressed an opinion that a higher degree of rank ought to be conferred. Mr. Pitt replied that he thought it needless to enter into that question. "Admiral Nelson's fame would be co-equal with the British name, and it would be remembered that he had obtained the greatest naval victory on record, when no man would think of asking whether he had been created a baron, a viscount, or an earl."

The Nile was the most skilful, as regards conception and execution, and the most complete, victory, perhaps, ever achieved on the sea, and its consequences were as far-reaching as those of Lord Howe's battle of the 1st June. It was far more meritorious than Sir John Jervis's victory on St. Valentine's Day, and yet that officer was created an earl and Nelson only received the dignity of a baron, the foolish reason advanced being that he was not commander-in-chief in the Mediterranean. Though Nelson throughout his life was only inspired by a sense of duty, he keenly felt the unworthy treatment to which he had been subjected on this and former occasions, and openly expressed his indignation.

We have neither room nor inclination to follow him through the only indefensible act of his life, which Campbell attributes to his attachment for Lady Hamilton. We refer to his giving his consent to the execution of the Republicans, after a treaty had been entered into with them by Captain Foote and the allied commanders. "Nothing," says this injured officer, "can be more evident than the fact that a solemn capitulation had been agreed upon, formally signed by the chief commander of the forces of the King of Naples, by the Russian commander, and by myself, all duly authorized to sign any capitulation in the absence of superior powers. This was not a treaty of peace subject to ratification, it was not a truce liable to be broken, it was a serious agreement for surrender upon terms which involved the lives and properties of men, which might have chosen to forfeit those lives and properties, had they not relied principally upon the faith of a British officer. Parts of this agreement were performed, and actual advantage was afterwards taken of those parts of the capitulation that had thus been executed, to seize the unhappy men who, having been thus deceived by a sacred pledge, were sacrificed in a cruel and despotic manner."

In the autumn of 1800, Nelson left the Mediterranean,* and returned to England by way of Vienna and Hamburg, accompanied by Sir William and Lady Hamilton.

* The following presents were received by Lord Nelson for his services in the Mediterranean between October 1st, 1798, and October 1st, 1799, besides a peerage and a pension of £2,000 a year from the British Parliament, and one

He arrived in England in November, and in the January following received orders to embark again. The Addington Administration was just formed, and Nelson was sent to the Baltic, under Sir Hyde Parker, by the Earl St. Vincent.* The capture of Copenhagen was a more difficult undertaking than the destruction of the French fleet at Aboukir, and displayed Nelson's unequalled genius for war and dauntless spirit. The Danes were prepared for defence. Upwards of 100 pieces of cannon were mounted upon the Crown batteries at the entrance of the harbour, and no less than 25 two-deckers, frigates, and floating batteries were moored across its mouth. The soundings were made under Nelson's own eye, and he was day and night in the boat, till his health had nearly sunk under the unremitting fatigue. The action was fought on the 2nd April. Nelson was given twelve ships-of-the-line with all the frigates and small craft, but three of the squadron grounded and were unable to take up their assigned stations. Of all the engagements in which Nelson had borne a part, this, he said, was the most terrible. It began at ten in the morning, and at one victory had not declared itself on either side. A shot through the mainmast knocked a few splinters about the admiral. "It is warm work," he observed, "and this day may be the last to any of us at any moment." "But mark you," said he, stopping short in his walk, "I would not be elsewhere for thousands." Just at this time Sir Hyde made a signal for the action to cease, and we have described elsewhere the characteristic manner in which the great admiral received it. His peace proposals were accepted in the course of the evening, and a suspension agreed on for four-and-twenty hours, during which it was resolved that he should negotiate in person with the Crown Prince. Accordingly, on the morning of the 4th he landed, when a strong guard protected him from the people, within

of £1,000 from the Irish Parliament, as Lords St. Vincent and Duncan had received for their victories:—From the East India Company, £10,000; from the Turkish Company, a piece of plate of great value; from Alexander Davidson, Esq., a gold medal; from the City of London, a sword of great value; from the Sultan of Turkey, a diamond aigrette, valued at £2,000, and a rich pelisse, valued at £1,000. The Sultan's mother presented him with a rose set with diamonds, of the value of £1,000. The Czar wrote him an autograph letter, and gave him a box, set with diamonds, valued at £2,500. From King Ferdinand, of the Two Sicilies, came a sword richly mounted with diamonds, with £5,000. And his Majesty also conferred on the admiral, who had saved the island of Sicily from being overrun by Napoleon's troops, the dukedom of Bronté, with an estate, supposed to be of the annual value of £3,000. The King of Sardinia presented a box set with diamonds, value £1,200; the people of Zante gave a gold-headed sword and cane, and the city of Palermo a gold box and chain.

* When the fleet sailed, it was sufficiently known that its destination was Copenhagen. Some Danish sailors, who were on board the *Amazon* frigate, went to Captain Riou and requested that he would get them exchanged into a ship bound on some other service; "they had no wish," they said, "to quit the British Navy, but they entreated that they might not be led to fight against their own country." There was not in our whole Navy a man who had a higher and more chivalrous sense of honour and duty than Riou. The tears came into his eyes while the men were addressing him, and he ordered his boat, and did not return to the *Amazon* till he had procured their exchange. The "good and gallant" Riou, as Nelson called him, fell at Copenhagen.

H.M.S. SPEEDWELL.
TORPEDO GUNBOAT.

whose sight the battle had been fought, and who were exasperated by witnessing the landing of the wounded on the preceding day. Some difficulty occurred in adjusting the duration of the armistice. He required sixteen weeks, bluntly giving, like a seaman, the true reason, that he might have time to act against the Russian fleet and return. This not being acceded to, a hint was thrown out by one of the Danish commissioners of the renewal of hostilities. "Renew hostilities!" said he to one of his friends—for he understood French enough to comprehend what was said, though not to answer it in the same language—"tell him we are ready at a moment, ready to bombard this very night."

Fourteen weeks were at length agreed to. The death of the Czar Paul intervened, and the Northern Confederacy was broken up. For this signal service, in which Nelson appeared not less conspicuous as a statesman than as an admiral, he was raised to the rank of a viscount. When England was alarmed by preparations at Boulogne, Nelson took command of a squadron in the Channel. His attack upon the flotilla failed, because the divisions did not all arrive in time, and the enemy's vessels were moored to the shore and to each other by chains. On the rupture that succeeded the peace of Amiens, Nelson was appointed commander-in-chief in the Mediterranean. We must pass to the concluding scene, the consummation of his labours and of his glory. After having watched the Toulon fleet for nearly two years, ready at any time to give them battle with an inferior force, he missed them, and they formed a junction with the Spaniards, and ran for the West Indies. With ten ships and three frigates he pursued 18 sail-of-the-line and six frigates, with 12,000 troops on board. "There is just a Frenchman apiece," he used to say to his captains, "leaving me for the Spaniards. When I haul down my colours, I expect you to do the same, but not till then." On his return to Europe Nelson made over his squadron to Admiral Cornwallis, lest the enemy should sail for Brest to liberate their fleet, and place him between two fires, and then he returned to England.

Nelson had not been at Merton a month, when Captain Blackwood, on his way to the Admiralty with despatches, called at five in the morning and found him already dressed. Upon seeing him, he exclaimed, "I am sure you bring me news of the French and Spanish fleets! I think I shall yet have to beat them!" It was as he supposed. They had liberated the squadron from Ferrol, and being now thirty-four sail-of-the-line, got safely into Cadiz. "Depend on it, Blackwood," he repeatedly said, "I shall give M. Villeneuve a drubbing!" but when Blackwood had left him, he wanted resolution to declare his wishes to his sister, and endeavoured to drive away the thought. He had done enough—"Let the man trudge it who has lost his budget," said he. As he was pacing one of the walks in his garden, which he used to call the quarter-deck, Lady Hamilton came up to him, and told him she saw he was uneasy. He smiled, and said "No, he was as happy as possible; he was surrounded by his family, his health was better since he came home, and he would not give sixpence to call the king his uncle." But the old spirit revived in him, and he could not be inactive while there was a chance of completing the discomfiture of the allied fleet.

Pitt accepted his services as willingly as they were offered, and Lord Barham, giving him the Navy List, bade him choose his own officers. He reached Portsmouth only twenty-five days after he had left it, and though the wind was against him, and blew strong, nevertheless such was his impatience to be upon the scene of action, that he worked down Channel, and, after a rough passage, arrived off Cadiz on his birthday, September 29th; the same day the French Admiral, Villeneuve, received orders to put to sea the first opportunity. From this time to the 21st October, when the battle of Trafalgar was fought, Nelson never came in sight of land, as he feared that if the enemy knew his force they would not venture out, notwithstanding their superiority. This was the case; for the Council of War Villeneuve called, on hearing that Nelson had taken the command, expressed their determination not to leave Cadiz unless they had reason to believe themselves one-third stronger than the British fleet. Many circumstances tended to deceive them into such an opinion, and in an unhappy hour for them, they sailed from Cadiz. On the 19th the signal was made that they were at sea. On the afternoon of the next day it was signified that they seemed determined to go to the westward, "and that," said Nelson in his journal, "they will not do if it be in the power of Nelson and Bronté to prevent them."

The British fleet consisted of twenty-seven sail-of-the-line, the enemy's of thirty-three, and their superiority was greater in size and weight of metal than in numbers. 4,000 troops were on board, and the best riflemen who could be selected were dispersed through the fleet. Nelson never went into a battle without a full sense of its danger, and always seemed rather to have prepared his mind for death than to have banished the thought of it. On the morning of the 21st he wrote a prayer in his journal, followed by a last testament, in which he bequeathed Lady Hamilton and his adopted daughter to the nation. "These," said he, "are the only favours I ask of my king and country at this moment, when I am going to fight their battle." He had put on the coat which he always wore in action, with the insignia of all his Orders. "In honour I have gained them," he said, "and in honour I will die with them." We have nothing to add to the detailed account given in the preceding pages of the battle of Trafalgar and the last moments of Lord Nelson.

The death of Nelson was felt in England as something more than a national calamity. Men started at the intelligence, and turned pale, as if they had heard of the loss of a dear friend.

The victory of Trafalgar was indeed celebrated with the usual forms of rejoicing, but they were joyless, for such was the glory of the British Navy, in great measure through Nelson's genius, that they scarcely seemed to receive any addition from this last triumph. The most signal victory that ever was achieved upon the seas, and the destruction of the allied fleet, hardly appeared to add to the strength and security of England, which felt as strong and secure while Nelson was living to guard the land as when he had removed all danger.

About noon on the 4th December the *Victory* hove in sight at Portsmouth, and at two o'clock she came to anchor at St. Helens, with the great seaman's flag flying at half-mast, when the port-admiral made the signal for the ships at Spithead and in the harbour to lower their flags and pennants to half-mast. Having received the necessary repairs at Portsmouth, the *Victory*, with the body on board, got under weigh for the Nore on the 10th of the month. On the passage the remains of Lord Nelson were taken from the cask of spirits in which they had been immersed for preservation, and deposited in a plain elm coffin,* which was placed in the after cabin of the main-deck

---

* On the outer coffin was the following inscription:—

Depositum
The Most Noble Lord, Horatio Nelson,
Viscount and Baron Nelson of the Nile,
and of
Burnham Thorpe, in the County of Norfolk,
Baron Nelson of the Nile, and of Hillborough, in the said County;
Knight of the Most Honourable Order of the Bath;
and
Vice-Admiral of the White Squadron of the Fleet;
Commander-in-Chief of His Majesty's Ships and Vessels in the
Mediterranean.
Also
Duke of Bronté, in Sicily;
Knight Grand Cross of the Sicilian Order of St. Ferdinand,
And of Merit;
Member of the Ottoman Order of the Crescent;
and
Knight Grand Commander of the Order of St. Joachim.
Born September 29th, 1758.

under a canopy of colours. With the exception of a little discolourment in the left ancle, neither the features nor body had undergone a change of appearance. In this state the last tribute of respect was paid to his memory by a number of visitors, who daily went off for that purpose, during the stay of the *Victory* in the Downs and at Greenwich Hospital, where he lay in state. Nelson's funeral under the dome of St. Paul's Cathedral was a splendid spectacle, all the King's sons and the Ministers being present, together with representatives of all classes, and the seamen of the *Victory*. It is recorded that as the coffin was about to be lowered, these gallant fellows, who had made no effort to conceal their grief, with one accord seized his flag and tore it into shreds, each retaining a portion as a memento.

Thus, after a series of transcendent and heroic services, Lord Nelson fell gloriously at the moment he achieved a brilliant and decisive victory over the combined fleets of France and Spain, on the 21st October 1805. Without the advantages afforded in this country to the possessors of aristocratic connections, Nelson by his unaided genius alone made his way from the press of self-reliant men to the front rank, and by his pre-eminence gradually outdistanced all competitors. Such a galaxy of naval talent the world has not yet seen; but in a race where the stern ordeal of war weeded out the incompetent and mediocre, he asserted his supremacy over his compeers. So modestly did he bear himself as honours and rewards were showered on his head, that his success evoked no word of complaint from his rivals, and at length, when his last great victory and triumphant death crowned an unparalleled career, the admirals and captains of the British Navy echoed the sentiments of the nation, that England could not hope to look on his like again. Southey has eloquently said in his biography, doubtless one of the noblest pieces of literary work in the language:—"Yet he cannot be said to have fallen prematurely whose work was done; nor ought he to be lamented who died so full of honour and at the height of human fame. The most triumphant death is that of the martyr; the most awful that of the martyred patriot; the most splendid that of the hero in the hour of victory; and if the chariots and horses of fire had been vouchsafed for Nelson's translation, he could scarcely have departed in a brighter blaze of glory." The passage is worthy the mighty seaman and great patriot whose services the book describes.

Some account of the naval career of Sir Thomas Troubridge will well follow that of his friend Lord Nelson, with whom he was ever a great favourite. Young Troubridge went to sea first in 1773, proceeding in the *Seahorse*, 20, commanded by Captain Farmer, to the East Indies, among his brother midshipmen being an officer who became Admiral Sir Charles Pole, and the great Nelson, who thus had the best opportunity of forming the opinion he ever after entertained of his shipmate's professional acquirements.

In the East Troubridge remained for ten years, but little is known of his services, as he was naturally reticent of talking about himself. It is said that he was engaged as lieutenant in the action fought, on the 10th August 1778, off the Coromandel coast, between Sir Edward Vernon and Admiral Tranjolly, and in some, if not all, the subsequent desperate and sanguinary battles between Sir Edward Hughes and de Suffren. On the 1st January 1783, Troubridge, having passed through the intermediate rank of commander, was promoted to captain, and posted to the *Active*, a 32-gun frigate. In the following year Captain Troubridge returned to England with Sir Edward Hughes, as flag-captain of the *Sultan*, but in 1790 he returned to India in command of the *Phœnix*, 32. In the autumn of the following year Captain Troubridge was employed by Commodore Cornwallis with a squadron on the Malabar coast, to examine ships that were expected to arrive from France with ammunition and warlike stores for the army of Hyder Ali, the ruler of Mysore, with whom we were engaged in our long and desperate struggle for supremacy. After bringing to and searching several French merchantmen, he discovered the frigate *Résolue*, having two ships in company, and commanded her to lie to while he examined her. With this peremptory order the French captain declined to comply, and first resisted an attempt to board his ship, and then fired a broadside into the *Phœnix*, to which she replied. An action lasting twenty-five minutes ensued, when the *Résolue* hauled down her colours, having sustained a loss of 25 killed and 40 wounded, that of the *Phœnix* being six and 11 respectively.

Troubridge returned to England soon after this action, and in 1793, on the outbreak of war with France, was appointed to the command of the *Castor*, a 32-gun frigate. In May of the following year, while convoying fourteen trading ships from the Channel Islands to Newfoundland, he was captured close to his destination by a French squadron, together with all his convoy, but was fortunate enough, before the close of the month, to regain his freedom, as the *Castor* was overhauled and retaken by the *Carysfort*, 26-gun frigate, Captain Laforey. In the action, which lasted an hour and fifteen minutes, the enemy had 16 killed and nine wounded, and the *Carysfort* had only 17 casualties in all. Troubridge now received command of the

Culloden, 74, a ship he immortalised by his exploits almost as much as his old shipmate of the *Seahorse* did the *Agamemnon* and *Captain*, which he commanded during these eventful years. In the *Culloden* he served under Howe in February 1795, and cruised off Brest, blockading the French fleet until May, when he sailed for the Mediterranean, and participated in Admiral Hotham's indecisive action of the 13th July, in which Nelson took so prominent a part in the *Agamemnon*. Again in Sir John Jervis's ever-memorable victory over the Spanish fleet off Cape St. Vincent on St. Valentine's Day of 1797, the gallant commander of the *Culloden* led the fleet into action, and took a prominent part, one only second in glory to that of Nelson in the *Captain*. The commander-in-chief said in a private letter to the First Lord of the Admiralty, written two days after the battle: "Captain Troubridge, in the *Culloden*, led through the enemy in a masterly style." The brunt of the fighting, and the chief loss, fell on the *Captain*, *Excellent*, *Blenheim*, and *Culloden*, which lost 10 killed and 47 wounded.

Captain Troubridge accompanied Nelson in his unsuccessful attack on Santa Cruz, in the island of Teneriffe, and to him was entrusted the command* of the seamen and marines who were to be landed. We have given a detailed account of the expedition, which resulted in a sanguinary repulse for the British seamen and marines, for which, however, they were in no way to blame. The ill-success was not attributable either to the plan or its execution, but chiefly to the overwhelming superiority of the enemy, and in a lesser degree to the darkness of the night and the heavy surf beating inshore which filled some of the boats with water and rendered useless much of the ammunition in the men's pouches. That Captain Troubridge was enabled to bring back any of his landing party was due to the adroitness, audacity and fertility of resource for which he was remarkable even among his brother officers of the British Navy.

* The following is the letter addressed by Admiral Nelson to the captain of the *Culloden*, giving him his instructions:—"I desire you to take under your command the number of seamen and marines named in the margin, who will be landed under Captains Hood, Miller, Fremantle, Bowen, and Waller, and the marines under Captain Thomas Oldfield, and a detachment of the royal artillery under Lieutenant Baynes, all of whom are now embarked on board his Majesty's frigates *Seahorse*, *Terpsichore*, and *Emerald*. With this detachment you will proceed as near to the town of Santa Cruz as possible without endangering your being perceived, when you will embark as many men as the boats will carry, and force your landing on the north-east part of the bay of Santa Cruz, near a large battery. The moment you are on shore, I recommend you first to attack the battery, which, when carried, and your post secured, you will either proceed by storm against the town and mole-head battery, or send in my letter as you judge most proper, containing a summons of which I send you a copy, and the terms are either to be accepted or rejected in the time specified, unless you see good cause for prolonging it, as no alteration will be made in them, and you will pursue such other methods as you judge most proper for speedily effecting my orders, which are, to possess yourself of all cargoes and treasures which may be landed on the island of Teneriffe. Having the firmest confidence in the ability, bravery, and zeal of yourself, and of all placed under your command, I have only heartily to wish you success, and to assure you that I am your most obedient and faithful servant."

The following is his official letter to Sir Horatio Nelson of the events of the night of the 24th July, written on the following morning:—"From the darkness of the night I did not immediately hit the mole, the spot appointed to land at, but pushed on shore under the enemy's battery, close to the southward of the citadel. Captain Waller landed at the same time, and two or three other boats. The surf was so high many put back; the boats were full of water in an instant, and stove against the rocks, and most of the ammunition in the men's pouches was wet. As soon as I had collected a few men, I immediately advanced with Captain Waller to the square, the place of rendezvous, in hopes of meeting you and the remainder of your people; and I waited about an hour, during which time I sent a sergeant, with two gentlemen of the town, to summon the citadel. I fear the sergeant was shot on his way, as I heard nothing of him afterwards. The ladders being all lost in the surf, or not to be found, no immediate attempt could be made on the citadel; I therefore marched to join Captains Hood and Miller, who, I had intelligence, had made good their landing with a body of men to the southwest of the place. I then endeavoured to procure some account of you and the rest of the officers without success. By daybreak we had collected about 80 marines, 80 pikemen, and 180 small-arm seamen; these I found were all that remained alive that had made good their landing. With this force, having procured some ammunition from the Spanish prisoners we had made, we were marching to try what could be done with the citadel without ladders, when we found the whole of the streets commanded by field pieces, and upwards of 8,000 Spaniards and 100 Frenchmen under arms, approaching by every avenue. As the boats were all stove, and I saw no possibility of getting more men on shore, the ammunition wet, and no provisions, I sent Captain Hood with a flag of truce to the governor, to declare that I was prepared to burn the town, which I should immediately put in force, if he approached one inch farther."

Nelson, in his letter to Earl St. Vincent, expressed his "admiration of the firmness with which Captain Troubridge and his brave associates supported the honour of the British flag."

In May of 1798, Lord St. Vincent, being reinforced by a squadron from England under Sir Roger Curtis, detached from off Cadiz Captain Troubridge with ten 74's and a 50-gun ship to join Nelson, who had been sent on a cruise with three sail-of-the-line and three smaller vessels. Troubridge joined Sir Horatio on the 8th June, but some weeks were passed in an unsuccessful attempt to find the French fleet, which had sailed from Toulon, with Napoleon on board, for Egypt. It was not till the 1st August that the enemy's fleet was discovered in Aboukir Bay, and the same evening took place the battle of the Nile. To the great mortification of Captain Troubridge, the *Culloden* took the ground on a shoal, as she was standing in towards the French fleet, and thus failed to participate in the action, notwithstanding the most strenuous exertions of the gallant captain, officers, and crew to get her off, which they succeeded in doing on the following morning.*

Nelson, with that nobleness of nature which distinguished him, felt great commiseration for his early friend in not being able to take part in the action of the 1st August, and in Clarke and McArthur's Life of the hero he is represented as having addressed him in these terms:—"Let us, my dear Troubridge, rather rejoice that the ship that got on shore was commanded by an officer whose character is so thoroughly established in the service as your own." Captain Troubridge received the thanks of the Houses of Parliament, in common with the other commanding officers, but as he was not actually engaged there was some demur to granting him the gold medal presented by the King, and also to promoting the first lieutenant of the *Culloden*, a reward received by those of the other ships, in accordance with the practice after a great general engagement. On this point Nelson wrote privately to Lord St. Vincent:—" I received yesterday a private letter from Lord Spencer, of October 7th, declaring that the first lieutenants of all the ships engaged should be promoted. I sincerely hope this is not intended to exclude the first lieutenant of the *Culloden*; for Heaven's sake, for my sake, if it be so, get it altered. Our dear friend Troubridge has endured enough; his sufferings were, in every respect, more than those of any of us; he deserves every reward which a grateful country can bestow on the most meritorious sea officer of his standing in the service. I have felt his worth every hour of my command, and had before written to you, my dear lord, on this

---

* Troubridge says in a letter to Lord St. Vincent, written on the 16th August: "Your lordship will have learned by Sir Horatio Nelson's letters, and Captain Berry, of the misfortune that befell the *Culloden*, just as I got within gunshot of the enemy. As we had no knowledge of the place, and the soundings continued regular as we stood in, I did not conceive the smallest danger, the man at the lead calling out eleven fathoms when she struck. The only consolation I have to support me in this cruel case is, that I had just time to make the signal to the *Swiftsure* and *Alexander*, which saved them, or they must inevitably have been lost, as they would have been further on the reef from their hauling considerably within me. Every exertion in my power was used to save his Majesty's ship; but it was long doubtful whether I should be able to keep her afloat after I got her off, as the rudder was gone, and she was making seven feet of water an hour. However, by great labour on the third day we got a new rudder made and hung, and with thrummed sails reduced the leak considerably. The false keel is gone, and probably part of the main, as she struck very hard for nine hours with a heavy swell. I shall use every exertion to patch the poor *Culloden* up again, and I flatter myself I can still fight a good battle in her, if opportunity offers. I am now fagging hard at the leak, and the first harbour we make I must and will patch the old ship up and make her last as long as your lordship has the command. Two pumps going I shall not mind, we are fully equal to that. I endeavour, and believe succeed, in making my men believe that the leak is nothing, for they dance every evening as usual."

subject; therefore I place Troubridge in your hands." Lord St. Vincent's good offices were successful, as appears from the following passage in a letter from Lord Spencer:—
"The exception of the first lieutenant of the *Culloden* was necessary, on account of that ship not having got into action from the circumstance of being aground. I am, however, so fully convinced of the merit both of Captain Troubridge and his officers on all occasions, that I beg you would be so good as to give the first vacancy of commander that arises to the first lieutenant of the *Culloden*."

Captain Troubridge, in the *Culloden*, with the *Alexander* and *La Bonne Citoyenne*, arrived at Naples, on his return from Alexandria, about the middle of September, and in four or five days he was joined by Admiral Nelson in the *Vanguard*. Captain Troubridge was afterwards employed in the blockade of Alexandria till the 5th March, 1799, when he left Sir Sydney Smith in command, and returned to Lord Nelson at Palermo. Lord Nelson now appointed Troubridge to the command of a small squadron, with the object of blockading Naples and obtaining possession of the islands of Ischia and Capri in the bay, which he succeeded in doing.

In consequence of information received by Lord Nelson as to the French fleet, his lordship, who was then at Palermo, sent for Troubridge to join him, and put to sea, but returned to his anchorage without falling in with the enemy. In a letter written to Lord St. Vincent on his return, Nelson said of the subject of this notice:—"I have our dear Troubridge for my assistant, and in everything we are brothers. Hood and Hallowell are as active and good as ever; not that I mean to say that any are otherwise, but you know these are men of resources." On the evacuation of Naples by the French in June, 1799, Nelson proceeded thither from Palermo, and landed a strong detachment of seamen and marines, under the command of Captain Troubridge, to dispossess the French of the castle of St. Elmo. The siege lasted between the 3rd and 12th July, when the fort surrendered to Troubridge, of whom his lordship wrote to the Admiralty in the following terms:—"Although the abilities and resources of my brave friend Troubridge are well known to all the world, yet even he had difficulties to struggle with in every way, which the state of the capital will easily bring to your idea, that has raised his great character even higher than it was before." Before the close of September, articles of capitulation having been entered into with the French general, Captain Troubridge took possession of Civita Vecchia and other posts while Captain (afterwards Sir Thomas) Louis, of the *Minotaur*, occupied Rome.

For his services on this and former occasions Troubridge received a baronetcy, and on his return to England, in 1800, was nominated flag-captain of the Channel fleet, under Lord St. Vincent, and a few months later, one of the Lords Commissioners of the Admiralty, an office he held till May, 1804. In April, 1805, Troubridge, who had attained the rank of rear-admiral twelve months before, sailed in the *Blenheim*, 74, to assume command of the squadron in the East Indies, to the eastward of Ceylon, and early in the following year he was transferred to the command at the Cape of Good Hope. But the gallant officer, who, since the death of his early friend, had no superior in the British Navy, never reached his destination. The last seen of the *Blenheim*, and the *Java* frigate, sailing in company, was on the 1st March, when the *Harrier* sloop, commanded by a son of the admiral, lost sight of the two ships in a heavy gale off Mauritius. "The night," wrote an officer on board, "was dreadful beyond description; it blew a perfect hurricane, with a tremendous sea. The *Blenheim* was in a very decayed state, and was particularly bad in her hull. The *Java* was badly manned, and extremely crank. The principal hope is, that they have got into some harbour in the island of Madagascar."

In concluding the notice of Sir Thomas Troubridge, we will give Lord Nelson's opinion of his friend, as derived from his letters to Lord St. Vincent. On the 15th June 1798 he says:—"Troubridge possesses my full confidence, and has been my honoured acquaintance of twenty-five years' standing." Again on the 10th August, a few days after the battle of the Nile, in a moment of depression, he thus writes:—"Although I keep on, yet I feel I must soon leave my situation in the Mediterranean to Troubridge, than whom we both know no person is more equal to the task. I should have sunk under the fatigue of re-fitting the squadron but for him, Ball, Hood, and Hallowell; not but that all have done well, but these are my supporters." In the following month he wrote from Naples:—"Dear Troubridge, whom we went to visit yesterday, is better than I expected; the active business and the scolding he is obliged to be continually at does him good. I am not surprised you wish him near you, but I trust you will not take him from me. I well know he is my superior, and I so often want his advice and assistance."

One of the most heroic officers of that heroic age of our naval history was Captain George Nicholas Hardinge, who fell in 1808, at the early age of twenty-seven, about the same time that his relative, the late Field-Marshal Lord Hardinge, began to earn distinction under Sir Arthur Wellesley and Sir John Moore in the Peninsula. He was born on the 11th April, 1781, and adopted the sea as his profession at the age of twelve, being encouraged in this step by Sir John Borlase Warren, who saw him accidentally at Eton, and was so struck by his personal beauty and vivacious manner and address, that he assured him "he was better fitted for a naval hero than for a lawyer," for which profession he was presumably intended. At that early age young Hardinge was entered as a midshipman on board the *Meleager*, Captain Tyler, an officer of high character, who made it his constant duty to supervise the training and promote the welfare of the youngsters under his command. He was engaged in the operations in the Mediterranean under Lord Hood in the early years of the Revolutionary War, and a letter he wrote descriptive of the services performed by the Navy at Corsica, was shown to Mr. Pitt, who declared that "it was a most extraordinary performance at so youthful an age."

Captain Tyler was appointed to the command of the 40-gun frigate *Minerve*, captured from the French, which had been weighed by his exertions after having been sunk, and took the young midshipman with him to the ship, which was re-named the *San Fiorenzo*, after the port in Corsica where she was taken. Again, on Captain Tyler removing to the *Diadem*, of 64 guns, Hardinge accompanied his patron, and was engaged in the action, fought by Sir William Hotham, which has been described, when the *Ça Ira*, 80, and *Centaur*, 74, were captured, and the partial success of which aroused Nelson's anger.

In the spring of 1798, before he had attained his eighteenth year, Hardinge returned to England, but after only remaining on shore a month or two, went to sea again in the *Aigle* frigate, under his old captain, and accompanied by a former shipmate in the *San Fiorenzo*, of whom Captain Tyler wrote, after the action in the Mediterranean, "My two boys behaved like veterans."

Off the coast of Africa the frigate was wrecked, and our hero had a narrow escape of his life. Lord St. Vincent, the commander-in-chief, who displayed kindness to him at this time, placed him on board the *Theseus*, Captain Miller, one of Nelson's favourite officers, who commanded the *Captain* at the battle of St. Vincent, and the *Theseus* at the Nile. He served under Miller at the siege of Acre, and was present when the fearful explosion took place on board the *Theseus*, by which Captain Miller and 30 officers and men were killed on the spot, nine who jumped overboard were drowned, and 47, including six officers, were injured. Young Hardinge had a narrow escape from death on that occasion. During the siege of Acre our hero had command of a gunboat, and received the commendation of Sir Sydney Smith for his conduct. For a short time he was on board the *Tigre*, Commodore Smith's ship, and received promotion to the rank of lieutenant when he returned to England. Lieutenant Hardinge was now appointed to the *Foudroyant*, commanded by Sir Edward Berry, captain of the *Vanguard* at the battle of the Nile. In the *Foudroyant* he was present at the action, fought on the 1st April 1800, with the *Guillaume Tell*, 80, the last of the fleet that Nelson destroyed in Aboukir Bay. The *Guillaume Tell* was engaged by the *Foudroyant*, *Lion*, *Alexander*, and *Penelope*, and after a gallant resistance, struck her flag, having lost 200 men. In this action the *Foudroyant* had eight killed and 64 wounded, including the captain.

In the following year he was serving on board the *Santa Teresa*, and when Lord St. Vincent became First Lord of the Admiralty, received promotion in May, 1802, to the rank of commander. In March, 1803, we find him appointed to the command of the *Terror*, bomb, being then in his twenty-second year. In this vessel he assisted at the ineffectual bombardment of some of the French Channel ports, and served under Captain Owen and Sir James Saumarez, who both entertained the highest opinion of his professional attainments. When the *Terror* became of no further use for active service, Commander Hardinge was appointed to the sloop-of-war *Scorpion*, and joined Admiral Thornborough off the Texel. Here he captured, on the 31st March, 1804, the Dutch 16-gun brig *Atalante*, under circumstances which have been mentioned in a previous chapter, and equally displayed his bravery and generosity of character.*

* He thus describes the event in a private letter to a friend :—" I am on my way to the Nore, after six days of severe but unrepented fatigue, and have 60 Dutch prisoners on board. We are accompanied by the *Atalante*, a Dutch war-brig, of 16 guns, prize to us. I was ordered on the 28th to reconnoitre at Vlie, and perceived a couple of the enemy's brigs at anchor in the roads ; despairing to reach them with my ship, on account of the shoals that surrounded the entrance, I determined upon a dash at the outermost one in the boats, if a good opportunity could be found or made. It came unsolicited, March 31. Preparing to embark, we accidentally were joined by the *Beaver* sloop, who offered us her boats to act in concert with ours ; we accepted the reinforcement, under an impression that it would spare the lives on both sides, and would shorten the contest. At half-past nine in the evening we began the enterprise. Captain Pelly, an intelligent and spirited officer, did me the honour to serve under me, as a volunteer, in one of his boats. We had near 60 men, including officers, headed by your humble servant, in the foremost boat. As we rowed with flood tide, we arrived alongside the enemy at half-past eleven. I had the good fortune, or, as by some it has been considered, the honour, to be the first man who boarded her. She was prepared for us with boarding nettings up, and with all the other customary implements of defence. But the noise and alarm so intimidated her crew, that many of them ran below in a panic, leaving us the painful task of combating those whom we respected the most. The decks were slippery, in consequence of rain, so that grappling with my first opponent, a mate of the watch, I fell, but recovering my position, fought him on equal terms, and killed him. I then engaged the captain, as brave a man as any service ever boasted, who had almost killed one of my seamen. To my shame be it spoken, he disarmed me, and was on the point of killing me, when Mr. Williams, the master, came up, rescued me at the peril of his own life, and enabled me to recover my sword. At this time, all the men were come from the boats, and were in possession of the deck. Two were going to fall upon the captain at once ; I ran up, held them back, and then abjured him to accept quarter. With inflexible heroism, he disdained the gift, kept us at bay, and compelled us to kill him. He fell, covered with honourable wounds. The vessel was ours, and we secured the hatches, which, headed by a lieutenant, who had received a desperate wound, they attempted repeatedly to force. Thus far, we had been

For this spirited action Hardinge was promoted to the rank of captain, and in the following August was appointed to the command of the *Proselyte*, of 20 guns, formerly a Newcastle collier. He was ordered on convoy duty to the West Indies; but his friends, dreading for him the climate and the command of such an unseaworthy ship, secured an exchange for him to the *Valorous*, which, however, was almost as wretched a craft as the collier, and from her he was appointed to the command of the *Salsette*, a 36-gun frigate, then being constructed at Bombay. Captain Hardinge proceeded to India, but found on arrival there that the *Salsette* was far from completion, when Sir Edward Pellew, the commander-in-chief, appointed him to the *San Fiorenzo*, the ship in which he had served in 1794 in the Mediterranean, under Captain Tyler. It was his ill-fortune to be appointed to a succession of rotten ships, and in October, 1807, we find him writing of her, after she had been patched up, that she was "barely effective, but not eligible, and rather less safe than sound." He had long pined to bring to action the French frigate *Piemontaise*, which had been committing great depredations on British commerce; and at length, early in March, 1808, he had his wish gratified, but met an untimely and heroic end. The *San Fiorenzo*, which sailed from Point de Galle, in Ceylon, on the 4th March, two days later passed three Indiamen, and soon after sighted a man-of-war, which proved to be the long looked-for frigate.

Captain Hardinge made the private signal, which was not answered, and at five showed his colours, of which the stranger took no notice. At 11.40 P.M. he ranged alongside of him on the port tack, and received his broadside. After engaging ten

---

fortunate, but we had another enemy to fight in the elements; a sudden gale had shifted against us, impeded all the efforts we could make, but as we had made the capture, we determined, at all events, to sustain it, or to perish. We made the Dutch below surrender, put forty of them into their own irons, and stationed our men to their guns, brought the powder up, and made all the necessary arrangements to attack the other brig. But as the day broke, and without abatement of the wind, she was off at such a distance, and in such a position, that we had no chance to reach her. In this extremity of peril we remained eight-and-forty hours. Two of the boats had broken adrift from us, and two had swamped alongside; the wind shifted again, and we made a push to extricate ourselves, but found the navigation so difficult that it required the intense labour of three days to accomplish it. We carried the point at last, and were commended by the admiral for our perseverance. You will see in the Gazette my letter to him. I aimed at modesty, but am a little afraid that, in pursuit of that object, I may have left material facts a little too indefinite, if not obscure. The *Atalante's* captain and four others are killed; eleven are wounded, and so dreadfully, that our surgeon thinks every one of them will die. To the end of my experience I shall regret the captain; he was a perfect hero; and if his crew had been like him, critical, indeed, would have been our peril. The *Atalante* is much larger than my vessel, and she mounted 16 long 12-pounders; we had not a single brig that is equal to that calibre. Her intended complement was 200 men, but she had only, as it happened, 76 on board. In two days after the captain's death, he was buried with all the naval honours in my power to bestow upon him. During the ceremony of his interment, the English colours disappeared, and the Dutch were hoisted in their place. All the Dutch prisoners were liberated; one of them delivered an *éloge* upon the hero they had lost, and we fired three volleys over him, as he descended into the deep."

minutes within a cable's length, the enemy made sail ahead out of the range of the *Fiorenzo's* shot. The British frigate made all sail after him, gradually approaching him till daylight, when, finding he could not avoid an action, the enemy wore, as did the *Fiorenzo*, and at twenty-five minutes past six, recommenced the engagement at a distance of half a mile, gradually closing to a quarter of a mile. The fire was constant and well directed on both sides, though that of the *Piemontaise* slackened towards the latter part of the action. At 8.15 the enemy made all sail. The *Fiorenzo's* main-topsail yard being shot through, the main-royal mast, both main-topmast stays, and most of the standing and running rigging and sails, cut to pieces, and cartridges fired away, she ceased firing, and employed all hands in repairing the damages and fitting her again for action. They kept sight of the enemy during the night, and at nine A.M. on the 8th, being perfectly prepared for action, bore down under a press of sail, for the Frenchman, who did not endeavour to avoid the *San Fiorenzo* until she hauled athwart his stern, to gain the weather-gage and bring him to close fight, when the *Piemontaise* hauled up also and made all sail. On perceiving the *San Fiorenzo* coming up fast with him and that a battle was unavoidable, he tacked; and at three P.M. they passed each other on opposite tacks, and commenced action within a quarter of a cable's length. When the enemy was abaft the *Fiorenzo's* beam, he wore, and after an hour and twenty minutes close action, struck his colours.

The *Piemontaise* mounted 50 guns, long 18-pounders, on her main-deck, and 36-pound carronades on her quarter-deck, and had 530 Frenchmen on board and about 200 Lascars. In the action she lost 48 men killed and 120 wounded. The *Fiorenzo* had 48 killed and 25 wounded, among the former being the gallant Captain Hardinge, her commander, who was struck by a grape-shot in the second broadside in the last action, and Lieutenant Massy was badly wounded just before the enemy struck. Moreau, the second captain of the *Piemontaise*, was severely wounded, and either threw himself or caused himself to be thrown overboard. The French frigate had her rigging cut to pieces, and her masts and bowsprit so wounded that they went by the board during the night. Lieutenant Dawson succeeded Captain Hardinge, and brought the *San Fiorenzo* and *Piemontaise*, her prize, into Colombo on the 12th March. The death of Captain Hardinge was sincerely regretted by all who knew him. In Lieutenant-General Maitland's "general orders" on the following day, he speaks of "the action as second to none in the splendid annals of British valour," and says, "he feels it his duty, as representing his sovereign in this island (Ceylon), to direct that the flag at the flag-staff of this fort be hoisted half-mast high, and that minute guns be fired agreeably to the number of years Captain Hardinge had so honourably lived, when most unfortunately for his friends and for his country his career was cut off."

Captain Charles Lydiard was an officer formed to attain the highest position in the Navy, but was lost to his country prematurely, though not, like Captain Hardinge, at the hands of the enemy. He saw considerable service in several ships, including the *Captain*, 74, in the Mediterranean until July 1795, when he was appointed first lieutenant of the *Southampton*, 32, under his old friend, Captain Shields, and later, under Captain Macnamara, who appreciated the remarkable gallantry and professional attainments of his executive officer. The *Southampton* blockaded in the port of Genoa the French frigates *Vestale* and *Brun*, with several gunboats, which at the end of fifteen days ventured out, when they were attacked by the small British frigate. The *Vestale* struck her colours, but at the moment of hoisting out the boats to take possession, the foremast of the *Southampton* went over the side, when the *Vestale* re-hoisted her colours and succeeded in making her escape.

On the next occasion these gallant officers were engaged with the enemy, they succeeded in securing their prize. On the evening of the 9th July 1796, Sir John Jervis, the commander-in-chief, noticing a French cruiser working up Hyères Bay, near Toulon, selected the *Southampton* to engage her, and Captain Macnamara's account of the manner in which he effected this duty, and of the gallantry of Lieutenant Lydiard is better than any I can give:—" In obedience to the orders I received from you on the *Victory*'s quarter-deck last evening, I pushed through the Grand Pass, and hauled up under the batteries to the north-east with an easy sail, in hopes I should be taken for a French or neutral frigate, which I have great reason to believe succeeded, as I got within pistol-shot of the enemy's ship before I was discovered, and cautioned the captain, through a speaking trumpet, not to make a fruitless resistance, when he immediately snapped his pistol at me and fired his broadside. At this period, being very near the heavy battery of Fort Breganton, I laid him instantly on board, and Lieutenant Lydiard, at the head of the boarders, with an intrepidity no words can describe, entered and carried her in about ten minutes, although he met with a spirited resistance from the captain (who fell) and 100 men under arms to receive him. In this short conflict, the behaviour of all the officers and ship's company of the *Southampton* had my full approbation, and I do not mean to take from their merit by stating to you that the conduct of Lieutenant Lydiard was above all praise. Making sail on the two ships,

I found some difficulty in getting from under the battery, which kept up a heavy fire, and was not able to return through the Grand Pass before half-past one o'clock this morning, with *L'Utile*, corvette of 24 guns, French 6-pounders, commanded by Citoyen Francois Viza, and 130 men, 25 of whom were killed and wounded."

For his gallantry on this occasion, Lieutenant Lydiard was promoted and appointed to the command of the prize, which he commanded till September of the following year, when she was paid off. In May 1798, he received the command of the *Fury*, bomb, and then of the *Kate*, sloop-of-war, which he vacated on promotion to the rank of post-captain. In December 1805, after nearly five years on half-pay, he was appointed to the *Anson*, 44, in which he performed many gallant actions, until her loss two years later. Captain Lydiard brought the crew to a pitch of perfection which made her second to none in the service, not even excluding the *Arethusa*, commanded by Captain Brisbane, the *Nymphe*, Captain Pellew, or the other frigates which made themselves a name for smartness under the command of the best officers that any navy can boast. In company with the *Arethusa*, on the 14th August 1806, he captured, off Havannah, the French frigate *Pomona*, of 38 guns and 347 men, destroyed twelve gunboats and silenced a battery, mounting 16 guns, close to which they took up a position. The *Pomona* struck her colours after a twenty-five minutes' action, having lost her captain and 200 men; three gunboats were blown up, six were sunk, and three driven ashore.

On the 15th September following, Captain Lydiard fell in with the French 80-gun ship *Foudroyant* in a dismasted state off Havannah, and standing in engaged her, but at the end of half an hour, finding her fire too much for him, he was compelled to sheer off. For his intrepid conduct on this occasion, Captain Lydiard received the thanks of the admiral on the quarter-deck of his flagship at Port Royal. In company with the *Arethusa*, *Latona*, and *Fisgard*, Captain Lydiard was engaged in the capture of the island of Curaçoa, and the manner in which the captains of these frigates laid them on board the strong fortress, as though it was an enemy's ship, forms one of the most brilliant episodes in the history of the British Navy.

Fort Amsterdam, as the chief work was called, mounted 66 guns, and there were also a 36-gun frigate, a corvette of 22 guns, and two schooners, with some batteries on the heights, and Fort République, enfilading the harbour, the entrance to which was only fifty yards wide. The ships stood in together, and while the Dutch frigate was carried by Captain Brisbane, Captain Lydiard boarded the corvette from the port bow of the *Anson*, while her starboard guns kept up a fire on the batteries on shore. Upon securing the *Surinam*, as the corvette was named, Captain Lydiard landed with his men at the same time as the commodore, and these two noble seamen were the first upon the walls of Fort Amsterdam. By seven o'clock all the enemy's works in the town were in their possession, and three hours later the British flag was flying at Fort République. The execution of this enterprise was said with truth to be "perfectly in union with everything glorious in the past, and an example of everything glorious in the future." Captain Lydiard sailed for Jamaica with the prisoners and the captured colours, and proceeded to England with them, where he arrived on the 21st February 1807. He was greeted with popular demonstrations of applause, and introduced to the King, from whom he received, together with the other captains, a gold medal, in honour of the achievement, while Captain Brisbane was also knighted. The *Anson* soon after returned from the West Indies, when Captain Lydiard rejoined her, and she was stationed for service in the Channel.

But the frigate, which had originally been a 64-gun ship, and still carried the masts and spars of that class, was not sufficiently seaworthy to battle against the stormy weather she now experienced, and before the close of the year was lost, together with her gallant captain and the greater part of the crew.*

An officer who had a long and distinguished career in the Navy, for which he received high honours, was Lord Gardner. He first went to sea in 1755, at the age of 13, on board the *Medway*, Captain Dennis (one of Lord Anson's lieutenants in the *Centurion* in his voyage round the world), and was present at the capture of the *Duke of*

* The following account of the catastrophe is from one of the survivors :—"On the 27th December, 1807, when cruising off the Black Rocks in the Channel, Captain Lydiard, apprehending the approach of a gale, at nine o'clock shaped his course for Falmouth. Soon after land was seen about two miles distant, but as from the extreme thickness of the weather they could not ascertain what part, Captain Lydiard ordered the ship to be wore to the S.E., not thinking it safe to stand in any nearer under such circumstances of weather. Soon after one o'clock the master wished him to run in again and make the land which was supposed to be the Lizard, when he asked if it could be done without risk. The master replied in the affirmative, when the ship was wore, and they made all sail. Soon after three o'clock, as the captain was going to dinner, he looked out of the quarter gallery, from whence he saw the breakers close to us, and the land a long distance ahead. The ship was brought to an anchor and rode very well until four o'clock next morning, when the cable parted. The other anchor was immediately let go, and the lower yards and topmasts immediately struck. At daybreak the other cable parted, and as they were so close to the land that they had no alternative but to go on shore, Captain Lydiard desired the master to turn the ship into the best situation for saving the lives of the people. Fortunately a fine beach presented itself upon which the ship was run. Shortly afterwards she struck, and the mainmast went overboard. Captain Lydiard and Sullivan (a volunteer on board the *Anson*), with the first lieutenant, were resolved to remain by the ship as long as possible. Many people were killed on board, and the first lieutenant and a number of others washed overboard. It was the captain's great wish to save the lives of the ship's company, and he was employed in directing them the whole of the time. He had placed himself by the wheel, holding by the spokes, where he was exposed to the violence of the sea, which broke tremendously over him, and from continuing in this situation too long, waiting to see the people out of the ship, he became so weak that upon attempting to leave the ship himself he was washed away and drowned."

Aquitaine. Under the same captain he served in the *Dorsetshire*, 70, when she took the *Raisonable* of 60 guns, and in the general engagement off Belleisle between Lord Hawke and Admiral Conflans. On the 7th March, 1760, after five years' service, Mr. Gardner was raised to the rank of lieutenant, and was appointed to the *Bellona*, 74, of which Captain Dennis received the command, the only commander under whom he had yet served. Not many months after joining her, Captain Faulknor was appointed to the command of the *Bellona*, and captured the French 74-gun ship *Courageux*, after one of the most severe actions recorded in the annals of the British Navy, of which we have given an account elsewhere.

On the 12th April, 1762, our hero received his commission as commander, and was appointed to the *Raven* fireship. Four years later he was raised to post-rank, and shortly after received the command of the *Preston*, 50, flagship of Rear-Admiral Perry, commanding on the Jamaica station. In this ship and the *Levant* Captain Gardner served till the end of 1771, when he returned to England. After remaining on shore unemployed for four years, he was appointed to the *Maidstone*, 28, and sailed for the West Indies. When the war with our American colonies broke out, he was sent to that coast, and on the 3rd November, 1778, engaged the French armed merchantship *Lion*, carrying 40 guns and 216 men. On the first day he hauled off to repair damages, and on the following morning again attacked her and compelled her to strike her colours. Soon after this event Captain Gardner was promoted to the command of the *Sultan*, 74, and took part in Admiral Byron's indecisive action with Count D'Estaing, off Grenada, on the 6th July, 1779. The *Sultan* took a prominent part in the engagement, and lost 16 killed and 39 wounded, being a greater loss than was incurred by any other ships. Shortly after this Captain Gardner sailed for England, and was not again employed till the end of 1781, when he commissioned the *Duke*, 98, and sailed to join Sir George Rodney in the West Indies. In that great seaman's battle with Count de Grasse, on the 12th April, 1782, the *Duke* was second to the *Formidable* flagship, and was the first ship to pass through the enemy's line. During one period of the action, the *Duke*, in company with the *Namur* and the flagship, sustained the fire of eleven of the enemy's ships, and experienced a loss of 13 killed and 60 wounded. On the conclusion of peace in the following spring, Captain Gardner returned to England, when the *Duke* was paid off.

Three years later we find him acting commander-in-chief on the Jamaica station, with the rank of commodore, and in January, 1790, when he was elected member of Parliament, he was appointed one of the Lords of the Admiralty, an office he held till May, 1795.

On the outbreak of war with France, Gardner was raised to the rank of rear-admiral, and on the 6th March, 1793, sailed for the West Indies, where he assumed the command. In the autumn he returned to England, and was attached to the Channel fleet, under the command of Lord Howe, having his flag in the *Queen*, 98. Admiral Gardner had the good fortune to participate in the great victory achieved by Lord Howe over the French fleet on the 1st June, 1794. The *Queen* took a prominent part in the action of the 29th May, and suffered proportionately. Her loss that day was 21 killed, including the master, and 25 wounded, among whom were Captain Hutt, who lost a leg, and died of the wound on the 2nd July. At one time the *Queen* was almost unmanageable, owing to the damages she had received aloft, and being far in the rear with the *Royal George*, the enemy attempted to cut her off, on perceiving which Lord Howe wore to her assistance and both vans were again engaged. In the decisive action on the 1st June, the *Queen* again suffered considerably when running down to close, and engaged first the *Northumberland* and then the *Jemappes*, whose fore and mainmasts she shot away. The *Queen* also lost her mainmast, and during the day her losses were 14 killed, and three officers and 37 men wounded.

Admiral Gardner received several flattering marks of the King's favour. He was promoted to the rank of vice-admiral and was created a baronet, and received the thanks of Parliament. Sir Alan Gardner was second in command of the British fleet in the action off Lorient, on the 23rd of June, 1795, between Lord Bridport and Admiral Villaret-Joyeuse, but was not prominently engaged. This was the last occasion in which he was in action with the enemy, and his record, which includes ten engagements, was assuredly an honourable and distinguished one. On the 23rd December, 1800, Sir Alan Gardner received an Irish peerage, an honour he did not live many years to enjoy, as he expired on the 1st January, 1809.

Lord Collingwood's name is one of the most honoured in our Navy. An adequate memoir has been written of this fine specimen of a naval officer and English gentleman, by a relative, with selections from his correspondence, which exhibit him as one of the most amiable as well as gallant of men, and equally beloved by his seamen in the busy and exciting scenes of war as by his family in the quiet of home-life. Cuthbert Collingwood entered the navy in the year 1761, on board the *Shannon* frigate, commanded by his uncle, Captain Braithwaite. He served with him for many years, but his life was not particularly eventful, until he was made fourth lieutenant of the *Somerset*, in 1775, on the day of the battle of Bunker's Hill, where he commanded a party of seamen. Next year his ship, the *Hornet*, was sent to the West Indies, where Collingwood was much thrown with Nelson, who, though his junior in point of service, was then second lieutenant of the *Lowestoft*. These celebrated men had been on terms of friendship before, and now renewed the intimacy, which ripened into a warm friendship and mutual admiration. In 1780, he participated in the expedition to Nicaragua, and he succeeded to the command of the *Hinchinbrooke*, when Captain Nelson was appointed to the charge of the naval brigade on shore. Like Nelson he suffered greatly in health during the expedition, and it is stated that, during four months, he buried 180 out of 200 men, forming the complement of his ship. In December, Collingwood was appointed to the command of the *Pelican*, 24, but on the 1st of August in the following year, she was wrecked in a hurricane, on the barren islets known as Morant Keys. Here he and his ship's company remained for ten days, with little food or water, until a boat reached Jamaica, and the *Diamond* frigate came to their assistance. His next command was the *Surprise*, 64, till she was paid off in 1783, when he commissioned the *Mediator*, and sailed for the West Indies, where he met his friend, Nelson, then in command of the *Boreas*. At the end of 1786, the ship returned to England, and Collingwood, after twenty-five years' service, lived in retirement, which was only broken for a few weeks when, in the apprehended rupture with Spain, he was appointed to the command of the *Mermaid*, 32. But the war cloud blew over, though in 1793, on the outbreak of hostilities with France, we find him gazetted to the *Prince*, 98, Rear-Admiral Bowyer's flagship. Collingwood accompanied this officer to the *Barfleur*, 98, and was present at Lord Howe's great victory on the 1st June, 1794, in which the *Barfleur* took a prominent part. Admiral Bowyer lost his leg in the action, and as he ceased to fly his flag, Collingwood was appointed successively to the 74-gun ships *Hector* and *Excellent*, which latter he commanded at Sir John Jervis's memorable engagement off Cape St. Vincent. We have mentioned the valuable assistance he afforded the *Captain*, commanded by his friend Nelson, when he passed between that ship and the *San Nicolas*, 80, allowing the harassed crew an opportunity of replenishing their shot lockers. Collingwood then engaged the *Santissima Trinidada*, four-decker, and the *Excellent* stood fourth on the list of ships which suffered most in the action. So fully did Nelson appreciate the skill and gallantry of his friend that when, in the following year, he was sent to reinforce his squadron, after his victory at the Nile, his lordship exclaimed, "See, here comes the *Excellent*, which is as good as two added to our number." In January, 1799, his ship was paid off, and on the 14th February, the second anniversary of the battle of St. Vincent, Collingwood was promoted to the rank of rear-admiral. He now hoisted his flag in the *Triumph*, on the Channel Station, and then on board the *Barfleur*.

From May 1802 till the following March, Admiral Collingwood was unemployed, but on the rupture of the peace of Amiens, he was again afloat in blockading the enemy's fleet at Brest, under Admiral Cornwallis. In May, 1805, he was detached with some ships to blockade the ports on the coast of Spain. At one time he was left with only four ships-of-the-line off Cadiz, where lay a large French and Spanish fleet, and in this service displayed those qualities of unwearied patience, address, and resource, that marked him out specially among the admirals of his time. With two ships close in-shore, to watch the motions of the enemy, he made signals to his two other ships, which repeated them to others that had no existence, and quite succeeded in deceiving the enemy as to the strength of the blockading squadron. In September, Lord Nelson arrived and assumed charge of the fleet, with Collingwood for his second-in-command, and at the battle of Trafalgar it fell to the subject of this brief notice, who had his flag flying on board the *Royal Sovereign*, to lead the lee column into action and break the enemy's centre, which he did in a style that drew from his friend, the commander-in-chief, a warm tribute of admiration. "Look," said Nelson, "at that noble fellow, Collingwood; see how he carries his ship into action." A kindred spirit animated these great seamen, and it is recorded that Collingwood, when enjoying the honour he knew his friend wished to share, exclaimed to his flag-captain, "Rotherham, what would Nelson give to be here!"

It had been Collingwood's lot to succeed Nelson as lieutenant; again in the ship to which he was promoted as commander; a third time in the *Hinchinbrooke*; and now he was his successor as commander-in-chief of the fleet after death had finally removed him from the scene. But there was no vainglory or self-seeking about the man, and he only deplored the loss of one he had known throughout his professional life, and wrote to the Admiralty:—"I have not only to lament, in common with the British Navy and the British nation, the fall of the Commander-in-Chief, the loss of a hero whose name will be immortal, and his memory ever dear to his country, but my heart is rent with the most poignant grief for the death of a friend, to whom, by many years' intimacy, and a perfect knowledge of the virtues of his mind, which inspired ideas superior to the common race of men, I was bound by the strongest ties of affection, a grief to which even the glorious occasion on which he fell does not bring that consolation which perhaps it ought."

In the battle the *Royal Sovereign* lost her main and mizen masts, and the fore-mast was so much injured by shot that it went over the side during the subsequent severe weather. Collingwood shifted his flag into the *Euryalus*, commanded by Captain Blackwood, Nelson's friend, and carried out the expressed hope of his late chief that "humanity after victory might be the predominant feature in the British fleet," by proposing to the Governor of Cadiz that all the wounded prisoners should be landed for treatment in the hospitals of that city, a suggestion which was gratefully adopted. The Spaniards, not to be outdone in generosity, offered the use of these institutions for the wounded British seamen.

Collingwood was raised to the peerage, with a pension of £2,000 a year, which, however, he did not live many years to enjoy. Though in failing health, he continued to serve in command of the Mediterranean fleet until the spring of 1810, when he expired on board his ship, the *Ville-de-Paris*, on the 7th March, the day after she sailed from Minorca for England. His body was brought home in the *Nereus* frigate, and, as with Lord Nelson, lay in state for some days in the Painted Chamber at Greenwich, and was interred in St. Paul's, where it lies beside his beloved friend and chief.

Lord Collingwood never heeded fatigue or exposure to all weathers in the execution of his duty, and was generally on deck day and night in times of emergency. During the last five years of his life he had scarcely been on shore, and in January, 1805, he wrote to a friend:—"Since the year 1793 I have been only one year at home. To my children I am scarcely known, yet while I have health and strength to do it, I will serve, and if successfully, as I have ever done faithfully, my children will not want friends." In this confidence he was not disappointed, as on his death his widow became entitled to a pension of £1,000 a year, and each of his daughters to pensions of half the amount, voted by the liberality of Parliament.

Lord Bridport was the younger of two brothers who both gained peerages and a high position in the naval service of their country. Alexander Hood first distinguished himself in May, 1756, while commanding the *Antelope*, 50, when he engaged and drove ashore the *Aquilon*, of 48 guns and 450 men. This took place in Hyères Bay, and on the following day he took a privateer of 16 guns. In the ensuing year Captain Hood was appointed to the command of the *Minerva*, 32, which he retained till the close of 1761. In January of this year he captured a privateer carrying 14 guns and 122 men, and retook the *Warwick*, formerly a British 60-gun ship, but now carrying 34, with a crew of 221 men, and 75 soldiers she was conveying to Pondicherry. He describes the action in the following terms:—" At twenty minutes after ten, with a fresh gale easterly, and a great sea, I began a close engagement with her. At eleven her main and fore-top-mast went away, and soon after she came on board us on the starboard bow, and then fell alongside, but the sea soon parted us, and the enemy fell astern. About a quarter after eleven, the *Minerva's* bowsprit went away, and the foremast soon followed it. These were very unfortunate accidents, and I almost despaired of being able to attack the enemy again; however, I cut the wreck away as soon as possible, and about one o'clock cleared the ship of it. I then wore the ship, and stood for the enemy, who was then about three leagues to leeward of me. At four o'clock I came quite close up to the enemy, and renewed the attack. About a quarter before five she struck, when possession was taken of the *Warwick*, which sailed from Rochefort on the 20th January, and was bound to the Isle of France and Bourbon with provisions, ammunition, and stores. The enemy had 14 killed and 32 wounded. Our numbers are the boatswain and 13 killed and the gunner and 33 wounded. The former died on the 27th, together with two seamen. I have given my thanks to the officers and crew of his Majesty's ship for their firm and spirited behaviour, and have great pleasure in acquainting your lordships with it. At nine o'clock the main-mast of the *Minerva* went away, and at eleven the mizen-mast followed it."

Captain Hood was promoted the same year to the *Africa*, 64, but the conclusion of peace in 1763 denied him the chance of courting further distinction. He held various commands until the outbreak of war with France in 1778, and was engaged in the indecisive battle fought on the 27th July, off Ushant, between Admiral Keppel and Count D'Orvilliers. In September, 1780, he was promoted to the rank of rear-admiral, and two years later, hoisted his flag in the *Queen*, and commanded a division of ships at the relief of Gibraltar by Lord Howe. We find that Admiral Hood entered Parliament in 1784, was appointed a Knight of the Bath four years later, and on the declaration of war with France in 1793, served under Lord Howe in the Channel fleet. At the great victory of the 1st of June, Sir Alexander Hood had his flag on board the *Royal George*, 100. In the preliminary action of the 29th May she was hotly engaged, and had 15 killed and 23 wounded, and in the main battle, passing through the enemy's line, between the *Sanspareil*, 80, and the *Républicaine*, 100, the *Royal George* engaged both ships, and shot away the fore and mizen mast of the former, which lost 300 men. On the second day, Admiral Hood's flag-ship had a midshipman and four men killed, and a lieutenant, master, two midshipmen, and 44 seamen and marines wounded. She was assisted by the *Glory*, which suffered severely in the action with the two ships, but they inflicted greater loss on the enemy, and the *Républicaine*, bearing the flag of Admiral Bouvet, was compelled to retreat, and shortly afterwards her main and mizen masts went over the side. The *Royal George* also lost her fore-mast and maintopmast. For his share in this memorable engagement, Admiral Hood received an Irish peerage as Baron Bridport.

On the 22nd June in the following year (1795) Lord Bridport, when cruising in command of the Channel fleet, with seventeen sail-of-the-line and five frigates, sighted and gave chase to a French fleet of twelve line-of-battle-ships and eleven frigates. Early next morning six of his ships closed with the enemy, when three of their fleet were taken. The admiral was not able to come into action until the success had been achieved, when he fired a broadside into the *Peuple*, a three-decker, but the combatants were so close in with the land that Lord Bridport was compelled to throw out the signal for discontinuing the chase, and Villaret-Joyeuse, Lord Howe's old opponent on the 1st June, was enabled to bring to in safety close to the Port of Lorient. In the year following this considerable success, Lord Bridport received an English peerage as a reward for his services, which he enjoyed until his death in 1814.

His elder brother, Samuel, Lord Hood, was not less distinguished. The first engagement in which he was engaged after attaining the rank of lieutenant, was in 1746, when his ship, the *Winchelsea*, 20, captured a French frigate of superior force. In this action Lieutenant Hood received a severe wound. He accompanied Admiral Watson in the *Princess Louisa* to Louisburg, in 1748, and eight years later, when commanding the *Grafton*, bearing the broad pennant of Commodore Holmes, participated in an action off the same port with a French squadron. But he established his fame as an enterprising and gallant officer in an action near Brest with a French frigate of the same force. Captain Hood drove the enemy on shore, where she was totally destroyed, her loss in the engagement being 30 killed and 25 wounded, while the *Antelope* had only three and 13 respectively.

Not less spirited and successful was the action he fought on the 21st February, 1759, when in command of the *Vestal*, 32, with the *Bellona*, carrying 32 guns and

SIGNALLING.

220 men. The action continued at close quarters for four hours, when the *Bellona* struck her colours, with only the fore-mast left standing and that without yard or topmast. On taking possession, over 30 dead were found on her decks, besides 12 the French acknowledged they had thrown overboard, and there were 42 wounded. The *Vestal* had only lost five killed and 22 wounded, but all her top-masts were shot away, and her shrouds and rigging were cut to pieces. The prize was jury-rigged and brought to Spithead in safety, and was purchased into the Navy under the name of the *Repulse*. Many years after Captain Hood was created a baronet, and in 1780, after forty years' service, was advanced to flag rank. When the French Government threw in their lot with the Americans, Sir Samuel Hood was of great assistance to Sir George Rodney through the protracted operations that ensued, and in the action of the 9th April, 1782—three days before the decisive victory that great admiral gained over Count de Grasse, in the West Indies—Admiral Hood chased the enemy with the van division of the fleet, the rear and centre being still becalmed under the lee of the land. The French commander-in-chief, observing his isolated position, bore down before the wind to attack him, when Hood hove to, and with the broadsides of his eight ships directed to the enemy, engaged fifteen of them with such vigour that when the British centre caught the sea-breeze, the French admiral tacked and relinquished the action. In the great battle of the 12th April, the *Barfleur*, flying his flag, also took a prominent part when she was enabled to close. With the *Canada*, 74, Captain Hon. W. Cornwallis, she engaged de Grasse's flag-ship, the *Ville de Paris*, the finest ship afloat, and it is said that her first broadside killed 60 men. The French Admiral struck his flag to Sir Samuel Hood, who, a week afterwards, when despatched in pursuit, brought in the 64-gun ships *Jason* and *Caton*, thus bringing the total captured up to seven, besides two smaller vessels. For his distinguished conduct Admiral Hood was created an Irish peer, and later received an English viscount's coronet, and also the freedom of the City of London.

Lord Hood commanded the fleet which occupied Toulon, but was compelled eventually to evacuate the place, and also took Corsica, when he had under his command the immortal Nelson, whose genius he fully recognised. This eminent admiral died in 1816, two years after his equally distinguished brother.

His relative, Sir Samuel Hood, who added to the distinction gained by the two preceding owners of that name, went to sea in 1776, as midshipman of Lord Bridport's ship, the *Courageux*, and accompanied him to the *Robust*, in which he participated in the engagement between Admiral Keppel and Count D'Orvilliers. In 1779, he joined the *Lively* sloop, and was present at the capture of a French privateer in the English Channel.

When Lord Hood hoisted his flag in the *Barfleur*, he took his young relative with him, and Lieutenant Hood was present in the action with Count de Grasse off Martinique on the 29th April, 1781, in the engagements off the Chesapeake on the 5th September following, and at St. Kitts on the 25th and 26th January, 1782. Five days after this last affair he was promoted to the rank of commander, and appointed to the *Renard* sloop, and in Lord Rodney's great victory of the 12th April, and the partial action three days before, Captain Hood was present in the *Barfleur*, Lord Hood's flagship, as also at the capture of the French squadron in the Mona Passage.

In 1790, Captain Hood was appointed to the command of the *Juno* frigate, in which he served in the West Indies, and, on his return to Europe, commanded her when she formed a portion of the squadron engaged at Corsica under Commodore Linzee. Captain Hood was also employed under Nelson at the attack on Bastia, and during the siege of Calvi he served in the frigate *Aigle*, in which he remained until the year 1796, engaged with a small squadron protecting the trade in the Levant and blockading some of the enemy's frigates at Smyrna. In April of this year Captain Hood was appointed to the *Zealous*, 74, and participated in Nelson's disastrous attack on Teneriffe. At the battle of the Nile also he was prominently engaged, and first discovered the French fleet, which he was ordered by Nelson to reconnoitre as they lay in Aboukir Bay. About six in the evening the Admiral hailed Captain Hood to ask him "what he thought of attacking the enemy that night?" to which he replied, "We have now eleven fathoms water, and, if the admiral will give me leave, I will lead in, making known my soundings by signal, and bring the van ship of the enemy to action." Late as it was, Nelson decided to attack, and said, "Go on, and I wish you success." During this conversation, the *Goliath*, Captain Foley, passed, and took the lead, which she kept; but, not bringing up alongside the first ship, went on to engage the second. On this, Captain Hood exclaimed to his officers—"Thank God! my friend Foley has left me the van ship." He soon after took such a position on the bow of the *Guerrier*, the ship in question, as to shoot away all her masts, and effected her capture in twelve minutes from the time that the *Zealous* commenced her fire. Afterwards the *Zealous* engaged the four ships which escaped until recalled by signal.

Captain Hood continued to serve for some time on the station, blockading the port of Alexandria, and destroyed thirty of the enemy's transports. For his services he received from the Sultan a snuff-box set with diamonds, and a sword from the Corporation of London. In February, 1799, he joined Lord Nelson at Palermo, assisted in driving the French out of the kingdom of Naples, and was employed at the reduction of that city, for which the King of the Two Sicilies presented him with a snuff-box enriched with diamonds.

In 1800 the *Zealous* was paid off, when Captain Hood commissioned the *Courageux*, 74, and in the following January the *Venerable*, of like force, in which he was present at Sir James Saumarez' unsuccessful attack on a French squadron, moored under the protection of the batteries at Algeciras, and in the subsequent victory achieved by the same admiral over a superior French and Spanish squadron, in which, says Captain Hood, in his Memoir, the *Venerable* had 30 killed and 100 wounded, her previous loss at Algeciras being eight and 25 respectively. The British seventy-four engaged the *Formidable*, 80, Admiral Linois' flaghip, which shot away her masts, when she struck on a reef about twelve miles from Cadiz, but was brought off and reached Gibraltar, where she was fitted for sea in a few days by her energetic commander. A few months later the *Venerable* returned to England and was paid off, and her captain was appointed, in October 1802, to a civil post in the island of Trinidad, and then Commodore on the station. On the outbreak of hostilities he assisted at the reduction of the islands of Tobago and St. Lucia, and all the Dutch possessions in the West Indies. Captain Hood received the Bath for these services, and on his return to England in 1806, was appointed to the *Centaur*, and placed by Earl St. Vincent in command of a squadron of seven sail-of-the-line and some frigates off the port of Rochefort. On the 25th September Sir Samuel Hood encountered a French squadron, consisting of five frigates and two corvettes, with troops on board, and captured all but one of the former. In the action the Commodore lost his right arm. He was also engaged in the Baltic in action with the Russian 74, *Sewolod*, which struck her colours to the *Centaur*, which was the last important service rendered by this distinguished officer.

Lord Keith, known in his earlier service as Captain Elphinstone, was son of a Scotch peer of that name. He was engaged on the American coast during the War of Independence, and in 1781, when in command of the *Warwick*, 50, took a Dutch frigate of the same force. At the operation before Toulon in 1793, he commanded the *Robust*, and was in charge of the batteries on shore. In the following year, being then a rear-admiral, he served in command of a division of the Channel fleet, and in 1795 sailed to the Cape of Good Hope, the reduction of which he effected in conjunction with some troops.

He also caused the surrender of a squadron of Dutch ships in Saldanha Bay, and for his services was created a peer. In 1798, he proceeded to the Mediterranean, and in the following year succeeded to the command of the fleet in that sea, with his flag on board the *Queen Charlotte*, of 110 guns. This noble three-decker was burnt by accident off Leghorn on the 17th March, 1800. Lord Keith was on shore at the time, and used every exertion to reach his ship, which was seen to be in flames from the mole of the port. A few boats from the shore assisted in taking off a portion of the crew, but the service was attended with great danger as her guns kept discharging, and some of the boats were swamped by the numbers that dropped into them from the bowsprit and quarter galleries. After little more than an hour the *Queen Charlotte* blew up, when most of those not consumed by the fire were drowned. In this great catastrophe there perished Captain Todd, commanding the three-decker, with 32 officers and 640 men.

Lord Keith transferred his flag to the *Minotaur*, 74, Captain Louis, and was engaged blockading Genoa, then besieged by an Austrian army, until its capitulation. In Sir Ralph Abercromby's expedition to Egypt, Lord Keith acted in command of the fleet, and was present at the capture of Alexandria. This was the last important service rendered by the admiral, who, though he achieved no great victory, could show a record of excellent and honourable service. In 1814, on the conclusion of peace, Lord Keith was advanced to the dignity of viscount, and died nine years after at the age of seventy-six.

One of the most celebrated officers of the Navy in its palmiest days, was Sir William Sydney Smith. He was born in 1764, and entered the service at the age of thirteen, on board the *Sandwich*. Three years later he was promoted to a lieutenancy on board the *Alcide*, 74, and after two years was advanced to the rank of commander, and appointed to the *Fury*, 18-gun sloop, on the Jamaica station. Finally in 1783, when only nineteen years of age, we find him made a post-captain, and appointed to the 28-gun frigate *Nemesis*. In this rapid promotion he was even more fortunate than Lord Nelson, who was posted and received the command of the *Hinchinbrooke* frigate before attaining the age of twenty-one. On the conclusion of peace, Captain Smith was out of employment for nearly five years, when, tired of inaction, he obtained leave to enter the service of the King of Sweden. Here he greatly distinguished himself in the war with Russia, and on his return to England was knighted. On the conclusion of peace between the northern powers, Sir Sydney Smith served in the Turkish Navy, but on the outbreak of the Revolutionary War he left Smyrna, and offered his sword to Lord Hood at Toulon. This was gladly accepted, and Sir Sydney rendered great services at the conclusion of the siege, when he burnt the arsenal, dockyard, and storehouses, with ten ships of the French fleet. In the following year (1794) Sir Sydney commanded the *Diamond*, 38, and by his activity and dash, rendered his name a terror on the French sea-board. He was one of that unsurpassed band of frigate captains, which included the two Pellews, Cochrane, William Parker, Lydiard, and the two Brisbanes, who made the English name as famous at sea as Drake and his compeers had three centuries before.

But at length his daring carried him too far in the pursuit of the duties of his profession, and on the 18th April, 1796, under circumstances which have already been detailed, a French privateer lugger he had captured was retaken by a force of overwhelming strength, and he was made a prisoner, with 19 of the *Diamond's* crew. Sir Sydney Smith was confined in the Temple prison in Paris, but managed, after two years' detention, to escape and make his way to England. In June, 1798, he was appointed to the command of the *Tigre*, 80, and sailed for the Mediterranean, and rendered important services on the Egyptian and Syrian coasts, after Nelson had effected the destruction of the French fleet at the Nile. At Constantinople Commodore Smith was well received by the Turkish authorities, to whom he was familiar. In March, 1799, on hearing from the Turkish Governor of Syria of Buonaparte's incursion into that province and his approach to Acre, he proceeded there and undertook to assist in its defence. He arrived there two days before the French army, and to his aid and indomitable energy—assisted by the equally gallant Captain Miller, of the *Theseus*, who lost his life by an explosion on board his ship—he succeeded in beating off the greatest soldier of the age. By this achievement Sir Sydney Smith rendered a service scarcely inferior to that of Nelson at the Nile, for his repulse of Buonaparte before Acre put an end to all his projects for the founding of a great eastern empire and the invasion of India, to which so rude a shock had been administered on the preceding 1st of August. Sir Sydney Smith was not present at any of the great battles which have made this period of our naval chronicles so glorious; but had he rendered no other service than this, his name would go down in history as one of our greatest sea-captains.

It is only necessary to very briefly advert to the career and great achievements of Lords Howe, St. Vincent, and Duncan, as each of them is celebrated as the hero of a great victory, which has been fully described in the preceding pages, as well as the chief incidents in their lives. Lord Howe, at the time of the outbreak of war with France, was the most distinguished naval officer in the service of this country, and no long time elapsed before he enhanced his reputation by his great victory on the 1st of June. He was born in 1725, and at the age of fourteen, left Eton to enter the navy. As a midshipman he served in the *Severn*, which formed one of Anson's squadron, and sailed for the Pacific. When only twenty years of age he obtained the command of the *Baltimore* sloop, and was made post-captain for defeating two French ships bearing supplies to the Pretender in Scotland. He captured the *Alcide* in 1755, and served under Lord Hawke in his victory off Belleisle. In the war with America Howe commanded the fleet, and took part as well in the operations in the West Indies, where D'Estaing was in command of a powerful fleet. In 1782 Lord Howe effected the relief of Gibraltar, displaying on that occasion his consummate skill in the management of a fleet in the face of a superior force. In the following year he was appointed First Lord of the Admiralty, and ten years later, on the declaration of war, assumed command of the Channel fleet. Then took place his great victory over Villaret-Joyeuse, for which he received, among other honours, the Order of the Garter. Lord Howe continued in chief command of the British fleet while his health permitted, and in 1797 was enabled to render a great service to his country by conciliating the mutinous seamen of the fleet at Spithead. Two years later the veteran entered into his rest, beloved by all ranks in the Navy, and respected and trusted by his countrymen.

Lord Duncan, the hero of Camperdown, was born in 1731, and gained promotion in all the ranks of the Navy up to that of admiral by his devotion to duty, his professional skill, and the services he rendered. He was present under Pocock at the capture of Havannah, and had command of a ship-of-the-line under Sir George Rodney in his victory of the 12th April, 1782, and at the relief of Gibraltar by Howe in that year.

But he had a rare field for the display of his undaunted and untiring resolution during his command of the squadron in the North Sea. For two years Admiral Duncan watched the Dutch fleet in the Texel, which he tried to induce by all the arts at his command to put to sea to engage him. When by the mutiny of the crews under his command, he was rendered powerless to act against them had they accepted his challenge, he displayed resource in deceiving the enemy as to his true position, and he was ultimately rewarded for all his patience by Admiral Winter leaving the protection of his harbours and batteries, and venturing out to give him battle. The result was the glorious victory of Camperdown on the 11th June, 1797, which was of a complete and crushing character, though sanguinary to both combatants. Lord Duncan only survived for seven years to enjoy the peerage and pension of £3,000 he was awarded for his great success, but his name will survive in our annals as one of the most celebrated of naval heroes.

Earl St. Vincent was in no way inferior to the others in this trio of great commanders, ennobled for the services they rendered their country in a critical period of her history. The first war service he saw was in 1759, when a lieutenant on board the *Namur*, 90, carrying the flag of Admiral Sir Charles Saunders, in the joint military and naval expedition against Quebec. The same year he received double promotion to the rank of commander and captain, and on the 13th October, was appointed to the command of the *Gosport*, 44, and served in her throughout the war in the Channel and the North American stations. The *Gosport* was put out of commission in 1763, and six years later we find Captain Jervis appointed to the *Alarm*, 32, in which he served in the Mediterranean. In 1775, two years after surrendering the command of the *Alarm*, he hoisted his pennant on the *Foudroyant*, 80, and on the commencement of hostilities with France in 1778, joined the Channel fleet, with which he participated in Admiral Keppel's engagement off Ushant.

In April, 1782, Captain Jervis engaged and captured the *Pegase*, of 74 guns and 700 men, for which he received the riband of the Bath, and he was with Lord Howe at the relief of Gibraltar. In January of the following year, on his appointment to the command of a small squadron, Sir John Jervis hoisted his broad pennant on board the *Salisbury*, 50, but the conclusion of peace robbed him of the chance of earning fresh distinction. In 1787 Sir John Jervis was promoted to the rank of rear-admiral, and on the outbreak of war with France, six years afterwards, hoisted his flag in the *Boyne*, 98, and assumed command of the expedition despatched to the West Indies to reduce the French possessions, which he succeeded in effecting. Not long after Admiral Jervis was appointed Commander-in-Chief in the Mediterranean, whither he sailed with his flag in the *Victory*. The French fleet remained close in Toulon, and Sir John Jervis repaired to Lisbon, when the Spanish Court threw in its lot with the French Directory. On the 14th February, 1797, took place the great achievement of his naval career, the defeat of the Spanish fleet. With only fifteen sail-of-the-line, he did not scruple to attack twenty-seven, but his fleet was drawn up in two compact lines, while that of the Spanish admiral was very scattered, his line being irregular and ill-formed. Carrying a press of sail, with a portion of his fleet he cut off nine of their ships from the rest, which were so far to leeward that it was not till the close of the day they were enabled to rejoin the van. When the conflict ceased at four o'clock, Sir John Jervis was rewarded for his intrepidity by the capture of two ships of 112 guns, one of 84, and a 74, two of which had surrendered to Commodore Nelson. Admiral de Cordova, having his flag in the great four-decker, *Santissima Trinidada*, which was much shattered, effected his retreat with the remainder of the van division, on being joined by the ships which had been cut off at the beginning of the action. Throughout the day Sir John Jervis exhibited the highest seamanlike skill, and it was only by a fresh exhibition of this talent—for which British officers were as much indebted for their victories as the gallantry and good gunnery of their crews —that the British admiral, covering his prizes and disabled ships, was enabled to carry off the fruits of victory. Earl St. Vincent, as he now was, long commanded the Mediterranean fleet, but could never again bring the French or Spanish fleets to action. It was greatly owing to the constant training in gunnery he enforced among the crews of the ships under his command, that the British Navy owed this and subsequent victories, and it was only when, rendered careless by success, this continuous practice was relaxed, with a consequent diminution of skill, that the crews of our frigates found more than their match in some encounters with American ships, who had cultivated this art, so essential to success in naval warfare. Lord St. Vincent survived to attain the great age of eighty-eight, and died in 1823, full of years and honours.

Space forbids us to give, as we could have wished, brief biographical notices of admirals who rendered services only less important than those described in the preceding pages, or of captains as distinguished as Captains Lydiard and Hardinge, but who did not acquire that claim of special recognition which is conceded to those who die in the service of their country. Among such may be named Admiral the Hon. William Cornwallis, who was distinguished by the courage with which, in 1780, when in command of two ships-of-the-line and three frigates, he beat off the attack of La Mothe Picquet, who commanded a squadron of double that strength, and again in Lord Rodney's action of the 12th April, 1782, when in the *Canada*, 74, he attacked the *Ville-de-Paris*, of 110 guns, flagship of the Comte de Grasse. Still more is he renowned, strange as it may sound, for his masterly retreat with only five sail-of-the-line and one frigate before a French fleet of thirteen ships and fourteen frigates. He showed a determined face to the enemy, and brought off his squadron without loss, for which he received the thanks of Parliament.

Sir Thomas Louis was one of the most capable officers of the Navy, and was thought highly of by Admirals Rodney, Jervis, and Nelson, under whom he commanded the *Minotaur*, 74, at the Nile and on the coast of Italy. In March, 1805, his lordship applied for the services of Rear-Admiral Louis, who accompanied him in the *Canopus*, 80 (the prize, *Franklin*, taken at the Nile), in his pursuit of the French fleet to the West Indies, but was not so fortunate as to be present at Trafalgar. A few days before the battle he was detached with five sail to Tetuan, to which circumstance is attributable the resolution of Villeneuve to venture out of Cadiz and hazard the chances of a naval engagement. Admiral Louis was present in Sir John Duckworth's action with the French off St. Domingo, on the 6th Feburary, 1806, for which he received a baronetcy. He also served under that officer in the unfortunate attempt to force the Dardanelles, and on the 17th May, 1807, expired on board his flagship before Alexandria.

Another flag-officer of eminence who died in this year was Sir Hyde Parker. He served in four ships under the command of his father—for the family had been represented in the Navy for a century and a half—and saw a great deal of service in the East Indies, and was engaged at the reduction of Manilla. He also displayed great gallantry and address in the operations against our rebellious colonists in America, and was knighted. On the shipwreck of the *Phœnix*, 44, Sir Hyde Parker was appointed to the *Latona*, 38, and again served under his father, Vice-Admiral Hyde Parker, who subsequently perished at sea on board the *Cato*, with all hands, while on his way to assume the command in the East Indies. With Admiral Parker he was present in the indecisive action with a superior Dutch squadron, and in April, 1794, became a rear-admiral. Sir Hyde Parker served under Lords Hood and Hotham in the Mediterranean, and held a command at Jamaica; and when, in 1800, it was determined to coerce Denmark, Admiral Parker was appointed to be commander-in-chief of the fleet. But the honour of the bombardment and surrender of Copenhagen was won by his second-in-command, Lord Nelson, and after his return to England Sir Hyde Parker was not again actively employed.

Sir John Duckworth was also a useful officer, but not possessed of pre-eminent talent. He commanded the *Orion*, 74, in Lord Howe's great victory, and served in the Mediterranean under Lords Bridport, St. Vincent, and Keith, until promoted to flag-rank in the last year of the century. At a later period he was appointed to the command at Jamaica, and gained the really brilliant victory at St. Domingo; but he failed to bring the Porte to terms, when, after forcing the Dardanelles, he arrived before Constantinople.

Sir Charles Cotton, one of the most famous admirals of his day, made his first trial of the sea in an East Indiaman, and in 1772, when in his twentieth year, entered the Navy. He served with credit on the American coast, and within seven years of entering the royal service, was promoted to the rank of post-captain, a result, in a measure, due to his being a *protégé* of the Earl of Sandwich, First Lord of the Admiralty. In 1781 Captain Cotton was appointed to the command of the *Alarm*, the first copper-bottomed frigate in the service, which in Rodney's action of the 9th and 12th April, 1782, was one of the repeating ships. He was also present at Lord Howe's victory, when he commanded the *Majestic*, 74, which was stationed second astern of the *Royal George*, flagship of Lord Bridport. On the 28th November, 1794, Sir Charles Cotton was appointed to the *Mars*, 74, one of the five ships comprising Admiral Cornwallis's squadron in his masterly retreat alluded to above. "The *Mars* and *Triumph*," wrote the Admiral, "being the sternmost ships, were, of course, more exposed to the enemy's fire, and I cannot too much commend the spirited conduct of Sir Charles Cotton and Sir Erasmus Gower, the captains of these ships."

Captain Cotton was promoted to rear-admiral in February, 1797, and two years later hoisted his flag in the *Prince*, as third in command of the Channel Fleet, under Lord Bridport. Later in the year he joined Lord St. Vincent in the Mediterranean, under whom and Lord Keith he served to the satisfaction of both those commanders. In the following year he was second in command in the Channel, and we find him appointed to the fleet off Lisbon, where he superseded Sir Sydney Smith. Sir Charles commanded on the coast of Portugal before Sir Arthur Wellesley opened his brief but successful campaign against Marshal Junot, who led the French army which had overrun the Portuguese kingdom at the time of the departure of the royal family for Brazil, escorted by a British squadron. The admiral issued a proclamation to the Portuguese on the 10th June, urging them to throw off the French yoke and follow the example of Spain in resisting the invader. He had great difficulties to encounter in obtaining supplies of food and water, but remained off the Tagus and assisted in the disembarkation of the British army, when its great commander gained the victories of Rolcia and Vimiero. When Sir Arthur Wellesley's successors, Generals Burrard and Dalrymple, assumed command, and concluded the convention of Cintra, by which the British army was deprived of the fruits of its victories, it was owing to the firmness of Sir Charles Cotton in resisting the first Article, on his own responsibility, that the Russian squadron then lying in the Tagus was not ranged under the flag of the enemy. This was the last service he was enabled to render his country, and on the 23rd February, 1812, Sir Charles Cotton expired suddenly, in his fifty-eighth year, when residing at his home near Plymouth.

There is no need to particularize the services of the great Lord Cochrane, afterwards Earl of Dundonald, as they can be found in his well-known "Autobiography of a Seaman," and we have already given them in detail; and the exigencies of space prevent our doing more than name his relatives, Sir Thomas and Sir Alexander Cochrane, both officers of great renown. A Memoir has been published of Sir Edward Pellew, afterwards Lord Exmouth, who captured the *Cleopatra*, after a long and sanguinary action, and throughout the war, maintained the high reputation he then acquired as a frigate captain, ending his career by the victory he gained at Algiers.

The "Life" has also been written, by Admiral Phillimore, of Sir William Parker, captain of the *Amazon*, one of Nelson's personal friends and favourite officers, who sailed with him in that frigate. Sir William Parker attained the highest rank in the Navy, and commanded the British fleet in the China War of 1840-42. Another famous officer was Sir Edward Berry, first lieutenant of the *Agamemnon*, who accompanied Nelson as a volunteer in the *Captain*, which carried his broad pennant at the battle of St. Vincent, and was captain of the *Vanguard*, the great Admiral's flagship at the Nile. Berry was a passenger on board the *Leander*, 50, Captain Thompson, when she long but unsuccessfully defended herself against the *Généreux*, 80, while on her passage to England with Nelson's despatches. For their gallantry both these officers were knighted, and received the freedom of the City of London. Sir Edward Berry returned to the Mediterranean as captain of the *Foudroyant*, 80, Lord Nelson's flagship, and after his lordship left her in Sicily, was present at the capture of the *Guillaume Tell*, 80, by a British squadron, and at Sir John Duckworth's victory off St. Domingo, where he commanded his and Nelson's old ship, the *Agamemnon*, which not long after was wrecked in European waters.

Other famous captains, who served under the victor of Trafalgar, and were honoured by his personal friendship, were Sir Alexander Ball, captain of the *Alexander* at the Nile, and first governor of Malta; Sir Benjamin Hallowell, captain of the *Swiftsure* at the same battle, and Captain Miller, who commanded the *Captain* at St. Vincent and the *Theseus* at the Nile, whose career was cut short in a terrible manner when the explosion took place on board his ship off Acre. Then there was Foley, captain of the *Goliath*, on the 1st August, 1798, and of the *Elephant*, which bore Nelson's flag at Copenhagen; Fremantle, who commanded the *Seahorse* at Teneriffe, where he was wounded, and was present with his chief in the hand-to-hand conflict between Nelson's barge and that of the Spanish commodore, and commanded the *Ganges* at Copenhagen; and most celebrated of all, Captain Thomas Masterman Hardy, into whose arms the great admiral fell when he received his mortal wound, and whom he loved so deeply, that, when dying, he said to him, "Kiss me, Hardy."

These were some only of the officers which their master moulded into congenial form, and whose proudest boast it was to be his disciples. The names of not less distinguished seamen are too numerous to do more than specify the chiefest among them. These were Sir Robert Calder, flag-captain to Jervis at St. Vincent, who received rather hard treatment after his action with a French squadron on the 22nd July, for the great victory of Trafalgar, a few months later, had set up a standard of success such as few admirals could hope to attain; Sir Richard Strachan, who gave a better account of the enemy on the 4th November following that great day; Sir Roger Curtis, Lord Howe's flag-captain on the 1st June; Sir James (afterwards Lord) Saumarez, an officer of the highest distinction, Nelson's second in command at the Nile, who, after his repulse by Admiral Linois at Algeciras, on the 7th July, 1801, took a handsome revenge on the enemy a few days later; and Sir Richard Goodwin Keats, captain of the *Superb*, the true hero of that memorable encounter, who also commanded her when she carried Sir John Duckworth's flag, and was altogether one of the best officers of his day. Also should be mentioned Sir John Borlase Warren, who long commanded a squadron of frigates, and, in 1798, defeated a French fleet off the coast of Ireland, and took the *Hoche*, 80, and four frigates; Admiral Owen, who, when captain of the *Immortalité*, was equally energetic and successful in counteracting the efforts of Napoleon's invasion flotilla to cross the Channel; Sir Edward Hamilton, the hero of the recapture of the *Hermione*; Sir Nesbit Willoughby, a seaman of the same grand fighting stock, who had the distinction of having been, perhaps, more often, and certainly more desperately, wounded than any officer in the service, but survived all the sanguinary fighting in the East and West Indies to receive the honour of knighthood in his old age; and finally, Sir James Lucas Yeo, who has a long record of vessels cut out and boarded, forts stormed, as at El Muros, on the coast of Spain, and who effected the conquest of French Guiana.

CHAPTER VII.

Lord Exmouth's Victory at Algiers—Details of the Action—Some particulars of the Queen Charlotte, Canopus, and Implacable—The Battle of Navarino—Defeat and Destruction of the Turkish Fleet—Anecdotes of the Battle—The Syrian War—Capture of Sidon—Bombardment of Acre.

THE British Government having resolved to punish the Dey of Algiers, whose atrocities had aroused the indignation of Europe, Admiral Lord Exmouth, so well known in these pages as Sir Edward Fleetwood Pellew, sailed on the 28th July, 1816, from Plymouth Sound with the following ships:—

100.	*Queen Charlotte*	{ Admiral Lord Exmouth, G.C.B. { Captain James Brisbane, C.B.	74 {	*Minden* *Albion*	Captain William Paterson. ,, John Coode.
			50	*Leander*	,, Edward Chetham, C.B.
98.	*Impregnable*	{ Rear-Admiral David Milne. { Captain Edward Bruce, C.B.	40 {	*Severn* *Glasgow*	,, Aylmer. ,, Anthony Maitland.
74.	*Superb*	Captain Charles Ekins.	36 {	*Granicus* *Hebrus*	,, William Wise. ,, Edward Palmer, C.B.

Also four bomb-vessels, and five brigs.

At Gibraltar Lord Exmouth found a Dutch squadron, and the officer commanding, Vice-Admiral Van de Cappellen, having solicited permission to assist in the praiseworthy task of bringing the Dey to his senses, Lord Exmouth accepted his services. The fleet, strengthened by four Dutch 40-gun frigates and two smaller vessels, carrying respectively 30 and 18 guns, five British gun-boats, and an explosion vessel, arrived in sight of Algiers on the 27th August.

Upon the various batteries on the north side of the city, including a battery over the north gate, were mounted, says James, about 80 pieces of cannon and six or eight mortars; but the shoalness of the water would scarcely admit the approach of a heavy ship within reach of them. Between the north wall of the city and the commencement of the pier, which is about 250 yards in length, and connects the town with the lighthouse, were about 20 guns; at the north mole-head stood a semicircular battery of two tiers of guns, about 44 in all; and to the southward, and nearly in line with the pier, was the Lighthouse Battery, of three tiers of guns, 48 in all. Then came a battery, also of three tiers, called the Eastern Battery, mounting 66 guns. This was flanked by four other batteries, of two tiers each, mounting altogether 60 guns;

and on the mole-head were two long 68-pounders, the other guns being 32, 24, and 18-pounders. Then there was the Fishmarket Battery of 15 guns in three tiers, and between that and the southern extremity of the city were two batteries of four and five guns each. Beyond the city, in this direction, were a castle and three other batteries, mounting between them 60 or 70 guns.

Thus the defences of Algiers were of a formidable character, and the Dey, having received notice of the intended attack, had brought in from the country about 40,000 men to serve the guns and defend the city to the last extremity. In addition there were four 44-gun frigates, five corvettes, mounting between 24 and 30 guns, and over 30 mortar boats. In all it was said over 1,000 guns could be brought into play on the sea and land faces of the fortifications.

Before noon on the 27th August, Lord Exmouth sent a demand for the abolition of Christian slavery and the release of all European slaves, as well as of the British consul, and two boats' crews of the *Prometheus*, detained by the Dey, and receiving no reply, the fleet bore up for the attack in the order already prescribed. At 2.35 the *Queen Charlotte* anchored with springs, about 50 yards from the mole-head. Ahead of her, rather on the port bow, lay the *Leander*, with her after guns on the starboard side bearing upon the mole and her foremost ones upon the Fishmarket Battery. Ahead of the *Leander* lay the *Severn*, with the whole of her starboard guns bearing on the Fishmarket Battery, and close to the *Severn* was the *Glasgow*, with her port guns bearing on the town batteries.

Astern of the *Queen Charlotte* was the *Superb*, with her starboard broadside bearing upon the heavy battery next to that on the mole-head. Not being sufficiently advanced when the firing commenced to take up her proper station astern of the *Superb*, the *Impregnable* was obliged to bring to considerably outside of the line of bearing within which the attacking force had been ordered to assemble, and thus lay exposed at the distance of about 400 yards, as well to the Lighthouse Battery of three tiers, towards which she soon sprang her starboard broadside, as to the Eastern Battery. Observing the open space between the *Impregnable* and her second ahead, the *Superb*, the *Minden* stood on and took up a position about her own length astern of the latter. The *Albion*, following, brought up within her own length of the *Minden*, which passed her stream-cable out of the gun-room port to the *Albion's* bow, and hove the two ships together. In this way the eight heaviest ships of the fleet took their stations: the *Queen Charlotte, Superb, Minden, Albion, Impregnable*, from the mole-head in a north-easterly direction, and the *Leander*, *Severn*, and *Glasgow* from the Fish-market Battery in a curved direction to the south-west.

The station assigned to the Dutch squadron was against the batteries to the southward of the city, and the Dutch admiral anchored his flagship, the *Melampus*, with her jib-boom over the taffrail of the *Glasgow*. Two Dutch frigates anchored successively astern, and the remaining Dutch frigate further out, while the corvettes kept under way. The *Hebrus* got becalmed by the heavy cannonade, and was obliged to anchor a little without the line, on the *Queen Charlotte's* port quarter, but Captain Wise anchored his frigate, the *Granicus*, in a space scarcely exceeding her own length, between the *Queen Charlotte* and *Superb*, and bore a prominent part in the battle.

The sloops *Heron*, *Britomart*, *Prometheus*, and *Cordelia* remained under way, and the *Mutine* anchored on the port bow of the *Impregnable*. The four bomb-vessels took post at a range of about 2,000 yards from the enemy's works, as did also the battering flotilla, commanded by Captain Frederick Thomas Michell, consisting of thirty-five gunboats, mortar-boats, launches with carronades, rocket-boats, barges, and yawls.

Scarcely had the flagship anchored than a gun was fired at her, to which she replied by opening fire from her starboard batteries, all the ships of the British line following motions as their guns were brought to bear. So terrible were the broadsides of the three-decker, that at the third discharge she had demolished the south end of the mole, when she sprang her broadside until it bore upon the batteries over the town gate leading into the mole.

The *Leander*, also, by her accurate and rapid fire, destroyed the Algerine gunboats and row-galleys, whereby their intention to board the British frigates was frustrated. The admiral, having determined to set on fire the enemy's frigate moored across the mole, about one hundred and fifty yards from her, signalled the *Leander* to cease firing and sent his barge, under the command of Lieutenant Richards—who was accompanied by Major Fosset and Lieutenant Wolrige of the marines, and Midshipman Henry McClintock—to accomplish the duty. Lord Exmouth also sent a rocket-boat, commanded by Midshipman Symes, who, his lordship says, "although forbidden, was led by his ardent spirit to follow in support of the barge." The boat being flat-bottomed, could not keep up with the barge, and became exposed to a heavy fire that wounded Mr. Symes and killed another young officer and nine of the crew. Meanwhile Lieutenant Richards had succeeded in boarding and setting fire to the Algerine frigate, and returned to the flagship with the loss of only two men killed. Soon after four the burning ship drifted out to the *Queen Charlotte*, which had to shift her berth to let her pass.

Shortly after this, Admiral Milne sent word to the commander-in-chief that the *Impregnable* had lost 150 men killed and wounded, and requested that a frigate might be sent to divert the enemy's fire. The *Glasgow* thereupon went to his assistance, and became exposed to a severe raking fire from the Fishmarket and other batteries, which dismounted two guns and did other serious injuries. The *Leander* also suffered so severely from their fire that at 7 P.M. she brought her broadside to bear upon them by running a hawser out to the *Severn*. About this time all the ships and vessels within the harbour had been set on fire by the mortar boats and flotilla, and the flames communicated to the arsenal and storehouses on the mole, and the city also was set on fire by the shells from the bomb vessels.

About 9 P.M. the explosion vessel was run ashore close under the semicircular battery near the lighthouse, and her one hundred and forty-three barrels of powder were exploded, which added to the horrors of the scene of destruction. The fire of the fleet was continued with unabated vigour until about 10 P.M. when the upper tier of the batteries on the mole being in a state of dilapidation, the fire from the lower tiers nearly silenced, and the ammunition of the attacking ships reduced to a very small quantity, the *Queen Charlotte* cut her cables and springs, and stood out before a light air which had fortunately just sprung up from the land. The remaining British ships did the same, but owing to their disabled state they made very slow progress, and the *Leander*, *Superb*, and *Impregnable* suffered much in consequence from the raking fire of a fort at the upper angle of the city. Before 2 A.M. on the 28th, the allied fleet was anchored out of reach of shot or shells. At this time a terrific storm of thunder, lightning and rain broke over the city, which, with the arsenal and storehouses, was blazing fiercely.

The British loss in achieving this memorable success was 128 killed, including 15 officers, and 690 wounded, among whom were 57 officers, two mortally. The Dutch sustained a loss of 13 killed and 52 wounded. The greatest sufferer was the *Impregnable*, which had 50 slain and 160 wounded; next came the *Leander*, with 17 and 118 respectively; the *Queen Charlotte*, eight and 131; *Superb*, eight and 84; the *Granicus*, 16 and 40; and the *Glasgow*, 10 and 37. The expenditure of powder and round shot was prodigious, each of the five ships-of-the-line and *Leander* using between 20,000 and 30,000 pounds of powder, and between 3,680 round shot on the part of the *Leander*, and 6,730 by the *Impregnable*.

At daylight Lord Exmouth sent a note to the Dey repeating his demand, to which that potentate, now thoroughly humbled, expressed his adhesion, and as a principal result, 1,200 Christian slaves were given up.

For this memorable feat of arms Lord Exmouth was created a viscount, Admiral Milne received the ribbon of the Bath, and the captains of the ships-of-the-line and frigates the C.B. All the first lieutenants were promoted, and also Lieutenant Fleming, commanding the explosion vessel.

Some details of the *Queen Charlotte*, one of the historic ships in the Navy, will be of interest here. Up to the close of the last year (1891) the *Queen Charlotte*, Lord Exmouth's flagship at the attack on Algiers, was retained on the active list of the Navy under the name of the *Excellent*, in succession to the 74-gun ship of that name which carried Collingwood's pennant at the battle of St. Vincent. As she possesses much interest therefore to the present generation, to whom she is so well known, some particulars of her dimensions should be placed on record in this work.

The *Queen Charlotte* was laid down at Deptford in 1803, and launched in 1810. She was 190 feet in length on the gun-deck, 52 feet 4 inches beam, and measured 2,289 tons. Her displacement was 3,994 tons, so that this first-rate was about the same size as our modern second-class cruisers of the *Severn* class, and little more than one-fourth that of our newest first-rates. The ship was, in dimensions and form, a reproduction of the earlier and still more famous *Queen Charlotte*, laid down in 1780, launched in 1789, and burnt off Leghorn in 1800. Thus in the *Excellent* we have a facsimile (except for later alterations in her head and stern) of Lord Howe's flagship on June 1st, 1794.

Among other famous ships in existence at the present time are the still older *Canopus*, one of Nelson's prizes at the battle of the Nile, and among the six which reached Plymouth in safety. In the French navy this 80-gun ship was known as the *Franklin*, and she had a narrow escape of being destroyed when the *Orient* blew up, as she caught fire in several places from the burning wreck falling on board her. During the battle the *Franklin* was first engaged by the *Leander*, and subsequently sustained the attack of the 74's, *Defiance* and *Swiftsure*, and she only surrendered when her main and mizen masts had been shot away, and more than half her crew had fallen. The *Canopus* took part in Duckworth's memorable engagement with a French squadron in the

West Indies, on which occasion she bore the flag of Rear-Admiral Louis, and took a prominent part in the action, losing eight officers and men killed, and 22 wounded. So admirable were her lines considered by naval architects that the *Canopus* was long the model on which our finest two-deckers were built. This ship, with the *Implacable*, has been laid up in ordinary at Devonport up to the year 1892.

The *Implacable* took part in the battle of Trafalgar, where she was known as the *Duguay-Trouin*, 74. She formed part of Rear-Admiral Dumanoir's squadron, which escaped, only to be brought to action and captured by Sir Richard Strachan on the 2nd November following the great battle. The *Duguay-Trouin*, to call her by her name at this time, was reduced to the condition of a wreck, and lost 150 men killed and wounded. With the *Scipion*, also captured in this action, she was the only one of the four prizes that went to sea.

There is also in existence at this time (January, 1892) the *Foudroyant*, 74, built in 1798. This ship bears the same name as a French prize, which was long commanded by Captain Jervis (afterwards Earl St. Vincent), and was present in Keppel's action with Count d'Orvilliers on the 27th August, 1779, when the *Victory* bore the flag of the commander-in-chief. In 1780, the *Foudroyant*, under the same officer, engaged and captured the *Pegase*, of 74 guns and 750 men. Not less famous than the victor of St. Vincent was the captain who succeeded him in command of the *Foudroyant* —Captain Duncan, the hero of Camperdown, who commanded her till he attained flag-rank in September, 1789. The new *Foudroyant* was Nelson's flag-ship at Naples in 1799, on his return from attaining his great victory of the Nile, when he shifted into her from the *Vanguard*. The following is a list of the ships over seventy years of age still in existence:—*Victory*, 1765; *Foudroyant*, 1798; *Eagle*, *Hibernia*, 1804; *Implacable* (ex-*Duguay-Trouin*), 1805; *Leonidas*, 1807; *Conquestador*, *Excellent* (ex-*Queen Charlotte*), 1810; *Forte* (ex-*Pembroke*), 1812; *Cornwall* (ex-*Wellesley*), 1813; *Cornwallis*, *Briton*, 1814; *St. Vincent*, 1815; *Trincomalee*, *Myrtle* (ex-*Malabar*), 1819; *Pitt* (ex-*Camperdown*), 1820; and *Ganges*, 1821.

For an interval of eleven years the Navy did not fire a shot in Europe, but in 1827 took place what was called "the untoward affair" of Navarino. But looking at the results of that achievement, all lovers of Greece, and indeed of humanity, must consider that it was a very desirable event, and never did our sailors perform a nobler service than when they destroyed the naval power of Turkey at that memorable action, and freed the Greeks from a hateful and barbarous thraldom.

Ibrahim Pasha, commanding the fleet as well as the land forces of the Sultan, broke the terms of an armistice he had agreed to with Sir Edward Codrington, the British admiral, who prevented him from relieving Patras and effecting a junction between his land and sea forces. Ibrahim then made sail for Navarino, where he landed his troops, and committed the greatest atrocities on the unhappy people of the Morea. He was followed by the British fleet, which, on the 13th October, was joined by the Russian squadron, and, on the following day, arrived off Navarino, where the squadrons of England, France, and Russia were united under Codrington's command. The combined fleet consisted of the following ships:—

ENGLISH.

84	*Asia*	Vice-Admiral Sir Edward Codrington / Captain Edward Curzon	42	*Dartmouth*	Captain Thomas Fellowes, C.B.
			28	*Talbot*	,, Hon. Frederick Spencer
74	*Genoa*	Commodore Walter Bathurst	18	*Rose*	Commander Lewis Davies
	Albion	Captain John A. Ommanney		*Musquito*	,, George Bohun Martin
50	*Glasgow*	,, Hon. James Ashley Maude	10	*Brisk*	,, Hon. William Anson
48	*Cambrian*	,, Gawen Wm. Hamilton, C.B.		*Philomel*	,, Viscount Ingestre

FRENCH.

74	*Scipion*	Captain Milius
	Tridente	,, Maurice
	Breslau	,, De la Bretonnière
60	*Sirène*	Rear-Admiral H. de Rigny
44	*Armide*	Captain Hugon

RUSSIAN.

74	*Azof*	Rear-Admiral Count de Heyden
	Gargonte	
	Ezekiel	
	Alexander Newsky	
50	*Constantine*	
48	*Provesky*	
	Elena	
	Castor	

The Ottoman and Egyptian fleets, according to the statement made by the Capitan Bey's secretary, numbered 65 sail. Of these two were Turkish 84-gun ships, one 76-gun ship, fifteen 48-gun frigates, eighteen corvettes, and four brigs. The Egyptian squadron consisted of two 64-gun ships, eight corvettes, eight brigs, and five fire-vessels. Admiral Codrington, however, in his general order to the fleet, placed the total strength of the enemy at eighty-one ships of war. The comparative force in guns has been placed at 1,324 on the part of the allies, and 2,240 of the Ottoman fleet.

Like a gallant seaman, the British admiral, who had commanded the *Blake* at the bombardment of Flushing and the *Orion* at Trafalgar, proposed to take to himself the post of greatest danger. In his instructions to the allied commanders, he ordered the French admiral to "place his squadron across" the Egyptian ships, and then proceeded:—"The vessel coming after them appears to be the vessel of the line bearing the admiral's flag at the main-mast. I propose placing the *Asia* athwart it, and the *Genoa* and *Albion* astern and near the *Asia*. I desire that his Excellency Count Heyden will have the goodness to cast anchor at the stern of the English vessels. The Russian frigates will then be able to occupy the Turkish vessels near and at the stern of the Russian vessels of the line. The English frigates will form a line before those of the Turk, which may happen to be in the west part of the port, athwart the English vessels of the line; and the French frigates will form themselves in the same manner in order to occupy the Turkish frigates who may be alongside the French line-of-battle ships. If there should be time before hostilities are commenced with the Turkish fleet, the vessels are to be moored with a spring on each cable; not a single cannon-shot shall be fired by the combined fleet until the signal has been given, but if they be fired upon by a Turkish vessel, the latter may be fired upon in order that it may be immediately destroyed. The corvettes and brigs are placed under the command of the captain of the *Dartmouth*, in order to keep the fire-ships in check, and continue them in such a position that they can by no means disturb the combined fleet. In case a general engagement should take place, in the midst of the confusion which is calculated to arise in such a case, every one should remember these words of Lord Nelson, 'No captain can be better placed than when his vessel is alongside one of the enemy.'"

Though the harbour of Navarino is six miles in circumference, the entrance is only about six hundred yards in width, owing to the island of Sphacteria, which stretches across its mouth. On the right-hand side of this passage stood a fortress, mounting 125 guns, and on the extremity of the island, almost opposite to it, was another battery, while a third, at the northern end of the island, also commanded the harbour.

On the 20th October, the weather being fine, the combined squadrons stood towards Navarino. The Turko-Egyptian fleet, says Sir Edward Codrington in his despatch, were at anchor, moored in the form of a crescent, with springs on their cables, the larger ones presenting their broadsides towards the centre, the smaller ones in succession within them, filling in the intervals. The English and French squadrons formed the weather or starboard line, and the Russian division the lee line.

Sir Edward Codrington led in with the *Asia*, and anchored close alongside a ship-of-the-line, when she was moored with thirty fathoms on each cable. The *Genoa* came next, and the *Albion* followed. The *Asia's* opponent was the flagship of the

Capitan Bey, the *Genoa* anchored close to another ship-of-the-line, and the *Albion* alongside a double-banked frigate. The four ships to windward, part of the Egyptian squadron, were allotted to Rear-Admiral de Rigny, and those to leeward, in the bight of the crescent, were to mark the stations of the Russian squadron, the ships-of-the-line crossing those of the English line, and being followed up by their own frigates. The French frigate *Armide* was directed to place herself alongside the outermost frigate on the port hand entering the harbour, and the *Cambrian*, *Glasgow*, and *Talbot* next to her, and abreast of the *Asia*, *Genoa*, and *Albion*. The *Dartmouth*, with the *Musquito*, *Rose*, *Brisk*, and *Philomel*, was to look after six fire-vessels at the entrance of the harbour.

The Turkish admiral did not witness this anchorage of the allied fleet without alarm, and his ships were ready for all eventualities, the guns being loaded to their muzzles, and the crews ready at their quarters. On the fleet entering, the commandant of a fort sent a boat with a message that "as Ibrahim Pasha had given no orders or permission for the allied fleet to enter, it was requested that they would again put to sea." To this demand Sir Edward Codrington made a reply befitting a British admiral, "that he was not come to receive orders, but to give them, and that if any shot were fired at the allied ships, he would destroy the Turkish fleet."

All as yet remained peaceful, though the air was charged with electricity, when suddenly musketry fire was heard in the direction of the *Dartmouth*. This arose from the Turks firing on the boat sent, under the direction of Lieutenant Smyth, to one of the fire-ships from the *Dartmouth*, to request that they would remove a little further from the allied fleet. The Turks, apprehensive that force would be used, fired upon the *Dartmouth's* boat, when Lieutenant Fitzroy and several of the crew were killed. The *Dartmouth* immediately opened a defensive fire to cover the boat; the *Sirène*, Admiral de Rigny's ship, joined in the affray with musketry only; one of the Egyptian ships fired a shot, which was the first round shot discharged, and struck the *Sirène*, "which, of course," as the vice-admiral states in his letter, "brought on a return," and thus very shortly afterwards the battle became general.

The *Asia*, although placed alongside the Capitan Bey's ship, was even nearer to Moharem Bey's, the Egyptian commodore, and since his ship did not fire at the *Asia*, although the action was begun to windward, neither did the *Asia* fire at her. Moharem Bey indeed sent a message that he would not fire at all, and therefore no hostility took place between Moharem Bey and the English admiral for some time after the *Asia* had returned the fire of the Capitan Bey. In the meantime, however, the pilot who went to interpret to Moharem Bey the admiral's desire to avoid bloodshed, was killed by his people in the boat alongside, and his ship soon afterwards fired into the *Asia*, and brought upon herself the terrible broadsides of the starboard guns of the British flagship. The action now became general, and was well maintained by the Turks, but at the end of four hours, the Ottoman fleet had been nearly destroyed. Each ship, as she became disabled, was deserted by the crew, after having been set on fire, and the frequent explosions rendered the situation of the allied fleet dangerous in the extreme. Captain Fellowes cleared away the fireships, and saved the French admiral's ship, the *Sirène*, from being burnt. "The *Cambrian, Glasgow* and *Talbot*," says the admiral, "following the fine example of Captain Hugon, of the *Armide*, who was opposed to the leading frigate of that line, effectually destroyed their opponents and also silenced the batteries."

During the action between the Capitan Bey's ship and the *Asia*, the latter's stern became exposed to a raking fire from a frigate, from which she sustained considerable damage. About three o'clock her opponent's cable was cut by a shot or slipped, and she dropped to leeward, when the flagship engaged Moharem Bey's ship and his second ahead. The former was silenced and disabled, and the latter, catching fire, burnt to the water's edge and blew up. So rapid was the *Asia's* fire, that Admiral de Rigny compared the noise of her shot against her adversary's side "to the united efforts of all the caulkers of England and France." Sir Edward Codrington, speaking of the crushing effect of his guns, says that the Egyptian flagship was "effectually destroyed by the *Asia's* fire, sharing the same fate as his brother admiral on the starboard side, and falling to leeward a complete wreck." The inner ships of the enemy's line were now enabled to rake the *Asia*, which suffered severely in consequence. Her mizen-mast was shot away, several guns were disabled, and her crew began to fall fast, the admiral himself being struck by a musket-ball, which knocked his watch out of his pocket. During the action Sir Edward Codrington set a bright example of coolness and courage. "He stood the whole time," writes one who was present, "on the poop constantly shouting to encourage the brave fellows around him, and waving in the air a white hat he wore. It was astonishing how he escaped death in the exposed position he had assumed."

The French and Russian squadrons displayed not less resolution than our ships. The boats of the *Dartmouth* and *Rose* towed away a fireship which threatened the destruction of the *Scipion*, and the *Sirène*, whose fire set in flames a ship she was engaging, was saved from a like fate by the *Dartmouth*, to which a sailor swam with a rope. The action came to an end about five o'clock, when the greater portion of the Turko-Egyptian fleet was in flames, and the scene of devastation that met the eye testified to the terrible nature of the allied fire and the devotion of the Mussulman crews, who rather than any of their ships should fall into the hands of the Christians, set fire to some that were efficient.

The British loss in the action at Navarino, was 75 killed, including Commodore Bathurst, of the *Genoa*, the master and officer commanding the marines on board the *Asia*, and 13 other officers; and 197 wounded, among whom were Commander Campbell of the *Albion*, and 27 other officers.

Commodore Walter Bathurst was wounded early in the action by a splinter, which knocked off his hat and slightly tore his face. Shortly afterwards a shot took off the skirts of his coat, and at length a grape shot, entering his side, passed through his body and lodged on the opposite side of the ship. Commodore Bathurst survived for eleven hours in great suffering. About midnight, shortly before he expired, the dying seaman was visited by the admiral, who said, "Well, Wattie, if you die, you die gloriously."

"I know I shall die, and that soon," was the reply; "but, Codrington," he added, "I hope you will remember my officers."

The admiral promised to attend to this request, and very soon the veteran seaman passed away. As Sir William Napier, the historian of the "Peninsula War," says in his panegyric of Sir John Moore: "If glory be a distinction for such a man, death is not a leveller."

Commodore Bathurst, who died at the age of sixty-eight years, was buried with the pomp of a military funeral at Plymouth, amid universal demonstrations of respect.

The *Genoa* suffered most in the starboard quarter from the oblique elevated fire of the Turkish ships, their shot generally striking below the water-ways of the main-deck, and cutting through the upper deck. To this circumstance the great loss of life among the marines on the poop is attributed, ten men having been killed at that point before a shot was fired by the *Genoa*. The few marines left with their gallant officer, Lieutenant Miller, were at length ordered down to the quarter-deck.

The *Genoa* was struck by a stone shot, weighing about 102 pounds, which entered the lower deck, five feet above the water, leaving a gap that puzzled the carpenters of the squadron to patch up. It killed four men, and afterwards split in pieces on the deck. The *Albion* was also exposed to the fire of a cluster of ships, and after repulsing an attempt to board by a 64-gun ship, a party of the seamen boarded in turn, and captured the latter. The prize was, however, soon relinquished, as she was discovered to be on fire, and she presently blew up. After engaging others of the enemy's ships, the *Albion*, towards dusk, stood out to clear herself from the blazing mass. The *Dartmouth* and *Rose* were chiefly instrumental in destroying four of the fire-ships.

The three line-of-battle ships were the chief sufferers, the *Asia* being first, with 19 killed and 57 wounded; then the *Genoa*, with 26 and 33 respectively, and the *Albion*, 10 and 50. These three ships and the *Talbot*, which was closely engaged with a 64-gun ship, were sent to England after repairing their defects at Malta.

The French squadron had 43 killed and 133 wounded, and the Russians 59 slain and 139 wounded. The enemy had sixty ships destroyed, including one sail-of-the-line, three double-banked frigates, nine other frigates, and twenty-two corvettes. Their killed alone were estimated at 3,000.

Honours were profusely distributed for Navarino, more liberally indeed than for some greater engagements. Sir Edward Codrington received the Grand Cross of the Bath, and the captains, the Companionship of that Order. All the commanders serving at Navarino were promoted to captains, and the first lieutenants and senior mates also received promotion. The allied powers honoured Codrington, Nicholas sending him the Cross of St. George, and the King of France that of St. Louis. The former also wrote him the following handsome letter of acknowledgment:—

"St. Petersburg, November 8th, 1827.

"Vice-Admiral Codrington,—You have achieved a victory for which civilised Europe ought to be doubly grateful to you. The memorable battle of Navarino, and the bold manœuvres which preceded it, evince to the world not only the extent of the zeal of three great powers in favour of a cause the noble character of which is still more heightened by their own disinterestedness, but also prove what can be effected by firmness, though opposed to numbers, and what a well-directed valour can accomplish against blind courage, with whatever force that courage may be supported. Your name from this time forward belongs to posterity. By praise I should but weaken the glory which surrounds it. But I must offer to you a brilliant mark of the gratitude and esteem which you have inspired in Russia. With this view I send to you herewith the Military Order of St. George. The Russian Navy is proud of having obtained your commendation at Navarino, and on my part I feel the most lively pleasure in thus assuring you of the sentiments of consideration which I entertain towards you.

(Signed) "NICHOLAS."

Some anecdotes of the officers and men engaged in this famous battle, gathered from the *Naval and Military Magazine* of that day, will doubtless be of interest.

LIEUTENANT AND SIGNAL BOY.

Sir Edward Codrington offered, as we have said, a conspicuous example of gallantry to the fleet, and it was the marvel of all that he escaped with his life. It is related of this officer, who commanded the *Orion* at Trafalgar, that on the morning of that memorable day, as the *Defence*, 74, which had been one of the look-out squadron, was taking her place in the line of battle, and her commander, Captain (afterwards Sir George) Hope, exchanged the usual compliments, the latter, pointing to the enemy's fleet, observed, "They should be with them after dinner time."

"Yes," replied Captain Codrington, "and I have some tough mutton ready for them," a joke which tickled the fancies of the gallant tars who were as light-hearted at their quarters as if they were proceeding on "liberty" ashore.

When Commodore Bathurst was laid in bed after his mortal wounds had been dressed, his leg being in an uneasy position, he called the surgeon and requested him in a tone of apology to move the limb, saying, "I'm a little fidgety just now, but I hope you will excuse it." On Captain Moore of the Marines being brought down wounded, the Commodore, recognising his voice, exclaimed, "Ah, Moore, is that you?"

"Yes," said Captain Moore, "I'm wounded."

"Ah," replied the dying officer, "*fortune de guerre*."

Captain Moore soon followed his lamented chief, and was buried near Mount Etna, in Sicily.

Mr. Frederick Grey, one of the midshipmen of the *Genoa*, had his arm nearly severed from his body by a shot, and it was found necessary to take it off at the socket. On reaching the cock-pit he called out to the surgeon, "Bear a hand here, my hearty; make haste, will you? The fun is not half over yet, and I must have another touch at the fellows." He was not, however, suffered to go on deck again. His brother, Mr. Herbert Grey, midshipman, was struck in the left leg by a piece of langridge,* but escaped amputation. This young officer was in immediate attendance on Commodore Bathurst, and assisted in carrying him below when he received his mortal wound.

A seaman, having his leg shattered by a cannon-ball, underwent amputation with the greatest indifference. When the limb was taken off, it was thrown overboard, upon which Jack, after an objurgatory reflection on the eyes of his officious friend, called out jocularly, "I'll complain of you to the captain; although you were ordered to throw my leg overboard, you had no right to throw my shoe with it." A marine of

---

* Langridge is a kind of shot consisting of various fragments of iron bound together, and has been long disused in the Navy.

the name of Hill, who was stationed on the poop of the *Genoa*, had both his arms shot off, when he turned to Commander Dickson, who stood near him, and said, with the utmost coolness, "I hope that you'll allow, sir, that I have done my duty." After the fatigue of the action, one of the officers lay down to rest himself on a chest on which the poor mutilated fellow was sitting. Presently he was aroused by hearing some one near him singing, and recognising the voice, exclaimed with surprise, "What, Hill, is that you singing?" "Yes, sir," answered Hill, "I'm trying what I can do at ballad singing now I have lost my arms." The poor fellow, who was only twenty-one, died of his wounds in hospital.

Another marine in the same ship had one of his arms shot off in the heat of the action. He coolly took up the severed limb and laid it on the shelf-piece over him, saying, "There's an example for you all."

Here is a comic anecdote. After the action, an Irishman, named Phelan, who was the cook's mate of the *Genoa*, was observed to skip about with the most ludicrous manifestations of joy. On being questioned, he shouted out, "Oh, by the powers, I'm so glad the villains haven't spoilt the coppers; never a shot has touched them."

There were several women on board the ships, as was the custom in the Navy in those days, and they were eminently useful in tending to the wounded. During the action, two Greeks, who were chained to a gun in one of the vessels which blew up, escaped and swam to the *Genoa*. Immediately on getting on board they set to work at the guns, and behaved with great gallantry. Four boats were sunk alongside the *Genoa*, and two on the booms were very much damaged.

The two Turkish line-of-battle ships which had been engaged by the *Asia* and *Genoa*, presented after the battle the most deplorable spectacle. It is said that each of them had on board about 800 men, and very few escaped being killed or wounded. The *Albion* was at one time ordered to destroy these ships, but the order was countermanded. Their state baffles description—beams severed, decks fallen in, and generally so riven with the iron hail that not a space could anywhere be seen free from shot-holes. The Turkish admiral, on going on board the *Asia* after the battle, remarked, with Oriental impassiveness, "My head will pay for this."

The scene when hostilities ceased was described as awful and impressive. At twenty minutes after six in the evening, the enemy on all sides were completely beaten, and, with the exception of two line-of-battle ships, one frigate and a few small vessels were either on shore, sunk, burnt, or burning. Night threw her mantle over the dreadful scene, and served as a pall to hundreds of dead or dying victims. The wind had totally sunk and left a perfect calm, and not a sound was heard save that of a few random shots fired at intervals from the guns in the forts, and which added to rather than diminished the solemnity of the scene. The harbour, which had but a few hours before presented the most animated picture imaginable, was shrouded in darkness and filled with desolation, which was rendered occasionally visible by the momentary bursts of light from the burning vessels.

The smaller vessels of the British squadron distinguished themselves not less than the ships of the line; this was more particularly the case with the corvette *Rose*, the brig *Philomel*, and the cutter *Hind*, Lieutenant Robb. An officer says in his letter, "The *Dartmouth* fired first, and, I believe, the little *Philomel* next, who very soon blew up her fire-ship, and then sunk a twelve-gun brig; she then opened her fire on a frigate and two corvettes, and it really was a miracle she was not blown out of the water, but the Turks fired very high. A Russian frigate, which was standing in, seeing the perilous condition of the gallant little *Philomel*, ran in between her and her powerful opponents, and silenced them. It is supposed the Turks lost at least 10,000 men. They chained their men to their guns and, and as their wounded became useless, threw them overboard. Not less gallant was the behaviour of the *Rose* corvette. Her commanding officer, Commander Lewis Davies, engaged and silenced two Turkish corvettes, thereby relieving the French frigate *Armide*, which was exposed to the concentrated fire of five of the enemy's ships. Captain Davies was in the chains of a fire-ship at the moment she blew up, and was hurled into his own boat without receiving any considerable injury. His behaviour excited the admiration of everyone in the allied squadron, and Admiral De Rigny honourably mentioned him in his despatches.

Lieutenant Robb, of the *Hind*, also excited universal commendation by the distinguished gallantry with which he fought his little craft. The *Hind* was a cutter of one hundred and sixty tons, mounting 10 six-pounder carronades, and manned with a crew of 30 men; she was the tender of the flag-ship, and had been entrusted by the admiral to the command of Lieutenant John Robb, who had entered the service in 1812, and had distinguished himself at the bombardment of Algiers, by Lord Exmouth, in 1816. The *Hind* had been sent with despatches to Zante, and only arrived off Navarino as the allied squadrons were entering the port. Lieutenant Robb immediately cleared for action, got springs on her cables, and followed into the harbour. With the greatest coolness and gallantry he anchored his little craft with her broadside bearing on the stern of a Turkish frigate, within forty yards, and opened a steady raking fire from his foremost guns. Not a shot was thrown away, and the havoc he wrought was considerable on his great antagonist, which was unable to return his fire. The *Hind* did not, however, escape without injury, for she was exposed to the fire of a corvette on one bow, a brig on the other, and a frigate some distance on the quarter; in about three-quarters of an hour her cable was shot away, and until she dropped her second anchor, she drifted between the corvette and brig, and for half an hour kept up a fire from both broadsides upon her opponents, until the Turkish brig blew up. The action was then continued with the corvette for about a quarter of an hour, when the cutter's last cable was shot away. As he could no longer maintain his position, nor get a gun to bear effectually on the enemy, and finding his men suffering much from the fire which he could not return, Lieutenant Robb sent his crew below, only remaining on deck himself to observe and seize upon the first opportunity which should present itself of using his guns again with effect. After drifting about in the hottest part of the action for a considerable time, the *Hind* at length ran her bow into one of the main-deck ports of a large Turkish frigate; the men were instantly called, and notwithstanding the disparity of numbers, they succeeded in repulsing, with loss, the repeated attempts made by the enemy to board. The Turks, not meeting with success, tried another method; to the number of about sixty they crowded into a large boat astern, with the intention of boarding, while their companions engaged the attention of the handful of Britons, who were numerically too weak to be divided into two parties. But Lieutenant Robb was equal to the occasion. With the utmost coolness and presence of mind, he loaded some of his guns with grape and canister to the muzzle, and as they bore on the advancing boat fired two of them. The aim was true, and the boat with its occupants disappeared; almost at this instant his heroic exertions were rewarded with success, for the cutter drifted clear of the frigate. Of her small crew of 30 she had half killed and wounded; among the former was her mate, and among the latter a midshipman. Three guns were split and dismounted, twenty-three shots had passed through her hull, and her spars, sails, and riggings were cut to pieces. It is related of the assistant surgeon that he was dressing a wound, when, hearing Lieutenant Robb's call for the men to repel boarders, he immediately threw down his instruments, and seizing a pike, helped to drive off the enemy. This being done he went below and resumed his surgical operations.

Sir Edward Codrington issued a general order to the fleet, dated 24th October, in which, after thanking all engaged for their "gallant and steady conduct in the battle of the 20th," he observes that there is no instance of the fleet of any one country showing more complete union of spirit and of action than was exhibited by the squadrons of the three allied powers, and attributes the glorious result to the bright example of the French and Russian admirals, and the cordial co-operation and assistance afforded to each by the several squadrons. "Such union of spirit and of purpose," he adds, "such coolness and bravery under fire, and such consequent precision in the use of their guns, ensured a victory over the well-prepared arrangements of greatly superior numbers. Out of a fleet composed of eighty-one men-of-war, there remained only one frigate and fifteen smaller vessels in a state ever to again put to sea." The victory was complete and glorious, and, as the admiral said, consolation must have been afforded to the friends and relatives of those who died by the thought that they fell "in the service of their country, and in the cause of suffering humanity." The battle of Navarino put an end to the Turkish dominion in Greece. Ibrahim Pasha withdrew his troops from the Morea, and Capo d'Istrea was elected by the Greeks their first President.

Thirteen years later, in July, 1840, England, in alliance with Austria, Russia, and Prussia, concluded a treaty with Turkey, by which they agreed to curb the pretensions of Mehemet Ali, the Viceroy of Egypt, who claimed the whole of Syria, as well as the virtual independence of his own province. Sir Robert Stopford, commanding the Mediterranean fleet, arrived before Beyrout on the 9th September, 1840, and was joined by a Turkish squadron, under Captain Baldwin Walker, and two Austrian ships-of-war, commanded by the Archduke Charles Frederick. The admiral opened fire on the Egyptian army drawn up between the town and the sea, and drove them back, and dismantled the fortifications; but an attack made by Captain Martin, with the frigate *Carysfort*, the 18-gun sloop *Dido*, and the steamer *Cyclops*, Commander Austin, on the town of Djebail, was not equally successful. An attempt made by 200 marines to storm the castle was defeated with the loss of 23 men, but the enemy evacuated the place on the following day, when Captain Martin took possession of the town and fort. Another small squadron, consisting of the *Castor* and *Pique*, under the orders of Captain Collier, captured the strong town of Kaiffa, on the 17th September, and a week later, the ancient Tyre was taken after a brief bombardment.

On the same day Commodore Napier, with a battalion of marines and some Turkish troops, arrived before the important town of Sidon. Anchoring the *Thunderer*, 84, with the two Austrian frigates, in front of the town, with the brig *Wasp* and *Stromboli* steamer on one side, and the steamers *Cyclops*, *Gorgon*, and *Hydra* on the other, he opened fire on the enemy's works, which made a vigorous reply. The principal defences of Sidon were two castles, the larger of which was connected with the town by a narrow causeway, and the neighbouring quarter was loopholed and commanded by entrenchments. But the fire of the ships caused the enemy to evacuate these defences, when the Turkish battalion was landed by Captain Austin before one castle, and a mixed force of British and Austrian seamen and marines took possession of the other. Commodore Napier himself took command of a third detachment, and advancing on some barracks and works, took them by assault, compelling the surrender of over a thousand men. Dispirited by these vigorous measures, the Egyptian governor surrendered the town, together with vast stores and military supplies. This great success was achieved with the loss of only four killed and 32 wounded, and had important consequences in paralyzing Ibrahim Pasha's subsequent movements.

Under orders from Sir Robert Stopford, who still lay before Beyrout with the greater part of his fleet, Commodore Napier marched along the hills to the rear of the town with his Turkish troops, and on the 9th October, the Egyptian army evacuated Beyrout, leaving their tents, stores, and 26 field-pieces, while 2,000 men surrendered with their arms. Mehemet Ali's generals, quitting northern Syria, now concentrated their forces at Acre for the defence of the southern portion of that province.

The British admiral, who had a capable military adviser in Sir Charles Smith, of the Royal Engineers, resolved to attack this stronghold, and embarking 5,000 Turkish troops, arrived before Acre on the 2nd November with the following ships:—

104	*Princess Charlotte*	Admiral Hon. Sir Robert Stopford, G.C.B. Captain Arthur Fanshawe	80	*Bellerophon*	Captain Austen.
			76	*Revenge*	,, Waldegrave.
84	{ *Powerful* *Thunderer*	Commodore Charles Napier, C.B. Captain Berkeley	72	{ *Edinburgh* *Benbow*	,, Henderson. ,, Houston Stewart.

Also the frigates *Castor*, Captain Collier, and *Carysfort*, Captain Martin; the steamers *Phœnix*, *Vesuvius*, and *Stromboli*; two Austrian frigates, and a Turkish 74, bearing the flag of Captain Walker, and a corvette. On arriving before Acre, the British admiral found lying there the frigates *Pique*, Captain Boxer, and *Talbot*, Captain Henry Codrington, who was wounded when serving as a midshipman in his father's flagship at Navarino, and the brigs *Wasp* and *Hazard*.

Acre was stronger than when, some forty years before, it had defied the utmost power of Napoleon to capture it, and its walls were now mounted with 147 guns, manned by 5,000 disciplined troops. The fortress presented to the sea a west and a south face of defence, and as the former was, apparently, the more powerful, the admiral entrusted to Commodore Napier the task of reducing it with the *Princess Charlotte* (from whence he shifted his flag to the *Phœnix*), *Powerful*, *Bellerophon*, *Thunderer*, and *Pique*; while the southern face was to be attacked by the *Edinburgh*, *Benbow*, three frigates, and the sloops, led by Captain Collier in the *Castor*.

Commodore Napier, in the *Powerful*, failed to conform to his instructions, and dropped his anchor at a spot where her fire was not considered by the admiral to be wholly effective, whereupon Sir Robert Stopford signalled the *Thunderer* to pass ahead of the *Powerful*; this, however, she was unable to do, being unable to extricate herself from her position between the *Princess Charlotte* and the *Bellerophon*, and the *Revenge* moved up and took the assigned position, engaging a great earthwork at the projecting angle of the enemy's defences, between the west and south faces. The division on the southern side brought up in its proper berth, led by Captain Stewart in the *Benbow*, and at 2·17 P.M. exactly, the fleet opened fire.

It soon became apparent that the Egyptian gunners could make no head against the terrific cannonade brought to bear upon them, but they continued to serve their guns with unabated vigour, though with ineffectual aim, until about four o'clock, when the principal magazine, containing, it is said, some thousands of barrels of powder, exploded, laying a great portion of the town in ruins, and killing two entire regiments, drawn up on the ramparts in the expectation of an assault.

The enemy's fire was only partially resumed after this catastrophe, which had damped the ardour of the gunners, and at dusk it ceased on both sides.

At daybreak news was received that the Egyptians were deserting, and Sir Charles Smith landed with the Turkish troops and took possession of the town, which presented an appalling scene of desolation, though the walls had not been breached, and any attempt to scale them would have involved great slaughter.

The allied loss was small, that in the British squadron being 12 killed and 32 wounded, and in the Austrian and Turkish ships six and 19 respectively. In their rigging and hulls they were little injured, the chief sufferer being the *Castor*, Captain Collier, which had taken a post between the *Edinburgh* and *Benbow*, the most exposed position in the line. To account for this immunity from severe loss, it was said that the Egyptian gunners, mistaking the buoys, laid down by the masters of the *Pique* and *Talbot* to mark the shoals, as denoting the positions the ships of the fleet would take up, levelled their guns for these marks, and then wedged them into the embrasures.

The capture of Acre virtually concluded the war, for though Ibrahim Pasha concentrated his army at Baalbec, it was considered by his father, Mehemet Ali, and by everyone in the East, that the power which, in a few hours, could capture a stronghold that had taken Ibrahim ten months to reduce with 40,000 men, was irresistible.

Sir Robert Stopford withdrew with his fleet to Marmorice, and Commodore Napier, whom he sent to Alexandria, negotiated a convention with Mehemet Ali, by which he conceded his hereditary claim to Egypt. In doing this the commodore exceeded his instructions, but Lord Palmerston, then Foreign Minister, overlooked his indiscretion, and the treaty was ratified, with the exception of a guarantee by the four allied powers to Mehemet Ali and his heirs of the Viceroyalty of Egypt. One important condition, the restitution of the Turkish ships that deserted to him, was carried into effect at Alexandria, and on the 11th January, 1841, Captain Baldwin Walker received possession of them on behalf of the Sultan.

The British commander-in-chief and the fleet were voted the thanks of Parliament for their brilliant success at Acre, Commodore Napier and Captain Walker received the ribbon of the Bath, and all the captains the C.B. Ten commanders, twenty-three lieutenants, and fifty mates, were also promoted; but, as usual, the marine officers were passed over in the distribution of rewards.

CHAPTER VIII.

Expeditions against the Pirates of the Persian Gulf in 1809 and 1819—Capture of Ras-ul-Khymah—Expedition against the Beni-Boo-Ali Arabs—The first Burmese War—Operations on the Irrawaddy—The first Chinese War—Capture of Chusan and the Bogue Forts—The Navy on the Seaboard of China and on the Yang-tse-Kiang—Captain Harry Keppel and the Pirates of Borneo—The second Burmese War—Capture of Rangoon—Other Operations of the War—Forcing of the Parana River in South America—Actions with Slavers—The Persian and New Zealand Wars—A Brief Survey of Arctic Exploration—Sir Edward Parry's Voyages towards the North Pole—Sir James Ross's Discoveries in the Arctic and Antarctic Regions—Sir John Franklin—Expeditions in Search of the Great Explorer—McClure and the North-West Passage—Collinson's Voyage in the *Enterprise*—McClintock discovers traces of the Franklin Expedition.

EVER since the year 1797 the maritime tribes of the Persian Gulf had given trouble to the Indian Government, and the Joasmis, who had embraced the religion of Abd-ul-Wahab, the great Mussulman reformer and founder of Wahabeeism, turned pirates and levied blackmail on the commerce of the Persian Gulf. This maritime tribe occupied that part of the Arabian coast extending from about 150 miles from a point near Cape Mussendom to Abu Thubee. The towns on this coast, which was generally designated by navigators 'the Pirate Coast,' are all built at the entrance of a Khor, or salt-water inlet, and the maritime robbers, established here from a very remote period, defied the efforts to subdue them of the Portuguese (who for two centuries claimed the whole coast of Oman until expelled by the Arabs) and even carried their depredations to the shores of India and the Red Sea. Their chief towns in the early years of the present century were Sharjah or Shargah, the residence of Sultan Sugger, the noted Joasmi chief, and Ras-ul-Khymah, formerly called Julfa, a large town built on a sandy peninsula, or spit, projecting into the sea, and enclosing a deep narrow bay protected by a bar, over which, even at spring tides, there is scarcely eleven feet of water.

These piratical tribes, though they preyed on native commerce, respected the ships-of-war of the Indian Navy, the commanders of which were enjoined by the Bombay Government to forbear from attacking them unless first fired upon. Emboldened by impunity, a squadron of dhows engaged the Hon. Company's 14-gun brig *Viper* as she lay off Bushire, when a desperate action ensued. It was about eight o'clock in the morning, and the crew of the Company's cruiser were at breakfast on the upper deck, when suddenly two of the dhows, which were passing under the *Viper's* stern, opened fire with round shot upon the little craft. The officers who were below rushed up, and Lieutenant Carruthers, the senior, called the men to quarters, and none too soon, for the dhows, crammed full of men, bore down on the little man-of-war, intending to capture her by boarding. The crew of the *Viper* cut the cable and made sail on the ship, while the guns were cast loose and soon opened a well-directed fire on their treacherous assailants. The superior seamanship of the Englishmen told in their favour, and, by dint of smart manœuvring, Lieutenant Carruthers succeeded, not only in preventing the enemy from carrying into execution their intention to board, when their numerical superiority must have given them the victory, but beat the dhows off, and ended the conflict by chasing them out to sea. Unfortunately the gallant young officer was killed towards the latter part of the action. He had been previously wounded by a musket-ball in the loins, but refused to leave the deck, and soon after was shot through the forehead. Mr. Salter, the senior midshipman, who took command on the death of his superior, fought the ship with determined bravery, and the great loss she incurred, thirty-two out of a total of sixty-five, testified to the severity of the action.

Notwithstanding the glaring nature of this outrage, no hostilities were ordered by the Bombay Government, but the Joasmis had received so severe a lesson that many years elapsed before a second attempt was made to attack a British vessel of war. The Company's Resident at Bushire wrote to the Joasmi Chief demanding explanations as to the treacherous attack on the *Viper*, but his remonstrances were met on the part of Sheikh Sugger by professions of regard for the English, and the contention that the cruiser had fired first upon the dhows.

In 1805 the Joasmis captured two English merchant brigs, and put to death a portion of the crew. These vessels were then armed with guns, and sent to cruise in the Persian Gulf. At first the Bombay Government left these marauders unpunished, and they had the temerity to attack the Hon. Company's cruiser *Mornington*, of 22 guns. Though the assailants numbered forty dhows the *Mornington*, manœuvring under sail, beat them off with great loss. "The Governor of that period," says the traveller, J. S. Buckingham, " from ignorance of the character of these people, could never be persuaded that they were the aggressors, and constantly upbraided the officers with having, in some way, provoked the attacks of which they complained, continuing still to insist on the observance of the orders, in not firing on these vessels until they had been first fired at by them." But at length the Company's ships were directed to operate against the Joasmis in conjunction with the government of the Imaum of Muscat, an old and faithful ally. The combined forces accordingly proceeded, in the year 1806, to the island of Kishm, where they blockaded the Joasmi fleet, which was reduced to such distress that they sued for peace. Captain David Seton, the British political agent, agreed to grant them a truce until the pleasure of his government should be known, and a treaty was concluded at Bundar Abbas, during the year 1806, by which they agreed to give up the brigs, and to "respect the flag and property of the Hon. East India Company and their subjects," and "to assist and protect" any English vessels touching on their coasts. Captain Seton represented to his government that "the whole bulk of the Joasmis were desirous of returning to their former mercantile pursuits," but the event proved he had suffered himself to be cajoled. Piracy was bred in the bone among these restless, truculent Arabs, and the fleets of large and heavily armed dhows, moored in the harbours of Shargah and Ras-ul-Khymah, were not destined for the peaceful pursuit of pearl-fishing on the Bahrein Coast, but for deeds of rapine and blood.

For a brief period the Joasmis continued true to the provisions of the treaty of 1806, so far as regarded the British ships cruising in the Gulf; but it is probable that this temporary abstention from acts of piracy on the British flag was induced only by a fear of the consequences, as we find that during the year 1807, owing to the exigencies of European politics, there was a powerful fleet of ships-of-war in the Persian Gulf, whither, in order to assist in bringing Turkey to her senses through her Asiatic possessions, a squadron had been despatched from Bombay, consisting of H.M.S. *Fox*, Captain Hon. A. Cochrane, and eight of the Company's cruisers. The additional cruisers remained in the Persian Gulf for a year, and hence there was a brief cessation of piracy on the part of the Joasmis. In the month of April, 1808, after the return of the squadron to Bombay, Joasmi dhows from Rams, Shargah, and other places on the coast, made their appearance on the coast to the northward of Bombay, and Captain Seton reported that the acts of piracy "can only be considered as a general one at the instigation of the Wahabees."

While off the Guzerat coast, in command of the schooner *Lively*, Lieutenant Macdonald fought a gallant action with four piratical dhows, each larger and carrying more men than his own little craft. During the year 1808, the pirates captured twenty native vessels, which so elated them that they despatched a fleet of fifty sail towards

Cutch and Scinde, and attacked the Hon. Company's cruiser *Fury*, of six guns, commanded by Lieutenant Gowan, when carrying despatches from Bussorah to Bombay. "The attack," says Buckingham, "was made by several dhows in company, and during a calm; but the resistance made was determined and effectual, and the dhows were made to sheer off with the loss of a great number of men. On the arrival of the *Fury* at Bombay, the commander waited on the governor in the usual way; but on reporting the affair of the battle, instead of being applauded for his spirited resistance, and his preservation of the despatches under his charge, he received a severe reprimand from the governor himself in person, for disobeying the orders given, and daring to molest the innocent and unoffending Arabs of these seas."

During the latter part of 1808, they attacked the merchant ship *Minerva*, while on her voyage from Bombay to Bussorah. The ship was taken to Ras-ul-Khymah, where twenty guns were mounted on her, and she was sent to cruise in the Gulf. On the 20th October, only a few weeks after this, they mastered the Hon. Company's cruiser *Sylph*, a small schooner of only 78 tons, and mounting eight guns, the commander's hands being tied by the instructions of his government until it was too late to offer any effectual resistance. The *Sylph* formed one of a squadron carrying the mission, under Sir Harford Jones, to the Court of the Shah of Persia, and, on being separated from the rest of the ships, a fleet of dhows was seen bearing down on her. Lieutenant Graham, her commander, was alive to the peril of his position, but he could take no steps to keep them at bay, as they had committed no hostile act; and he had peremptory orders, any infringement of which would involve dismissal, on no account to fire on the Arab craft, until they first opened fire upon him. These orders placed a small cruiser absolutely at their mercy, for the Joasmis did not care to engage in a gunnery duel with British seamen, even with long odds in their favour; their tactics consisted in running on board an enemy, and throwing some hundreds of desperate men, armed to the teeth, on the deck of a vessel, thus bearing down all resistance. Thus it happened that the decks of the *Sylph* were boarded by a host of desperadoes. Lieutenant Graham fell, covered with wounds,* down the fore hatchway, where one or two of the crew, who had been hurled below, dragged him into a store-room, of which they barricaded the door from within by a crowbar. His chief officer, Acting-Lieutenant Denton, who had served as a midshipman on board the *Colossus*, at Trafalgar, only

* Lieutenant Graham, who subsequently held a shore appointment at Bombay, survived for half a century the terrible wounds he received on this occasion on the head and shoulders.

survived the wound he had received on that great day to be butchered by these murderous pirates; and, in a few minutes, almost the entire crew had perished fighting desperately.

The Joasmis now made sail on the schooner, and were bearing her off in triumph to their own ports, when an unexpected event snatched the prize from their hands. This was the appearance of His Majesty's 36-gun frigate *Néréide*, Commodore Corbet, forming part of the squadron, which hove in sight, and, perceiving the *Sylph* in company with the dhows, divined what had occurred, and made sail in pursuit. On nearing the prize, the Joasmis quitted her and took to their dhows, to which the commodore gave chase, but without success, as owing to their superior sailing, they were enabled to effect their escape.

Only three days after this affair, the Joasmi pirates attempted to capture the Hon. Company's brig *Nautilus*, 14 guns, in a similar manner, but met with a warm reception at the hands of the commander, Lieutenant Bennett. "The *Nautilus*," says Buckingham, "was proceeding up the Gulf with despatches, and in passing the island of Anjar, on the south side of Kishm, near the Persian shore, was attacked by a squadron, consisting of a baghalah, a dhow, and two trankies; the two former mounting great guns, the others having oars as well as sails, and all being full of armed men. The attack was made in the most skilful and regular manner, the two larger vessels bearing down on the starboard bow, and the smaller ones on the quarter. As Lieutenant Bennett had received the same positive orders as his brother officers, not to commence an attack until fired on, he reserved his guns until they were so close to him that their dancing and brandishing of spears, the attitude with which they menace death, could be distinctly seen, and their songs and war shouts heard. The bow gun was then fired across their hawse as a signal for them to desist, and the British colours were displayed. This being disregarded, it was followed by a second shot, which had no more effect. A moment's consultation was then held by the officers, when it was thought a want of regard for their own safety to use further forbearance, and a broadside was instantly discharged among them all." An action now commenced between the *Nautilus* and the two largest of the boats mounting cannon, and continued for nearly an hour, the "trankies" lying on their oars during the contest to await its result, and seize the first favourable opportunity to board. As the superiority on the part of the cruiser became more decidedly apparent, these latter, however, fled, and were soon followed by the others, the whole of whom the *Nautilus* pursued, and fired on during the chase as long as her guns would tell. Among the killed in this action was the boatswain, and the wounded included Lieutenant Thomas Tanner,* who survived to a great age, and in the year 1859 was elected Mayor of Exeter, his native town.

These repeated aggressions of the Joasmi, coupled with an insolent demand from the chief of Ras-ul-Khymah, whose harbour was the principal resort of the larger craft, for the payment of tribute by the Bombay Government, in order that their merchant ships might be permitted to traverse the waters of the Gulf unmolested, at length opened the eyes of the Governor of Bombay and Court of Directors to the fatal impolicy, and indeed absurdity, of the instructions enjoined upon their naval officers. The public voice called for the punishment of the piratical horde which had heaped insults and injuries on the English name, and when the blood-red Joasmi flag was seen flaunting itself on the coasts of Cutch and Scinde, and twenty craft were captured in Indian waters, the authorities awoke to a sense of shame, and considered it high time to make a hostile move if British trade was not to be driven out of the Persian Gulf. These counsels were quickened by the aggressions of the Wahabees, who had established a preponderance throughout Oman, so that the Imaum was virtually dependent upon them, while, in another direction, their armies appeared before the walls of Bussorah, and their fleet of twenty-two vessels attacked and defeated that of the Governor of Bushire at Khor Hassan, where they captured six ships. According to a well-authenticated calculation, the Joasmi fleet consisted of sixty-three large vessels and eight hundred and thirteen of smaller size, and this truly formidable armada was manned by 19,000 men. This force was increasing, and, in the month following the capture of the *Minerva*, a fleet of seventy sail, with crews averaging between 80 and 200 men, was cruising about the Gulf and threatening Bushire. The Bombay Government, having determined to relieve the Imaum† from the power of the Wahabees, and, at the same

---

* Lieutenant Tanner entered the Royal Navy on board the *Fisgard* frigate, under command of Captain (afterwards admiral of the fleet) Byam Martin, and assisted in blockading the combined French and Spanish fleets in the port of Brest. He was also employed against the enemy on the coasts of France and Spain, and in cutting out from under the batteries at Corunna, the 20-gun ship *Neptune*, a gunboat, and some merchantmen. After the peace of Amiens, in 1802, Mr. Tanner entered the Indian Navy, and served under Commodore Hayes and other officers, on the coast of India, and among the eastern islands of Borneo and the Moluccas, before proceeding to the Persian Gulf.

† The first treaty on record entered into by the Imaum of Muscat with the Indian Government was, according to the Rev. J. P. Badger, that dated the 12th August, 1798. Its object was to secure his alliance against the suspected designs of the French and the commercial rivalry of the Dutch factory and garrison at Gomboon or Bunda Abbas. The second, which is dated 18th January, 1800, and signed on the part of the Company by Sir John Malcolm, Envoy to Persia, provides for the reception of a British Political Resident at Muscat. In these documents Seyyid Sultan is styled "Imaum."

time, to suppress the Joasmi pirates, organised an expedition which proceeded to the Gulf in 1809. The naval portion, under command of Commodore John Wainwright, consisted of Her Majesty's 36-gun frigates *Chiffonne* and *Caroline*, and the Company's cruisers *Mornington*, 22 guns, *Ternate*, 16 guns, 14 gun-brigs *Aurora, Mercury, Nautilus, Prince of Wales*, 10-gun brigs *Vestal* and *Ariel, Fury*, 8, and *Stromboli*, bomb-ketch. The troops, embarked on board four transports, consisted of His Majesty's 65th Regiment, flank companies of His Majesty's 47th Regiment, a detachment of the Bombay Artillery, and about 1,000 Sepoys, the whole under the command of Colonel Lionel Smith, of the 65th Regiment. The fleet sailed from Bombay in September, and it had not quitted the harbour twenty-four hours before an accident occurred involving loss of life. The *Stromboli* bomb-ketch was in tow astern of the *Mornington*, when suddenly her bottom fell out, and she foundered, carrying with her Lieutenants Taylor, of the Indian Navy, and Sealy, of the Bombay Artillery, and the greater portion of her crew. The despatch of this vessel, laden with a heavy cargo of ordnance and shot and shell on such a mission was due to the most culpable carelessness. It appears that a long period anterior to this she had been condemned as unfit for service and for three years lay moored as a floating battery off the entrance of Tannah River, as is called the strait which separates the island of Salsette from the mainland. From thence she had been removed to Bombay harbour, and moored off a sunken rock, whence she was taken on the strength of the squadron, and fitted out to carry the heaviest and least buoyant cargo that a ship can be freighted with.

On arriving at Muscat the Imaum, on whose behalf the expedition had been, in a great measure, undertaken, regarded the project of an attack on Ras-ul-Khymah with so small a force as ill-advised, but the British officers were sanguine of success. The ships arrived off that town on the afternoon of the 11th November, but, in consequence of the shallowness of the water, the frigates were not able to approach within four miles; the Company's cruisers, however, owing to their small draught, anchored nearer, and with the ships' boats attacked the enemy's works on the following day. The troops were landed in the early morning of the 13th, and after prolonged fighting gained the centre of the town at two in the afternoon. By four o'clock the boats of the squadron had set fire to upwards of fifty vessels, twenty of them being large war dhows,* the guns of some of which were loaded. Many of the houses had depots of gunpowder, the explosion of which, with the general conflagration in the town and harbour, added

* *See* Commodore Wainwright's despatch of the 14th November, 1809.

to the scene of desolation and misery presented by Ras-ul-Khymah. No looting was permitted, and the town with its contents was set on fire, and the flames quickly reduced all to ashes. The British loss was trifling, considering the resistance encountered, while some hundred of the Joasmis were slain. The punishment thus meted out was condign, but the effects were in a great measure neutralised by Colonel Smith hastily re-embarking the troops on the morning of the 14th, on receipt of a report that a large body of Arabs was nearing the place from the interior. This hurried exit reassured the Joasmis, who assembled on the shore, defiantly displaying their colours, brandishing their swords and spears, and discharging their muskets. From Ras-ul-Khymah the expedition proceeded to Linjah, a flourishing port of the Joasmis on the Persian coast, near the island of Kishm, and probably containing at that time nearly 10,000 inhabitants. On the 17th November Linjah was occupied without resistance, and burned to the ground, and the vessels, amounting to twenty, some of them being large war dhows, were destroyed. The squadron arrived at noon of the 26th off the town of Luft, a Joasmi port on the north side of the island of Kishm. The channel being narrow and difficult of approach, the *Ternate*, *Nautilus*, and *Fury* were warped into their stations, and the troops, preceded by the gunboats, were landed under Colonel Smith about two o'clock on the following day, and advanced towards the fortress, which is described as having walls fourteen feet thick, pierced with loop-holes, and only one entrance through a small gate cased with iron bars and bolts. It was intended to have blown the gate open with an howitzer, but the men were picked off so rapidly from the loop-holes above that a general retreat took place, the howitzer was abandoned even before it had been fired, and the troops sought shelter by lying down behind the ridges of sand and little hillocks; the night favoured their retreat to the beach, whence they re-embarked without molestation. Meantime, says Commodore Wainwright, in his despatch of the 7th December, "the gunboats and the *Fury*, which being of light draught, had been towed within musket shot of the fort, kept up a ruinous fire, which very much shattered the strong fort by sunset." With the dawn of morning all eyes were directed to the fortress, when a man was seen waving the Union Jack on the summit of its walls. It was an officer of the Indian Navy, Lieutenant Hall, who had commanded the *Stromboli* bomb-vessel at the time of her sinking, but had saved himself by swimming, and now commanded the *Fury*, the vessel nearest the shore. "During the night," says Buckingham, "he had gone ashore alone, taking an Union Jack in his hand, and advanced singly to the castle-gate. The fortress had already been abandoned by the greater number of the inhabitants, but some few still remained there. These, however, fled at the approach of an individual, either from deeming all further resistance unavailing, or from supposing, probably, that no one would come singly, but as a herald to others immediately following for his support. Be this as it may, the castle was entirely abandoned, and our flag was planted on its walls by this daring officer, to the surprise and admiration of the whole force." The town and fortifications, together with eleven dhows, were taken possession of, and the latter were burnt. As Luft had been taken by the Joasmis from the Imaum of Muscat, it was delivered over to his Highness. In this affair the squadron had 27 killed and wounded, including three officers.

The squadron visited several other ports on the coast near Ras-ul-Khymah, and all the vessels were destroyed. Thence, in company with a large body of troops, under the command of the Imaum of Muscat, the expedition sailed to attack Shinas, a considerable town, with a strong fort, on the Batnah coast. The Wahabee general was summoned to surrender, but on his refusing to do so, the ships cannonaded the castle, and the British and native troops were landed. A strong battery was completed on the 2nd January, 1810. Throughout the night the squadron continued their fire, and some 4,000 shot and shell were discharged, until the walls of the fortress were reduced to ruins, and a breach was effected. Twice Colonel Lionel Smith summoned the brave governor, but at length, when the troops were on the point of advancing to storm, and above 1,000 men had fallen in its defence, the place was surrendered. The British troops now returned to Bombay, but the squadron continued cruising for some time in the Persian Gulf.

Notwithstanding the severe chastisement they had received, the maritime Arabs of the Pirate Coast were too much addicted to their nefarious calling to return to a peaceful and regular mode of earning a livelihood. They rebuilt their towns and constructed a fleet of war dhows, and recommenced their depredations on commerce on a larger scale than before. At first they confined themselves to preying on native ships, but in 1815, they captured off Muscat a vessel sailing from Bombay under British colours, and put the greater portion of the crew to death. In this year, also, a Joasmi fleet of twenty-five sail attacked the Imaum while cruising with some of his ships, and his Highness narrowly escaped capture. Upon this Seyyid Said wrote to the Bombay Government, imploring their aid, and early in the following year a British squadron blockaded Ras-ul-Khymah for four months, but this had no effect. They soon appeared off the coast of India, and captured a Government armed vessel, after a desperate resistance, in which nearly all the crew were slain, and, emboldened by impunity, attempted to cut off a large native craft laden with treasure, towing astern of the Hon. Company's 14-gun cruiser, *Aurora*. But they "caught a tartar" on this occasion, for the *Aurora*, casting the vessel adrift, wore round and engaged the squadron, consisting of fifteen sail, with such effect that she sunk three of them, when the remainder made sail and escaped. The Joasmis attacked ships of all nations, among them being an American, and a French sail bound from Mauritius to Bussorah. Many others flying English colours were taken, and the crews murdered, so that native vessels were compelled to sail under convoy of ships-of-war. During the year 1816, they took four Surat ships, on which H.M.S. *Challenger* and three of the Company's cruisers proceeded to Ras-ul-Khymah, with the British political agent in the Persian Gulf, to demand satisfaction. But none was afforded, when the ships cannonaded the defences of the town, though with small effect, and received a return fire. So matters continued, the Joasmis gaining confidence and cruising off the Indian and Arabian coasts, thus creating a terror in all these waters.

On the 21st December, 1818, the Hon. Company's 18-gun brig *Antelope*, Lieutenant Tanner in command, fought a spirited action with eight Joasmi war-dhows, which attempted to board her from different quarters. It was only by smart seamanship that the *Antelope* was enabled to keep the enemy at bay. The latter carried an aggregate of 29 guns and 1,070 men, of whom it was afterwards ascertained that 117 were slain, mostly while trying to grapple the cruiser at close quarters. About this time H.M.S. *Eden*, with the Company's cruisers, *Psyche* and *Thetis*, encountered eight Joasmi sail off the island of Kishm, when they succeeded in sinking two of them.

At length the patience of the long-suffering Government of Bombay was worn out, and in 1819, an expedition was despatched to punish the piratical tribes. It consisted of a force of over 3,000 soldiers, of whom 1,649 were Europeans, under the command of General Sir William Grant Kier, and the following Royal ships-of-war, one of which was in the Persian Gulf:—*Liverpool*, 50 guns, Commodore F. A. Collier, C.B., who arrived on the 25th September from Mauritius to assume naval command of the expedition; *Eden*, 26 guns, Captain Loch; and *Curlew*, 18 guns, Captain Walpole—which arrived at Bombay only a few days before from the Persian Gulf, having been attacked on her way down by fifteen Joasmi boats. The Hon. Company's ships were:—the 16-gun brigs *Teignmouth*, Captain Hall (senior officer), and *Benares*, Commander Arthur; the 14-gun brigs *Aurora*, Commander Mallard, and *Nautilus*, Lieutenant Faithful; and 10-gun brigs *Ariel*, Lieutenant Greenway, and *Vestal*, Lieutenant Watson. Besides these cruisers, which actually participated in the ensuing operations, the Hon. Company's ships *Ternate*, 16 guns, *Mercury*, 14 guns, and *Psyche*, 10 guns, were engaged cruising about the Gulf, and, during the month of November, the former was sent to Bushire to bring Mr. Bruce to Ras-ul-Khymah to confer with the general, who was invested with supreme political authority. On the 3rd November, Sir W. Grant Kier having embarked on board the *Liverpool*, the first division of transports sailed under convoy of the *Liverpool*, *Curlew*, and *Aurora*. The remaining part of the expedition followed a few days later for the Persian Gulf. It was about time that active steps should be taken to extirpate the audacious horde of pirates, for by accounts published in the *Bombay Gazette* of October 27th, it appears that the Joasmi fleet, cruising off the coasts of Kattywar and Cutch, consisted "of 64 vessels, having on board a crew of 7,000 men," and the *Bombay Courier*, of October 23rd, mentions that thirty-five sail of Joasmi had proceeded on a cruise off the coasts of Mekran and Scinde.

The fleet proceeded to the rendezvous at Kishm, while the *Liverpool* sailed to Muscat, which she reached on the 13th November, and on the 17th the military and naval chiefs had an interview with the Imaum, who promised to co-operate with 4,000 men and three vessels of war. As it was desirable that Ras-ul-Khymah should be blockaded, the Commodore ordered the *Benares* to accompany the *Liverpool* to assist in the operation, and on the same day the two ships arrived off the place. The military commander, accompanied by his staff and the commanding engineer, reconnoitred the town during the 26th and 27th November; and on the arrival of the fleet with the transports on the 2nd December, immediate arrangements were made for disembarking the troops. On the following day this was done under cover of the gun-boats and armed launches of the squadron with celerity and good order, considering the great distance the ships were obliged to anchor from the town, and the lack of a sufficiency of means for transporting so large a force with all the guns, supplies, and stores necessary for a regular siege. In order to create a diversion while this was in progress, the *Aurora* and *Nautilus* brought up near the mouth of the creek and opened a heavy fire in that direction, and to assist in the siege operations, a body of 500 seamen was landed from His Majesty's and the Hon. Company's ships.

The following condensed narrative of the operations before Ras-ul-Khymah is from an officer of the Royal Army who was present:—"The batteries of the town bore directly on the entrance of the port—the harbour was full of shipping—the mainland on the opposite coast appeared picturesque and verdant with innumerable date trees, and the mountains of Arabia reared their dim, hazy outline in the background. The place of our encampment and soil of the tongue of land was parched, sandy, and herbless. 2,000 of the Imaum's troops joined us; they had forced the passes in the hills, deemed impregnable, and brought in some prisoners. Parties of seamen were landed to assist in the erection of the batteries. Smart skirmishing took place during the 4th, and the gun-boats particularly distinguished themselves by their activity. The first line of trenches having been made by means of sand-bags, an advanced battery opened on the place at a distance of three hundred yards. A mortar battery on the right was served very effectively. Early in the siege Major Molesworth, of the 47th Regiment, was killed by a round shot. The ships-of-war having approached nearer the town, in conjunction with our batteries, opened a vigorous fire on the morning of the 5th. Shells were thrown with evident effect, the gun-boats contributing, as before, their powerful assistance. The duties of the seamen in the trenches were severe and unremitting. While the soldiers were relieved every four hours, the sailors remained frequently twenty-four hours without any rest or respite.

"The firing from the ships and batteries still continued on the 6th; that of the Arabs was very faint, and they evidently did not possess much ammunition. The firing had terminated for the day, the men had been relieved, silence reigned in the batteries, the night was very dark, and the picket, as usual, on the alert. About one, a dark object, like a large black dog, was seen creeping along on all fours, several similar objects following. The advanced pickets were cut down; all was hurry, shout, and bustle. The trenches were filled with a large party of Arabs, engaged in a close contest with our men, who were speared and stabbed in a twinkling. Already the Arabs had succeeded in dragging away a howitzer in triumph. The alarm spread like wildfire through the trenches. A party of the 65th Foot, under Major Warren, instantly advanced in double-quick time, attacked the assailants, drove them out of the trenches, and re-captured the howitzer. A desperate conflict ensued; the Arabs fought like furies, but they were soon bayonetted. They had divested themselves of their upper garments to facilitate their onset; and, if we mistake not, their bodies were anointed with oil. It being found that our 12 and 18-pounders produced but a slight impression on the walls and towers, it was resolved that 24-pounders should be erected as a breaching battery. Two were accordingly landed with considerable exertion from the *Liverpool*, and had to be dragged a long way through heavy, deep sand. The battery was erected nearer the town, and a party of seamen and marines, under the command of Lieutenant Mills, was landed to work the guns. The 24-pounders opened on the 8th with marked effect, and the walls and towers appeared to crumble under the force of the shot. The cannonade was recommenced at an early hour the next morning, and when the breach was reported practicable, the necessary arrangements were made to assault the works. But the enemy did not wait to be attacked, but evacuated the town." Hassan Bin Rahma, chief of Ras-ul-Khymah, surrendered with nearly one thousand followers, his loss in action being estimated at the same figure by the British general. About eighty vessels, varying in size from two hundred and fifty to forty tons, were captured.

The only other service of importance was the siege of the hill fort of Zayah, situated at the head of a creek about two miles from the coast. In this a detachment of sailors took part, and worked two 24-pounders, which were placed in battery with other guns. The fort was breached, when the garrison surrendered. The British loss was only four killed and 16 wounded. Major Warren of the 65th, commanding on this occasion, paid a tribute to the zeal of the officers and men of the Naval detachment, which enabled them to "overcome the difficulties attending the landing of the supplies and stores, particularly the guns, which, after being brought up a narrow, intricate, and shallow creek, a distance of upwards of three miles, had to be dragged through a muddy swamp, and afterwards over a considerable space of rocky and intersected ground, before they could be placed in the batteries." The commander of the expedition in his field orders to the army, dated Ras-ul-Khymah, 25th December, 1819, says of the services of the sister service:—"The Major-general feels at a loss to express in adequate terms his obligations to the Navy, but the value of their services will be estimated when he declares that the enterprise must have failed without their assistance." The column, after destroying the fortifications, returned to the camp before Ras-ul-Khymah on the 26th December.

The squadron now visited all the Joasmi ports on the coast, destroying their dhows and blowing up the forts, but on the 8th January, 1820, the chiefs came to terms, and a treaty of peace was signed, by which they agreed to abandon piracy for ever, a promise, notwithstanding occasional isolated outbursts, they have loyally carried out.

Scarcely was this matter settled than trouble arose with the Beni-Boo-Ali tribe of Arabs, whose habitat is near Ras-ul-Had. A detachment of native infantry, sent from the Persian Gulf, was overpowered by the Arabs, who adopted the tactics the Soudanese put in practice in 1884-85, and fell upon the troops, sword in hand, breaking their ranks. No less than 270 men were slain, together with six out of the eight British officers engaged, and had it not been for the entrenched camp to which the remnant fled, all would have been slaughtered. On the 11th January, 1821, an expedition, consisting of 4,676 soldiers, and four of the Hon. Company's cruisers, sailed for Sohar, where the troops were disembarked. Accompanied by a detachment of seamen, the army marched for the interior, and after repulsing a night attack, in which 17 officers and men were killed and 26 wounded, they inflicted a crushing defeat on the brave Arabs, who again tried with desperate bravery to break through the ranks. Of less than 1,000 warriors engaged, 500 were left on the field, and 236 were made prisoners, of whom 96 were wounded. The right brigade, on which the main attack was made, lost 29 killed and 173 wounded, but the success was decisive. The settlement was destroyed, even the date groves being cut down and the water courses turned away; and then the expedition returned to Bombay, having turned a smiling oasis into a desert. Two years afterwards, Mr. Mountstuart Elphinstone, the great and humane Governor of Bombay, sent back to their country the remainder of the Beni-Boo-Ali tribe, who had little cause to bless the British, as the demand made in the first instance for the surrender of their arms was unjustifiable and such as a proud race like the Arabs would never concede.

The British Navy was frequently engaged in the Eastern seas in assisting to extend the limits of the Empire. Though the army, from the nature of things, had the chief part in conquering our great Indian dependency beyond the boundary of Hindostan, the Navy afforded valuable aid.* The forts of Mocha, in 1817 and 1821, were attacked and reduced by a combined squadron of Royal and Indian ships, and the important fortress of Aden, "the Gibraltar of the East," was captured by them after a sharp action, in 1840, the same year that Kurrachee surrendered, almost without resistance. More important from a military point of view were the operations against Burmah in 1824-26, the first of three wars we waged with that country. The result of the first was the acquisition of the provinces of Assam, Arracan, and Tenasserim, of the second, the conquest of Pegu, and of the third, the annexation of the whole of Upper Burmah, so that the great kingdom of Alompra, extending to the confines of China and Siam, has been added to the vast Empire ruled by the Queen of England and Empress of India.

The naval portion of the expedition to Burmah, in 1824, consisted of the *Liffey*, Commodore Grant, and the sloops *Slaney*, *Larne*, and *Sophie*, Commanders Mitchell, Marryat (the famous novelist), and Ryves. There were, in addition, four cruisers of the Indian Navy, under Captain Hardy of the *Hastings*, eighteen brigs and schooners, and

* A detailed account of the operations against the maritime tribes in the Persian Gulf, at Mocha, Aden, and elsewhere in the East, may be found in the author's "History of the Indian Navy" (2 vols., Bentley & Son).

other small craft, each armed with two carronades and four swivels, and twenty row-boats, lugger-rigged, each carrying an 18-pounder, about forty sail of transports, and finally the *Diana*, steam-vessel, the first used for war purposes propelled by this newly applied agency.

Rangoon was captured on the 11th May by the squadron, led by the *Liffey*, only a few rounds being exchanged between her and a 14-gun battery. The enemy were then driven out of Kemmendine, three miles above Rangoon, and some stockades higher up the Irrawaddy were also taken. The Burmese were constant in their attacks on the position at Rangoon, which were repulsed with loss. But the ships-of-war were in great danger from the fire-rafts sent down the river. In order to minimize the danger, Kemmendine was permanently occupied, when some severe fighting ensued. The enemy made strenuous efforts to retake the stockades, but the zeal of the officers and seamen rendered abortive all their attempts.

Commodore Grant was compelled from severe sickness to leave Rangoon a few weeks after his arrival, and died in July, when Marryat assumed temporary command, but he also suffered much, as did the crews of the ships, to such an extent that they were almost non-effective. On the 15th September, Captain Henry Ducie Chads, the same gallant officer who had taken the *Java* out of action after the death of Captain Lambert, arrived at Rangoon from Madras in the *Arachne*, 18, and took command of the squadron as senior naval officer. At the capture of Kemmerut and Cheduba Island, and in the operations at Syriam and at Dalla, on the opposite side of the river to Rangoon, the sailors of both Royal and Indian Navies performed good service. Gun-boats also took part in the capture of Tavoy and Mergui in Tenasserim, and at Dalla, the *Kitty*, gun-boat, under the command of Mr. Crawford, of the Hon. Company's service, repulsed with great gallantry an attack of the enemy until the boats of the *Larne* came to her assistance. The Navy participated in the attack on Tantabain and on the city of Martaban, under Colonel Godwin, of the 41st Regiment, who afterwards commanded in the Burmese war of 1852-3; and in all the numerous attacks on Rangoon and Kemmendine by the enemy, under the energetic Bundoola, they materially assisted their brethren on shore and were also engaged in towing clear the numerous fire-rafts launched upstream.* The attacks of the enemy recommenced on the 13th December, and Lieutenant Kellett was sent up the

---

* A full account of the part taken by the Navy in the operations in Burmah will be found in the pages of the historian, Marshall, but though arduous and most praiseworthy, they were not of a sufficiently important character to demand a detailed description.

Lyne branch of the Rangoon river, where he took thirty of the enemy's war-boats and destroyed many more. During this expedition, excellent service was rendered by Lieutenants Goldfinch, of the *Sophie*, and Collinson, commanding the Hon. Company's cruiser *Prince of Wales*. After his great defeat on the 18th December, Bundoola returned to Donabew and made no further offensive movement, and on the 13th February, 1825, Sir Archibald Campbell began his adventurous march on the capital, distant some 600 miles, which was made by the river, as the army was destitute of carriage. The troops were organised in two divisions, one under his own command—with a column detached to Bassein, under Colonel Godwin, with the *Larne* and Company's cruiser *Mercury* acting in co-operation—and the second, under General Willoughby Cotton, numbering 800 Europeans, 250 Sepoys, and 108 artillerymen, embarked in the flotilla, of which Captain Alexander, of the *Alligator*, now senior naval officer, assumed command. This flotilla consisted of two mortar-boats, six gun-vessels, thirty armed row-boats, about sixty launches, flats and canoes, and all the boats of the men-of-war remaining at Rangoon, together with the *Diana* and *Satellite*. General Cotton and Captain Alexander, after capturing the stockade at Panlang, were repulsed on the 7th March at Donabew, when the Commander-in-chief returned to their aid, and the place was captured on the 2nd April, the flotilla acting in co-operation by cannonading the stockade. The death of Bundoola, who had been killed on the previous night by a shell, quite disheartened his followers. Prome was taken possession of without resistance on the 25th April, and here the combined force remained during the monsoon until the following September. A chain of posts was formed between Rangoon and Prome by the gun-boats, placed at equal distances, by which means, says Marshall, "provisions were forwarded to form a depot at that station for the ensuing campaign." The Burmese professed themselves anxious to negotiate for terms of peace. Accordingly Sir Archibald Campbell and Commodore Sir James Brisbane, who had arrived from Rangoon, held a conference with a minister of high rank, but the Court of Ava would not consent to surrender territory, and on the 15th November hostilities were resumed. At this time the Navy sustained a loss in the death of Captain Alexander, and soon after Captain Dawson, of the *Arachne*, died of disease.

On the 1st December the British army took the offensive, and while Commodore Brisbane cannonaded the enemy's centre on the heights of Napadee, the General made an attack in the direction of Simbike. The Burmese were driven from their positions on that and the following day with slaughter. Pushing up the river, on the 17th, the

LANDING ORDER.

expedition arrived before Meaday, which was reconnoitred by Captain Chads, and evacuated by the enemy after a slight resistance. The army, continuing its march on Melloun, carried the place by assault with the loss of only nine killed and 35 wounded. The fall of this stronghold even failed to convince the King of Ava of the fruitlessness of resistance, but on the 9th February the defeat of his choicest troops at Pagahm Mew opened his eyes, and at length, with the small English army within 45 miles of his capital, he consented to conclude a humiliating peace, which involved the cession of territory and the payment of twenty-five lacs of rupees, or over a quarter of a million sterling. Sir James Brisbane had, before this, been compelled by sickness to retire to the coast, and he died on the 19th December following. The Navy received the thanks of the Houses of Parliament for their services, and Captains Chads, Marryat, and Ryves were awarded the C.B., while every lieutenant and passed midshipman employed in the expedition was promoted.

The same year that witnessed the fall of Acre (1840), saw us embarked in the first of our wars with the Empire of China. Ever since the abrogation of the East India Company's Charter in 1833, by which the trade of China was thrown open to all merchants, and the mission of Lord Napier to Canton in the following year to regulate the trade, there had been constant friction with the officials of the Celestial Empire in the southern capital. These treated Lord Napier with insolence, and even fired on the British frigates *Imogene*, Captain Blackland, and *Andromache*, Captain Chads, from the batteries on the islands of Chuenpee and Tycocktoo. As their guns did no injury the squadron continued its course to Whampoa, without firing a shot, but the Bogue forts and the Tiger battery in the Bocca Tigris opened a more destructive fire, to which the frigates replied with effect. This lesson brought the authorities at Canton to their senses, and they acceded to our demands, including the opening of trade. Lord Napier died a few days after this success, and his successor, Captain Elliott, was too credulous and pliant to receive the respect of the arrogant mandarins. Presuming on the supposed weakness of the British squadron, consisting in November, 1839, of only the *Volage*, 28, Captain Smith, and *Hyacinth*, 18, Commander Warren, a Chinese flotilla of war-junks and fire-ships moved down to Lankeet, a few miles below Chuenpee, where they lay to attack them. Captain Smith at once took the offensive, and speedily routed the flotilla, sinking one junk and blowing up three others. In the following June Sir Gordon Bremer in the *Wellesley*, 74, arrived in the Canton river, and leaving a few ships to blockade that port, sailed for the Chusan group of islands, with a squadron of four sailing ships and the *Atalanta* and *Queen*, steam-sloops of the Indian Navy, with four transports, having on board some troops.

The Chinese authorities were so confident in the ability of their fortifications and fleet of war-junks to repel the British squadron, that they would listen to no terms, and on the 5th July the troops were landed and advanced against the town, on the chief island of the group, while the ships opened a heavy cannonade. The Chinese soldiers soon abandoned their works, and the town and whole island were surrendered. A few days before, the island of Amoy, between Chusan and the mainland, submitted to Captain Bourchier, of the *Blonde*, 44, after the loss of much time in negotiations for peace, for which the Chinese had no real desire. Sir Gordon Bremer, in January, 1841, attacked the forts at Chuenpee and Tycocktoo, which were silenced by the fire of the fleet, and then stormed by the troops and a brigade of seamen. This so intimidated the Chinese that the Bogue Forts struck their colours, without firing a shot, and Keshen, a high mandarin sent from Pekin, signed a preliminary treaty, restoring the trade, agreeing to the payment of an indemnity, and ceding the island of Hong Kong. The last stipulation was carried into effect, but the treaty was a mere blind, and when the armed steamer *Nemesis* proceeded up the river she was fired upon by the Bogue Forts, which had been strengthened to bar the passage of the fleet.

The British commodore thereupon sailed with a powerful squadron, and on the 25th of February attacked these formidable batteries, mounting 172 guns, which were situated on the island of Anunghoy, and 167 on the island of North Wantung. A battery was constructed on the South Wantung and opened fire on the enemy, while Sir Henry Senhouse, with the *Blenheim*, *Melville*, *Queen*, and four rocket-boats, attacked Anunghoy, and the commodore, North Wantung. Having silenced the batteries by the fire of the ships, the soldiers and marines were landed and stormed the works with a loss to the Chinese of 2,500 prisoners and 500 killed, that of the British being almost nominal. Following up this success, a battery and a fleet of forty war-junks, off Whampoa, were attacked and captured by Captain Herbert, with the frigates and smaller vessels. Sir Gordon Bremer prosecuted his operations with vigour and success, and sent up a channel, about two miles above Canton, Captains Scott and Herbert, with the steamers *Nemesis* and *Madagascar*, the *Modeste* and some armed boats. The passage was forced, the Chinese were shelled and driven out of five forts, and nine war-junks were boarded by the boats and destroyed, when both officers, who had proceeded by different passages, rejoined the commodore with small loss.

Sir Hugh Gough had now arrived with reinforcements of troops and assumed command. As it was resolved to occupy Canton, in order to bring the Emperor of China to his senses, in May, the fleet, with the transports, having on board 2,000 soldiers, approached the city, and while Captain Herbert directed the operations on the river, the troops and naval brigade were landed and stormed the forts, and forced their way to the gates, when the garrison sued for peace. Canton was ransomed by the payment of six millions of dollars, and the fleet returned to the mouth of the river. But still the Central Government at Pekin remained obstinate. On the 9th August, 1841, the Hon. Company's steamer *Sesostris*, 68 days from England* (an unheard-of passage in those days) arrived at Hong Kong, with Sir Henry Pottinger, who assumed control of political affairs, and a new Commander-in-Chief in Rear-Admiral Sir William Parker, one of Nelson's favourite frigate captains, who commanded the *Amazon* when she took the *Belle Poule*.

The first operation undertaken by Admiral Parker was an attack on Amoy, the fortifications of which had been greatly strengthened since its first capture. He sailed with the seventy-fours *Blenheim* and *Wellesley*, two 44-gun frigates, the Hon. Company's steam-sloops *Phlegethon* and *Nemesis*, and steam-frigates *Queen* and *Sesostris*, and six smaller vessels, having on board 2,000 soldiers. On the arrival of the expedition before the city on the 25th August, the action was commenced by the *Queen* and *Sesostris*, which opened fire with their heavy guns, while the other ships, anchoring by the stern, took up their appointed stations. At the end of an hour the Chinese fire slackened, and Sir Hugh Gough landed at the head of his troops, who carried the works. The admiral also sent ashore a strong party of seamen and marines, who captured the batteries on the sea-face. Meanwhile the defences on the island of Kalungsoo, on the western side of the harbour, were attacked by the frigates under Captain Bourchier, and on their fire being silenced, marines and troops were landed and took possession of the island.

The next step was the re-occupation of the Chusan group of islands. The fleet, with some troops, arrived before the town of Chusan on the 1st of October, but only the *Nemesis*, *Queen* and *Modeste* could take up a position sufficiently near the enemy's batteries to attack and silence them. The troops and a naval brigade, under Captain Herbert, were landed and the British flag soon floated over Chusan. The expedition then proceeded to attack the town of Chinhae, on the mainland. The *Sesostris*, Commander Ormsby, towed the line-of-battle ships to their respective berths, and their

* See "Life of Admiral Sir William Parker," by Admiral Phillimore.

fire speedily silenced the great fort and the sea defences, when the troops and seamen were landed, captured the fort, and descending, drove the Chinese gunners from their batteries, and scaled the walls of the city.* Ningpo, fifteen miles higher up the river, was surrendered without resistance. In all these operations the steamers were chiefly engaged, and great praise was due to Commander (the late Admiral Sir Richard) Collinson for piloting the ships up these hitherto unknown Chinese rivers.

Emboldened by the inactivity of the military and naval commanders, the enemy marched against Chinhae and Ningpo, and sent fire-rafts to destroy the ships, but their troops were routed with great slaughter, and the fire-ships were towed to the bank where they exploded or burnt without doing any damage. Taking the offensive again, Sir Hugh Gough, with 850 troops and 400 seamen, under Captain Bourchier, marched inland, and after some sharp fighting, inflicted a severe defeat on the enemy. The Chinese, however, displayed considerable enterprise, and again tried to destroy the squadron at Chusan with fire-ships, but the attempt ended in failure. It was now resolved to ascend the great Yang-tse-Kiang and attack Nankin, with the object of bringing the Imperial Government to terms. First Chapoo, situated on the same great bay as Chinhae, was taken, after the usual combined attack by the troops and seamen, and then the fleet sailed for the entrance of the mighty river forming one of the chief arteries of the Celestial Empire. The long line of batteries at the mouth was first cannonaded and silenced by the ships, when the seamen and troops were landed, and took possession of the works and also of Shanghai, now the great emporium of European trade in China. The expedition, consisting of seventy-three men-of-war and transports, with a strong body of troops, sailed from Woosung on the 6th of July, and on the 21st the great city of Chin-Kiang-foo was taken by assault by the troops, assisted by a naval brigade. The task of ascending 170 miles up an unknown river was one of great difficulty, but it was successfully surmounted. The admiral says that, "it is with renewed pleasure that he again reports the zeal and gallantry evinced by every officer and man of the Royal and Indian Navy and the Royal Marines under his command, which has been equally manifested in bringing the fleet up this river, as in subsequent operations on shore." The expedition thence proceeded to Nankin, but it was a relief to all when a repetition of the sanguinary scenes at Chin-Kiang-foo was averted by the submission of the Emperor of China and his advisers,

---

* A full report of the operations is found in "Sir William Parker's Life," in a letter he addressed to Lord Auckland, Governor-General of India, dated 11th of October, 1841.

who had at length taken to heart the lessons of a long and sad experience. Commissioners from Pekin arrived to sue for peace, and a treaty was signed on the 29th August on board the flag-ship *Cornwallis*, by which twenty-one millions of dollars were to be paid towards the expenses of the war, and the ports of Canton, Ningpo, Amoy, Shanghai and Foochow were opened to British trade.

Though the Chinese Government was reduced to reason, much trouble was caused in the East, on the seaboard of that empire, as well as in the Malay Archipelago, in Borneo and its neighbouring waters, by the pirates, who had carried on depredations unchecked from time immemorial. In 1843, our countryman, the late Sir James Brooke, was recognised by the Sultan of Borneo as Rajah of Sarawak, on the west coast of the island, and to assist him in extirpating piracy, Sir William Parker, on the conclusion of the war, sent Captain Henry Keppel in the *Dido*. This officer was a worthy coadjutor of Rajah Brooke, and their names are now famous as " household words" throughout further Asia for the enterprise they displayed, and the success which rewarded their exertions.

In June, 1843, 80 men from the *Dido*, with about 300 native auxiliaries, under Rajah Brooke, ascended the River Sarebas, and by simple audacity our sailors carried all before them, and the pirates agreed to the terms dictated by the two British commanders. Returning down the same river, the expedition beat up the Dyak pirates in their other strongholds.

Captain Keppel now proceeded to China, but in the following year returned with the Hon. Company's steamer *Phlegethon*, and an attack was made on the Sikarran pirates, a more numerous and powerful tribe than those of Sarebas. Proceeding up the Batang Lupan river, with the boats of the *Dido* and *Phlegethon*, on the 7th August, the expedition arrived off their chief town, and the sailors, landing as before, regardless of numbers, captured the stockades. Thence Captain Keppel pulled up the streams Undop and Sikarran, and beat the pirates in detail. But not without loss, as at the former, Lieutenant Wade, first of the *Dido*, was killed, and at the attack on Karangan, on the Sikarran river, where the enemy mustered in overwhelming force, they cut off a party of 30 men of our allies, all of whom, with an English volunteer, were slain, fighting desperately.

In the year 1845, Sir Thomas Cochrane, now Commander-in-Chief in India, sent Captain Talbot, with twenty-seven boats, containing 350 seamen and marines, to attack the pirates up the Songibasar river, in the northern part of the island, near Labuan. The expedition was completely successful, and the pirates were defeated with great loss, all their fortifications and vessels being destroyed. In achieving this success, Captain Talbot's loss was 21 killed and wounded. In the following year Sir Thomas Cochrane in person conducted an expedition, numbering 600 seamen and marines, against the Sultan of Bruné. On the way up the river, they found, at a place called Pulo Bungore, five batteries, which were stormed in succession. On arriving at Bruné, the *Phlegethon* opened fire on a battery of 10 heavy guns, with such effect that the enemy deserted the works.

Every year active operations were undertaken against the pirates infesting these seas, and the *Encounter*, *Rattler*, and *Bittern*, under Captains O'Callaghan, Fellowes, and Vansittart, who fell at the attack on the Peiho forts, rendered good service in assisting to destroy these pests of the sea. Lieutenant Wildman, in the gunboat *Staunch*, gained his promotion for an act of signal gallantry on the China coast in 1858, and the same year Commander Cresswell, in the *Surprise*, near Hong Kong, either destroyed or captured a flotilla of twenty-six pirate vessels after a spirited action, and Captain Vansittart, with the *Magicienne*, *Inflexible*, and gun-boats *Plover* and *Algerine*, had great success in rooting out piracy along the seaboard to the westward of that port.

In 1852 broke out the second of our Burmese wars, which resulted in the annexation of Pegu. The Indian Government despatched an army of 5,760 men, under the command of General Godwin, an officer who had served with distinction in the war twenty-six years before, and a fleet of Royal and Indian Navy ships acted in conjunction. The former, under Rear-Admiral Austen, consisted of the *Fox*, 40, *Rattler*, *Serpent*, *Hermes*, and *Salamander*, and the latter of a fine squadron of steam-frigates of the Indian Navy, under Commodore Lynch, and some armed steamships of the Bengal Marine. Martaban was taken on the 5th April after a brief bombardment, but the Burmese offered a determined resistance at Rangoon, where the Hon. Company's steam-frigates, *Feroze*, *Moozuffer*, and *Sesostris*—which had taken part in the China War in 1842—as well as the *Fox* and *Rattler*, silenced the guns and captured the stockades. This was on the 11th and 12th April, and on the following day the *Feroze*, *Moozuffer*, H.M. brig *Serpent*, and the *Phlegethon* steamship, engaged the stockade at Kemmendine, after which a party from the ships landed and burnt it.

The chief military achievement was the storming on the 14th April of the great Shoé Dagon Pagoda, a vast temple, strongly fortified and defended by several thousand men. A detachment of seamen assisted on shore, and the fall of what was practically the citadel of Rangoon put an end to all further resistance. The ships co-operated in the attack by their shell fire, and Commander Campbell, of the *Sesostris*, fired red-hot shot from his 68-pounders, and blew up the magazine in a stockade, as detailed in a letter to the *Times* of the 1st June, 1852. Admiral Austen now surrendered the command to Commodore Lambert, and returned to Calcutta.

General Godwin, embarking with 800 men in the *Moozuffer* and *Sesostris*, and the steamships *Pluto* and *Tenasserim*, accompanied by Commodore Lambert, sailed to make an attack on Bassein, an important town held by about 6,000 Burmese troops. On the 20th May the ships opened fire on the works, consisting, says the commodore, " of a very extensive fort, a long line of stockades, and a strong work round the Pagoda," and on the opposite, or right bank, of the Bassein river was a large and strong stockade. These works were silenced by the fire of the steam frigates, under Commander Campbell, I.N., and while the troops stormed the enemy's works, a strong detachment of seamen took the stockade on the right bank. Commodore Lambert thanked Commanders Campbell and Hewett "for the skill and ability with which they brought their ships up a river imperfectly surveyed for more than 60 miles;" and to the officers and men he expressed his thanks "for their steady, gallant, and cheerful conduct." Fifty-four guns, besides 32 jingalls, were captured at Bassein, and the Governor-General issued a special notification of thanks to the troops and seamen engaged.

Some fighting took place at Martaban, which was held by our troops, but the enemy were driven off with great loss, to which the fire of the *Feroze* contributed. In June, an expedition, consisting of troops and ships' boats, under Commander Tarleton, of the *Fox*, proceeded to Pegu, which was captured, and in July the same officer embarked in the Hon. Company's steamship *Medusa*, Lieutenant Fraser, with three other steamers and some boats from the *Fox*, and made his way up the river to Prome, where 28 guns were captured. In this affair, Acting-Lieutenant Hunter, I.N., of the *Medusa*, lost an arm, and Commander Tarleton spoke in high terms of the zeal and attention shown by all in their duties. Tarleton received promotion for his services, and Commander Shadwell was appointed to the command of the Irrawaddy flotilla.

On the arrival of large military reinforcements, General Godwin and Commodore Lambert proceeded up the river to Prome with a strong combined force, including the *Sesostris* and *Medusa*, with the steam-vessels and nine boats from the ships. This important Burmese town was taken, after some fighting, in which the gallant commander of the *Sesostris* received special commendation from the commodore. This ship and the *Medusa* remained to assist in the defence of Prome, and were engaged in repelling the repeated attempts made by the enemy to retake the place. The *Winchester* now arrived at Rangoon, and Captain Loch, C.B., in conjunction with Sir John Cheape, commanding at Prome, undertook active operations against the enemy, with the boats of his ship and of the two steam-frigates, among those engaged at this time under his orders being Commander Beauchamp Seymour, since so well known as Lord Alcester.

In March, Pegu, which had been evacuated, was re-occupied by us, but the enemy made great efforts to retake the town, and in the operations which ensued, the boats of the *Fox*, *Sphinx*, and *Moozuffer*, under Commander Shadwell, suffered a loss of over 30 killed and wounded. General Godwin proceeded to relieve the place, attacked on all sides by the Burmese, and was assisted by Captain Tarleton with the boats of the squadron, and a strong detachment of seamen and marines serving on shore. The fighting round Pegu at this time was very severe, and the Navy received great commendation from the General for the assistance afforded on the river with the convoy, and in transporting the field-pieces " a distance of eight or nine miles through a difficult country under an ardent sun."

In May, 1853, General Steel set out for Tonghoo from Martaban, which received sufficient protection throughout these months from the guns of the *Feroze*. Her first Lieutenant, Hellard, afforded the General material assistance by forcing his way up the Sittang with three boats from his ship, which escorted a convoy of craft laden with provisions for the military force. The Governor-General specially thanked this officer for the important service rendered on this occasion.

Myatoon, the notorious Burmese dacoit (or patriot, as his countrymen regarded him), made himself very obnoxious by burning Donabew and other villages, and by his active hostility against the British. In December, 1852, Commodore Hewett, of the *Moozuffer*, with the boats of his ship and of the *Fox*, surprised 3,000 of Myatoon's men, and killed a large number of them, but a second attack, made in the following January, by the boats of the *Fox*, *Moozuffer*, and *Zenobia*, under Commander Lambert of the flagship, was not equally successful, and the boats were forced to retire with the loss of 12 men, including Lieutenant Michison, of the *Zenobia*, who lost a leg. Myatoon now took up a strong position at Donabew, and, on the 4th February, Captain Loch proceeded to dislodge him with 225 seamen and marines from the *Fox*, *Sphinx*, and

Winchester, 300 Sepoys of the 67th Bengal N.I., under Major Minchin, and two three-pounders from the *Phlegethon*. Captain Loch was an officer of dash and enterprise, but he was out of his element in jungle warfare. The first intimation he had of the position of the enemy was a heavy and destructive fire, and in a vain but gallant effort to get at close quarters with the unseen foe, he was killed, as well as Lieutenant Kennedy, first of the *Fox*, and Captain Price, of the 67th, and 80 men were placed *hors de combat*. The column retreated, leaving behind the two field-pieces, and the disaster necessitated the dispatch of a second expedition under the command of Sir John Cheape. This was completely successful, after some severe fighting in which Lord Wolseley, then a subaltern in the 80th Regiment, first brought himself into notice by heading two storming parties in one day. Acting in co-operation with the main column was Commander Rennie, I.N., of the *Zenobia*, with 80 seamen. This officer, who had served in the China War as First Lieutenant of the *Sesostris*, and had done good service in the preceding January near Bassein, engaged and routed with much loss 800 Burmese regular soldiers. The dispersion of Myatoon's followers was the last important service of the Burmese War, but the army of occupation and the Indian Navy ships and flotilla had much harassing work dealing with dacoits and reducing the newly acquired province of Pegu to subjection. The Burmese, though of little account in regular warfare, are adepts at dacoiting on a large scale, as we have found to our cost in the recent conquest and annexation of Upper Burmah.

In another quarter of the globe, a few years before, the prowess of our seamen received a conspicuous illustration. Rosas, the dictator of Buenos Ayres, closed the Parana river to commerce, and a British and French squadron, the former under Captain Hotham, undertook to free the navigation. Shortly before Garibaldi, who afterwards attained a world-wide reputation, under protection of the British admiral, had made his way up the Uruguay river as far as Paysandu, but the freeing of the Parana river was known to be a far more difficult task, as Rosas had established strong batteries at Obligado, about 100 miles from its entrance. In November, 1845, this was attempted by the combined English and French squadrons, the former consisting of the steamers *Gorgon*, *Firebrand*, and *Fulton*, and sailing vessels *Philomel*, *Comus*, and *Dolphin*, with the tender *Fairy*. Captain Hotham commanded, and the squadron was piloted by Commander Sulivan, in the surveying vessel *Philomel*, who later did such conspicuous service in the same capacity in the Baltic, during the

Russian War. This officer examined the batteries on the right bank of the river, here about 800 yards wide, which were found to mount 22 heavy guns. There was also a barrier of twenty-four boats, moored across the stream, with gun-boats to protect them, and eight field-pieces were posted in the rear of the batteries. The sailing vessels of both squadrons commenced the attack, the steamers being held in reserve, and gallantly they engaged the batteries for two hours, the *Philomel* and *Dolphin* being conspicuous on the English side, and the *San Martin* on the French. At length Captain Hope, of the *Firebrand*—the same officer who displayed such heroism at the attack on the Peiho forts — dashed forward, and under a hot fire, severed the iron chains holding together the barrier, when the three steamers passed through and engaged the batteries, while below, the English *Comus* and a French gun-boat continued the action at close range. The enemy's fire being almost silenced, at 5 o'clock Captains Hotham and Sulivan landed at the head of 300 seamen and marines, and stormed the upper fort, while Commander Hope drove the enemy out of the wood. The other batteries were also carried, the British loss being 33 killed and wounded and that of the French rather more.

Pushing up the river Parana to Corrientes, 800 miles from its mouth, Captain Hotham negotiated with the chiefs, but Rosas was exasperated with his defeat, and on the return of the allied squadron, they found their way barred by strong batteries at San Lorenzo. A smart action took place on the 4th June, but the fire of the *Gorgon*, *Firebrand*, *Fulton*, and the French *Gassendi* enabled the convoy of twenty sail they were escorting, to run the gauntlet with slight loss. This concluded the operations in this quarter of the globe, which, as regards their success and daring, reflected great credit on all the officers and men engaged.

A chapter, and a long and honourable one, might be written on the services of the British Navy in the suppression of slavery, a duty distasteful to officers and men from the nature of the climate on the West Coast of Africa, and the small opportunities afforded for earning distinction. Occasionally the slavers showed fight, as in 1830, when the *Primrose*, 16, Commander Broughton, engaged the *Veloz Passagera*, of 20 guns and a crew of 150 desperadoes of all nations, bound from the Guinea coast to Havannah. The slaver resisted the demand to search her, and an action was fought at pistol-shot range, which was terminated by Captain Broughton running alongside the ship, and boarding her at the head of his men. A severe hand-to-hand combat ensued, but the slaver was captured, with the loss of 46 of her crew killed, the cruiser losing three killed and 12 wounded, including her gallant commander. On this occasion 550 slaves were released.

Not long after, an equally meritorious capture was made by the *Black Joke*, Lieutenant Ramsay, mounting a pivot 68-pounder and a carronade, with a crew of 44 men and boys. Her opponent was a notorious slaver, carrying five 18-pounders and 77 men. The *Marinerito*, as she was called, was brought to action off the old Calabar river, after a long chase and pull at the sweeps, during which the slaver kept up a running fire, when Lieutenant Ramsay ran alongside and brought matters to a crisis by boarding at the head of his brave fellows. Owing to the shock when the ships came into collision, the *Black Joke* rebounded, leaving the gallant officer on the slaver's deck with only 10 men at his back, but the cruiser was speedily pulled alongside again, and almost every man of her crew jumped on board the *Marinerito*, which was carried after a severe struggle, in which Ramsay was wounded, together with eight of his men, the slaver losing 15 killed alone. Her living cargo of nearly 500 slaves was landed at Fernando Po, and the gallant lieutenant received well-earned promotion.

But to make the steps for the extirpation of the slave trade really effective it was necessary to destroy the barracoons, or fortified slave depots ashore. The first to adopt this step was Commander the Hon. J. Denman, at that time senior naval officer on the West Coast of Africa. With this view he made treaties with the native chiefs on the Guinea coast, and destroyed their depots, a precedent that was followed by his successors. In January, 1851, the squadron made an attempt on Lagos, then held by one Kosoko, who had expelled the legitimate ruler, and some severe fighting took place, in which a midshipman and many men were killed when attempting to land in face of a heavy fire from the stockade. Captain Lyster was more successful, and stormed a battery, and on the following day Kosoko fled and Lagos was taken possession of and ultimately became a British colony. In effecting this service, our loss was 17 killed and over 70 wounded, including Captain Lyster and Commander Hillyer. Since that period small expeditions have constantly proceeded up the rivers and creeks of the Bight of Benin and West Coast generally, to keep the peace or punish aggression among the "kings," as the petty chiefs delight to call themselves. On the Zanzibar coast of Africa, the cruisers of the Indian Navy, until the abolition of that service in 1863, and the ships-of-war of the British Navy, both before and since, have been engaged in noble and self-denying efforts to eradicate this great evil, against which our common humanity cries out.

In another quarter of the globe, during the war with Persia in 1856-57, important services were rendered by our seamen in bringing the enemy to terms. In this case the Indian Navy were engaged without any aid from their royal brethren, and therefore we will only briefly mention two of the most striking events of the war in which they had the chief part. After occupying the island of Kharrack in the Persian Gulf, and disembarking the army at Hallilah Bay, near Bushire, the Indian Navy squadron bombarded Bushire, which surrendered on the 10th December. Sir James Outram, on his arrival to assume command of the expedition, advanced from Bushire as far as Boorazgoon, 46 miles into the interior, and on his return march fought an action at Kooshaub, where he totally defeated a superior Persian force. With 5,000 men the gallant general then sailed up the Shatt-ul-Arab, as the river is called into which flow the waters of the classic Tigris and Euphrates, and the Indian Navy squadron engaged the earthworks at Mohamrah, near the confluence of these rivers. The defences were of very great strength, being 20 feet thick and 18 feet high, with casemated embrasures, mounted with heavy guns, and were held by a Persian army of 13,000 men, with 30 guns. The attack by the Indian Navy squadron of four steam-frigates, one steam-sloop and two sailing sloops-of-war, under Commodore Young, was made on the 26th March, 1857, first at a range of 800 yards and then of 300. After the fire had continued for more than an hour, the *Feroze*, Commander Rennie, flying the commodore's broad pennant, and *Assaye*, Commander Adams, took up a position within 60 yards of the great north fort, while the other ships lay in line astern. At the end of three hours the north fort blew up, and gradually the enemy's fire slackened. At 1 o'clock, the works being silenced, the steam transports moved up and landed the troops a mile above the earthworks, and while Lieutenant Clarkson, first of the *Assaye*, landed and took possession of the north fort, General Havelock, advancing through the date groves, entered the entrenched camp, whence the enemy fled, leaving behind 16 guns and an enormous quantity of ammunition and stores. As that great soldier, who was soon to earn deathless renown in the suppression of the Indian Mutiny, remarked in a letter to his wife:—"The gentlemen in blue had it all to themselves, and left us naught to do." The loss in the squadron was only 10 killed and 30 wounded, a result attributable to the enemy's guns being elevated for a much greater range than that at which the forts actually engaged, and to the wise prevision of Commander Rennie in placing round the ships' hulls trusses of pressed hay, which, at the termination of the action, were found to be full of bullets. The same officer conducted a successful expedition up the river Karoon to the town of Ahwaz, situated about 100 miles up that stream. The naval portion consisted of three armed steamers, with three gun-boats and some ships' boats, and the military, of 300 men from the 64th Regiment and 78th Highlanders under Captain Hunt. On arriving near Ahwaz the troops were landed, and advancing under cover of the fire of the flotilla, captured the town, from which a Persian force of 7,000 men, with six guns, precipitately retreated. The conclusion of peace at Paris, on the 4th March, brought this admirably conducted war to a conclusion, and fortunate indeed it was so, for within a few months our Indian Empire was engaged in a desperate struggle with the mutinous Indian army, and every available European soldier was required in Bengal, where the 64th and 78th Regiments, under Generals Outram and Havelock, specially distinguished themselves.

The last of the "little wars" we shall refer to here before detailing the share taken by the Navy in the great struggle with Russia, was that in New Zealand. Here little glory could be acquired, while there was much hard fighting, as the enemy displayed considerable ingenuity in the construction of their "pahs," or stockades, and conspicuous valour in defending them. There was fighting in 1845-6, before Kawiti's pah, in which detachments of seamen from H.M.S. *North Star*, *Racehorse*, and *Osprey*, and from the Hon. Company's sloop-of-war *Elphinstone*, numbering 35 officers and 360 men, co-operated with 720 troops drawn from the 58th and 99th Regiments, the whole under Colonel Despard. With much labour the guns and stores were transported inland, and after a bombardment of 24 hours, on the night of the 10th May, 1846, the enemy abandoned the works, described by Colonel Despard as "the strongest fortress which the New Zealanders had ever erected." The British loss in this affair was 12 killed and 30 wounded.

In 1860 broke out the first Taranaki war, which gave rise to some heavy fighting, with considerable loss to us. In the attack on the Rangiriri pah, 200 seamen and 1,100 soldiers were engaged, and four attempts to assault before a breach had been made were repulsed, with the loss of 35 killed and 85 wounded. The next day the Maori defenders, numbering 183, surrendered. At the attack on Orakau, our troops again suffered severely, and the enemy managed to effect their escape. But the most disastrous affair was the "Gate pah," on the 28th February, 1864, when 300 men, half seamen from the *Esk* and *Harrier*, and the remainder soldiers of the 43rd Regiment, after entering the works, were seized with panic, and fled. In this lamentable business the British loss was 27 killed, including nine officers, among whom were Colonel Booth, commanding the 43rd, and Commander Hay, of the *Esk*, and 66 wounded. Again the enemy escaped during the night through the British lines, but in the action of "Te Ranga," on the 21st June, they were defeated by Colonel Greer, and after hostilities had languished for some time, their chiefs were constrained to sue for terms. Doubtless the tactics adopted by the commanders were not suitable against a wily and brave foe, who might easily have been shelled out of their stockades, which, moreover, were assaulted before they had been breached.

At the commencement of the long peace in 1815, the attention of the Navy was turned to the more peaceful pursuits of marine surveying and exploration. The southern and eastern seas had been explored during the previous century by Cook and other great navigators, and early in the present century, Flinders examined the coasts of Australia. Attention was now directed to survey in greater detail the shores, not only of our colonies, but of foreign states.

One portion of the waters of the globe remained unexplored, and to this our Naval officers, now that war no longer offered its more exciting incidents, turned their eager attention. The Arctic and Antarctic seas afforded fresh fields for the display of that generous ardour which has made our Navy pre-eminent, and men like Franklin—who had served under Nelson at Copenhagen in 1801, and during the two succeeding years assisted Flinders in his explorations—entered with spirit and success on the great task of solving the problem of the North-West Passage, that will-o'-the-wisp which has brought honour and glory to few and lured many seamen to their end.

In 1818 Captains John Ross and Buchan started to reach the "North Pole," but effected nothing, though among those engaged under Ross were two famous officers, Lieutenant Edward Parry, second in command, and Midshipman James Ross, a relation of his. In the following year Parry was in command of an expedition to discover the North-West Passage, and between 1819-26, he made three voyages to the Polar regions. In the first—conducted with the *Hecla* and *Griper*—Parry found that Lancaster Sound was a strait and not a bay, as was hitherto supposed. He named it Prince Regent's Inlet, and penetrated to 110° W. Long., thus gaining the bounty of £5,000 promised by Act of Parliament. The headland he called Bounty Cape, and the island he named after Lord Melville, First Lord of the Admiralty. Near this spot he wintered, and with the assistance of Captain Sabine, R.A. (afterwards President of the Royal Society), and others of his officers, he made valuable astronomical and meteorological observations. The long wintry nights were made amusing to the men by theatrical performances, and a magazine was published for their edification.

In August, 1820, the work of exploration commenced, and Captain Parry named Banks' Land after the President of the Royal Society, and he discovered a new strait on the south side of Lancaster Sound, communicating with Prince Regent's Inlet, which he called Admiralty Inlet. More than thirty years afterwards, Captains Collinson and McClure, working from the Behring's Straits end, actually reached a point within a few miles of the spot attained by Parry in 1820, and which that great explorer beheld from Melville Island.

On his return to England, Parry again sailed with the *Hecla* and *Fury*, accompanied by James Ross and a young officer of the name of Crozier, who was destined to become a martyr to his enthusiasm for Arctic exploration. Nothing was discovered in this voyage, and in May, 1824, he proceeded for the third time with the same ships to prosecute the attempt to complete the North-West Passage. But again failure resulted, and the *Fury* was so greatly injured by the pressure of the ice that she had to be abandoned. In 1827, Parry made an effort to reach the North Pole, adopting the route by Spitzbergen, whence he made a journey by boats and sledges. Again James Ross and Crozier were his companions, and they reached 82° 45′ N. Lat., the most northerly point yet attained. So great was the drift of the ice that they lost ground, and after thirty-five days' hard work, retraced their steps to Spitzbergen.

In 1829, a civilian named Felix Booth and James Ross explored the land named after the former, and two years later, Ross, while absent from the ship on an overland journey, discovered what was considered to be the Magnetic Pole, though it has since been ascertained that "the true centre of magnetic intensity is a movable point within the frigid zone." Ross was unable to extricate his ship, and indeed his crew were only saved from starvation by reaching Barrow's Straits in August, 1832, where they discovered the stores abandoned by the *Fury*. In July of the following year they embarked in their boats, and made their way to open water, and returned to England in a whaler. Early in the same year, the *Terror* was despatched to the assistance of the long-lost voyagers, under the late Sir John Back, who, on hearing of their safety, continued his investigations in the Arctic regions until the autumn of 1835.

Attention was now directed to the Antarctic seas, and in 1839, Captain James Ross and Commander Crozier sailed in the *Erebus* and *Terror*, but it was not until New Year's Day, 1841, that the ships actually crossed the Antarctic Circle, and ten days later they reached 71° 15', the highest latitude attained by Captain Cook. They coasted along an inhospitable shore, and sighted a range of mountains, to the highest peak of which Ross gave the name of Mount Sabine, and further southwards they came upon a still loftier mountain, which was named after the *Erebus,* and an extinct volcano he called Mount Terror, while the whole continent was designated Victoria Land. Pushing on, he penetrated to 78° South Lat., nearly four degrees further than had been reached by a whaling captain, named Weddell, in 1823.

Ross now proceeded to Tasmania, Sydney, and New Zealand, and in 1842 again crossed the Antarctic Circle at a point forty degrees more to the eastward, and thence proceeded to the Falkland Islands. Having examined Tierra del Fuego, he made a third visit in 1843 to the Southern Polar seas, and finally returned to England, where he was hailed as an explorer second to none, with the exception of Cook, Parry, and Franklin. This last is perhaps the greatest navigator of the nineteenth century, and his sad fate has added to his name an element of romantic interest such as only enshrines the memory of the great Cook.

In 1821, while Parry was striving to discover the North-West Passage, Captain Franklin was engaged exploring by land the northern coast of America, eastward from the Coppermine River. It was not until July in that year, after an absence of two years from England, that he arrived at the mouth of the Coppermine, and embarking in canoes, got as far as the cape he named Point Turnagain, whence he was compelled to return to the Hudson's Bay Company's settlement before the advent of winter. Franklin on another occasion penetrated to 149° W. Long., but some years were yet to elapse before he undertook the crowning exploit of his life. Meantime, he was appointed Governor of Tasmania, and in that capacity rendered assistance and advice to his brother officers, James Ross and Crozier, when they twice put in at Hobart Town, during their great expedition to the Antarctic seas.

In 1845, soon after his return from Tasmania, the Government, acceding to the pressing request of the Royal and other learned societies, resolved to despatch an expedition to the Polar Seas, in order to establish the existence of a water communication between the mouth of the Great Fish River and Barrow's Strait or Melville Sound, which had been traversed by Parry in his first voyage, and was the sole link required to complete the discovery of the problem known as the North-West Passage. Captain Markham, R.N., writes in his "Life of Sir John Franklin":—"The post of leader of the expedition of 1845 Sir John Franklin claimed as his special right, as being the senior

Arctic officer alive in a position to assume it. No service, he said, is nearer to my heart than the completion of the survey of the north coast of America, and the accomplishment of a North-West Passage. Lord Haddington, the First Lord of the Admiralty, on being informed that Sir John was desirous of being appointed to the command, at once sent for him, and gladdened his heart by complying with his wishes, but intimated that perhaps his age might be a bar to his being selected, as he was informed that he was sixty years of age. 'No, my lord,' was Franklin's ready and earnest response, 'You have been misinformed—I am only fifty-nine.'" Franklin was accordingly appointed to the command. He was in every respect well fitted to be the leader of the expedition which achieved the honour of accomplishing the task, described by old Purchas some two hundred and fifty years before, as "that thing yet undone whereby a notable mind might be made from us."

With Captain Crozier as his second-in-command, an officer of experience in Arctic exploration inferior to few, Sir John Franklin sailed from the Thames in May, 1845, with the *Erebus* and *Terror*. The last seen of the expedition, save by the wandering Eskimo, was on the 26th July, when some whalers sighted the ships near Lancaster Sound. When no news was heard of them for two years, Sir John Ross volunteered to go in search, but as the expedition was victualled for three years, the Government declined the offer, though, indeed, their fate was decided by the autumn of that year. In 1848, however, the Admiralty yielded to the public anxiety, and despatched two relief expeditions, one under Captain Kellett, in the *Herald*, by Behring's Straits, and the second, by the Baffin's Bay route, under the veteran Sir John Ross, who had under his command the *Enterprise* and *Investigator*. Both these expeditions failed of their purpose, and in January, 1850, Captains Collinson and McClure recommissioned the *Enterprise* and *Investigator*. The ships parted company, and Captain McClure, not finding his senior officer at Cape Lisburne, the last rendezvous, proceeded alone on a voyage pregnant with memorable results. On the 14th August the *Investigator* had passed Return Reef, Franklin's farthest on his second expedition, and by the 5th September she reached Cape Parry. Beyond this was sighted land which Captain McClure named after Sir Francis Baring, First Lord of the Admiralty, under the impression that he was its discoverer, though Parry had named the northern district of the same island Banks' Land. On the following day he saw land which he named after Prince Albert, and eagerly pushing on along the channel between the two, on the 11th reached a point which Parry, on his first voyage in 1821, had sighted from Melville Island. The ship was now wedged in by the ice close to an island which her captain named after the Princess Royal, and the channel in which it lay, running along the southern shore of Banks' Island, he called Prince of Wales's Strait. McClure started in October with a sledge party along the coast towards the point on Melville Sound attained by Parry, and on the 26th sighted the eastern entrance of the strait in which his ship lay and thus achieved the North-West Passage, and made his name for ever famous. But the great enterprise had been accomplished two years before by Sir John Franklin's companions, the survivors of the crews of the *Erebus* and *Terror*, while seeking to escape from the starvation which ultimately overtook them.

In the summer of 1851 Captain McClure made an attempt to pass the short intervening space of 30 miles between him and Melville Sound, but was compelled to winter in a bay he called Mercy. In the following spring he crossed in a sledge to Melville Island, and visited Parry's winter quarters, but the ice bound him in, and he passed a second winter in Mercy Bay. As starvation threatened the destruction of his crew, in April, 1853, he made preparations to send a portion overland, while with 30 men he remained by the ship in the hope of forcing his way through the ice.

His long absence from England had excited apprehensions as to his safety, and in the spring of 1852 an expedition was despatched to his rescue, under Sir Edward Belcher in the *Assistance*. The other ships were the *Pioneer*, Commander Richards, the *Resolute*, Captain Kellett, and the *Intrepid*, Commander McClintock. The two latter reached Melville Island, where one of the search parties, under Lieutenant Mecham, discovered a record McClure had cut on the sandstone. In the following spring Lieutenant Pim, of the *Resolute*, was despatched to Banks' Island, and there discovered the *Investigator* just in time to save the crew. The ships were now abandoned, and Captain Kellett and Commander McClintock proposed to navigate the *Resolute* and *Intrepid* to England, when Sir Edward Belcher, who had had no previous experience of Arctic exploration, issued orders that all the four ships were to be abandoned in the ice. Kellett and McClintock vainly protested, but Belcher was peremptory, and the crews were divided between the *North Star, Phœnix* and *Talbot*, which had arrived from England. The *Resolute*, indeed, drifted out of the ice into Baffin's Bay in the course of the summer, and was picked up by a Yankee whaler, and eventually the American Government restored her to the Queen.

Captain Collinson, in the *Enterprise*, also made discoveries of great importance, though they were thrown into the shade by the achievement of his subordinate officer, McClure who was knighted, and with his men fêted with great honour on his return to England. Collinson passed the winter of 1851 off Prince Albert Land, and one of his sledging parties, crossing the channel, reached Melville Island, where the *Investigator* then was wintering, without seeing her. He found that Prince Albert Land, Wollaston Land, and Victoria Land were all portions of one island, and discovered traces of Franklin's ships. Indeed, in the spring of 1853 he reached a point within 40 miles of the spot where the *Erebus* and *Terror* had been abandoned five years before. The *Enterprise* returned by the Behring Sea, and in May, 1855, anchored at Portsmouth after an absence of over five years. Before this, however, intelligence of Franklin's party was learned by Dr. Rae, an officer of the Hudson's Bay Company, from the Eskimos, who reported that a party of 40 men had been seen some years before travelling with sledges over the ice, and that their dead bodies were afterwards found beyond the Great Fish River. As the Government were satisfied that Sir John Franklin and his party were beyond human aid, the gallant officer's widow herself, with the assistance of friends, purchased and equipped the steam yacht *Fox*, in command of which Commander McClintock sailed from Aberdeen in July, 1857.

For eight months the little *Fox* drifted about in the pack ice, and in August in the following year her progress was arrested by the ice in Peel Sound. Descending Regent's Inlet, she wintered at the western outlet of Bellot Strait, so called after a gallant French naval officer serving in one of our expeditions, who lost his life there, about 100 miles from the spot where the Eskimos asserted they had seen the relics of the Franklin expedition. Early in the spring of 1859 McClintock despatched sledging parties, one of which, under his own command, discovered, near Cape Herschell, on King William's Island, the skeleton of a member of the missing crews.

More important was the find of Lieutenant Hobson, who had directed his course towards Cape Felix, on the north-eastern extremity of the same island. Tents, blankets, clothes, and a boat's flag rewarded his search, and, proceeding, he found, a few miles further on, at Point Victory, a cairn, manifestly erected by Franklin's men, in which a tin case had been deposited, containing a paper with the brief but piteous narrative, written at intervals of nearly a year apart, the last being dated the very day before the survivors started on their sad journey to the Great Fish River. It told that in the first year of his voyage Franklin had conducted his ships successfully up Wellington Channel, penetrating as far as the seventy-seventh degree of latitude, to the north of Bathurst Island, returning through the narrow strait which separates it from

Cornwallis Island, and wintering at Beechey Island. The next year he worked down Peel Channel, and was hemmed in by the ice a few miles to the north-west of the cape where this record was found. In the following spring he sent out travelling parties, and when those who penned the first portion of this record left the ships on May 24th, 1847, all was still well.

In less than three weeks from that time a different tale had to be told. On the 11th June Franklin died. In the course of the next ten months twenty-three more shared his fate, and during the whole of that summer and winter the ice held the ships in its unyielding grasp. Crozier still survived, but when spring returned, as their provisions were almost exhausted, he resolved to abandon the ships, and on the 26th April, 1848, he started with 104 men for the Great Fish River. From that day the only record was that supplied by the Eskimos, which related to a portion only of the crews. Crozier and his gallant comrades reached the mouth of the Great Fish River during the year, and as the line of coast from the west bank of that stream to Behring's sea had been already traced, these British seamen, in their last despairing efforts to save their lives, had actually completed the discovery of the North-West Passage, thus anticipating McClure's great feat by two years.

The enthusiasm for Arctic discovery flagged somewhat after these events, but the work of exploring the Polar area was slowly but surely carried on by all the nautical powers, America and Austria, with England, taking the lead. The most important and successful expedition undertaken by this country was that under the leadership of Captain George Nares. A sledging party, under Commander Markham, reached a point considerably nearer the Pole than had before been attained, and the observations of the expedition in these high latitudes were of an extended and valuable character.

CHAPTER IX.

The War with Russia—Expedition to the Black Sea—Bombardment of Odessa—Siege of Sebastopol—The Expedition to Kertch and Yenikale—Commander Lyons, of the *Miranda*—Expedition to Kinburn—Operations in the Baltic—Capture of the Forts of Bomarsund—Commander Lyons at Kola—The Failure at Petropaulovski—The Baltic Fleet in 1855—Bombardment of Sweaborg—The Indian Mutiny—Services of the *Shannon* Brigade at the Relief and Siege of Lucknow—The Indian Navy Detachments serving on Shore.

ON the causes of the war with Russia, the first struggle with a European power in which we have been involved since the Napoleonic period, we will not dilate, as being foreign to the purpose and scope of this work.

Soon after the destruction of the Turkish squadron at Sinope, when all the ships, with the exception of one small steamer, were sunk, and over 3,000 men were slaughtered, the allied French and British fleets entered the Black Sea, and on the 28th March, 1854, this country declared war against Russia. On the 17th April, the combined fleets sailed for Odessa. The British contingent consisted of ten sail-of-the-line, eleven frigates—two of which, as well as the *Agamemnon* and *Sanspareil*, ships-of-the-line, were auxiliary screws—four paddle steam-frigates, and nine paddle steam-sloops. Admiral Dundas was in command, with his flag in the *Britannia*, 120, and Sir Edmund Lyons, in the *Agamemnon*, 90, was second in command, and before the close of the year, became commander-in-chief, a position he filled with great honour to his country.

The French fleet, commanded by Admiral Hamelin, who hoisted his flag on board the *Ville de Paris*, 120, consisted of fifteen ships-of-the-line and twenty-one frigates and smaller vessels.

On arriving before Odessa the allied admirals demanded the surrender of the Russian fleet, as a punishment for having fired on the *Furious* when under a flag of truce, but as no answer was received, on the 22nd April the steamships *Terrible*, *Tiger*, *Retribution*, and *Furious*, under Captain Jones, and three belonging to our allies, stood in and opened fire on the enemy's works. The squadron moved in a circle, delivering their fire each time on passing the works. The frigate, *Arethusa*, Captain Mends, also stood in and engaged the mole, the fort at the extremity of which she blew up. The batteries gradually ceased to reply, when Captain Jones stood closer in, and sunk or set on fire the ships-of-war behind the mole, and soon the arsenal and storehouses, as well as the docks and batteries, were in flames. Admiral Dundas left a few vessels to cruise off the coast, but the *Tiger* unfortunately ran ashore about four miles from Odessa, where she was attacked by a field battery and some Russian infantry. Captain Giffard was mortally wounded, and ultimately was compelled to haul down his colours, and set the ship on fire.

Admiral Dundas arrived on the 28th April before Sebastopol, the defences of which Sir Edmund Lyons and Captain Mends reconnoitred, and ascertained that the enemy consisted of eleven ships-of-the-line, four frigates and some smaller vessels, which made no attempt throughout the ensuing siege to break the blockade that was rigidly enforced. In the course of the summer Captain Hyde Parker, with the *Firebrand* and *Fury*, destroyed the batteries at the Sulina mouth of the Danube.

When, after the abandonment of the siege of Silistria by the Russian army, and their retreat across the Danube, the English Government resolved to dispatch the British army to the Crimea, the conduct of the transport of the troops from Varna to its shores was committed to Sir Edmund Lyons, who had great experience of the Black Sea, having formerly surveyed its waters.

The army of 26,000 men, with 54 guns, and the stores, was landed without loss, at Old Fort, near Eupatoria, between the 14th and midnight of the 18th September, and two days later was fought the battle of the Alma. The Russian commander at Sebastopol, Prince Menschikoff, scuttled and sunk most of his ships, and as the British fleet had no enemy to contend with afloat, a naval brigade of 1,000 men, with 50 guns, was landed from the fleet, and under command of Captain Lushington, rendered valuable assistance to the army.

On the 16th October took place the first bombardment of Sebastopol, in which the allied fleet took part, the French attacking the southern side where the besieging army lay, and the British fleet engaging the defences on the north side of the harbour, including Fort Constantine, mounting over 100 heavy guns, the Telegraph battery, of 17 guns, which, being on a hill, brought a plunging fire to bear upon our ships, and the Star Fort.

Sir Edmund Lyons commanded the inshore squadron, consisting of the *Agamemnon*, *London*, *Albion*, and *Sanspareil*, to whom was entrusted the task of engaging Fort Constantine, within 750 yards of which the flagship brought up in five fathoms of water. The admiral was not unworthy to fly his flag in a ship whose name is immortalized in our history by the daring deeds of Nelson and his crew in 1794-96; and in Captain Mends of the *Arethusa*, he had one of the best officers in the Navy. The squadron opened fire about two o'clock, and a lucky shell from the flagship caused the explosion of a magazine, but soon the Russian gunners got the range of our ships, which suffered severely. The *Albion*, *Sanspareil*, and *London* were compelled to haul off, and the *Agamemnon* sustained alone the enemy's concentrated fire until the two former returned, and the admiral signalled the *Queen*, *Rodney*, *Bellerophon*, and *Arethusa* to come to his assistance. The *Queen* was set on fire by a shell, and the *Rodney* grounded, though she was towed off by the *Spitfire*, all the time continuing her fire, and at length, towards evening, the squadron retired, having effected nothing of importance, though among the slain was Admiral Nachimoff, the officer who had so wantonly destroyed the Turkish ships at Sinope. The British loss was 44 killed and 262 wounded, the chief sufferer being the *Albion*. This ship and the *Arethusa* had been so much injured by the Russian fire that they were sent to Malta for repairs.

On shore the Naval Brigade did excellent service throughout the siege, especially with the 8-inch guns landed from the *Terrible* and *Retribution*, and on the 26th October a young mate, Mr. Hewett (afterwards Admiral Sir William Hewett), performed an act of gallantry for which he was awarded the Victoria Cross. A body of Russians made a sortie and advanced within three hundred yards of a Lancaster gun under his command, which he was ordered to spike, and fall back, but the young sailor refused to do so until he had received instructions from Captain Lushington, and when the Russian column retreated, he brought his gun to bear on them with good effect. At the battle of Inkerman, on the 5th November, Lieutenant Hewett (as he now was) again distinguished himself, and Captain (afterwards Sir William) Peel, of the *Diamond*, frigate, who was serving ashore with the Naval Brigade, was engaged with the Guards in the desperate conflict at the Sandbag battery.

A terrible storm broke over the fleet on the 14th November, when the ships-of-war escaped with trifling damage; but it was otherwise with the transports, which were riding at anchor outside Balaclava Bay. No less than forty vessels foundered or went to pieces on the rocks, including the *Prince*, transport, which had only arrived from England a few days before with ammunition and stores, and in all some 400 seamen were drowned. The French and Turkish fleets each lost a ship-of-the-line in this memorable storm, besides some smaller vessels, and the loss of stores, urgently needed by the army, aggravated their miserable condition during the winter, which had now set in with Arctic rigour.

On the 17th February, 1855, Captain Hastings, with the *Curacoa, Furious, Valorous,* and *Viper*, and a French steamer, assisted Omar Pasha in repelling the attack of General Liprandi. Bringing his squadron close in shore he supported the Turkish right flank by the fire of his guns. No more attacks were made on the sea-forts, but some of the ships steamed in at night, and assisted the besiegers by their fire.

In May, a combined military and naval expedition, drawn from the British and French services, consisting of nine sail-of-the-line and forty-seven frigates and smaller vessels, with 16,000 troops, sailed to attack Kertch, at the eastern extremity of the Crimea, which the Russians abandoned at their approach. Yenikale also fell into the hands of the allies, who, after taking what stores could be embarked, destroyed the remainder. Commander Lyons, of the *Miranda*, steamed into the sea of Azof, with thirteen English and four French gunboats, and burnt or sunk no less than two hundred and fifty vessels laden with stores. In the operations at Genitchesk, Lieutenants McKenzie and Buckley, of the *Miranda*, and Lieutenant Burgoyne, of the *Wrangler*, performed excellent service, and the boats were engaged with a detachment of Russian troops and a battery. Thence Commander Lyons proceeded to Taganrog, and, aided by the launches of the fleet and some light gunboats, engaged the batteries, while the boats of the squadron, under Commander Coles and Lieutenants McKenzie and Buckley, destroyed the magazine, though the place was defended by 3,000 troops. Mariopol, at the entrance of the Gulf of Azof, was subjected to the same treatment, and also Gheisk, on the other side. Though the military results of the expedition to Kertch and the Sea of Azof were small, the Russian army was greatly crippled by the loss of the vast accumulation of stores and ammunition. Unhappily Commander Lyons did not survive to receive the promotion he had so well earned. On rejoining the fleet before Sebastopol, while engaged with the smaller vessels in making night attacks on the outer defences, he was wounded in the leg by a shell, and died within a week in the hospital at Therapia, to which he had been removed.

Commander Sherard Osborn, of the *Vesuvius*, an officer of equal energy and gallantry, succeeded to the command of the Sea of Azof squadron, and continued the task of harassing the Russian commanders, and destroying their magazines on the shore of that inland sea. In this service he was assisted by a host of gallant young officers, including, besides those already mentioned, Lieutenants Lambert of the *Curlew*, Commerell of the *Weser*, Hewett of the *Beagle*, Hudson of the *Jasper*, and Day of the *Recruit*. On the institution of the Victoria Cross, in the following year,

H.M.S. BLENHEIM.
1st CLASS CRUISER.

Hewett, Commerell, Burgoyne and other officers were among its first recipients. On the two nights preceding the attack of the 18th June on the Redan and other defences of Sebastopol, a portion of the fleet co-operated together with their launches fitted as rocket-boats, and the Naval Brigade, under Captain Peel, assisted at the assault. The two ladder-parties, of 60 men each, were led by Captain Peel, who was severely wounded, and 14 men were killed and 47 wounded, including all the officers except three. A young midshipman was present on that occasion and was severely wounded, named Evelyn Wood, who lived to become one of the greatest ornaments of the sister service. In the following July, Captain Lushington, on attaining flag-rank, was succeeded by Captain Hon. Henry Keppel, who remained in command of the Naval Brigade till the close of the siege, including the final bombardment on the 7th September, the day preceding the last memorable but unsuccessful assault of the Redan.

In the autumn, a combined military and naval expedition was planned by the allied commanders for an attack on the Russian ports at the mouth of the Dnieper and Bog. The British contingent consisted of six sail-of-the-line, nine steam frigates, and twenty-four smaller vessels, with 4,000 troops, which sailed, together with our allies, for Odessa. On the 14th October the expedition arrived before Kinburn, forty miles to the eastward of Odessa, where was a strong casemated fort, mounting nearly 70 guns, with two earthworks armed with 10 guns each. The waters here were shallow and difficult, but Captain Spratt, of the *Spitfire*, had surveyed them, and on the 17th the attack was commenced by the English mortar-boats supported by three French floating batteries. Later in the day the line-of-battle ships, headed by the *Royal Albert*, 130, flagship of Sir Edmund Lyons, now Commander-in-Chief, attacked the forts on the southern side at a range of 1,200 yards, while the opposite face was engaged by the steam frigates, led by Sir Houston Stewart and Admiral Pellion. So irresistible was the fire that, in ten minutes, the Governor surrendered Kinburn to the allied commanders, and the fort of Oczakow, on the other side of the bay, was blown up to prevent its falling into their hands. Sir Edmund Lyons, leaving a French garrison in Kinburn, sailed with a small squadron for Kazatch Bay, where he arrived on the 2nd November, and thus were concluded, so far as the Black Sea was concerned, the naval operations of the Russian war.

On the outbreak of hostilities, a powerful fleet was fitted out to attack the enemy in the Baltic, and was placed in command of Sir Charles Napier, a veteran officer who had repeatedly distinguished himself during the great Napoleonic struggle, and was second in command under Admiral Stopford at Acre. But the gallant officer, though eager to crown his early achievements by one greater than all, and confident in his unimpaired ability to do so, had not taken sufficient account of the inroads that age makes on the strongest nerve and the most iron frame, and though Lord Howe won his proudest triumph when sixty-nine, a year older than Sir Charles Napier now was, his was an exceptional case, and experience, especially that of the Crimean War, has shown the unwisdom of entrusting officers over threescore with the conduct of warlike operations.

The admiral sailed in March, 1854, with a fleet consisting of nineteen ships-of-the-line, the greater portion having auxiliary screws, and twenty frigates and steam-ships. Expectation ran high as to the outcome of the expedition to the Baltic, but the people of England were grievously disappointed. As regards the ships themselves the fleet was magnificent, but the *personnel* was not equally good, for the complement of some of the crews was made up by landsmen, who had never before set foot on board ship. However, with such first-rate officers as Chads, Michael Seymour, Elliott, Keppel, Hope, Warden, Hall, Key, Yelverton, and a host of others, the raw material was rapidly worked up into the British man-o'-war's-man. The fleet arrived at Hango Head, where it lay inactive for a few weeks, during which an attack was made on some forts, but the ships were recalled by signal without effecting anything. Some small squadrons cruised about, inflicting damage on Russian commerce, and Captain Yelverton, with the *Arrogant*, 46, and the *Hecla*, steamer, of 6 guns, Commander Hall, engaged and silenced some batteries at Ekness, in a narrow creek, eight miles from the sea.

On being joined by nine French ships-of-the-line under Admirals Dechasnes and Penaud, Sir Charles Napier sailed for Cronstadt; but Captain Sulivan, of the *Lightning*, who reconnoitred the defences, found them too strong to be attacked save by mortars, of which the fleet had none. He reported the presence of eighteen sail-of-the-line in the port, but as they could not be induced to venture out, though only confronted by an equal number of allied ships, the combined fleet retired to Baro Sound.

Meanwhile Captain Key, with the *Amphion* and *Conflict*, blockaded the Gulf of Riga, and some desultory operations with boats were undertaken at Uleaborg, at the top of the Gulf of Bothnia, where thirty-four Russian trading ships were destroyed, and on the Finnish coast, where the boats of the *Odin* and *Vulture* met with a repulse.

Acting on the information supplied by the indefatigable Captain Sulivan, Sir Charles Napier resolved on making an attack on Bomarsund; and the French Emperor having, at the request of our Government, dispatched General Baraguay d'Hilliers with 9,000 men to aid him, early in August the plan was put into execution. The French troops were landed on the south-west side of the principal fort, and the British detachment, consisting of 700 seamen and marines, and a party of sappers, under Brigadier-General Harry Jones, were disembarked near one to the northward. Batteries were erected and both forts were reduced, the squadron, meanwhile, pouring a heavy fire on the principal fort, which capitulated on the morning of the 16th August, and finally the battery on Presto Island was silenced, and thus the whole of the works fell into the hands of the allied commanders. This success concluded the operations for that year, as Sir Charles Napier declined to adopt the plans of General Jones for an attack on Sweaborg, after Cronstadt the most important Russian fortress in the Baltic, and returned with his fleet to England, where disappointment was loudly expressed at the small results of the naval campaign.

During the summer, however, Commander Lyons, of the *Miranda*, who afterwards died of wounds received before Sebastopol, performed excellent service in the White Sea, at the northern extremity of Russia. With his ship and the *Brisk* he silenced some guns on an island, and then with the gallantry and enterprise for which he was distinguished, proceeded up a narrow river a distance of 30 miles, and attacked Kola, the capital of Russian Lapland. With the *Miranda* alone he engaged the battery, set the town and storehouses on fire, and returned without loss to the mouth of the river. The success of the enterprise showed what could be effected with small means by a resolute seaman, and the failure of another at the other extremity of the Russian Empire also demonstrated that adequate means would not ensure success, if wielded by an incompetent or timid officer. At Petropaulovski, the principal seaport of Kamtschatka, lay two Russian ships, the *Aurora*, 44, partially disarmed, and the 20-gun corvette *Dwina*, whose capture or destruction Captain Sir Frederick Nicolson undertook with a squadron consisting of the *President*, 50, *Pique*, 40, and *Virago*, steamship of 6 guns, a force which, in combination with three French ships, respectively of 60, 22, and 12 guns, was amply sufficient for the purpose if judiciously and boldly handled. The enemy's ships lay moored behind the point of a sandbank, and the entrance to the harbour was protected by some batteries, mounting about 22 guns. On the 31st August the British frigates *President* and *Pique*, and the 60-gunship *Forte*, carrying the French Admiral's flag, engaged the batteries, but at so long a range that the fire had no effect. The *Virago*, on the other hand, attacked and disabled a three-gun battery, and landing a party, spiked the guns, after which she stood in to engage the enemy's ships.

"Presently," says a writer, "having received a heavy shot between wind and water, she signalled for assistance, but instead of getting it, Sir F. Nicolson went on board and ordered her out to tow off the French admiral, who had asked for such aid, and at the close of the day the frigates hauled off, contented with having expended a great quantity of ammunition, and with having done but little more." Three days passed away, when the allied commanders attacked two batteries of seven and five guns, and having silenced them, landed a party of 700 seamen and marines, under Captain Burridge, of the *President*, and La Grandière, of the *Eurydice*, to capture a fort on high ground in the rear commanding the town. Hardly, however, had they landed than they were suddenly attacked by a body of Russian troops, and were compelled to retreat. In this ill-considered enterprise the British loss was 26 killed and a large number wounded and prisoners, and our allies suffered equally.

In March and April, 1855, a powerful fleet for the second time sailed for the Baltic, under the command of Rear-Admiral Hon. R. Dundas, with Rear-Admiral Michael Seymour as second in command. The fleet consisted of twenty sail-of-the-line, five frigates, nine sloops-of-war, and thirteen smaller vessels, besides a flotilla of gun-boats. The Russians made a treacherous attack at Hango Head on a boat of the *Cossack*, which was landing prisoners, when four of her crew were killed, and the remainder, some of whom were wounded, were made prisoners. In retaliation for this outrage the British admiral dispatched a squadron, under Captain Yelverton, of the *Magicienne*, along the coast of Finland, which destroyed several fortified posts and routed bodies of Russian troops. Squadrons, under Admiral Seymour and Captain Warden, of the *Ajax*, also attacked other points. Meantime the preparations were matured for the bombardment of Sweaborg, on the plan suggested by Captain Sulivan in the preceding year, with the exception that mortar boats instead of mortar-batteries on the islets were employed. Sixteen of these vessels, and an equal number of gun-boats, specially prepared in England for the purpose, aided by five French mortar-rafts, were employed in the attack on the defences of this fortress, which consisted of five fortified islands; while the adjacent mainland, on which stood Helsingfors, the capital of Finland, bristled with earthworks armed with heavy guns. The channels were either blocked with sunk ships, or sown with submarine mines, and the three principal islands presented an almost unbroken line of batteries. The mortar-boats, which were moored 3,900 yards from the enemy's batteries, opened fire under the direction of Captain Wemyss of the Marine Artillery, sending 30 shells an hour from each piece of ordnance, and so accurately had they been laid that speedily the public buildings, arsenal, and store-houses were set in flames. Within the mortar-boats, the gun-boats, under the command of Commodore Pelham, manœuvred in a circle, firing their heavy guns as they were brought to bear on the enemy's works. Outside of all, the allied admirals took post with six ships-of-the-line and most of the sailing and steam frigates. Within three hours of opening fire the government buildings on the principal island of Vargon were well alight, and loud explosions, greeted with cheers by the seamen, showed the accuracy of the fire. Meanwhile Captains Yelverton and Wellesley engaged the subsidiary batteries with some of the ships, thus diverting the attention of the garrisons. The attack was discontinued at nightfall, the rocket-boats of the fleet taking their place, but at 5.30 on the following morning was resumed, one division of English mortar-boats and three out of the five French vessels being moored 400 yards nearer in order to attack the arsenal and works on East Svarto. So admirably were the mortars laid that by evening the whole of these works and the magazines in rear of Vargon were in flames, and at nightfall the rocket-boats again took up the conflict, thus giving no opportunity to the enemy to extinguish the conflagration. By daybreak on the 11th August the whole of the public buildings, except the batteries on the sea front, which had not been attacked, were destroyed, and the allied admirals, who had succeeded beyond expectation, withdrew to their anchorage at Nargen. While their loss had been merely nominal, the Russians had suffered severely, though the exact amount was never known. This was the last event of the war in the Baltic, and early in December the whole fleet returned to England.

In May, 1857, after only a brief respite from the exhausting struggle with Russia, this country was involved in a desperate conflict for the retention of our Eastern Empire. The Sepoys of the Bengal army rose in rebellion, and the utmost efforts of our small European force were exerted to maintain our hold of India until reinforcements could arrive from England. In this anxious crisis the Navy afforded a welcome accession of strength. Sir Michael Seymour, commanding the fleet in China, where we were engaged in hostilities, dispatched to Calcutta the *Sanspareil*, 74, Captain Key, the *Shannon*, 50, Captain Peel, and the *Pearl*, 21, Captain Sotheby. On the arrival of the squadron in the Hooghly, Captain Key landed his marines at Fort William, while Peel formed his crew into a naval brigade, and on the 13th August proceeded up the river in a steamer, with 408 seamen and marines. They remained in garrison at Allahabad, where they were joined a month later by Lieutenant Vaughan with a detachment of 120 seamen, recruited from the merchant ships in port. In October, Captain Peel, with a portion of the brigade, was engaged in action with a body of mutineers, in which Colonel Powell of the 53rd was killed, when he assumed command of the force, and totally routed the enemy. The seamen acted as gunners throughout the operations, their artillery consisting of the following ship-guns:—six 55-cwt. 8-inch guns (commonly called 68-pounders), two 8-inch howitzers, eight 24-pounders, two ships' field-pieces, and eight rocket tubes. For the first time in the history of war heavy ordnance were worked as field-pieces, and the dexterity and ease with which the sailors of the *Shannon* handled their 24 and 68-pounders during the ensuing operations called forth expressions of surprise and admiration from Sir Colin Campbell. In a letter to Sir Michael Seymour, dated Camp Oonao, 23rd February, 1858, Captain Peel says: "It is the most formidable field artillery the world has seen, for it is a truth and not a jest that in battle we are with the skirmishers." After the action near Allahabad the *Shannon* naval brigade participated in the second relief of Lucknow in November, 1857, and battered the Dilkhoosha, the Martinière, and the Shah Nujeef. The commander-in-chief, in his official report, says, "Captain Peel brought up his heavy guns with extraordinary gallantry within a few yards of the Shah Nujeef, to batter the massive stone walls. It was an action almost unexampled in war, and Captain Peel behaved very much as if he had been laying the *Shannon* alongside an enemy's frigate." On this occasion the brigade lost 17 killed and wounded. When Sir Colin Campbell recrossed the Ganges he was compelled on the 6th December to fight a severe action for the relief of Cawnpore, which the rebels had beleaguered after defeating General Windham, and he says of the *Shannon* brigade: "I must here draw attention to the manner in which the heavy 24-pounders were impelled and managed by Captain Peel and his gallant sailors. Through the extraordinary energy and goodwill with which the latter worked, their guns have been constantly in advance throughout the late operations, from the relief of Lucknow till now, as if they were light field-pieces, and the service rendered by them in clearing our front has been incalculable. On this occasion there was the sight of 24-pounders advancing with the first line of skirmishers." The brigade was engaged at Kalla Nuddee on the 2nd January, 1858, and at the attack on Futtyghur, but little of importance was done until the siege of Cawnpore in March, when the brigade, mustering 430 officers and men, performed excellent service. Captain Peel, unhappily, when recovering from a wound, was attacked by small-pox, of which he expired on the 27th April, universally regretted as an officer of rare promise and an ornament to the British Navy.

The *Pearl* brigade, under Captain Sotheby, first numbering 155 officers and men, and afterwards raised to 250 of all ranks, also played a distinguished part in the suppression of the revolt in the Gorruckpoor district, under Brigadier Rowcroft, and during the fifteen months it was embodied, was ten times engaged with the enemy. Captain Sotheby received the C.B. for his services, and, as in the case of the *Shannon*, all the officers were promoted.

Some months before these brigades were landed from their ships, four steam frigates of the Indian Navy* arrived at Calcutta, and the confidence inspired by their presence, in the critical days between May and August, will be remembered by all who were at the Presidency capital in those exciting times. A strong detachment of seamen from the *Punjaub*, under Commander Foulerton, with some European troops, accomplished the seizure and removal of the King of Oude, who lived at Garden Reach with regal pomp, surrounded by thousands of armed retainers, and brigades were landed from these four steam frigates and other ships of the Indian Navy, the whole being placed under the command of Captain Campbell, who had done such good service in Burmah, and whose experience was of the greatest service to the supreme Government, while his tact enabled him to conduct with success the delicate relations with the military and civil authorities at the capital.

Not only were seamen from the Hon. Company's ships drafted ashore, but a large body of men was recruited from the merchant ships lying in port, and drilled into shape as efficient gunners and light infantry. No less than 60 Indian Navy officers and 1,800 European seamen, with 42 field-pieces, were engaged in the suppression of the Mutiny, and performed excellent service in the field and in overawing or disarming the mutineers. At Dacca 90 officers and men, under Lieutenant Lewis, first of the *Punjaub*, attacked in their barracks the 13th Bengal N.I. and a detachment of native artillery with two field-pieces, and after a smart action, in which they lost 19 killed and wounded, routed and dispersed the rebels with heavy loss. On this occasion Midshipman Mayo gained the V.C. for charging the guns loaded with grape. Equally meritorious service was rendered by Lieutenants Lewis and Davies in Assam, during which one-third of the seamen were placed *hors de combat*, and the latter officer was severely

* A detachment of seamen from the ships-of-war of the Indian Navy took part in the siege of Mooltan, under the command of Captain Powell. They constructed two batteries, armed them with ships' guns, and worked them throughout the siege. Sir Herbert Edwardes speaks highly of the services of the Indian Naval brigade, and particularly eulogizes the senior lieutenant, Mr. Christopher, an officer as eminent for his scientific attainments as for his amiability of character and high courage. Lieutenant Christopher died of wounds received at the assault of Mooltan. Naval brigades, landed from the ships of the Indian Navy, had participated in military operations long before the time of Clive at Surat and elsewhere. (See the author's "History of the Indian Navy.")

wounded by a poisoned arrow, from the effects of which he never recovered. Lieutenant Carew, first of the *Auckland*, in command of over 100 officers and men, with two nine-pounders and two $5\frac{1}{2}$-inch mortars, participated in the operations against Koer Singh, in the Jugdeespore district, Lieutenant Duval, of the *Coromandel*, was enabled to do excellent service in the Gya district, with his brigade of 200 men and six field-pieces, as did also Lieutenants Barron and Burnes, and Lieutenant Windus, who was engaged in arduous field operations against the Coles in Chota Nagpore, in the height of the rainy season. Lieutenant Batt, who was in command of the *Zenobia*, proceeded up country in July, 1857, with 100 men and four field-pieces, and with the 90th Regiment disarmed the disaffected Sepoy regiments at Berhampore. Proceeding up the Ganges from Allahabad in a river steamer, Lieutenant Batt engaged the enemy for six hours, and shelled them out of their positions. When in command at Buxar, this officer took the field with two guns, the only artillery with the detachment under Major Carr, and his excellent practice assisted materially in defeating a strong force of rebels. The Indian Navy also manned four screw gun-boats which patrolled the river, cleared the banks of rebels, carried supplies, and kept open the communications.

On the west coast of India the cruisers of the Indian Navy landed brigades at Surat, Rutnagherry, and Bombay itself, where they took part in disarming rebellious Sepoys, holding the dockyards and other public buildings, or otherwise assisting the civil power. Before the final suppression of the great revolt which convulsed all India, a squadron of ships of the Indian Navy was engaged in reducing to subjection the disaffected inhabitants of the island of Beyt, and a strong detachment of seamen was landed from the ships to assist at the siege of Dwarka, where there was some severe fighting.

CHAPTER X.

The China War of 1856-60—Action at Fatshan Creek—The Operations off the Peiho—Repulse of Admiral Hope before the Taku Forts—The Abyssinian and Ashantee Expeditions—The Naval Brigade in South Africa—The defence of Ekowe—The War in Egypt—The Seizure of the Suez Canal—The Bombardment of Alexandria—The Naval Brigade at Suakin—The Nile Expedition—Conclusion.

IN 1856 hostilities broke out in China in consequence of the seizure of the *Arrow* by the authorities at Canton. As the Commander-in-chief, Sir Michael Seymour, could obtain no redress, on the 23rd October he seized the Barrier forts and pushed on to the city. But Yeh, the Imperial commissioner, remained obstinate, and even attacked the outposts of the force landed to protect the English factories, when the Admiral opened fire on the defences of the city, which he entered, though it was too extensive to be conquered or held. Yeh being still intractable, he attacked the fleet of war-junks which lay under the protection of the fort, which was silenced and all the junks were burnt or sunk. Sir Michael now made himself master of the Bogue forts, which mounted upwards of 200 guns, and thus gained command of the entire river. Much desultory fighting ensued, always with the same result, the defeat of the enemy, but the admiral, in order to terminate this state of affairs, which was ruinous to trade, appealed to the Governor-General of India for 5,000 troops, and to the Home Government for a division of gunboats. In May, 1857, on the arrival of the latter, Commodore Elliot attacked the fleet of war-junks, stationed in Escape Creek, when he succeeded in sinking and destroying the whole.

But these operations were only subsidiary to the main attack by the Admiral on the great fleet of eighty junks of the largest size, manned by 6,000 men, which was stationed off Fatshan Creek, their main station and arsenal. The attack was completely successful, and the whole flotilla, with the exception of three, was taken and set on fire. The city of Fatshan was spared, but the blow struck was complete, and was attained with the loss of 13 killed, including two officers, and 40 wounded. The greater part of the loss was incurred by the division of gunboats under the gallant Commodore Keppel, while attacking twenty junks moored in compact order.

The outbreak of the great Mutiny in India caused a lull in the operations, as the troops which had been sent out to China, and some of the ships, were diverted thither. However, at the end of September, 1857, Lord Elgin, who had gone to Calcutta, returned to China, and soon after the remainder of the gunboats arrived from England, and some Sepoys from India, as well as a French squadron. A demand was made for the surrender of Canton, but as Yeh treated the allies with sovereign contempt, on the 25th December a heavy fire was brought to bear on the defences, both on the river face as well as the heights and outer forts, from mortars and rockets, and the long 32-pounders of the gunboats. Besides the marines and 1,500 sailors, a detachment of 800 troops, with a French naval brigade, was landed by the allied commanders, and the city was taken, though the resistance was continued for some days. The British loss was 130 killed and wounded, of whom one-half belonged to the Naval Brigade, which mourned the loss of the gallant Captain Bate, of the *Actæon*. The success was made complete by the capture, by Captain Key, of the *Sanspareil*, of the redoubtable Yeh himself, whose arrogance was the cause of the war. The tyrant, who had bathed in blood the province he had long misgoverned, was sent a prisoner to Calcutta.

Lord Elgin and Baron Gros, the British and French ministers, sent the conditions of peace they intended to exact to the Emperor at Pekin, but no answer being returned, in April, 1858, they anchored off the Peiho, and the allied admirals made a demand for the surrender of the Taku forts, guarding the entrance to that river. Sir Michael Seymour shifted his flag to the gunboat *Slaney*, where he was joined by his French colleague and, on the 20th May, the British squadron, assisted by four French gunboats, attacked the earthworks and batteries extending for nearly a mile on both banks of the river, which were silenced in a little over an hour. Strong parties of seamen and marines were now landed, and the whole line of defences changed hands, with a loss to the British of 21 killed and wounded, that of the French being 67, including 50 by the explosion of a magazine. This defeat quickly brought the Chinese Emperor to his senses, and peace was signed at Tientsin, about 40 miles up the Peiho. Sir Michael Seymour now proceeded to England, and was succeeded by Sir James Hope, who had distinguished himself so greatly on the Parana.

On his arrival in the Peiho on the 18th June, 1859, Admiral Hope reconnoitred the defences, and found that they been greatly strengthened since his predecessor had effected their capture, and that the two great forts on the left bank, whose fire raked the ships attacking the batteries lower down on the opposite bank, had more guns mounted on them, and that to prevent any attempt to storm these latter, mounting over 50 heavy guns, they had cut two ditches, in rear of the last of which were sharp-pointed stakes, and that a boom had been thrown across the river with the object of delaying the advance of the gunboats while under fire. The British admiral only received evasive answers to his demands for the removal of the boom in order that he might take the allied ambassadors to Tientsin, to exchange the ratifications of peace at Pekin, as agreed upon, and on the 24th June took his gunboats within the bar and made preparations to land 700 marines to storm the forts after they had been breached. During the night Captain Willes blew open the boom and examined an inner raft, when he was fired upon and forced to retire. On the following morning the *Nimrod*, *Cormorant*, and nine gunboats took up their positions, the right division under Captain Shadwell in the *Banterer*, and the left under Captain Vansittart in the *Forester*, while Admiral Hope, in order to direct the operations in person, shifted his flag into the *Plover*. About two o'clock the *Opossum* advanced to pull up the iron stakes in front of the boom, which was found to have been repaired during the night, and this gave the signal to the batteries on both banks to open fire. The admiral, flying the signal to engage, advanced to the boom, the *Opossum*, *Lee*, and *Haughty* being astern, and soon all the gunboats were engaged except the *Starling*, which, with the *Banterer*, had run aground, the former in such a position that she could take no part in the action. So severe was the cross-fire to which the squadron was exposed, that Lieutenant Rasen, commanding the *Plover*, was killed, and of her crew of 40, nine only remained uninjured. The Admiral, who was severely wounded in the thigh, sent her downstream to procure more men, and shifted his flag into the *Opossum*, directing the flag-captain, Willes, to take her close under the forts. He was again wounded, and as the ship became unmanageable, owing to her screw fouling, and drifted down the river, the brave old admiral left her and proceeded to the *Cormorant*, where, lying on her deck, he directed the battle with all the spirit of a Blake or Benbow. At length the loss of blood prevented him from taking any further part in the operations, and he surrendered the command to Captain Shadwell.

Meantime the *Opossum* and *Plover* had resumed their positions in the line of battle, but the *Kestrel* was in a sinking state, the *Lee* was so disabled that her commander had to run her aground to save her from a like fate, and the *Haughty* was in little better plight. Owing also to the fall of the tide the gunboats were several feet below the level of the forts, which rendered their fire less effective. But the Chinese guns on both banks were nearly silenced, and Captains Shadwell and Willes, with the sanction of the Admiral, resolved to land and attempt to storm the works, which, all previous experience had shown, the Chinese were little likely to defend. Accordingly, soon after seven, these officers, with Colonel Lemon, of the Marines, landed on the right bank with all the available men, who advanced through the soft mud in a gallant attempt to reach the batteries, exposed the whole time to a heavy gun and musketry fire. All the three senior officers were shot down, and the command devolved upon Commander Commerell. At the head of the leading division he crossed the first ditch, which was dry, but the second was full, and here he found himself with only 50 followers, about 150 men having reached the first ditch. As a further attempt to advance could only end in failure, the party, with the reserve under Captain Willes, retired to the boats and were embarked in safety.

In this unfortunate affair the loss had been 80 killed and 350 wounded, many of whom died, including Captain Vansittart, one of the most gallant and distinguished officers in the Navy. The *Cormorant*, *Lee*, and *Plover* were all aground, and no efforts could get them afloat, but the *Starling* was rescued, and owing to an unusually high tide the next morning the *Kestrel* and *Haughty* were saved. In the following week Admiral Hope withdrew his fleet to an anchorage near Ningpoo, and awaited, with unabated resolution, the time when he could retrieve the disaster. Throughout the action he had been accompanied by Captain Tricault, of the French ship *Duchayla*, who, with a detachment of his men, took part in the assault, and a noteworthy incident was the sympathy and assistance afforded by Flag-officer Tatnall, of the American Navy, commanding the *Toeywan*. This officer not only went on board the *Cormorant*, through the thickest of the fight, to visit the wounded admiral, when his boat was sunk alongside by a cannon-shot, and his coxswain was killed, but he assisted in embarking a detachment of our seamen, and gave expression to the noble sentiment, that " blood was thicker than water."

The British and French Governments resolved to punish the perfidy of the Chinese, and in the following year, an army of 13,000 Europeans and Sepoys was despatched from India under Sir Hope Grant, exclusive of 5,000 detained at Hong Kong, and of 6,700 French troops, under General Montauban. A large fleet was concentrated, including a squadron of the Indian navy, and on the 31st July, 1860, a landing was effected without opposition at Pehtang, in the Gulf of Pechili. As the history of the operations that ensued rather concerns the Army than the sister service, it will suffice to say that the formidable Taku works and batteries were surrendered after the great fort on the north bank had been breached and stormed by the troops under the command of Sir Robert (afterwards Field-Marshal Lord) Napier. This experienced and skilful officer had foreseen that this result would follow, and it was on his advice that Sir Hope Grant determined to make the attack on this side, and not on the south bank, as his colleague, General Montauban, desired. The gunboats and rocket-boats of the allied fleets assisted by shelling the forts, but the glory and loss of the achievement fell to the soldiers. The Chinese army was defeated on the 18th and 21st September, and finally, on the 13th October, when the allied batteries were on the point of opening fire on Pekin, the city was surrendered, and the treaty of Tientsin was ratified within the walls of the capital of the Chinese Empire.

Nearly two years after these events, during the Taeping rebellion, a brigade of British and French seamen and marines assisted Colonel Ward in defeating the rebels near Woosung, and on another occasion Sir James Hope received a severe wound in the leg when rallying a party of Ward's men who had fallen into confusion. In May the rebels at Ningpo fired on the allied ships, when the admiral silenced the batteries, and, landing with some men, gained possession of the town, which he gave over to the Imperial troops. Other places were captured, at one of which Admiral Protet, commanding the French fleet, was slain.

In our subsequent "little wars," as in all since the peace of 1815, the British Navy played a part subordinate to the Army. In the expedition to Abyssinia they earned the commendation of Sir Robert Napier for the cheerful manner in which officers and men, under Admiral Leopold Heath, performed their arduous duties of disembarking the Army,* and keeping up the supplies, and a rocket battery, under Commander Fellowes, took part in the defeat of King Theodore's troops at Arogie.

In 1873, the state of affairs on the West Coast of Africa, where the Ashantees had invaded the Fantee Protectorate, and dominated the country to the walls of Cape Coast Castle, led the British Government to undertake an expedition to drive them back, and restore our influence and prestige in those regions. Before the arrival of Sir Garnet Wolseley, in October of that year, the only troops at Cape Coast, besides 200 Houssas, employed as native police, were 100 marines, under Colonel Festing, who landed on the 9th June, and kept the Ashantees in check at Elmina until the arrival of the British troops. Commodore Commerell, V.C., assumed command of the squadron on the station

* There were 235 sailing-ships and 94 steamers employed in the Abyssinian expedition, which conveyed to Annesley Bay, near Massowah, 42,699 persons, of whom 14,683 were soldiers; also 36,094 transport animals, including 44 elephants.

on the 5th July, and on the following day, the *Himalaya* arrived with the 2nd West India Regiment. Owing to the sickness that prevailed, the greater portion of the Marines returned in that ship to England. Commodore Commerell took immediate steps to meet an apprehended attack by the Ashantees on Discove and Secondee, at the mouth of the Prah. With the boats of the *Rattlesnake* and *Argus* he made a reconnoissance up that river, when he was fired upon by the natives concealed in the bush. Four men were killed and 16 wounded, among the latter being the Commodore, and Commander Luxmoore, of the *Argus*. The ships then shelled and destroyed the town of Chamah. Commodore Commerell's wound was so severe as to disqualify him for further service, and on the 22nd August he sailed from the West Coast for the Cape of Good Hope, when Captain Fremantle succeeded to the command until the arrival of Sir William Hewett. Captain Fremantle continued hostile operations with the *Barracouta* and *Argus*, which shelled and destroyed some villages near the mouth of the Prah, but a landing party suffered some loss. Other ships engaged on the coast were the *Druid*, Captain Blake, and the gunboats *Decoy*, *Merlin*, and *Bittern*.

Sir Garnet Wolseley arrived at Cape Coast Castle on the 2nd October, and assumed the political and military command, and among the officers most prominent under his orders was Commander Glover, R.N., who was appointed Commissioner to the friendly native tribes in the district east of the Gold Coast. Commander Glover raised a mixed force of Houssas and friendly natives, and, advancing from the mouth of the Volta, caused a diversion by acting in the rear of the Ashantee army, when the British troops advanced on Coomassie.

Sir Garnet Wolseley resolved to strike a blow with the assistance of Captain Fremantle, and on the 13th October sailed in the *Barracouta*, on board which were embarked 150 Marines and 50 sailors, with one 7-pounder and a rocket-trough, accompanied by the *Decoy*, conveying the West India Regiment and some Houssas. Disembarking at Elmina, the column, with some troops under Sir Garnet and Colonel Evelyn Wood, encountered the enemy in the bush, and inflicted on them a severe defeat. Among the wounded on our side were Captain Fremantle, Colonel McNeill, chief of the staff, and Captain Redvers Buller. The Ashantees were panic-struck at the energy and celerity displayed by Sir Garnet Wolseley, and retreated precipitately across the Prah, thus evacuating the Fantee Protectorate. Before the close of the year, two regiments of British infantry arrived from England, but ere this there was some desultory fighting, and a small force, under Lieutenant Wells, R.N., did good service at Abrakrampa. The enemy pressed hardly on this post, and on the 6th November, a detachment of 22 officers and 300 men, drawn from the ships, under command of Captain Fremantle, and accompanied by Sir Garnet, made a forced march to relieve that post. This was done, but at the cost of great suffering, as the heat was so excessive that only 140 men were in a condition to complete the march from Assaybo, 20 miles from Cape Coast.

On the 27th December, the Naval Brigade of 250 officers and men, under the command of Captain Blake, accompanied by Sir William Hewett and Captain Hunt-Grubbe, marched for Prahsu. Here Captain Blake was compelled to return to the coast, owing to sickness, but the gallant officer did not survive to embark for England. Commander Luxmoore now assumed the command. After crossing the Prah and advancing into Ashantee, the sailors were engaged in the reconnoissance at Borborassie, and at the action, on the 31st January, of Amoaful, which decided the fate of the campaign. On this occasion the brigade was divided into two wings, the right under Captain Hunt-Grubbe, and the left under Commander Luxmoore, who was placed under the orders of Colonel Evelyn Wood, himself an old sailor, who had served with distinction before Sebastopol. The fire of the enemy was so heavy, that Colonel Wood directed the detachment of seamen to lie down, after cutting a clearing, when they engaged in a musketry duel with the Ashantees. At this time, and in the subsequent advance, which ended in the utter rout of the enemy, the sailors had six officers and 23 men wounded from slugs, but none of their number were killed. At the attack on Becqua, under Colonel Macleod, on the following day, the Naval Brigade were again engaged, and the place was burnt.

Sir Garnet Wolseley now made a rapid march on Coomassie, giving the enemy no time to rally, and throughout the advance the sailors brought up the rear. The whole force was constantly engaged, and nothing could stay the magnificent dash with which the 42nd Highlanders, with bagpipes playing, carried all before them until the capital was entered. Sir Garnet Wolseley left Coomassie on the 6th February, but King Koffee refused at the time to treat for terms, though on hearing of the advance of Commander Glover from the Volta, he sent envoys to sue for peace. The Naval Brigade was now disbanded, and returned to their ships. Though but few had fallen in action, a large number had been wounded, and no less than 95 per cent., practically the whole of the 250 engaged, suffered from sickness, and

39 per cent. were actually invalided to England. Throughout the trying operations, their conduct in the field had been such as to gain from Sir Garnet Wolseley the expression of opinion that "all have fought with the dashing courage for which seamen and Marines are so celebrated."

Not many years elapsed before a Naval Brigade was again employed, and indeed it had become the recognised thing for a detachment of seamen to serve on shore with their brethren of the Army. In 1877, the country was engaged in one of the numerous South African wars which we have waged during the present century, and in December of that year, 300 seamen and Marines, with seven guns, were landed at East London, from H.M.S. *Active*, to take part in what is known in South African history as the Transkei Campaign. A portion of the brigade, under Captain Wright, R.N., was attached to Colonel Glyn's column, which was engaged scouring the country towards the Quora, and the Marines formed part of another column operating beyond that river. In the skirmishing on the 13th and 29th January, 1878, the seamen performed good service, and at the action at Quintana Mountain, on the 7th February, they were again of material assistance. Their services being no longer required in this quarter, they embarked at East London on the 16th March, after three months' fighting and hard marching.

While a portion of the Naval Brigade rejoined the *Active* at Simon's Bay, a detachment under Captain Wright proceeded to reinforce the troops under Lord Chelmsford, who had succeeded Sir Arthur Cunningham, and they were engaged in the action with the Gaikas at the Peri bush, where the rocket-battery was of special service. This detachment also now rejoined the *Active*. Before the close of the year 1878, the British army in those regions was involved in a life-and-death struggle with the Zulus, the most warlike tribe in South Africa, who possessed a military organization that rendered them no contemptible foe for the best-disciplined European troops. Not only were they bold fighters, but their powers of mobilization and hard marching were remarkable, and they numbered not less than 40,000 warriors, whose prowess was acknowledged by the heterogeneous races of Europeans and natives inhabiting the southern portion of the African continent.

On the 19th November a detachment of seamen and Marines was landed from H.M.S. *Active* at Durban, and marched to guard the important ford, or "drift," in the lower Tugela, until Lord Chelmsford had matured his plans for the invasion of Zululand. The brigade consisted of 172 men, with a Gatling and two other guns, and two rocket-tubes, under the command of Captain Campbell, among the officers being Lieutenants Craigie and Hamilton, who had done good service in the Transkei Campaign. The sailors garrisoned an earthwork, to which was given the name of Fort Pearson, after the officer commanding the column, and at this place, distant 104 miles from Keshwayo's capital of Ulundi, took place the meeting between the Indunas, or chiefs, of the Zulu monarch, and the Commissioners appointed by Sir Bartle Frere, the British High Commissioner for South Africa, whose policy it was either to bring about a disarmament or precipitate a war. Keshwayo conceded most of the demands in Sir Bartle's ultimatum, but he could not be brought to disarm his savage warriors, who entertained an overweening idea of their ability to meet British soldiers on the battle-field.

On the 4th January Colonel Pearson arrived with 800 bayonets of the 3rd Foot (the "Buffs"), and the Naval Brigade was reinforced by 40 men from the *Tenedos*. Six days later, the time given in the ultimatum having expired, a state of war existed between the Zulu King and the British army. The column, under the command of Colonel Pearson, was conveyed in five days across the Tugela by the sailors, and on the morning of the 18th January, 1879, commenced its march into Zululand. The total strength of the column, which was organised in two divisions, was 2,055 Europeans—including the Naval Brigade, the "Buffs," and 99th Regiment, some Royal Artillery and Engineers, with Volunteer Horse—and 2,342 native troops. On the 22nd took place the action of Inyezane, at which only a portion of the force, including the Naval Brigade, was present. The Zulus were in great force, their numbers being variously estimated between 5,000 and 8,000, and held the ground stubbornly, but the sailors and Royal Artillery did considerable execution with their guns and rocket-tubes, and then the former, led by Captain Campbell and Lieutenant Hamilton, with a company of the Buffs, under the personal command of Colonel Pearson, who had his horse shot under him, advanced upon the enemy, who, after three hours' fighting, retired in good order, leaving 300 dead on the field. The British loss was only two officers and seven men killed, and 15 wounded.

At noon on the following day, a place called Ekowe was reached, and here was received the astonishing news of the destruction of a portion of the column under the immediate command of Lord Chelmsford, which took place on the same day as the successful action at Inyezane. There was only one sailor, a signalman of the *Active*, present at that massacre, and he was seen, says Colonel Parr, in his interesting sketch of the war, "with his back against a wagon-wheel, keeping the Zulus at bay with his cutlass, but a Zulu crept behind him, and stabbed him through the spokes." The first rumour of the disaster was received at Ekowe on the 26th January, and two days later arrived a letter from Lord Chelmsford, informing Colonel Pearson that he might "expect the whole Zulu army" to attack him, requesting him to take steps for the safety of his column, and directing him to retire to the Tugela if he was not in sufficient strength to hold Ekowe. But Colonel Pearson resolved to remain in Zululand, although his was the only one of the three columns that did so, and by the aid of Captain Wynne, the able Engineer officer attached to his force, he was soon enabled to place the position in a state of defence impregnable to any force unprovided with artillery. A portion of the column was sent back, and with 1,400 Europeans, including the Naval Brigade, and 460 natives, Fort Ekowe was held without being attacked until the 3rd April, when Lord Chelmsford, having crossed the Tugela and defeated the Zulus in the action at Gingilhovo, arrived at the post and found the garrison in good condition and heart, save for some sickness which had carried off 28 officers and men. A Naval Brigade, drawn from H.M.S. *Shah*, *Tenedos*, and *Boadicea*, under the command of Captain Brackenbury, was present at Gingilhovo, and their battery of two guns, two Gatlings, and two rocket-tubes, materially assisted in driving back the Zulus, when they made a desperate attempt to capture the British laager. Lord Chelmsford recrossed the Tugela, leaving a detachment of seamen to hold a post on the Inyezane, and others to occupy Forts Pearson and Tenedos, until he had completed his arrangements for the final defeat of the Zulus. When all was ready, the Naval Brigade, under the command of Captain Campbell, numbered 41 officers and 812 men, of whom 535 formed part of the First, or Coast, Division, commanded by General Crealock. But for reasons into which we will not enter here, this division, though encamped at Fort Durnford, within seventy miles of Ulundi, took no part in the decisive engagement of the war, which was won by the divisions of Generals Evelyn Wood and Newdigate. On the 7th July, three days after the action at Ulundi, Sir Garnet Wolseley arrived at the camp, and on the 21st he inspected the Naval Brigade, of whom he said, in a General Order, that their "conduct had been admirable, and their bearing in action in every way worthy of the service to which they belonged." On the same day they embarked at Fort Durnford, and at Durban rejoined the *Shah*, which sailed for Simon's Bay. The last occasion on which our sailors were engaged in South Africa is not one that can arouse any feelings of pride, but we must not deviate from our practice of recording defeats as well as victories. We refer to the disaster at Majuba Hill, at which a party of seamen were present and suffered severely, among the slain being their gallant leader, Commander Romilly, of the *Boadicea*.

In 1882 took place the bombardment of Alexandria, one of the most successful of this class of services rendered by the British Navy. Though it cannot compare in military importance with the attacks on Copenhagen or Algiers, yet its political results have been very considerable, and from the former point of view, it is of interest as being the first occasion on which an ironclad fleet attacked fortifications constructed on the latest and most improved method of modern war, and mounted with the heaviest ordnance then in use.

On the 11th June took place the massacre at Alexandria of the Europeans, but nothing was done to restore order by the Egyptian Government, which indeed was powerless, or by the Porte, the suzerain Power. The British and French fleets arrived off Alexandria, but no steps were taken to avenge the massacre until the 11th July, when Admiral Sir Beauchamp Seymour made his famous attack on the defences of the city, and his colleague, Admiral Conrad, acting under instructions from the French Government, quitted the port, and steered for Port Said, thus resigning to England the task of coercing the Egyptian insurgents, and tacitly surrendering the Dual Control, on which the French nation had hitherto set so much store. The English commander, a man of tried experience and remarkable for his professional attainments, eagerly hailed the opportunity of acting without having to consult an ally. The Egyptians, under the orders of Arabi Pasha, who was in rebellion against the Khedive Tewfik, continued working on the fortifications, strengthening the ramparts and mounting fresh guns, which bore on the British fleet. Sir Beauchamp Seymour addressed a remonstrance to Ragheb Pasha, President of the Khedive's Government, pointing out that these preparations menaced the safety of his ships, but though promises were made he failed to obtain a discontinuance of the works, which the search lights of the fleet showed were mostly carried out at night. As it became evident that each day added to the strength of the means of attack, on the 10th July, the fugitives having by that time embarked, Sir Beauchamp Seymour addressed a formal demand for the surrender to him, within twelve hours, of the batteries on the isthmus of Ras-el-Teen. The Egyptian authorities, however, paid no heed to this ultimatum, and at seven A.M. on the 11th July Sir Beauchamp Seymour opened fire on the enemy's forts and batteries.

The following were the ships and gunboats of his fleet. The crews of all had been trained, by the experienced officers who commanded them, to a pitch of excellence as regards gunnery that promised well for any trial of strength, but that they had no contemptible foe to deal with soon became apparent.

Battle-ships—

Sultan	Captain W. J. Hunt-Grubbe, A.D.C., C.B.
Superb	,, T. le H. Ward
Alexandra	,, F. Hotham
Invincible (flagship)	,, R. H. More Molyneux
Monarch	,, H. Fairfax, C.B.
Penelope	,, St. George d'Arcy Irvine
Inflexible	,, J. A. Fisher
Téméraire	,, H. F. Nicholson

Gunboats—

Beacon	Commander G. W. Hand
Condor	,, Lord Charles Beresford
Bittern	,, T. S. Brand
Cygnet	Lieutenant C. D. Ryder
Decoy	,, A. H. Boldero
Helicon (despatch-boat)	,, W. L. Morrison

The plan of operations embraced two attacks, one by Captain Hunt-Grubbe, second-in-command, with the *Sultan, Superb,* and *Alexandra,* on the northern face of the batteries of Ras-el-Teen, supported by an enfilading fire from the 80-ton gun in the aftermost turret of the *Inflexible.* The other attack was by the *Invincible,* bearing the admiral's flag, *Monarch* and *Penelope,* from inside the reef, aided by the fire of the *Inflexible's* foremost turret, and the *Téméraire,* which took up a position close to the fairway buoy of the principal entrance (called the Boghaz Pass) leading into Alexandria harbour. The *Helicon* and *Condor,* the latter commanded by Lord Charles Beresford, were detailed for duty as repeating ships, and the gunboats *Beacon, Bittern, Cygnet,* and *Decoy* were directed to assist the heavy ships by their fire as required.

It was seven o'clock when Sir Beauchamp Seymour signalled from the *Invincible* to the *Alexandra* to fire a shell into the newly-armed earthworks, termed the "Hospital Battery," and followed this by a general signal to the fleet, "Attack the enemy's batteries." The action soon became general between the ships and the whole of the forts, mounting 59 guns, commanding the entrance to the harbour of Alexandria.

A steady fire, says the admiral in his despatch, was maintained on all sides until 10.30 A.M., when the *Sultan, Superb,* and *Alexandra,** which had been hitherto under weigh, anchored off the Lighthouse Fort, and by their well-directed fire, assisted by that of the *Inflexible,* which weighed and joined them at 12.30 P.M., succeeded in silencing most of the guns in the forts on Ras-el-Teen, though some heavy ordnance in Fort Ada, mounting 25 guns, kept up a desultory fire. About 1.30, a shell from the *Superb,* whose practice excited admiration, blew up the magazine, and caused the immediate retreat of the remaining garrison. These ships then directed their attention to Fort Pharos, commanding the entrance to the New Port, mounting 45 guns, which were silenced with the assistance of the *Téméraire,* who joined them at 2.30, when a shot from the *Inflexible* dismounted one of the heavy guns. The Hospital Battery was well fought, and although silenced for a time by a shell from the *Inflexible,* it was not until 5 P.M. that the artillerymen were compelled to retire from their guns. The *Invincible,* supported by the *Penelope,* both ships being at anchor, and assisted by the *Monarch,* under weigh inside the reefs, as well as by the *Inflexible* and *Téméraire,* succeeded, after an engagement of some hours, in silencing and partially destroying the batteries and lines of Meks, on the seashore. Fort Marsa-el-Kanat, still farther to the west than Meks, was destroyed by the explosion of the magazine, after an hour's action with the *Monarch.*

Early in the day, when the firing had become general, Lord Charles Beresford, of the *Condor,* stationed as repeating ship, performed a gallant action. Seeing the accuracy with which two 10-inch rifled guns in Fort Marabout were playing upon the ships engaged off Fort Meks, he steamed up to within range, and, by excellent practice, soon drew off the enemy's fire. The admiral sent to his assistance the *Beacon, Bittern, Cygnet,* and *Decoy,* the *Cygnet* having been engaged with the Ras-el-Teen batteries during the early part of the day. About two P.M., seeing that the artillerymen in Meks had abandoned their guns, the admiral, under cover of the fire of the gunboats, landed a party of volunteers, under Lieutenant E. Bradford, of the *Invincible,* accompanied by Lieutenant Richard Poore, of that ship, Lieutenant the Hon. Hedworth Lambton (Flag-Lieutenant), Major Tulloch, Welsh Regiment, and Mr. Hardy, midshipman, who reached

---

* Early in the action, an act of great heroism was performed on board the *Alexandra.* A 10-inch spherical shell passed through the ship's side and lodged in the main deck, when Mr. Harding, gunner, hearing the shout, "There is a live shell just above the hatchway," rushed up the ladder from below, and observing that the fuse was burning, took some water from a tub standing near, and threw it over the projectile, which he then picked up and put in the tub. Had the shell burst, it would probably have destroyed many lives. For this act of devoted bravery, Mr. Harding received the Victoria Cross, and never was it better earned.

the shore through the surf, and having destroyed with charges of gun-cotton two 10-inch muzzle-loading rifled guns, and spiked six smooth-bore guns in the water battery at Meks, re-embarked without a casualty beyond the loss of one of their boats on the rocks, due to the heavy surf.

The action was over at 5.30 P.M., when the ships anchored for the night. The victory was complete; but, says the admiral, the force opposed to us would have been more formidable had every gun mounted on the line of forts been brought into action. In the Ras-el-Teen batteries, few of the large smooth-bores, and fewer of the French 36-pounders, mounted in the time of Mehemet Ali, were manned, the Egyptians preferring to use the English 10-inch, and smaller muzzle-loading rifled ordnance. These guns, which were identical with those then in use in the British Navy, were abundantly supplied with projectiles of the latest description, and their sighting was excellent. The same may be said of the guns in the Meks lines, excepting that in them the 36-pounders were more used, and that one, if not two, 15-inch smooth-bores were brought into action, in addition to the 10-inch and smaller guns fired. Fort Marabout employed two 10-inch guns at long range, shell after shell of which came up towards the in-shore squadron in excellent line, falling from ten to thirty yards short, but not one shell from the guns in the southern batteries burst on board the fleet.

As might have been anticipated, Sir Beauchamp Seymour handled his ships with great skill, and was ably seconded by Captain Hunt-Grubbe (the same officer who had done such good service in the Ashantee War), who commanded the outside squadron, operating against the Ras-el-Teen batteries, which bore the brunt of the action. All the captains and commanders of gunboats maintained the reputation of their noble service. The ships that sustained the greatest damage were the *Sultan*, *Superb*, and *Alexandra*, and the upper works of the *Invincible*, *Inflexible*, and *Penelope* were also a good deal knocked about, but the *Téméraire* and *Monarch* suffered no damage. The losses sustained by the fleet were surprisingly small, Lieutenant Jackson and Mr. Shannon, carpenter, both of the *Inflexible*, and four seamen being killed, and 27 wounded, including Lieutenant Davies, of the *Penelope*, and Mr. Lumsden, midshipman of the *Invincible*. It is due to the Egyptian artillerymen to say that they stood to their guns under a crushing fire, and amid the masses of falling masonry, with a devotion that elicited the encomiums of the British admiral and all observers.

On the morning of the 12th July, the *Inflexible* and *Téméraire* engaged Fort Pharos, which hoisted a flag of truce after a few shots were fired, as did also the Meks Barracks

Battery in reply to a similar appeal. On the following day, the admiral steamed into the harbour with the *Invincible, Penelope,* and *Monarch,* and landed a party of seamen and Marines, under Captain Fairfax, to take possession of Ras-el-Teen, but owing to the absence of a sufficiently strong landing-party to occupy the town, the retiring Egyptian army set fire to it, almost destroying the European quarter, containing some buildings that would have adorned any city, which those will admit who remember the beauty of the great square called after Mehemet Ali. During the afternoon of the 13th, the Khedive, Tewfik Pasha, who had been practically a prisoner of Arabi, arrived from Ramleh, and took up his residence at Ras-el-Teen palace, under the protection of 700 Marines, and in the evening the admiral landed all the Marines from the off-shore squadron, with some Gatling guns, and cleared the streets of the Arabs, who were burning and pillaging.* During the whole of the 14th, as many men from the fleet as could be spared were landed, under command of Captain Fisher, and by evening the most important positions were occupied. On the 17th, the Channel Squadron, consisting of the *Northumberland, Agincourt,* and despatch-vessel *Salamis,* arrived; also the *Tamar,* from England, with soldiers and Marines. Major-General Sir Archibald Alison, than whom there are few more experienced officers in the Army, now took command of the troops, consisting of the 1st Stafford Regiment, the King's Royal Rifles, and a battalion of Marines, and the greater portion of the seamen rejoined their ships. Mention should be made of the services of a detachment of sailors, under Lord Charles Beresford, detailed for police duty during the days immediately succeeding the burning of the city, when the streets were crowded with incendiaries and thieves.

The strength of the force in Alexandria was 3,755, including seamen and Marines, who had with them seven 9-pounders, two 7-pounders, six Gatlings, and four rocket-tubes. In the event of attack, the admiral had arranged to land 1,200 more men, while the line of approach on the side of Aboukir was completely covered by the guns of the fleet. Sir Archibald Alison took the offensive, and sent a force at daylight on the 24th to seize the position in the direction of Ramleh. Accompanying this column were four guns, manned by the sailors. The original intention had been to protect the right flank by floating rafts, or flat-bottomed boats, but the shallowness of the water and the rapid fall of Lake Mariotis, made this impossible. To meet the difficulty,

---

* The bombardment was a costly affair, not only to the Egyptian exchequer, which ultimately had to pay an indemnity of a million for the firing of the city of Alexandria, but to the English taxpayer. Every shot from the 80-ton guns cost £25 10s.; from the 25-ton guns, £7; from the 18-ton guns, £4 4s.; and so on in proportion for the projectiles from the smaller ordnance.

Captain Fisher, commanding the *Inflexible*, with sailor-like resource, devised an armoured train, consisting of two trucks fitted with iron-plating and sand-bags as protecting cover, and mounted with a Nordenfeldt and two Gatling guns. A 9-pounder was also placed on one of the trucks, with a crane, by means of which it could be quickly taken out; and the crews were formed of 200 seamen, with small-arms, in other trucks, also protected by sand-bags and boiler plating.

This novel engine of war was soon brought into use. In order to repair the railway-line, which had been destroyed by the enemy, a small force was despatched by Sir Archibald Alison, including the armoured train, and the line was completed. Arabi's outposts showed fight, and fired some shots over the train. The position at Ramleh was now connected with Alexandria by a second line of railway. The armoured train was further improved by Captain Fisher, who placed one or two empty wagons in front of it, and a 40-pounder upon a truck, protected by an iron mantlet. At the same time the engine was placed in the middle of the train, and was protected by sand-bags and railway iron.

Meanwhile, on the 16th July, the Khedive Tewfik, who had placed himself under the protection of British bayonets, issued an order dismissing Arabi Pasha from his post of Minister of War, and from that time forward action was taken by us in the Egyptian *imbroglio* in the name of the Khedive. On the 27th July, the House of Commons passed a credit, by 275 votes to 19, of £2,300,000, and two days later the French Chambers, by a majority of 216 to 75, refused any money for the expedition, thus leaving on this country the onus of establishing order in Egypt. Three days before this, orders were sent to Sir Beauchamp Seymour and Sir Archibald Alison, warning them to be ready in case of necessity to seize Port Said or Ismailia, and on the 27th, the day of the adoption of the vote of credit, H.M.S. *Orion* passed into the Canal toward Ismailia, in accordance with the authority obtained from the Khedive, and on the 30th July, Sir William Hewett, commanding on the East India station, arrived off Suez, and Admiral Hoskins, at Port Said, with some ships, ready, when the time arrived for action, to seize the Canal from both ends. On the last day of July all the French ships-of-war still remaining at Alexandria withdrew, with the exception of one gunboat.

Almost daily reconnoissances were carried out at Alexandria by Sir Archibald Alison, and in one of them, Midshipman de Chair, who had been sent with despatches, was captured by the enemy, and taken to Cairo, where it was given out that the prisoner was Sir Beauchamp Seymour.

In order to keep up the belief that the attack on the Egyptian army was to be from Alexandria, General Alison, on the 5th August, undertook a reconnoissance in force with two columns, each consisting of 1,000 troops. The left column advanced along the bank of the Canal, and the right along the railway. The most interesting incident of the action was the good service done by the 40-pounder from the armoured train, which, with four guns dragged by the sailors, was the only ordnance employed. The enemy only yielded their successive positions as the artillery fire became too much for them, or as their flanks were turned. On the arrival of reinforcements, they appeared resolved to fight, but the object of keeping Arabi alarmed, and encouraging the belief that the attack on his army was to be from Alexandria, had been attained by the British general, who retired to his positions.

A portion of Arabi's reserves had been called out on the 27th July, and between the 30th of that month, when the *Orient* sailed from England with a battalion of the Scots Guards, and the 11th August, the various transports, conveying the troops of the expeditionary force, cleared from the ports of this country. Sir Garnet Wolseley sailed on the 2nd August in the *Calabria* for the seat of war. It had been his intention to proceed overland, *viâ* Brindisi, but when returning from a visit to Osborne to wait on the Queen, he caught a chill which resulted in an attack of erysipelas, and under medical advice, he took the sea route as the best means of restoring him to health. On the 10th August, Sir Garnet touched at Gibraltar, and despatched a telegram to Sir John Adye, his Chief of the Staff and second-in-command, who had arrived that day at Alexandria, requesting him to have all ready for the movement on the Suez Canal, immediately on his arrival.

Long before quitting England, and, indeed, early in July, Sir Garnet Wolseley had decided to make the line of advance on Cairo, the objective of the expedition, by Ismailia, lying midway in the Canal, and distant only 75 miles from the capital, Alexandria being 120. This course was dictated by necessity, as during the months of August, September, and October, the period of "high Nile," the whole delta is laid under water by the irrigation works, while the desert between Ismailia and Cairo afforded fair marching ground for infantry and cavalry, though difficult for artillery and wheeled transport because of the sandy patches interspersed through its entire route. Further, an advance from Ismailia would cover and protect the Canal, where also the troops from India could more easily concentrate. Accordingly, on the 2nd August, Admiral Hewett landed some Marines, and occupied Suez without resistance.

The task entrusted to the British Navy of seizing the Canal, and disembarking a large army with all its stores, was both complex and arduous, which will be apparent by a consideration of the difficulties involved in the navigation of the Canal, and by the fact that M. de Lesseps had taken up a hostile attitude to the expedition, and commanded the services of the Canal pilots. The narrowness of the channel, and the character of the banks, made it impossible for a large ship to pass down rapidly, and any attempt to do so caused a wash upon the banks, and a consequent backwater. Then special steering-gear is required in ships using this route, and the services of experienced officers. At this time, only one small pier existed at Ismailia, and ships did not anchor in Lake Timsah nearer than half a mile from the shore, so that every man and horse and gun, as well as all the stores, had to be transhipped from the transports into barges and small boats before being landed. The organization was placed in the hands of Captain Fisher, under the orders of Admiral Hoskins.

On the night of the 15th August, Sir Garnet Wolseley arrived at Alexandria, and on the following day, the whole of the arrangements for seizing the Canal, and for the movement of the Army on Ismailia, was worked out between the General and Sir Beauchamp Seymour, and the same evening, Admiral Hoskins left, in the *Iris*, for Port Said, to communicate the plan of operations to Sir William Hewett, at Suez, and to make arrangements with him for the effective military occupation of the Canal throughout its entire length on the morning of Sunday, the 20th August, for which he had a mandate from the Khedive, dated the 1st of the month. Admiral Hoskins reached Port Said at ten A.M. on the 17th August, and on the following morning, Captain Fitzroy, who was at Ismailia with his ship, the *Orion*, together with the *Carysfort* and *Coquette*, watching over the security of the Canal, arrived at Port Said, and received from the admiral instructions for seizing Ismailia before daybreak on the 20th August. Captain Fairfax, of H.M.S. *Monarch*, was ordered to occupy Port Said, at the same time, and Commander Edwards, of H.M. gunboat *Ready*, started at eight in the evening of the 19th August, to take possession of all barges and dredges along the line to Ismailia, the property of the Canal Company, to seize the telegraph-station at Kantara, in order to command the communications between Port Said and Ismailia, and to require all vessels in the Canal bound for Port Said to move into the "gares," points where the Canal is widened to admit of ships passing each other. The *Ready* and the *Dee* embarked three companies of Marines to assist in carrying out the undertaking, and 100 seamen were sent in the *Nyanza*, to reinforce the squadron at Ismailia.

At the Suez end, Admiral Hewett was directed to permit no ship to enter the Canal on the 19th, to drive the enemy out of Shalouf on the following morning, and attempt the capture of Serapeum. In this way the whole of the maritime waterway was to be occupied and cleared from Port Said to Suez, so as to be ready, soon after daybreak on the 20th, for the passage of the expedition from Alexandria. The whole of the arrangements were successfully carried into execution just as directed, and the result speaks well for the sagacity of the heads that planned the scheme, and the boldness and spirit with which it was put into execution. All the various craft on the Canal were taken possession of, an officer and 15 men being detailed to each. The whole of the passing ships were detained in the "gares," with the exception of the French ship *Melbourne*, which, as carrying the mails, was permitted to proceed as an act of international courtesy, and two English steamers which followed in her wake. Thus by dawn of the 20th August the Canal was clear.

Captain Fairfax was equally successful in his forcible occupation of Port Said. At sunset on the previous evening, in order to distract attention, the *Falcon* had been sent to anchor off the coast midway between the port and Fort Gemil, off which, during the night, the *Northumberland* brought to. Before the attacking parties left the ships, Colonel Tulloch landed with six Marines, and surprised the sentries. This done, the seamen of the *Monarch*, under Commander Hammill, passed ashore by an ingeniously-constructed floating bridge, formed of a lighter, planked over, and the ship's launch. Lieutenant Cook, of the *Iris*, also landed with a party of men from that ship, and, meeting the detachment from the *Monarch*, the united party formed a chain of sentries stretching across the neck of land between Lake Menzaleh and the sea, thus effectually cutting off all retreat from the town, and preventing all communication between it and the neighbouring country. Meantime, a company of Marines from the *Iris*, with a Gatling, under Captain Coffin, moved upon the barracks, while another company from the *Monarch*, with a Gatling, under Captain Eden, marched to effect a junction on the other side of the barracks. Thus surrounded, the soldiers laid down their arms without resistance, and the Khedive's governor, who had been expelled by the rebels, was reinstated in his office. Kantara was occupied without resistance, and by four in the morning the town of Ismailia was also seized. An hour before, 565 officers and men, from the *Orion*, *Northumberland*, and *Coquette*, and the *Nyanza*, troopship, with two Gatlings and a 7-pounder gun, under Captain Stephenson, were landed, and before they were discovered, surrounded the lock guard, who fired off their rifles, wounding an officer, Commander Kane. The guard over the governor's house laid down their arms, but there was some skirmishing at a small village outside the town, occupied by the enemy, who were, however, dislodged by the seamen and Marines, advancing under a covering fire from the ships. At the telegraph-office, it was ascertained, from the messages there, that the enemy, who had about 2,000 men at Nefisha, intended to reinforce that station, with the object of attacking Ismailia and the British ships. Accordingly, the *Orion* and *Carysfort* shelled the railway-station at Nefisha, and though the distance was about 4,000 yards, a train was struck by a shell, and the enemy's camp so much exposed that it was abandoned.

An amusing instance now took place of the uses to which a telegraph can be put against an unsuspecting enemy. Messages addressed to the manager were received from the War Office at Cairo, which, like the whole military resources of Egypt, was worked in the interests of Arabi, and a reply was sent in the name of the traffic manager, to the effect that 5,000 English troops had landed, and any attempt to relieve Ismailia would now be too late. The War Minister thereupon acknowledged the message, and added that he had informed all concerned.

Meanwhile at Suez, Admiral Hewett had taken equally energetic measures, and with not less success. It was of the first importance to seize Shalouf, not only because it gave possession of the maritime canal between Suez and the Bitter Lakes, but as there was a lock there of the fresh-water canal, by which its waters could be emptied into the Suez Canal. Admiral Hewett therefore sent a detachment of the Seaforth Highlanders, with seamen and Marines from the gunboats *Seagull* and *Mosquito*, who seized the lock and closed the gates, which had already been opened. The enemy showed in some force on the further bank of the fresh-water canal, and opened fire, but Lieutenant Lang, of the Highlanders, gallantly swam across under fire, and brought over a boat, by means of which the troops and seamen crossed the canal, and with the assistance of a well-directed fire of small-arms, and of a Gatling and 7-pounder from the tops of the *Seagull* and *Mosquito*, speedily drove back and dispersed the Egyptians. Thus it came about that the whole of the Suez Canal from sea to sea passed into the possession of the British commander, in spite of the vehement protestations of M. Lesseps, and became available for the unrestricted transport of troops to the new seat of active hostilities designed by Sir Garnet Wolseley. The plan had been carried out without a hitch, and was of so novel a character, that we have deemed the details of sufficient interest to merit description.

Meantime, it had been given out at Alexandria, so that it might come to the ears of Arabi, that the fleet would proceed to the bombardment of Aboukir, and that the whole of the forces at Alexandria would take part in the subsequent operations. Sir Edward Hamley, commanding the Second Division, was not let into the secret, and he and his brigadiers, Sir Archibald Alison and Sir Evelyn Wood, worked out the arrangements for advancing from Alexandria on Arabi's works in the neighbourhood, while the rest of the army was to co-operate from Aboukir Bay, and on communicating his proposals to the Commander-in-chief, Sir Garnet gave them his full approval. On the same day, the 18th August, the brigade of Guards and the cavalry and artillery which had been landed, were re-embarked, as well as four locomotives and 80 railway-carriages, and in the evening, the whole fleet anchored outside the outer harbour of Alexandria. At noon of the following day, the ships, consisting of eight ironclads and 17 transports, each of the former having charge of two of the latter, together with the despatch-boats, *Salamis* and *Helicon*, having on board respectively the military and naval commanders-in-chief, weighed anchor, and, forming in five lines, stood to the eastward. At four P.M. the same day, the fleet anchored in Aboukir Bay, and there they remained until nightfall, when the small craft stood close in shore and opened fire, while the remainder of the expedition, with the transports, steamed full power towards Port Said, which was reached soon after sunrise on the 20th August, by which time the Suez Canal throughout its length was in possession of the British Navy.

General Gerald Graham, commanding one of the two brigades of the First (General Willis's) Division, proceeded in the *Falcon*, with a wing of the West Kent, to reinforce Ismailia, which was reached at ten that night. The same day, several of the transports, with troops, had reached Kantara, and the remainder had anchored in the Canal. Sir Garnet Wolseley himself arrived at Ismailia at nine on the following morning, and immediately sent forward General Graham with the West Kent and a naval Gatling gun to occupy Nefisha. Serapeum, in advance of Shalouf, was seized by the Seaforth Highlanders on this day, and thus the main line of railway and fresh-water canal between Suez and Ismailia was in the hands of the British commander, and communications by land had been secured with the Indian Contingent, a portion of which had arrived at Suez. The rest of the operations, from the action at Magfar to the battle of Tel-el-Kebir and occupation of Cairo, are of a military character, though a strong detachment of seamen and Marines was also engaged.

The prescient character of Sir Garnet Wolseley in the conduct of this, as in all his other campaigns, is manifest in the fact that before leaving England he had expressed his opinion that the decisive battle of the war would take place at the earthworks of Tel-el-Kebir, and in a private letter, written just before he left Alexandria, he said:— "I shall want every available man I can get for my fight near Tel-el-Kebir, if Arabi will only in kindness stay to fight me there."

In the action of the advanced guard, on the 24th August, at which Sir Garnet was present, a party of seamen from H.M.S. *Orion*, with two Gatling guns, under Lieutenant King-Harman, was engaged, with two guns of the Horse Artillery. One machine-gun was placed in the line, and a shelter pit was made for it, while the second Gatling took post on the left flank of the York and Lancaster Regiment, between the freshwater canal and railway. The enemy were in greatly superior force, and the position was an anxious one, for had the small artillery force fallen back, owing either to the extreme heat of the day, or the explosion of an ammunition waggon from one of the shells, "there could be little doubt," says Colonel Maurice, the official historian of the war, to whose account we are indebted, "the enemy would have acquired a confidence which would have induced him to try his greatly superior numbers in a close attack, which we had barely sufficient numbers to meet." The four remaining guns of the battery of Horse Artillery arrived later in the day, and on the arrival of the Guards' Brigade and some cavalry the enemy withdrew into camp. Sir Garnet Wolseley returned to Ismailia for the night, and early on the morning of the 25th August, advanced with the First Division, when the enemy abandoned the camp at Mahsama, with seven Krupp guns, stores, ammunition, and 75 railway-waggons. A battalion of Royal Marines, under Colonel Jones, and a second of Royal Marine Artillery, under Colonel Tuson, both of which added to the reputation of their corps, took part in the operations ending with the battle of Tel-el-Kebir, on the 13th September, and the capture of Cairo. A naval brigade of 210 seamen, with six Gatlings, under Captain Fitzroy, was attached to the Indian Contingent, and marched along the line of railway, on the northern bank of the Canal, the main body of the infantry advancing on the southern side, connection between them being maintained by pontoons, under charge of the Royal Engineers. The Gatlings gave effective support to the Seaforth Highlanders, who, with the Native Infantry, captured the entrenchments on the southern bank, and of the 58 guns taken in the battle, General Macpherson's force was credited with eight Krupp field-guns, and four 7-pounder rifled bronze guns.

The services of one of our naval officers were of such importance as to merit special notice. Lieutenant Rawson was employed on shore as naval aide-de-camp to Sir Garnet Wolseley, and was present in the memorable march on Tel-el-Kebir. The night of the 12th September was more than usually dark, and it was some time before the troops could be placed in the positions assigned to them. About eleven P.M., when this was done, Sir Garnet rode on the ground, and went round the whole of the bivouac. As the sole means of direction depended on the stars, he instructed Lieutenant Rawson to guide the Highland Brigade, "as a man well accustomed to steer his way by the stars, and familiar with the desert from having accompanied the Commander-in-chief in his many journeyings to and from Ismailia by night."

The army marched off at 1.30 A.M. on the 13th September, the right company of the Cameron Highlanders, guided by Lieutenant Rawson, being the company of direction. So well did he perform his task, that the Highlanders, leading the Second Division, arrived at the enemy's entrenchments before the First Division, although it was supposed that the latter would strike the line of works first, as it trended forward towards its left. Absolute silence prevailed, and "sight or sound at 100 yards from any column there was none, save of the desert and the stars." After marching for about an hour and three-quarters, the Highland Brigade halted and laid down for twenty minutes in order to refresh the men, but some confusion was caused by the flanks continuing to advance until the brigade stood in a crescent-shaped formation. However, with the assistance of Lieutenant Rawson, Sir Archibald Alison drew back the other battalions and companies, and the brigade resumed its march in perfect order, and about five minutes to five, the Highlanders, being quite 600 or 700 yards in advance of the leading brigade (General Graham's) of the First Division, charged the entrenchments, and after a long and severe struggle, made good their footing within it.

The gallant Rawson, who was among the first to top the crest of the entrenchments, received a wound, from which he expired before receiving the news of his promotion to the rank of commander. Sir Garnet Wolseley rode back from the field of battle on the same afternoon to express to his dying subaltern his appreciation of his gallantry and devotion. "Did I not lead them straight?" was the eager question of the dying officer, who, though *in articulo mortis*, smiled gratefully, when his chief, pressing his hand, expressed his satisfaction with his conduct, and said he hoped he might survive to enjoy the hardly-earned promotion to the rank of commander, which a cruel fate, however, denied him.

Sir Garnet Wolseley says of this officer, who had earned his thanks by his gallantry at Ashantee:—" Of my aides-de-camp, I have to regret the loss of Lieutenant Rawson, R.N., who was mortally wounded at Tel-el-Kebir. During the many journeys I made by night, I found him of great use in directing our line of march correctly, through his knowledge of the stars. On the 13th inst., I selected him to conduct the Highland Brigade during the night to the portion of the enemy's works where I explained to him I wished them to storm. This duty he performed with the utmost coolness and success, but lost his life in its execution. No man more gallant fell on that occasion."

Throughout the succeeding operations near Suakin, in the Eastern Soudan, and in the campaign on the Nile for the relief of General Gordon, the Navy took an important, if a subordinate, part, and added a fresh page to the glorious records of the service. Sir William Hewett, commanding the fleet on the East India Station, was Governor of Suakin, and on the 24th February, 1884, accompanied Sir Gerald Graham to Trinkitat, where the troops were disembarked for the march to relieve Tokar. Here the malcontents had taken post under the irrepressible Osman Digna, who was so often reported as killed, but again and again turned up to engage his combined British and Egyptian enemies, and harass "the friendlies," who suffered greatly by their adhesion to the cause of England. A naval brigade accompanied the army under Commander Ernest Rolfe, who had served ashore in the Ashantee Campaign, and was an officer of great promise, and much experience of native warfare. The brigade numbered 150 seamen, with six machine-guns, and accompanying the expedition was a battalion of Royal Marines, light infantry and artillery, nearly 400 strong, commanded by Colonel Tuson. A hotly-contested battle took place on the 29th February at El Teb, the scene of Valentine Baker's rout, when his ill-disciplined *gendarmerie* were slaughtered by the warlike Arabs of the desert. The Naval Brigade, with their machine-guns, were stationed in the angles in the front of the advancing square, and the Royal Artillery with their guns on the rear face, and when the hand-to-hand fighting took place, the seamen and their officers greatly distinguished themselves by their cool intrepidity. One of the latter, Captain Wilson, of the *Hecla*, a volunteer, gained the Victoria Cross. He was attached to the right half battery of machine-guns, and when the troops charged a work armed with two Krupp guns, the enemy attacked the corner of the square, where the seamen were dragging forward a Gardner gun, in order to bring it into action. Captain Wilson sprang to the front and engaged the Arabs until he was assisted by some men of the York and Lancaster Regiment. In the action, Lieutenant

SHIP'S COOK.

Royds, of the *Carysfort*, who had been engaged at Kassassin and Tel-el-Kebir, was slain, together with three seamen, but the services rendered by the detachment received the approval of Sir Gerald Graham, who wrote :—" The general officer thanks the Naval Brigade for their cheerful endurance during the severe work of dragging the guns over difficult country, when suffering from heat and scarcity of water; and for their ready gallantry and steadiness under fire while serving the guns. The Naval Brigade contributed materially to the success of the action, and the general officer commanding cannot too highly express his thanks for their services." The expedition returned to Suakin, but on the 11th March again took the field to disperse the Arabs, who were beleaguering Sinkat, where some Egyptian troops still held out.

The Naval Brigade had arduous work in dragging the machine-guns through the scrub and sand, and at Tamai the column came into collision with the Arabs. Undaunted by their experiences at El Teb, they threw themselves recklessly on the British square, under command of General Davis, to which was attached the Naval Brigade and Marine battalion, numbering 14 officers and 464 men. The seamen, with the machine-guns, were posted inside the square, formed by the Second Brigade, but owing to the rapidity of the advance, which was made at the double, the formation was broken, and the enemy charged from a nullah in which they were secreted, on the right corner of the square, formed by the York and Lancaster Regiment, where there was a gap. The brigade fell back in confusion, and the Arabs captured the guns, by which, says the general, the men " stood to the last." It was at this time, when bravely defending their charges, that Lieutenants Almack, Houston Stewart, and Montresor, with seven seamen, were killed, Lieutenant Conybeare and seven others being wounded.

The brigade quickly rallied, and the steady advance of the First Brigade, under Sir Redvers Buller, whose volleys swept all before them, completed the discomfiture of the Arabs, when the guns were retaken. After occupying the camp and village of Tamai, on the same day, the column returned to Suakin, and a body of 200 seamen, landed from the squadron, afforded valuable assistance in carrying the wounded. The campaign was concluded by an unopposed advance on Tamanieb, when the troops returned to Cairo or England, with the exception of a small garrison for Suakin, including a battalion of Marines.

In the autumn of 1885 took place the expedition, under Lord Wolseley, for the relief of General Gordon at Khartoum. In the arduous task of transporting men and stores along the reaches of the Nile to Korti, the Navy rendered valuable assistance, under Commander Hammill, of the *Monarch*, and received the thanks of his lordship for its co-operation, and also had part in the advance from Korti to Metemmeh, on the Nile, under the command of Sir Herbert Stewart. Small in numbers, but excellent in discipline and valour, the Naval Brigade was commanded by Lord Charles Beresford, who had already earned a reputation for gallantry when in command of the *Condor* at Alexandria. On the 5th January, 1885, a portion of the Brigade, consisting of four officers and 51 seamen, arrived at Korti, under Lieutenant Pigott, and shortly after, the remainder followed, consisting of six officers and 50 seamen, under the command of Lieutenant Van Koughnet, including some men of the Naval Engineer Department, to assist on board the steamers.

On the 8th January, the column of 100 officers and 1,500 men, of whom a portion were mounted on camels, marched from Korti under command of Sir Herbert Stewart, and Gakdul Wells was reached four days later without any opposition being encountered. The column marched after a halt of two days, and on the 16th, the scouts first had touch of the enemy, and from this point till the Nile was reached the fighting was of a desperate character, and the Naval detachment of 55 officers and men suffered its full share in the loss sustained and the honour achieved.

On the night of the 16th, when the small British force was encamped in a zareba, or breastwork of prickly camel-thorn bushes, about four miles from the wells of Abu Klea, the Arabs commenced to annoy them by a distant rifle fire, but no organized attack was made. At six on the following morning, after breakfast, the column was formed up outside the zareba, about 800 yards from which the enemy appeared in dense masses, and showed every disposition to try conclusions at close quarters. The artillery, with a half battery of 7-pounders, and 40 seamen with the Gardner gun, took up a position on the right front, the remainder of the Naval Brigade remaining in the zareba.

For some time the British column remained drawn up in expectation of an attack, but as the enemy showed a disinclination to take the offensive, shortly after nine A.M. General Stewart ordered the greater portion of the troops to take up a fresh position in front of the zareba, in which a detachment with the transport camels still remained. Accompanying the column was the main portion of the Naval Brigade, with the Gardner gun, under the command of Lord Charles Beresford. The troops advanced in square formation a distance of about two miles, the enemy meanwhile keeping up a hot fire, and as they cleared a hill on their left flank, a large number of flags was seen planted in the high grass, which was about 400 yards distant. Still none of the Arabs showed themselves, but when the square halted abreast of the flags, suddenly they were seen to spring up, to the number of about 6,000, and advance rapidly upon the British position. Accompanying them was a body of some 40 horsemen, all carrying flags. To meet the attack, Beresford brought the Gardner gun from its position on the rear face of the square to the centre of the left flank, on which the enemy were advancing with speed. His lordship succeeded in getting off 40 rounds, or five turns of the lever, when, perceiving that the elevation was too great, he gave the order to cease firing until the gun was brought to bear on the foe. Again he fired 30 rounds, when the gun jammed, the Arabs being then about 200 yards distant from its muzzle. In a moment the enemy were upon them, and a hand-to-hand melée ensued, in which Lord Charles Beresford was knocked down, and some of his men were killed and wounded.*

The Arabs now diverged to their right, and bore down on the rear face of the square. Lord Charles Beresford, as soon as he was relieved from the pressure, and regained his legs, used his best endeavours to clear the jam in the Gardner gun, and succeeding in doing so, opened fire on the enemy, but was not able to effect much, as by that time they were under cover beyond range. In the brief struggle, the detachment had suffered severely, two officers and six men being killed, and seven wounded, out of 40 engaged. The officers were Commander Alfred Pigott and Lieutenant Rudolf de Lisle, both described as "most excellent." The enemy lost heavily, quite 800 dead being visible in the grass, and one of their leaders, who was mounted, was killed inside the square.

The column halted while attention was given to the wounded, and about 2.30 continued the march to Abu Klea Wells, the Naval Brigade having a difficult task in dragging the Gardner gun over the rough ground, owing to their diminished numbers. Abu Klea was reached about five the same afternoon, and the column having constructed a zareba, bivouacked on the night of the 17th, without provisions or blankets. The

---

* His lordship says in his despatch:—"The captain of the gun (Rhodes, chief boatswain's mate) and myself unscrewed the plate to clear the barrel, or take the lock of the jammed barrel out, when the enemy were upon us. Rhodes was killed with a spear. Walter Miller, armourer, I also saw killed with a spear at the same moment on my left. I was knocked down in the rear of the gun, but uninjured, except a small spear scratch on the left hand. The crowd and crush of the enemy was very great at this point, and, as I struggled up, I was carried against the face of the square, which was literally pushed back by sheer weight of numbers, about twelve paces from the position of the gun. The crush was so great that at the moment few on either side were killed, but fortunately this flank of the square had been forced up a very steep little mound, which enabled the rear rank to open a tremendous fire over the heads of the front rank men: this relieved the pressure, and enabled the front rank to bayonet or shoot those of the enemy nearest them."

night was very cold, and the sufferings of the wounded were greatly aggravated by the low temperature. On the following morning, the detachment and camels joined the column at Abu Klea from the zareba in rear, and at two o'clock the same afternoon, the whole force continued the march for the Nile, with the determination of reaching it without a halt. All that day and through the night the troops moved on, and at half-past six on the morning of the 19th, the river was seen in front. It was a welcome sight, but the British soldiers and sailors had a hard day's fighting before them, and some were destined even now to be deprived of the anticipated pleasure of quenching their thirst in the waters of the Nile.

A halt was made for the purposes of rest and breakfast, when the enemy made their appearance on one of the neighbouring hills. While they were engaged in the construction of a zareba, the Arabs opened fire, and our men began to fall fast. Among those wounded was Sir Herbert Stewart, who received a bullet-wound in the groin, from the effects of which he eventually succumbed. Sub-Lieutenant Munro, R.N., was also severely wounded. The Gardner gun was taken to a point about ten yards outside the square, and opened fire, but it could not have been very effective, as the enemy's sharpshooters, on whom it was directed, were under cover or concealed in the grass.

At length, about ten A.M., the zareba was completed, and the troops formed outside, to the number of 1,000 men, to continue the march for Metemmeh, on the Nile, while to Lord Charles Beresford was entrusted the command of the position, in which all the camels, over 2,000 in number, and the wounded, were left under the protection of 300 men, composed of details from various regiments and departments, with the Naval Brigade.

Upon the square moving off for the river, the enemy appeared inclined to repeat the tactics of Abu Klea, but they met an equally warm reception. A fort had been constructed outside the zareba, on which two 7-pounders, under Captain Norton, R.A., and the Gardner gun had been mounted, and as the square, being still within range, was attacked by the Arabs, these pieces of ordnance opened fire on them with great accuracy and fatal effect. At length the column reached the Nile, but long before they reached the river, the enemy, disheartened by their want of success, desisted from making any further attack.

The position of the detachment left in the zareba, under Lord Charles Beresford, through that day and night, was a critical one, and when, on the following morning, the column returned to escort the camels and wounded men to the spot on the banks of the Nile selected for the temporary encampment, a sense of relief pervaded all hearts. At four o'clock the same afternoon the united column marched for the river, which they reached without experiencing opposition.

Instead of pushing on to the rescue of General Gordon without further loss of time than was absolutely necessary, Sir Charles Wilson undertook a useless reconnoissance towards Metemmeh, to which he took with him the Gardner gun, under charge of Mr. Webber, boatswain, every other naval officer being killed, wounded, or required for other duties.

In the interval the naval engineer with the column had effected what repairs were necessary to the engines of the four steamers Gordon had sent from Khartoum, and at three P.M. on the 22nd January, Lord Charles Beresford reported to Sir Charles Wilson that they were ready for service. But instead of despatching them immediately to effect the object of all the expenditure of treasure and blood involved since the despatch of the expedition from England, the officer in command detached Lord Charles Beresford to Shendy with two steamers—the *Bordein* and *Tull-Howeiya*—on board of which were their native crews and some of Gordon's black troops. After throwing a few shells into that place Beresford returned to Metemmeh, and it was not until seven o'clock on the morning of the 24th January that Sir Charles Wilson left for Khartoum with these two steamers, conveying a detachment of about 20 men of the Sussex Regiment and the Soudani troops, some 280 in all.

Lord Charles Beresford, who remained in camp with the Naval Brigade, employed the leisure at his disposal in again visiting Shendy, in the *Sofia* steamer, on board of which were embarked some British seamen and a Gardner gun. The enemy were engaged, and replied to the ship's fire, but were easily dispersed. The fourth steamer, *Tewfikea*, was utilised to bring food for the camels from an island in the river opposite the camp, garrisoned by some of Gordon's Egyptian troops, and to receive Sir Herbert Stewart, whose condition had become serious. Between the 25th and 30th January, Lord Charles Beresford daily patrolled the stream, and brought off such supplies of vegetables and sheep as he could raid from the adjacent villages. These excursions were conducted with comparative impunity from loss, owing to the precautions his lordship had taken in fitting bullet-proof screens on the bulwarks.

On the 31st January, the Second Division of the Naval Brigade, consisting of 56 officers and men, arrived at the camp from Korti, and on the following day, the anxiety with which the column were awaiting news from Khartoum was intensified by the intelligence that the city had fallen, that Gordon was slain, and that the two steamers had been wrecked. Lieutenant Stuart-Wortley, who brought this startling intelligence, had arrived in a boat from Sir Charles Wilson's party, which was encamped on an island about 30 miles up stream, with an urgent request from that officer, addressed to Lord Charles Beresford, to proceed to his assistance. Immediately his lordship selected a crew for the *Sofia* from the Naval Brigade, and taking with him 20 picked shots from the Mounted Infantry, and mounting in the steamer the two Gardners, now at his disposal, sailed on the 2nd February for the rescue of the ship-wrecked party. At seven on the following morning he came abreast of a strong earthwork, about a quarter of a mile from the island where they were encamped, which opened on them from some heavy guns, and also kept up a continuous fusillade. Owing to the depth of water, the *Sofia* had to pass within 80 yards of the fort, but by directing the fire from his Gardners and the ship's howitzer into the embrasures, he was enabled to pass by without accident. He had increased his distance to 200 yards, when the enemy sent a shot into the boiler, which rendered the machinery powerless. Lord Charles headed the steamer at once for the opposite bank, and when she had lost her way, dropped his anchor. The Arabs now redoubled their fire, when his lordship mounted one of the Gardners on the after part, and directed a hot fire from it and from the 7-pounder, as well as from the rifles, on the embrasures of the battery, facing up stream. About eleven o'clock, when the boiler had cooled, Mr. Benbow, the chief engineer, began its repair, a job which took ten hours to accomplish. "Too much credit," says Lord Charles, "cannot be given to this officer, as he had to shape the plate, bore the holes in plate and boiler, and run down the screws and nuts, almost entirely with his own hands, the artificers and every one in the stoke-hole having been scalded severely by the explosion when the shot entered the boilers. The plate was 16 inches by 14, so that some idea can be formed of the work entailed upon him."

Lord Charles Beresford, having communicated with Sir Charles Wilson, arranged to march down the right bank of the river, while his sick and wounded were removed in a nuggah, or large native boat. On the vessel making its appearance, the enemy opened fire from the earthwork, but with little effect, owing to the darkness. After it had passed, they took their guns out of the fort, and fired several rounds on the steamer, but not receiving any return, came to the conclusion apparently that it was deserted, which was what Lord Charles Beresford desired, and ceased firing for the night.

The repair of the boiler having been completed at nine in the evening, early on the following morning, the 4th February, fires were lit, and at 5.30, within a few minutes of daylight, steam was up, and all ready for a start. On perceiving the ruse that had been successfully practised, the enemy began yelling, and opened fire on the steamer, but it was then too late to stop her progress, and she steamed up stream, and proceeded a distance of three-quarters of a mile to one of the reaches of the river, where there was room to turn, when she steamed past the fort at a good speed, and opened fire with her guns and rifles. But all difficulties and dangers were not yet surmounted, for it was discovered that the nuggah had grounded on a rock within range of the fort. His lordship sent Sub-Lieutenant Keppel to assist in getting her afloat, and when this was done, while exposed to a heavy fire, Beresford embarked the military party from the shore, and the steamer proceeded to camp, where she arrived at 5.45 the same evening, without further incident.

The successful termination of the undertaking was due to the skilful management and coolness of Lord Charles Beresford, who, however, gave the credit to others. He says in his despatch:—"I consider that we owe our safety in the steamer, as well as the safety of Sir Charles Wilson and his party, who undoubtedly would have been killed if the steamer had been destroyed, to the untiring energy of Sub-Lieutenant Keppel and Mr. Webber, boatswain (who worked the howitzer), to Lieutenant Bower, who commanded the picked shots of the Mounted Infantry, and Mr. Ingram, of the Yeomanry, who is attached by order to the Naval Brigade, and who attended to the working of the Gardner, after Lieutenant Van Koughnet was wounded at the moment the fort bore on our beam. Surgeon May, R.N., was also very attentive to the wounded. Testimony must be borne to the splendid discipline maintained by the men, one and all, during a tremendous fire which lasted thirteen hours." The steamer was patched up for temporary service, but she leaked badly, owing to the concussion of the gun in the action of the 3rd February, there not being sufficient room for its recoil.

Sir Redvers Buller now arrived from Korti to assume command of the column, which set out on its return march at daybreak on the 14th February. On the previous day, Lord Charles Beresford spiked the guns on board the two remaining steamers, *Sofia* and *Tewfikea*, and threw them overboard, together with the ammunition, and also removed the eccentric bands from the engines of both vessels. The column halted at Abu Klea Wells from noon on the following day till the 23rd February, and had a skirmish with the enemy, but on the evening of that day the march was resumed for

Gakdul. This place was reached on the 26th, and two days later the Naval Brigade left with a portion of the force for Korti, which they entered without molestation. The return march of 200 miles from Metemmeh was made without a man falling out.

On their arrival, Lord Wolseley inspected the Naval Brigade, and made an address expressive of his thanks and recognition of their good conduct. He highly complimented Lord Charles Beresford, and presented his own cigarette-case to Mr. Benbow, the engineer who patched the boiler, and thus enabled the steamer to return, and saved the lives of all the party. The expedition marched for Cairo without any further incident, and the Naval Brigade was broken up and the men returned to their ships.

Meantime, a detachment of seamen participated in the operations in the neighbourhood of Suakin, having for its object to assist Lord Wolseley by opening up the Berber-Suakin route. In the occupation of Hasheen a battalion of Royal Marines did excellent service, and in the surprise at Tofrek, when the Arabs nearly overpowered Sir John McNeill's brigade, heavy loss was sustained by the detachment of seamen drawn from the ships in port—*Carysfort*, *Condor*, *Dolphin*, *Coquette*, and *Sphinx*. The Naval Brigade was divided into two portions, each having two Gardner guns, stationed in two redoubts, constructed at the apex of the zareba, and therefore exposed more than any other point to attack. The redoubts were unfinished at the time of the onset of the Arabs, who carried the northern one by a rush, the weight of numbers overbearing all attempts to make a stand. Lieutenant Seymour, of the *Dolphin*, in command at this point, was killed, together with six seamen, and many were wounded. The other redoubt, where Lieutenant Paget commanded, escaped attack, and the fire that officer brought to bear on the front of the Arab masses, largely contributed to drive them off. Over 1,000 dead bodies lay close to the works, and our own men suffered severely, about 400 being slain, while the loss of 600 camels, besides other baggage animals, seriously crippled the force. But the Arabs had received a severe lesson, and when, in April, 1885, Sir Gerald Graham advanced and burnt Tamai, Osman Digna could not bring his followers to offer any opposition, although they made desultory attacks on convoys. The Naval Brigade now rejoined their ships, and thus terminated the last service ashore or afloat which our sailors have been called on to render to their country. A special word of praise is due to the Royal Marines, who garrisoned Suakin at a time when Osman Digna was in great strength in the neighbourhood, and the alarms and attacks were constant and harassing. The seamen from the ships already named, as well as from H.M. ships *Briton*, *Tyne*, *Woodlark*, *Myrmidon*, and *Albacore*, were constantly landed to assist in the defence of the town and outlying forts and redoubts, while in all the expeditions, especially the last, the Navy Transport Department, under Captains Fellowes and Morrison, had an arduous duty to perform in providing for a force of 12,000 men in the field. Among the officers who specially distinguished themselves in superintending the working of the land mines, which were used to defend the causeway communicating with the town and the flank of the position, were Lieutenants Kirby, of the *Briton,* Talbot, of the *Carysfort*, and Seymour, of the *Dolphin*, who afterwards fell. Lieutenant Smythies, of the *Albacore*, also rendered good service in protecting the south side of the town, and the gunboat was frequently under fire from the enemy, sheltered in quarries near the harbour. Finally, a word of praise is due to Commodore Molyneux, the officer commanding the Red Sea Division of the Mediterranean fleet, whose "tact, intelligence, and judgment, in dealing with an infinite variety of circumstances," was commended by Lord John Hay, the commander-in-chief.

And now our survey of the matchless services rendered by the British Navy is completed. Who can tell the nationality of the enemy with whom our sailors will next have to contend on their own native element? These shore expeditions, in which they have been so much engaged since the war with Russia, are but as interludes or by-plays in the great historic drama of the deeds of our Navy. It is on their own element that their glory has been achieved in the past, and it is from their deeds afloat that a due estimate of their efficiency can be formed.

Enigmatical are the conditions of warfare, or even the weapons that will be employed at sea with most deadly effect. It may be the torpedo, as many think, or the ram, as in the action between the Italian and Austrian fleets, and on a memorable occasion in America during the great War of Secession. It may be that the powers of offence, as represented by the gun, will triumph over the armour-plate. Each have their advocates in the race of competition, and only a battle between the fleets of the great European maritime powers can solve the question. New explosives, hitherto undreamt of, may revolutionize warfare on the sea, and the navy that possesses the most deadly agent of destruction may carry all before it. All we can do is to use our best endeavours to be foremost in the race of invention and manufacture, and to deny no expenditure that may be necessary to make England the Mistress of the Seas, as in the past. Even a man of pacific views, like Cobden, who was denounced in his time as one of the "Manchester School," or the "Peace at any Price" party, was alive to this necessity, and expressed an opinion that England should build two ships for every one constructed by France. In the present day, with the development of naval strength on the part of Italy and Russia, not to speak of Germany, the youngest aspirant for nautical honours, whose ships are little likely to be employed against this country, it behoves us to increase our comparative strength as regards the European states which may be found in combination against us. "*Si vis pacem para bellum*" is a very old, and a not less wise, dictum, and we should act upon it if we would preserve our ancient dominion of the sea, as well as our colonies, our trade, nay, our very existence !

We cannot do better than conclude this history of the British Navy by the warning addressed to the Government by England's great and patriotic poet, Lord Tennyson, at a time when the attention of his countrymen was directed to the inadequacy of the Navy for the due fulfilment of its multifarious needs. It should act as a spur to Ministers and people in the event of their neglecting hereafter to maintain our fleet in the position of supremacy demanded by the necessities of this great nation.

> You—you—*if* you have fail'd to understand—
> The Fleet of England is her all in all—
> On you will come the curse of all the land,
>   If that Old England fall,
>   Which Nelson left so great—
>
> This isle, the mightiest naval power on earth,
> This one small isle, the lord of every sea—
> Poor England, what would all these votes be worth,
>   And what avail thine ancient fame of "Free,"
>   Wert thou a fallen State ?
>
> You—you—who had the ordering of her Fleet,
> *If* you have only compass'd her disgrace,
> When all men starve, the wild mob's million feet
>   Will kick you from your place—
>   But **then**—too late, too late.

CHAPTER XI.

(*SUPPLEMENTARY.*)

The *Materiel* of the British Navy in 1892—England's Responsibilities and the Condition of the Fleet—The Transition from Wooden Ships to Ironclads—British Ships-of-war of the Past and Present—The Guns of our Day—The Naval Defence Act of 1889, and the New Programme of Shipbuilding—The *Royal Sovereign*—Some other Battle Ships—Our Cruisers—Our Torpedo Flotilla—Comparison of British with Foreign Navies—The *Personnel* of the Navy—Our Reserves.

NOT among the least sagacious remarks of the great Francis Bacon was the following, in which he dealt with the necessity of maintaining the command of the sea: "He that commands the sea is at great liberty, and may take as much and as little of the war as he will. Whereas those that be strongest by land are nevertheless many times in great straits. Surely, at this day, with us of Europe, the vantage of strength at sea (which is one of the principal dowries of this Kingdom of Great Britain) is great, both because most of the kingdoms of Europe are not only inland, but girt with the sea most part of their compass, and because the wealth of both Indies seems, in great part, but an accessory to the command of the seas."

The British Navy, as now constituted, is a highly complex machine, with manifold duties to perform, the due execution of which demands a variety in the type of its constituent parts such as was never dreamt of in past times by the Boards of Admiralty and great sea captains who guarded our native seas, and kept the island free from the invader's foot. For coast defence, for cruising purposes, for the protection of India and our colonies, for convoy to our merchantmen, and, finally, to fight general engagements and blockade the enemy in their ports—for all these objects and needs a multiform and diverse machine is demanded by the exigencies of modern war, and woe be to the country if in one detail alone she is unable to meet her requirements. Thus any inability to protect our colonies would result in their secession, while impotence on the high seas, either to keep clear the great ocean highways, or meet in battle any power, or combination of powers, would result in the loss of our freedom, and in any case would so raise the price of bread and other necessaries of life, that popular riots, if not revolution, would threaten the existence of society, if not cause its disintegration. For these reasons it behoves the people of the three kingdoms to keep their navy in such a state of efficiency as to defy half the world in arms, as we did at the time of Napoleon, when, although the Northern Powers, as well as France and Spain, were banded against us, we drove their combined fleets from the seas, and seized or blockaded the ships in their ports.

A survey of our comparative strength at the present time, will attest the fact that England is insufficiently powerful at sea to undertake hostilities on this gigantic scale, and whereas in those days most of our colonies had no existence, or were too poor to invite attack, they now embrace a great portion of the most fertile regions of the globe, and are the wonder and envy of all nations. England has an unequalled prestige at sea, but in this, as in all instances recorded in history, lies the danger, as tending to breed over-confidence. What has been in the past, it is thought, will be in the future, so long as the spirit of the country suffers no deterioration. But this is a fatal mistake. High spirit, unaccompanied by preparedness, will not ensure success in war, either on shore or afloat, and it behoves us therefore to keep ahead of other nations in numerical superiority, as well as in professional skill.

Apparently our officers and seamen are equal, and we hope superior, at the present day, in training and experience to those of any other nation, but we should not allow this belief, the soundness of which can only be tested by actual hostilities, to induce us to relax in our endeavours to make the Navy stronger in ships and men, as it was in the time of the Revolutionary war in 1793, than any possible combination of powers. As also the conditions of success may be entirely altered by the intrusion of some new element, or invention, of which we have no idea at present, it becomes our duty to give ceaseless attention to the problems of naval science, as they become modified or entirely changed by the introduction of new motive powers for propelling ships and projectiles, improvements in the form or nature of either, or altogether novel agencies and weapons for maritime warfare.

On the sea our commerce is our most assailable point, and it is certain that France, or any other naval power with which we might be at war, would use every endeavour to cripple us by fast cruisers, or the employment of swift armed mercantile steamships. The unlimited rights of belligerents have been advocated by most Continental writers, and it is certain that they would be enforced by the employment of torpedo boats. The knowledge of this would in all probability result in the transfer, on the declaration of war, of a large portion of our carrying trade to other powers, and the experience of the United States shows that when commerce is diverted, it is slow to return to its old channels. As regards the ruthless characteristics of such a war, it has been insisted by Continental writers of weight, including Admiral Aube, late French Minister of Marine, that not only should merchant ships be tracked and destroyed by torpedo boats, but that seaports should be burnt, even though unarmed, the coasts harried by fire and sword, and every means put in practice to bring hostilities to a speedy close by striking terror into the population, and causing ruin to the community. These being the accepted principles of a large section of writers and men of action, who might have it in their power to enforce their views, a sense of self-preservation requires that the nation should possess a force of powerful and swift cruisers, as well as torpedo-catchers, to clear the seas. The country which has the command of the sea is enabled to select its point of attack, and suddenly assail places accessible to a fleet, which is an incalculable advantage. It is one we have ever enjoyed in all our wars, and has been a main cause of their success. This superiority enabled us to capture Belleisle in the middle of the last century, and land an army in Egypt, which resulted in the expulsion of the French in 1801. By this power we were placed in a position to wrest from France her settlements in India and Canada, and from Holland and Spain their colonial possessions. Again, in our war with Russia, the command of the sea enabled us to land in the Crimea, and supply with stores a comparatively small army, to combat which drained the resources of the Russian Empire, and compelled the Czar to negotiate a humiliating peace.

Very different is the man-of-war of the present day from that of thirty years ago. In 1862 the wooden line-of-battle ship *Victoria*,* of which we give an illustration, was considered the *ne plus ultra* of naval ship-building science, and justly so as regards beauty of appearance and strength to resist the action of the elements and the guns of the period, of which the 95-cwt. 68-pounder, or 8-inch gun, was still the heaviest afloat. But between the wooden three-decker of that time and the *Royal Sovereign* † of 1892, there is a wider difference in construction than between the *Duke of Wellington,* now in Portsmouth harbour, and the *Sovereign of the Seas* of Drake's day.

In 1810, when the British Navy possessed no less than two hundred and forty-eight ships-of-the-line fit for sea, and two hundred and ninety frigates, the largest vessel was only 205 feet in length on the main-deck, and the proportion between the length and beam of battle-ships had undergone but little change in two hundred years. Thus in the *Sovereign of the Seas* it was 3.46 to 1, and in the *Caledonia*, the largest ship in commission in 1810, the proportion was 3.82 to 1. As any one can

* See illustration, Vol. II., page 286.   † See illustration, Vol. III., page 332.

see, the old *Victory* * of 1765 is not very different in construction from the *Duke of Wellington* of ninety years later, though Seppings had introduced a more efficient system of framing the hull, and Symonds gave loftier decks and more roomy batteries. Fifty years ago we had paddle steamships, which took part in the attack on Acre, but it was not until just before the time of the Crimean war that the screw system displaced the side-wheel as a means of propulsion. Up to that time our ships-of-war retained their beauty of outline, and carried the sails which had inspired poets.† After the invention of the auxiliary screw came the introduction of armour, then the ram, iron instead of wood, steel in place of iron, the turret, the barbette, and, lastly, the torpedo. Thus between the ship-of-war now and thirty years back there is little in common, except that both are armed with guns and propelled by steam.

It is an undeniable fact that to the United States *Monitor* is due the change in the construction of ships-of-war which has revolutionized the navies of the world. That strange innovation upon the wooden vessels of the past, which was due to the genius of Ericsson, startled the world by her performances in the great internecine struggle in America some thirty years ago.‡

The first ironclad of the British Navy was the *Warrior*, 380 feet in length, the same as the *Royal Sovereign* of 1892, a ship of great beauty in her lines, and provided with masts and sails, but with her ends unprotected by armour, and having only a central battery. She was succeeded by a long series of full-rigged ironclads, though gradually sails were discontinued. The *Black Prince*, her sister ship, and the reduced *Warriors*, *Defence* and *Resistance*, had unarmoured ends, but the *Minotaur* and *Agin-*

---

* See illustration, Vol. III., page 20.

† Mr. Ruskin, writing in 1856, when such ships as the *Marlborough*—now employed in Portsmouth to berth engineer apprentices—were considered the triumph of the naval architect, describes in eloquent terms the impressions produced on his mind by a line-of-battle ship, which was only an improved *Victory*, with the auxiliary screw as an additional means of propulsion. He says in his "Harbours of England":—"One thing this century will in after ages be considered to have done in a superb manner, and one thing only. Take it all in all, a ship-of-the line is the most honourable thing that man, as a gregarious animal, has ever produced. By himself, unhelped, he can do better things than ships-of-the-line; he can make poems and pictures, and other such concentrations of what is best in him. But as a being living in flocks, and hammering out with alternate strokes and mutual agreement what is necessary for him in those flocks, to produce the ship-of-the-line is his first work. Into that he has put as much of his human patience, common sense, forethought, experimental philosophy, self-control, habits of order and obedience, thoroughly-wrought handiwork, defiance of brute elements, careless courage, careful patriotism, and calm expectation of the judgment of God, as can well be put into a space of 300 feet long by 80 broad, and I am thankful to have lived in an age when I could see this thing so done."

‡ The ship in our navy which nearest approaches the type of the *Monitor* is the *Glatton*, designed by Sir Edward Reed; but in her case, as in all his turret-ships, the base of the turret and the hatchways over the machinery were protected with an armoured breastwork standing high above the deck, whereas in the American *Monitor* the turret rested upon the deck, which was near the surface of the sea.

court, both of the same size as the *Warrior*, were protected from stem to stern. The *Achilles*, smaller than these ships, was also furnished with a complete belt at the water-line, but the *Hector* and *Valiant* resembled the *Defence* class, and had their ends unarmoured at the water-line. The *Northumberland* resembled the *Minotaur*, but had the armour reduced above the water at both ends, though she carried a protected bow breastwork, in which were placed two heavy guns firing ahead. With this exception all the early ironclads were without any other protected guns than those on the broadside.

Sir Edward Reed designed the succeeding ships, all with hulls of iron, or iron and steel combined, and all rigged. These were the *Bellerophon, Hercules, Sultan, Penelope, Invincible, Iron Duke, Vanguard, Swiftsure,* and *Triumph*, together with the *Enterprise, Research, Favourite, Pallas, Lord Warden, Lord Clyde,* and *Repulse*. All these ships were protected by armour throughout the entire length along the water-line, but in most of them the armour above the belt was limited to the central battery. In several of them a fire ahead and astern, within about 20 degrees, was obtained by means of ports cut through the transverse armoured bulkheads. In others these bulkheads were turned inwards towards the battery near the sides of the ship in order to facilitate the working of the guns when firing approximately ahead and astern. In the *Sultan* an upper-deck armoured battery was adopted, and in the five ships of the *Invincible* class, a direct head-and-stern fire was obtained from a somewhat similar structure, which projected a few feet beyond the side of the ship. The rigged ships of later design present a greater variety in the disposition of their guns and armour. The *Alexandra*, launched in 1875, which was of 9,492 tons and 8,615 horse-power, and carried 12 guns (two of 11-inch 25 ton, and ten of 18 tons), had a thickness of armour in the central part of the ship varying between 12 and 6 inches. This ship bore the flag successively of two of our most distinguished living naval officers, Admirals Sir Geoffrey Hornby and Sir Beauchamp Seymour, now Lord Alcester. The *Alexandra* presented a development of the combined broadside and fore-and-aft fire of the central battery ships which preceded her. Besides the broadside battery on the main-deck, she could bring a cross-fire on the same deck, and a direct bow-and-stern fire on the upper deck from within the armour, as in the *Invincible* class, and all these guns were available for broadside fire; but the upper-deck battery did not project beyond the main-deck, as in that class the forward and after parts of the ship above the main-deck were greatly contracted in breadth in order to allow the guns to fire clear fore and aft.

The *Téméraire* may be taken as an example of another class of ship constructed after Sir E. Reed's tenancy of the post of chief-constructor had ceased. She had a displacement of 8,540 tons, with 7,700 horse-power, and was constructed to carry four 11-inch and four 10-inch guns. Two of these guns were mounted above the upper deck, in armoured turrets, within which they were made to revolve and rise and fall on Colonel Moncrieff's disappearing principle, by hydraulic machinery, which was also employed to load and supply them with ammunition. Her thickness of armour above the water-line in the central battery varied between 11 and 8 inches, and her cost, including the charge for guns and engines, was £472,000, or £44,000 less than the *Alexandra*. The *Nelson*, and her sister-ship, the *Northampton*, are types of a smaller class than either the preceding. Their displacement is 7,320 tons, and they have only a partial armour-belt, not all of their guns being enclosed within armour protection.

Even less protection than this was given to the *Shannon*, which has a displacement of 5,439 tons, and was built to carry nine guns—two 10-inch of 18 tons, and seven 9-inch of 12 tons. The *Shannon* had a thickness of armour-plating above water on the central part varying between 9 and 7 inches. Competent naval critics were opposed to the construction of such practically unarmoured ironclads.

A more formidable ship than any of these was the *Inflexible*, which was long the most powerful vessel in the British Navy. The *Inflexible*, which, as well as the *Alexandra* and *Téméraire*, participated in the bombardment of Alexandria, was of 11,500 tons displacement, and carried four guns only, but they were 16-inch, and weighed 80 tons; and her thickness of armour in the central part varied between 24 and 16 inches. Her length was 320 feet, 60 less than the *Warrior* and *Royal Sovereign*, the first and last launched of our ironclad fleet.

Of an altogether different class were the turret-ships, among the earliest of which were the *Prince Albert*, *Scorpion*, *Wyvern*, and *Royal Sovereign* (a former one of that name), which embodied the views of Captain Cowper Coles, who was lost in the Bay of Biscay on board the *Captain*, a turret-ship of his own design, which foundered owing to her freeboard being insufficient to enable her, when under canvas in a moderate gale, to resist the pressure of the wind. The *Hotspur* and *Rupert* had 11-inch armour extending from stem to stern, and dipping down forward to strengthen the ram, for which these ships were specially designed. They carried one 25-ton gun, which was mounted in a revolving turret. We have referred to the *Glatton*, the nearest approach to the type of the American *Monitor*. The first sea-going turret-ship was the *Monarch*, constructed to carry Captain Coles's revolving turrets, which was in every way a success. Designed purely for coast defence were four other turret-ships, *Cyclops*, *Gorgon*, *Hecate*, and *Hydra*, but they were comparatively small, and were hastily ordered in 1870, at the time of the scare consequent on the outbreak of war between France and Germany.

The same sort of ill-regulated expenditure occurred in 1878, when the country appeared likely to be involved in the Turko-Russian War. A sum of two millions was voted by the House of Commons, and four ships built for other states in our ports were purchased for the Navy. These were the *Neptune*, *Superb*, *Orion*, and *Belleisle*. The *Neptune*, constructed for the Brazilian Government, was 9,170 tons displacement, and carried six guns—four of $12\frac{1}{2}$-inch and 38 tons, and two of 9-inch and 12 tons—with a thickness of armour varying between 13 and 8 inches. The *Superb* was of the same size, and the other two ironclads were each of 4,380 tons. Though differing widely in many respects, the *Thunderer*, *Devastation*, and *Dreadnought*, which, when launched, were regarded as the most formidable ships-of-war afloat, all owe their origin to the Ericsson turret, and the *Times* declared that the "American *Monitors* were certainly the progenitors of our *Devastation* type." The *Dreadnought* had a displacement of 10,886 tons, and carried four $12\frac{1}{2}$-inch guns, with a thickness of armour varying between 14 and 10 inches. She has been in every respect a success, both for her serviceable qualities as a sea-boat and a ship-of-war, and all the admirals who have hoisted their flags in her have expressed satisfaction with the ship.

Up to the year 1889, when the Naval Defence Act was passed, involving a large special expenditure for shipbuilding purposes, the condition of the British Navy, relatively to that of other great powers, had been in a declining state, and in 1888 it was described by a very high authority as "deplorable," a result due to the attempts made by successive Governments to keep the naval expenditure within the fixed annual amount, although it was admitted that the cost of building ships was increasing, as also were the naval requirements of the Empire.

While other countries were increasing the tonnage of their battle-ships, which, as in the past, must form the backbone of the Navy, the Admiralty, during the decade elapsing between the date of the launching of the *Devastation* and of the *Inflexible*, had constructed no single ship of which the displacement exceeded 10,000 tons. Further, a system was initiated of reducing the armour on ships, so that they would have been incapable of engaging an enemy wholly armoured from end to end, like the French *Admiral Duperré*. It was sought to make up for this, in the case of the

Inflexible, by making the armour of her citadel of excessive thickness, though this would in no way have compensated in action for a reduction elsewhere, but in some more recent ships the thickness was only 18 inches to 22 in the French ships.

Before the passing of the Naval Defence Act, it may be said that the only three totally unarmoured ships of the large cruiser class were the *Inconstant*, *Shah*, and *Raleigh*. Two others, the *Impérieuse* and *Warspite*, having a displacement of 8,400 tons, had 140 feet armoured of their total length of 315 feet. All five ships were constructed with great coal capacity, in order to cruise in distant seas for the protection of British commerce, and the two last have been flagships on the Channel and Pacific stations. Equally devoid of armour with the three cruisers named above, were the *Scio* and *Mercury*, built for great speed, and the corvettes, *Active*, *Bacchante*, *Boadicea*, *Euryalus*, *Rover*, and *Volage*, all over 3,000 tons displacement, and having a speed in excess of fourteen knots. There were also thirty-six smaller and slower corvettes, nearly half of which were built of wood, and about an equal number of sloops of even less speed and tonnage, in addition to the gunboats and gun-vessels.

Of ships which, though not armoured, have thick-plated decks to protect the engines, there were, in 1889, eight of 3,500 tons, built and under construction, namely, the *Amphion*, *Arethusa*, *Leander*, *Phaeton*, *Mersey*, *Severn*, *Forth*, and *Thames*.* Battle-ships not wholly armoured were the *Ajax*, *Agamemnon*, *Colossus*,† and *Edinburgh*; and there were the six first-class ships of the *Admiral* class, *Anson*, *Collingwood*, *Camperdown*, *Rodney*,‡ *Howe*, and *Benbow*, all of 10,400 tons displacement. The *Inflexible* also had her ends unarmoured, but unlike some of those named above, it was claimed for her that even were these ends destroyed, her stability could not be impaired. Sir Edward Reed declared that in the *Admiral* class is found a dangerous combination, from which the *Inflexible* and *Agamemnon* and other like ships are exempt—"the combination of

---

* The *Thames* and *Severn*, like their sister-ships, *Mersey* and *Forth*, had a complete protective deck, the horizontal portion of which extended one foot above, and the inclined portion three inches below, the water-line. The principal guns were two of 8-inch calibre, mounted on central pivots forward and abaft a covered deck, which contained ten 6-inch guns. The secondary battery was ten 1-inch Nordenfeldts and two Gardner machine-guns, and the ships were fitted with six above-water torpedo-tubes in the broadside. A development of this class were the partially-armoured cruisers *Orlando* and her sister-ships, which had a displacement of 5,000 tons. Their length was 300 feet, with 10-inch armour, and they carried two 18-ton guns, one well forward, and the second right aft, as well as five 6-inch guns in each broadside, the foremost and aftermost of which were placed on projecting sponsons, so that they were enabled to fire right ahead and astern. These cruisers were followed by others, named the *Immortalité* and *Aurora*, of 600 tons more displacement, given to enable them to carry a 5½-foot water-line belt, 10 inches in thickness, extending for 190 feet amidships, and they had an armoured deck from 2 to 3 inches thick, and a conning tower of iron 13 inches in thickness.

† See illustration, Vol. II., page 176. ‡ See illustration, Vol. II., page 224.

long, unarmoured ends, comprising about 45 per cent. of the water-line area, with so shallow a belt of armour that, when the unarmoured ends are injured and filled by the sea (as they would be in action), there would remain so little armour left above water that a very slight inclination of the ship would put it all below water." He declared that there was great danger of these ships capsizing in action when injured by shot.

During the year 1888, twenty-five ships were completed and added to the First Class Reserve, including, besides some of those already named, the partially armoured cruisers *Orlando, Narcissus, Australia, Galatea,* and *Undaunted,** six torpedo-cruisers of the *Archer* class, and one of the *Scout* class, three torpedo-gunboats of the *Rattlesnake* class, and three composite gunboats and sloops of the *Buzzard* and *Rattler* class. The battle-ships *Victoria* † and *Sanspareil,* of the same tonnage as those of the *Admiral* class, and carrying two 110-ton guns, besides a secondary battery, with 18 inches of armour, were constructed by Messrs. Armstrong. The armour belt in these ships extended over about one-half their length, which was 340 feet, and to a height of $2\frac{1}{2}$ feet above the water. Before and abaft the belt, under-water armoured decks extended to the bows and stern respectively, as in the *Admiral* class.

The Admiralty proceeded to the construction of ships even larger than the *Victoria* and *Sanspareil,* which received the name of *Trafalgar* and *Nile,* and had a displacement of 11,940 tons. Their design is a departure from the central citadel type, and they carry revolving turrets on the fore-and-aft line amidships, with an intermediate broadside battery mounted on a superstructure. A water-belt line 230 feet in length rises in the waist for a distance of 193 feet, and both belt and citadel are covered by a three-inch steel deck, which is carried forward and aft to strengthen the ram and protect the steering-gear. The armour is 18 inches thick in the turret, and 20 inches as a maximum at the water-line, and to support the backing there is an inner skin two inches thick. The armament consists of four $13\frac{1}{2}$-inch 67-ton breech-loading rifled guns, distributed in pairs in the turrets, and eight 5-inch guns in the broadside battery on a covered deck, protected by three inches of vertical armour, besides some machine-guns.

But, notwithstanding these additions, a general feeling of alarm at the condition of the Navy found vent in 1889, and the Admiralty, which at one time spoke in such vaunting terms of the superiority of the service over any possible combination of European powers, yielded to the clamour, which was only too well founded, and in the end

* See illustration, Vol. II., page 112. † See illustration, Vol. II., page 318.

a large measure, termed the "Naval Defence Act" was passed through the House of Commons, involving an expenditure, distributed over a term of years, of twenty-one and a half millions. The Act authorized the construction and equipment, between the years 1889 and 1894, of ten battle-ships, nine first class protected cruisers, twenty-nine second class and four third class protected cruisers, and eighteen first class torpedo gunboats, of the *Sharpshooter* class, two-thirds of the contracts for shipbuilding being given to private firms.* These numbers were in addition to the ships then in progress, which included, besides the first class battle-ships *Trafalgar* and *Nile*, the *Camperdown*, the last laid down of the *Admiral* class, and the following protected cruisers—first class, *Blake* and *Blenheim*,† of 9,000 tons, and no less than 20,000 horse-power; second class, *Melpomene*, *Magicienne*,‡ and *Marathon*, of 2,950 tons displacement, and 9,000 horse-power; the five cruisers for Australia, of 2,575 tons displacement, and 7,500 horse-power, and the six third class cruisers *Barham*, *Bellona*, *Barrosa*, *Blanche*, *Blonde*, and *Barracouta*, the two first of 1,830 tons and 6,000 horse-power, and the others of 1,580 tons and 3,000 horse-power. Also the torpedo depôt-ship, *Vulcan*, of 6,620 tons displacement and 12,000 horse-power; the sloops, *Beagle* and *Basilisk*, of 1,170 tons and 2,000 horse-power; seven torpedo gunboats of 735 tons and 4,500 horse-power; and two of the same class for Australia.

The change carried through in the past ten years of substituting breech-loaders for muzzle-loading guns, was of prime importance in developing the fighting powers of our Navy. It was curious and not very edifying to regard the tenacity with which the Ordnance Department clung to the exploded system of loading by the muzzle. It had been made manifest to the world many years before that

---

* The following table gives the number and character of the ships to be built under the Naval Defence Act.

CLASS OF SHIP.	Displacement Tonnage.	Indicted Horse Power.	Number to be built.
Battle Ships, 1st Class	14,150	13,000	8
,, ,, 2nd Class	9,000	10,000	2
Cruisers, 1st Class	7,350	12,000	9
,, 2nd Class	3,400	9,000	29
,, 3rd Class	2,575	7,500	4
Torpedo Gunboats	735	4,500	18
Total	...	...	70

† See illustration, Vol. III., page 268. ‡ See illustration, Vol. I., page 192.

the adoption of the breech-loading rifle had given the Austrians into the hands of Prussia in the Schleswig-Holstein campaign; but when Woolwich yielded to the demand of the nation that our troops should be armed with the breech-loader, it offered a resolute resistance to the adoption of the system in the field-batteries of the Royal Artillery; and yet again a determined stand was made against breech-loading ordnance in our guns of position, and on board our ships-of-war. But they had to give way when it was seen that all the nations of Europe had discarded the old method, and that in the event of war, disaster would be certain to ensue were our seamen to be exposed to fire while loading the heavy guns that were universally adopted in the navies of the world. Our breech-loading ordnance now range in calibre from 16·25-inch (110 tons), forming the armament of the *Victoria*,[*] *Sanspareil*, and *Benbow*, and 13·5-inch (67 tons), carried by the *Trafalgar*, *Nile*, *Royal Sovereign*[†] and other ships, to the small quick-firing guns forming the secondary battery of our battle-ships.[‡] Though considerably smaller than the 80-ton gun of the *Inflexible*, the 67-ton gun has a greater penetrative power, which is mostly due to the improvements in manufacture and the powder employed.

It would seem, however, that we are distanced by the gunmakers on the Continent in weight of gun and projectile, and also in velocity and penetrative power. The French have had afloat for some years 75-ton guns, with a calibre of $16\frac{1}{2}$ inches, and now possess, we believe, one of 124 tons, having a calibre of 18 inches, which fires a projectile weighing 2,465 pounds, or over a ton. The Italians have long had a 106-ton gun, and the Germans one of 120 tons, designed by the famous Krupp, of Essen, which fires a projectile 500 pounds heavier than the Armstrong 110-ton gun, and develops an energy greater by 10,000 foot-tons.

Lord Brassey has given his views on the cardinal point of armament in a lecture delivered on the 18th March, 1891, before the Institution of Naval Architects, on "The Future Policy of Warship Building." In the armaments of our battle-ships, he thought the ponderous pieces which had of late been mounted on board ship should be excluded. The objections to monster guns were the limited endurance, difficulty of manufacture, excessive cost, slowness of fire, length, and hence liability to be struck, and possibly disabled, and dependence on hydraulic loading gear, perfect in its working

---

[*] See illustration, Vol. II., page 318. [†] See illustration, Vol. III., page 332.

[‡] The 110-ton gun carries an armour-piercing projectile of 1,800 pounds, capable at 1,000 yards of penetrating nearly $27\frac{1}{2}$ inches of steel, with a bursting charge of 180 pounds in the common shell. The 67-ton gun propels a projectile weighing 1,250 pounds with a charge of 54 pounds.

under peace conditions, but too susceptible of injury for the practical purposes of war, and requiring armour for its protection. The naval advisers recently consulted by the Admiralty considered that the heaviest gun for battle-ships should not exceed 50 tons, while Admiral Scott placed the limit of weight at 30 tons. Lord Brassey stood by the principle that no gun too ponderous to be worked by manual power should be mounted on board ship, and to this thesis our present naval advisers appear to give their adhesion. He considered that a 29-ton gun was relatively cheap, durable, and easy of manufacture, while its power of penetration was equal to 21 inches of armour at 1,000 yards, which was sufficient for all practical purposes. The number of heavy guns which could be carried must depend on the displacement, and a battle-ship should be able to carry at least four 29-ton guns, exclusive of the quick-firing armament. With reference to the outcry against our heavy breech-loading guns, which have been compared unfavourably with the ordnance of other powers, Lord Brassey asserts that in all the essentials that constitute an effective gun—accuracy and rapidity of fire, handiness, penetration, and durability, our guns are equal to any in existence in foreign navies. This opinion is endorsed by all naval officers who have actually handled them at sea. Every gun, after it has passed proof, is tried afloat with full service charges to test the mountings upon which it is placed; and once in every quarter, while the ship is in commission, the guns are again tested.

The earlier ironclads had the old broadside system, which was followed by the *belt and battery* type, as it was called, where the heavy guns, now reduced in numbers, were carried amidships in a box battery, and had a fore-and-aft fire by means of recessed ports. In 1869 the *breastwork monitor* was adopted, a type of ship having a low freeboard—that is, the height above the sea of the upper-deck—which was plated from stem to stern along the water-line, and had amidships an armoured breastwork, or citadel, carrying at each end a revolving turret. A prejudice was created against turret-ships as unsafe when the *Captain* foundered with between 400 and 500 men, and when this type was modified, the complete water-line belt and the central citadel were retained, which were the essential features of Sir Edward Reed's type of fighting ship. The *Inflexible*, among other ships, had her engines and the bases of two turrets protected by this box-shaped citadel, from the extremities of which an armoured deck extended fore and aft below the water-line, while above this deck an armoured superstructure completed the freeboard.

The Italian Admiralty, in 1872, adopted Sir Edward Reed's principle of an elevated battery, and the result was the construction of the *Duilio* and *Dandolo*, though these ships lacked high speed and coal-carrying power. In 1878 the *Italia* was constructed, in which protection was afforded, not by vertical or side armour, but by an armoured deck, which extends six feet below the water-line at the sides, while fore and aft it dips so as to strengthen the ram and cover the steering gear.

To cope with this formidable fighting ship the "Admiral" class of ships was designed by our Admiralty, in which the main battery is mounted in two barbettes, or armoured parapets built high out of the water near the extremities of the vessel, while in the centre are carried the armour-piercing and rapid-firing guns. The engines and barbette communications are protected by a water-line belt of thick armour, which covers nearly half of the ship's entire length, at the upper edge of which is an armoured deck, and at its ends bulk-heads, erected athwart-ships. Before and abaft the belt and beneath the water-line is a similar iron deck, with the usual water-tight compartments. The *Trafalgar* and *Nile*, and the *Royal Sovereign** and her sister ships, which are the latest development of the "Admiral" class, will receive a more detailed description when we speak of the results of the Naval Defence Act.

The relative value of long guns and defensive armour can only be decided by the experience acquired in actual war. Both these main factors in the problem of attack and defence have advocates. The French generally, it may be said, incline towards the claim of the guns to superiority, and many writers and practical men of eminence in England hold the same view, but on the other hand, equally great authorities entertain the view that the days of heavily-armoured ships are not yet ended. All alike concede the importance of rams and torpedoes, and a high French authority, Gabriel Charmes, has laid down the dictum that a "squadron attacked at night by torpedo boats is a squadron lost." Equally regarding the thickness of armour are the authorities divided, but Lord Brassey, after a review of all the circumstances, has expressed an opinion that to meet the conditions of warfare, 12 inches of armour-plating in wake of machinery, boilers, magazines, and on the turrets and conning towers, would suffice; and as, since the introduction of quick-firing guns, it is no longer possible for crews to stand in the open without some protection, the batteries should be protected by five inches of steel or compound plating, as side armour. But, added Lord Brassey, no practicable thickness of armour is impenetrable, and captains of ships and guns must under all circumstances be exposed. In the *Huascar's* conning towers three commanders were slain in half an

* See illustration, Vol. III., page 332.

hour. On the necessity of high speed alone is there any agreement. This is a cardinal point both in battle-ships and ocean cruisers, without which efficiency in other respects can avail little in the day of trial. Up to 1875, the highest speed attained under the most favourable circumstances by the battle-ship was fourteen knots, while some fast cruisers could steam fifteen and sixteen knots. But their coal-carrying capacity was limited, whereas now fighting ships are constructed that can steam thousands of miles at sea, at a speed of twenty knots, without re-coaling. So exacting have our censors in naval matters recently become, that the inability of the *Blake*, sister ship of the *Blenheim*, to steam more than $19\frac{1}{2}$ knots with natural draught, or half a knot less than the promised speed, brought down on the Admiralty the unsparing censure of some critics.

The speed of torpedo vessels has been increased to an even greater ratio within recent years. Thus, in their infancy, in 1873, the fastest were constructed to steam 14 knots, but now a speed of over 20 is easily attained, and their size has also greatly increased. A first-class torpedo boat, lately constructed for the Government of Victoria, is stated to have attained a speed of 22 knots while fully equipped with all her weights. The *Gleaner*, one of eighteen steel torpedo gunboats of the *Grasshopper* type, ordered to be constructed under the Naval Defence Act, attained an average speed of 18 knots throughout her steam trial, and with forced draught 20 knots.

In our earliest ironclads, including the *Warrior*, wrought iron was employed, but this was replaced in later ships by a compound metal faced with steel for the purpose of breaking up the projectiles on impact. This is the description of vertical protection hitherto used in our ships, though the practice in the French and other Continental navies has been to employ only steel armour. Recently English manufacturers have turned their attention to this point, and success has been attained at a trial of all-steel armour manufactured by Messrs. Charles Cammell and Company, of the Cyclops Works, in Sheffield, the firm who contracted for the whole of the armour of the new battle-ship *Royal Sovereign*. The Wilson compound plates, with a thick backing of iron to prevent cracking or breaking up under impact, will probably give place to Cammell's all-steel plates, which, in December, 1891, were tested with eminent success on board the *Nettle* at Portsmouth.

It is a comforting consideration to the much-enduring British taxpayer that the relative strength of England and France has changed to the advantage of this country within the last few years. Sir Spencer Robinson, formerly Controller of the Navy, declared in 1887 that "the number of armoured ships of the two countries may be stated as fifty-five for England and fifty-one for France." But since that day England has awakened to a sense of her insecurity, and the responsibilities entailed upon her by her world-wide commerce and possessions.

Some critics have decried the necessity of building large and expensive battle-ships, as the torpedo, say they, and the other conditions of modern war, point to the greater utility of smaller and handier ships. The policy adopted in Italy of constructing once in two years or so a battle-ship of exceptional size, was vindicated on the ground that as Italy was unable to vie with others in the amount of tonnage constructed, it was necessary to secure the utmost development of power in a limited number of ships. The wisdom of this policy is at least doubtful, though since ships have been constructed with the swiftness and handiness of the *Royal Sovereign*, the argument against size has lost half its force, and it is now mostly a question of money. Few will disagree with Rear-Admiral Ince, of the United States Navy, who declared that now, as in the past, "the battle-ship is the very foundation of a navy." Further it may be assumed that, given other conditions of equality, a heavy battle-ship is superior to a light one. As to the necessity of keeping up our fleet of battle-ships, the same authority observed: "Supposing Great Britain had no battle-ships, how long could she hold Gibraltar and Malta, control the Suez Canal, and maintain her Indian Empire by the eastern route? How long could she hold the line from London to Halifax, Esquimalt, and India by the western route? How long could she prevent Germany from establishing a military port on the Scheldt? How long could she hold the great strategic points at Jamaica, Barbados, and St. Lucia, which dominate the West Indies, the Spanish Main, and the Panama Canal? . . . Without battle ships the whole British Empire would crumble to pieces."

A competent writer in a daily journal gives as follows the number of battle-ships that will be possessed in 1894 by the six great powers of Europe.*

	1st Class. No.	1st Class. Tonnage.	2nd Class. No.	2nd Class. Tonnage.	3rd Class. No.	3rd Class. Tonnage.
Great Britain	30.	333,950	16.	108,720	6.	55,660
France	14.	148,063	15.	108,225	4.	29,280
Italy	11.	139,694	2.	12,248	9.	34,801
Russia	9.	81,907	1.	5,860	5.	19,380
Germany	4.	40,000	9.	50,140	2.	11,280
Austria	1.	6,790	7.	39,860	3.	10,500

* This table excludes armoured cruisers, and classifies each new vessel as if she formed part of the British Navy. It may be taken that, as a rule, the first class ships are of above 14 knots speed, carry modern breech-loading guns of

No comparison of the battle-ship strength of the six fleets would be complete without a table showing the number and size of the heavy guns—namely those of 4-inch calibre and upwards—which each will possess. These, by the year 1894, according to the same authority, will be as follows:—

	Over 13 inches.	12 inches to 13 inches.	10 inches to 12 inches.	7 inches to 10 inches.	5 inches to 7 inches.	4 inches to 5 inches.	Total.
Great Britain	66	40	54	188	160	81	589
France	57	6	64	32	249	16	424
Italy	44	...	16	20	87	111	278
Russia	...	36	10	34	62	34	176
Germany	...	16	48	57	54	...	175
Austria	...	5	14	68	6	6	99

Great Britain, it will be seen, would therefore possess 160 guns of 10-inch and upwards against 127 of France, and 429 of smaller calibres against France's 297; but some of our guns of between 7-inch and 13-inch calibre are muzzle-loaders, while all the guns of France, whatever may be their faults in other respects, are breech-loaders.

As the battle-ships of the powers will fight the general engagements, so the cruisers will be employed in scouting, protecting convoys, and harassing an enemy's communications. Wherefore, as the former class should have, as their chief characteristic, offensive and defensive power, the cruisers should first of all possess extreme mobility. In the next table is shown, from the same authority, the number of cruisers, of the three classes into which the Navy List divides our own vessels of this type, the six Great Powers will possess by the year 1894. Our cruisers, it should be explained, are classified in the Navy List, not according to their speed, but according to their size and armament.*

	1st Class. No.	1st Class. Tonnage.	2nd Class. No.	2nd Class. Tonnage.	3rd Class. No.	3rd Class. Tonnage.
Great Britain	23.	162,250	48.	178,540	54.	114,545
France	12.	65,584	16.	64,830	55.	64,835
Italy	...	...	7.	23,680	14.	30,274
Russia	8.	53,239	9.	29,400	14.	29,650
Germany	1.	5,200	6.	24,640	19.	40,120
Austria	3.	11,800	2.	6,760	12.	21,620

8-inch calibre or over, and have at least twelve inches of armour on some part of them. The speed of the second class ships averages about 12 knots, the minimum calibre of their heaviest guns is eight inches, and the minimum thickness of their armour is about seven inches. The third class includes all the remainder of the battle-ships that cannot be considered obsolete. In battle-ships England's strength in 1894 will thus be, relatively to France, as 52 to 33, and she will be considerably stronger than any two powers taken together, or than Italy, Russia, Germany and Austria combined.

* The first class is composed of cruisers armoured, or of upwards of 7,000 tons displacement; the second class of vessels of from 3,000 to 7,000 tons, and the third of vessels of between 3,000 and 1,300 tons. Each country has,

An examination of the relative value of the cruiser fleets of the six European Great Powers from the point of speed shows that out of one hundred and sixty-six cruisers having a nominal extreme speed of 16 knots and over, Great Britain possesses, or will possess by 1894, ninety-three as compared with seventy-three possessed by the remaining five Powers, and that, in fact, the majority of the cruisers owned by the other powers are slow craft, while the majority of ours are fast. It may be accepted, moreover, that most of the slow cruisers are old and comparatively valueless, while nearly all the fast ones are modern and armed with the newest weapons, besides having a relatively wider radius of action. The writer quoted arrives at the conclusion that practically the cruiser-force of Great Britain is a little superior to those of the five remaining Powers combined; but, lest it should be supposed that we may have more cruisers than we need, it may be well to add that the duties which, in time of war, would be imposed upon our cruisers are greater than those of all the other Powers together. For example, Great Britain and her colonies have to protect twelve thousand merchant vessels, while France, Italy, Russia, Germany, and Austria combined own only six thousand six hundred. Again, we are an island power, and all our external food supply must come to us by water, the routes across which we must therefore guard at the peril of national starvation. Finally, our empire rests on every sea, and it is incumbent upon us to preserve free communication at all times with even the most distant part of our possessions. In these respects we differ from any of the other nations, and, far from having too large a cruising fleet, we have, in fact, too small a one. This will be conceded when it is understood that we possess, roughly speaking, 455,000 tons of cruisers to insure nearly 11,000,000 tons of merchant shipping, while France has about 195,000 tons of cruisers to insure 985,000 tons of merchant shipping. If we had cruisers in proportion to France, we should have not 455,000, but over 2,000,000 tons of them, or, say, six hundred and fifty ships instead of one hundred and twenty-five.

The coast defence vessels built and building by the six Powers may be summarised as follows:—Britain, ten having a displacement of 30,670 tons; France, fifteen and 46,000 respectively; Russia, seventeen and 32,577; and Germany, sixteen

---

besides, a number of sloops and gun-vessels, but these are craft which could be increased at very short notice, and need not here be taken into consideration. The cruiser fleet proper may be thus divided: Great Britain, one hundred and twenty-five ships, of which twelve are armoured on the sides, averaging 3,642 tons; France, sixty-three ships, of which twelve have side armour, averaging 3,099 tons; Italy, twenty-one ships, of which none have side armour, having an average displacement of 2,960 tons; Russia, thirty-one ships, of which eight are armoured on the sides averaging 3,622 tons; Germany, twenty-six ships, of which one has side armour, averaging 2,690 tons; and Austria, seventeen ships, of which three are armoured on the sides, having an average of 2,363 tons.

ships and 27,382 tons. Italy and Austria have no ships of this category. The relative smallness of the British coast defence force—which includes four vessels which are practically useless—may be attributed to the fact that our naval policy has always been to take the offensive, and seek the enemy on the seas and blockade him in his ports. Whether such a policy can in future be carried out as successfully as it was in the old wars, is a problem affected by the introduction of the torpedo, and it is one which can only be decided by the rough experience of war.

A large class of naval officers, with reason as we think, claims for the power that has a predominating number of swift torpedo-boats and torpedo gun-vessels, or "catchers," a good prospect of success in the next naval war. It is contended that if our large ships are allowed to go into action in the vicinity of ports without an accompanying flotilla capable of warding off the attack of torpedo-boats, we may have bitter cause to regret our short-sightedness. The question arises which description of these craft is most needed; whether it is the torpedo-boats of 100 tons or upwards, or the torpedo gun-vessels of from 575 to 1,000 tons displacement. The former have the advantage of speed in ordinary weather, as their engine-power already reaches 18 horses per ton of weight driven, while in the fastest of the torpedo-catchers it does not exceed $4\frac{1}{2}$ horse-power. The speed of the latter has been hitherto below nineteen knots, while the speed of the first-class torpedo-boats is two knots in excess. As regards cost, four of the former can be produced for one of the latter, and though they cannot keep the sea, they have made ocean voyages in safety. According to the Report of the French Budget Commission, the torpedo flotillas of England and France, exclusive of boats of less than 25 tons displacement, and of "catchers," are at the present time as follows:—Over 100 tons, England, 8; France, 21. Under 100 tons, England, 76; France, 163. Total, England, 84; France, 184.

A great change will probably soon be made in the relative strength of the torpedo-boat flotillas of the two Powers, which stands now as follows:

	Great Britain.	France.
Seagoing	2	25
First Class, built and ordered ...	94	62
*Second Class, built	73	83
Third Class, built	—	41

* Our second-class boats are craft none of which exceed about 16 tons displacement and 66 feet in length. They are, therefore, entirely inferior to the French second class boats, which have a minimum displacement of 54 tons, and

Our inferiority in torpedo-boats of the seagoing class is partially compensated by our superiority in torpedo gun-vessels, a type of the first importance in a navy which must be prepared to act offensively. Of torpedo gun-vessels with 19 to 20 knots speed, and ranging from 575 tons to 1,070 tons displacement, we have 31 vessels. Adding to this class the *Polyphemus*, of 2,640 tons, our aggregate tonnage for the British Navy is 27,110 tons. The French have 14 vessels ranging in displacement from 320 to 925 tons, and in speed from 18 to $21\frac{1}{2}$ knots. The aggregate tonnage of the French torpedo gun-vessels is 6,210 tons. Our superiority is conspicuous, but it is not sufficient to justify any relaxation of effort in building.

As Lord Brassey observes, it is obvious that a blockading fleet required to keep the sea for a lengthened period, must be supported by torpedo vessels of a large and powerful class, while a torpedo-boat flotilla, acting on the defensive, and operating off the entrance to a port only when a dark night or hazy weather affords an opportunity for a sortie, may consist of comparatively small and inexpensive vessels. The manœuvres of the year 1892 have forcibly demonstrated that the torpedo is a deadly weapon even under the least favourable conditions, whereas a prolonged blockade in winter would expose the fleet outside to hazards which it is impossible to contemplate without misgivings, and which could only be averted by closing the entrance to the blockaded ports with a swarm of torpedo gun-vessels. For these reasons Lord Brassey proposes that for purposes of training and practice a small squadron of torpedo-boats should be always in commission, and the estuary of the Thames would be an admirable cruising-ground, while Sheerness dockyard could be readily adapted for building, fitting, and repairing the flotilla.

As a result of the Naval Defence Act, in 1889 no less than forty-nine vessels were commenced, of which twenty-five, with a displacement of 131,760 tons, were laid down in the royal dockyards, and twenty-four, with a displacement of 138,050, in the private dockyards of the kingdom. Of the above, the *Blake*, built at Chatham, and her sister-ship, the *Blenheim*,* constructed by the Thames Ironworks Company, are the most powerful cruisers ever built for the British Navy. The chief considerations Mr. White, of the Admiralty, had in view when designing them, were seaworthiness, speed, and coal capacity to enable them to keep the sea for a lengthened period. Of the battle-ships since laid down, Lord Brassey is of opinion that in the second class

---

a minimum length of 108 feet, and even to the French third-class boats, which have a minimum displacement of 34 tons, and a minimum length of 88 feet. The only French boats comparable with our second-class boats are the *torpilleurs-vedettes*, which are of 12 tons displacement and 59 feet in length.

* See illustration, Vol. III., page 268.

barbette battle-ships *Barfleur* and *Centurion*, of 9,000 tons, and armed with four 10-inch and ten 4·7-inch guns, besides a subsidiary armament, with a promised speed of eighteen knots—we have "a design which gives to the nation as good value for cost as under existing conditions it seems practicable to secure; and a further advantage offered by ships of their size is that the country could afford to construct a larger number for the same expenditure." But, apparently, this has not been the opinion of the late Board of Admiralty, to judge by their policy in respect of the battle-ships laid down under the Act of 1889, all of which, with these two exceptions, exceed 14,000 tons. Before this, however, as a result of the outcry against the ships of the *Admiral* type, of one of which, the *Rodney*,[*] we gave an illustration, the *Trafalgar* and *Nile* were constructed, with longer and higher armoured protection at the water-line, greater freeboard (combined with increased defence at the extremities against the fire of machine and quick-firing guns), and guns in a turret for their main armament, with larger displacement and augmented engine-power. But the *Nile* and *Trafalgar* yield the palm in size and fighting-power to the class represented by the *Royal Sovereign*, launched by Her Majesty the Queen on the 26th February, 1891, at Portsmouth Dockyard, together with the *Royal Arthur*, a first class cruiser. The *Royal Sovereign* is the earliest ready of the first class battle-ships built under the provisions of the Naval Defence Act of 1889, the others being the *Empress of India*, at Pembroke; the *Hood* and *Repulse*, at Chatham; and the contract-built ships, *Royal Oak*, at Birkenhead; *Ramillies* on the Clyde; and *Revenge* and *Resolution* on the Tyne. All these ships are of the same build, displacement, and armour, with their guns in barbettes, except the *Hood*, which carries them in turrets.

The *Royal Arthur*, laid down as the *Centaur*, but whose name was changed in compliment to Her Majesty and the Duke of Connaught, was the earliest launched of nine first class protected cruisers of the type known as "the improved *Mersey*"—the others being the *Endymion*, built at Hull; the *Edgar*, constructed at Devonport; the *Hawke*, at Chatham; and the *St. George*, *Grafton*, *Crescent*, *Gibraltar*, and *Theseus* in private yards.

Many of the twenty-nine second class cruisers, which were ordered under the Naval Defence Act, have been launched, and are being completed for sea with a rapidity unknown till recent years. Such of these cruisers as have been tested have attained a speed of 20 knots, and cost about £186,000. They carry two inches of armour plate,

[*] See illustration, Vol. II., page 224.

which extends three feet under water, and are built of steel, with plated decks. Their total length between perpendiculars is 300 feet, and their extreme breadth 43 feet. The displacement of these cruisers when fully equipped is 3,400 tons, and the indicated horse-power 9,200. The coal capacity is 400 tons, but storage is provided for 235 more, and their armament consists of two 6-inch breech-loading guns, one to be placed on the forecastle and the other on the poop, and on the broadside six 4·7-inch guns, and nine 3-pounders, all quick-firing guns. They will also be fitted with four torpedo tubes, and will have a complement of 253 officers and men.

The keel of the latest of our second-class cruisers was laid down at Portsmouth in January, 1892. This ship, called the *Fox*, is one of eight of a new type, or "improved *Apollo*," with 960 tons more displacement. She will carry a powerful armament of quick-firing guns, and be fitted with all the improvements known to ship-building science, and lighted throughout with electricity. The length of the *Fox*, which will be completed in about two years' time, is 320 feet, extreme breadth 49 feet, and her displacement 4,360 tons, with a mean draught of 19 feet.

The hull will be constructed entirely of steel, with a protective deck running right fore and aft, and affording cover to the magazines, shell-rooms, steam-steering gear, boilers and engines, the cylinders of the latter being further defended against shell fire by an armoured combing carried to the height of the main-deck. Her bottom will be sheathed with teak and coppered, for the purpose of enabling her to continue on service for a lengthened period without requiring to be docked. The stern-post, rudder frame, and ram-shaped stern will be formed of strong phosphor-bronze castings. Two engine-rooms will be provided, one on each side of the middle line, separated by a water-tight bulkhead. The engines will be of the triple-expansion type, designed to develop 9,000 and 7,000 indicated horse-power, with and without forced draught respectively. The maximum speed of the *Fox* will be 19.5 knots under forced draught, and 18·25 under natural draught, and her armament will consist of two 6-inch guns, eight 4·7-inch guns, four 6-pounder guns, and one 3-pounder, carried on the upper deck, four 6-pounders on the main-deck, four Nordenfeldt guns on the shelter-deck, and one 9-pounder gun. She will carry Whitehead torpedoes, and four tubes will be fitted, of which two, on the broadside, will be on the main-deck, one direct ahead through the stem, and one through the stern-post.

The Navy estimates for the year 1892-93 mount up to £14,240,200, of which the Royal Marines absorb £1,070,217, and the Coastguard £452,569, the latter being thus maintained at a cost of £117 per head per annum, while each marine costs the country £80.* This total of fourteen millions is independent of the expenditure to be covered by the money voted in the Naval Defence Act of 1889.

The number of ships to be built and equipped under this Act by contract with private firms is thirty-two, and comprises four first class battle-ships, five first class cruisers, seventeen second-class cruisers, and six torpedo gunboats. The ships to be built in the royal dockyards, under the same statute, number thirty-eight, which will all be completed by April, 1894. They consist of four first class and two second class battle-ships, four first class, twelve second class, and four third class cruisers, and twelve torpedo gunboats.

All the first class battle-ships building in the royal dockyards under the Act of 1889, were floated early in 1892. Besides the *Royal Sovereign*, the *Renown* (re-named the *Empress of India*) was launched at Pembroke on May 7th, 1891, the *Hood* was floated at Chatham on the 30th July, and the *Repulse* at Pembroke in February of the following year. The first of the four contract-built first class battle-ships to take the water was the *Ramillies*, at Thomson's yard on the Clyde, and the second was the *Resolution*, from Palmer's yard at Jarrow-on-Tyne.

There is also a further source of strength to the Empire provided by the agreement arrived at, in 1887, between the representatives of the Australian Colonies and the mother country, by which a squadron of five cruisers was to be provided for the exclusive protection of commerce in Australian waters. By this agreement, which was embodied in the Imperial Defence Act of 1888, the Home Government were to provide the funds for the construction and armament of these ships, as well as their officers and crews. In return the Colonies agreed to vote an annual subsidy for a period of twelve years for the protection thus afforded. A further annual payment has been made for some thirty years by the Indian Government, which refunds in full all the disbursements of the Admiralty for the naval protection afforded to India.

The *Royal Sovereign* and the other dockyard-built ships were constructed with greater rapidity than those contracted for by private firms. She was on the stocks only about seventeen months, and although she was the last to be begun, she was the first of them to be launched, and was completed for sea and commissioned within thirty-two months of the time her keel was laid. The *Empress of India* was twenty-two months in construction,

---

* See Navy returns No. 237, from which these figures are derived, though by the estimates they appear at about alf the amount above stated.

H.M.S. ROYAL SOVEREIGN.

1ST CLASS. BATTLESHIP

and the *Repulse*, thirty-four months. This was a great advance in rapidity even in comparison with the *Trafalgar*, which was launched in April, 1890, having been in the shed four years and two months, and with the *Victoria*,* a yet smaller ship, which the Elswick Company delivered within three years of the date the contract was signed. Some detailed account is required of the *Royal Sovereign*, a fit successor to the long line of battle-ships bearing the name, extending from the time of Elizabeth, and including the *Sovereign of the Seas*, and the ship which bore Collingwood's flag at Trafalgar.

The *Royal Sovereign* † is a steel, twin-screwed, double-barbette battle-ship, of 14,150 tons displacement, and 380 feet long by 75 broad. She is thus 35 feet longer than the *Trafalgar*, and is equal in length to the *Warrior*, the first of our ironclads. She carries vertical triple-expansion engines, which develop 9,000 horse-power with natural draught, and drive the ship at a speed of 16 knots, and with forced draught work up to 13,000 horse-power, and give a speed of $17\frac{1}{2}$ knots. The vessel carries 900 tons of coal, which will enable her to steam 5,000 knots at 10 miles an hour, without refilling her bunkers; but in case of necessity she will be able to stow about 400 tons more, and so obtain a radius of action of over 7,000 knots. In addition, the chief weights to be carried are the armament, 1,190 tons, and the armour, 4,530 tons.

At each end of the ship is a section, 65 feet long, which is entirely without vertical armour, the only protection there being afforded by a two and a half inch steel deck. The whole middle section of the ship is furnished with a water-line belt of a maximum thickness of 18 inches, 250 feet long, and extending five feet six inches below and three feet above the line of immersion. The ends of the belt are joined by transverse armoured bulkheads, which rest upon the armoured deck. At each end of the armoured enclosure, which is thus formed, there rises to above the level of the upper deck a barbette composed of 17-inch armour. On the top of the armoured belt rests a three-inch steel deck, and above this, to a height of some feet, the outer walls of the ship are composed of four-inch steel upon a one-inch steel skin. Again, above this there is armour in the shape of steel shields to the larger broadside guns. Finally, there are two armoured conning towers. The subdivision into water-tight compartments is very complete, and the whole framework of the hull is exceptionally strong. Just abaft the forward barbette, and immediately before the after one rise substantial masts, provided with tops, and nearly midway between them are the two funnels, which are placed abreast of one another. The ship carries twenty-one boats, including two 56-feet torpedo boats, all stowed amidships.

* See illustration, Vol. II., page 318.   † See illustration, Vol. III., page 332.

Each barbette is, in effect, a separate and very strong pear-shaped two-storeyed redoubt. In the upper storey is the turntable, carrying the guns; in the lower are the turning engines, and the whole structure is thickly armoured all the way down to five feet six inches below the water-line; thus there is obviously little danger of a hostile shell putting the heavy guns out of action by exploding beneath them, and so either disabling the guns themselves or destroying the ammunition hoists. The tops of the barbettes project but two feet nine inches above the upper deck, and consequently the axes of the guns are only about four feet six inches above that deck, an arrangement which, for general cruising purposes, has the great advantage of permitting the vessel to have a comparatively high freeboard. The freeboard of the battle-ships of the *Admiral* class is only 10 feet 3 inches, being so low that, when the vessels attempt to steam against a moderate sea, their forecastles are almost under water, and their forward barbette guns can scarcely be fought. But the freeboard of the *Royal Sovereign* and her sister ships is 18 feet aft, and slightly more forward, while the heavy guns are 25 feet above the water instead of 20 feet as in the improved "Admirals."

The chief armament of the *Royal Sovereign*, and the other battle-ships of her class, consists of four 13·5-inch 67-ton guns, disposed two in each barbette. These have arcs of training of about 200 degrees, and all four guns can be simultaneously discharged on either broadside. The secondary armament consists of the following quick-firing guns:— ten 6-inch, carried in the box battery, between the barbettes, two on each broadside, on the main deck in sponsons, and three on each broadside on the upper deck; sixteen 2·14-inch 6-pounders, twelve of which are on the main, and four on the upper deck; ten 1·85-inch 3-pounders on the upper deck and superstructure, and in the tops; eight machine-guns, and two 9-pounder fieldpieces. She also carries five above-water and two submerged 18-inch torpedo-tubes. The total actual cost for ship, engines, hydraulic gear, gun-mountings, and torpedo-fittings, was £770,000. This is exclusive of the guns, which cost £75,000, and the ammunition, which will come to probably twice as much, so that the ship, when complete for sea, represents nearly a million of money.

A writer in the *Times* gives the following comparison between the *Royal Sovereign* and the largest and most powerful battle-ships, built or under construction, of the chief maritime powers, except Russia, of which all that is known with certainty is that her heaviest ships are of about 11,000 tons displacement. The representative French class contains the sister-ships *Lazare*, *Carnot*, and *Charles Martel;* German, the sister-ships *Kurfürst Friedrich Wilhelm*, *Weissenburg*, and *Brandenburg*; American, *Indiana*, *Massachusetts*, and *Oregon*; and Italian, *Sardegna*, *Lepanto*, *Sicilia*, and *Re Umberto*.

	British.	French.	German.	American.	Italian.
Length, in feet	380	393·7	376·2	348	400
Beam, in feet	75	71·1	63·9	69·3	72·6
Tons	14,150	11,900	10,000	10,201	14,800
Maximum horse-power	13,000	13,275	15,000	9,000	13,300
Maximum speed, in knots	17·5	17·5	18	15	18
Thickest armour, in inches	18	17·7	16	17	14·2
Coal capacity, in tons	900			400	1,200
Torpedo tubes	7	6	7	7	5
Guns	4 13·5in. 10 6in. Q.F. 16 6-pdr. Q.F. 10 3-pdr. Q.F. 8 machine.	2 12in. 2 10·6in. 8 5·5in. Q.F. 26 small Q.F. & mach.	6 11in. 16 3·4in. Q.F.	4 13in. 8 8in. 4 6in. 20 Q.F. ...	4 13·5in. 8 6in. 16 4·7in. Q.F. ... ...

The *Royal Sovereign* is the fastest battle-ship actually afloat, except the *Lepanto* and her sister-ships, which are 20 feet longer, and have a displacement of 650 more tons, with a speed of 16·77 knots with 9,700 horse-power, and 18 knots with 13,300 horse-power.

The first-class cruisers are scarcely less formidable than the battle-ships, while their greater speed and handiness make them most useful adjuncts of our Navy. Among those completed are the *Blenheim*,* of which an illustration is given, and her sister-ship, the *Blake*, with a displacement of 9,000 tons, each of which cost the country £434,000. These cruisers were designed to steam 22 knots under forced draught of 20,000 horse-power, and 20 under natural draught of 13,000 horse-power. The *Blenheim* was stated in her trials to have exceeded the estimated speed under both conditions, but the boilers leaked. The same occurred at the trials of the *Vulcan*, torpedo-ship, and the *Blake*, built at Chatham, which failed in point of speed to realise the promise of her designers. On the other hand, the *Edgar*, first-class cruiser, built at Devonport, which was designed for 12,000 horse-power, gave 480 in excess, and attained a speed of nearly 22 knots, or two more than was anticipated. The ship also cost £60,000 less than the *Blake* and *Blenheim*, though this is accounted for by her tonnage being 7,350 instead of 9,000.

* See illustration, Vol. III., page 268.

The nine first class protected cruisers, authorised under the Act already mentioned, consist of six unsheathed ships, the *Edgar*, *Gibraltar*, *Hawke*, *Endymion*, *Grafton*, and *Theseus*, of 7,350 tons, and three sheathed and coppered, the *Royal Arthur* (late *Centaur*), *Crescent*, and *St. George*, each of 350 tons more displacement, owing to these additions to the weights. In other respects these cruisers are alike, and the following description will do for all.

They are 360 feet in length and 60 feet in breadth, and when ready for sea draw rather over 24 feet of water. The coal capacity is 850 tons, and the radius of action 10,000 miles. The armament consists of one 9·2-inch 22-ton gun, mounted on the poop, and the following quick-firing guns:—twelve 6-inch $5\frac{1}{2}$-ton, two mounted on the forecastle, and five on each broadside, six being on the upper, and four, in sponsons, on the main deck; 12 6-pounders and three 3-pounders, 8 machine-guns, and two fieldpieces, besides four 14-inch torpedo ejectors.

The protective deck of steel has a maximum thickness of five inches and a minimum thickness of two inches. As the engines rise somewhat above the steel deck, the upper parts are protected by 5-inch inclined plates, backed with teak. The conning tower is of 12-inch plates, with armoured communication tubes seven inches in thickness. The larger guns are protected by steel shields, and, in addition to twenty-seven water-tight compartments under the machinery space, the double bottom is extended nearly throughout the length of the ship.

In regard to the future policy of shipbuilding, the late Admiralty decided before leaving office to construct three battle-ships. There will be some modifications in these ships, with special reference to recent foreign shipbuilding policy, and the latest developments of armament, armour, and propelling machinery. It has been decided that the introduction of quick-firing guns of large calibre, and the use of high explosives, necessitate changes in the character and distribution of the protective hull armour, and the increase of protection to guns' crews. It has also been determined that further steps must be taken in the direction followed in the *Royal Sovereign* and *Centurion* class, so as to give even greater relative power and prominence to the secondary armament of quick-firing guns. The new battle-ships are described by the late First Lord as "of large displacement, of high freeboard and speed, large coal capacity, and carrying as a main armament four guns of large calibre, and as a subsidiary armament a large number of well-protected quick-firing 110-pounder guns."

With regard to the ten new torpedo gunboats, which are to be built by contract, the Admiralty propose that half should be of larger size than any preceding vessels of this kind. They will have the following dimensions:—length, 250 feet; breadth, 30 feet 6 inches; displacement, 1,070 tons; horse-power, with natural draught, 2,500, and with forced draught, 3,500: mean speed on natural draught, 17 to 17½ knots, and on forced draught, 19 knots. The armament will include two 4·7-inch quick-firing guns, four 6-pounders, and five 18-inch torpedo-tubes.

The battle-ships, cruisers, and smaller vessels selected by our artist for illustration, are diverse enough to display to the eye of the non-professional reader the special characteristics of the numerous types forming the British Fleet of our day. The *Royal Sovereign** is the most important and interesting of these, and scarcely inferior is the *Victoria*† first class battle-ship, the "counterfeit presentment" of which may be compared with that of her namesake, one of the last of the wooden three-deckers built before the *Warrior* initiated the new order of shipbuilding. The *Colossus*† is also of the same class, and represents a type of not wholly armoured ships, of which the *Ajax*, *Edinburgh*, and *Agamemnon* are examples. The *Rodney*† is a sample of the "Admiral" class, having armoured ends and carrying 67-ton guns in place of the 110-ton guns forming the armament of the *Victoria*. The *Hero*† is a type of the older second class battle-ship, which has given place to the *Barfleur* and *Centurion* class, declared by competent critics to be on the whole the best description of fighting ship we possess. The *Blenheim*,* like her sister ship, the *Blake*, is perhaps the noblest and fastest cruiser afloat, having a tonnage equal to the *Barfleur*, and a horse-power double hers. The *Undaunted*† is a cruiser of the *Orlando* type, having a displacement of 5,000 tons, and is partially armoured. The *Magicienne*‡ is one of the protected second class cruisers, under construction before the passing of the Naval Defence Act. The *Latona*† belongs to another type of cruiser, and the *Calliope*‡ is one of the older third class cruisers, and earned a world-wide fame by the seamanlike skill with which Captain Kane rescued her from the fate that overtook the war-ships of other nations in Samoa on the 16th March, 1889. The *Mohawk*‡ is a sister-ship of the ill-fated *Serpent*, which was lost on the north-west coast of Spain, and the *Nymphe*‡ is a specimen of the modern sloop-of-war, and bears a name rendered famous by Captain Edward Pellew who, while in command of her predecessor, captured the French *Cléopatre*. The *Bramble*† and *Thrush** are examples of our gunboats, and the latter carried the pennant of H.R.H. the Duke of York in his first command on the North American station. Finally, the *Speedwell**

---

* See illustration, Vol. III.   † See illustration, Vol. II.   ‡ See illustration, Vol. I.

is one of those torpedo-catchers which will doubtless play so important a part in future wars, and of which it were well, as of the more powerful class of torpedo-boats, we had a larger number to meet the enemy on the high seas and off his coast.

A continuous system of reconstructing and re-boilering is hardly less important than the constant prosecution of ship-building. The life of every ironclad as an effective fighting machine of the first order, in these days of constant improvement, is comparatively short, and it is false economy to put off necessary repairs. The relative number of ships of our own Navy and that of other powers on foreign stations is striking, and this necessitates greater wear in our ships which are constantly in motion. France, which, next to us, has the largest navy and the greatest colonial possessions of any European power, in December, 1891 (excluding the Mediterranean station), had only thirteen ships on foreign stations as against forty-seven of our Navy. The difference in numbers, great as it is, does not accurately convey a full sense of the disproportion between the foreign duties of the two navies, for the English ships, on the average, are larger and of more modern type. This work of reconstruction, so far from decreasing, must increase with the expansion of our Colonies. Four years ago the annual coal bill of the British Navy was £274,000, but now it is estimated at £530,000, and although a certain proportion of this increase is attributable to more auxiliary machinery and the electric light, the bulk is due to the greater activity of our ships on foreign stations. In future years larger sums must be allocated to the heads of reconstruction, re-engineering, re-boilering, and large repairs, if readiness for service is to be the condition of the ships in reserve.* Recently the *Nelson* has superseded the wooden line-of-battle-ship *Duke of Wellington* as flagship at Portsmouth, and the more modern *Swiftsure* has taken the place of the *Black Prince* at Plymouth, while the *Alexandra* has succeeded the *Northumberland* as flagship of the coastguard squadron.

The placing of orders for the guns simultaneously with the commencement of the

---

* The official summary of the work proposed to be done during 1892-93 is as follows:—

Under construction—Ten vessels will be completed. Twenty will be advanced sufficiently to be completed in 1893-94. Two ironclads will be commenced in the dockyards, and one by contract. Ten first-class torpedo gunboats will be commenced by contract.

Under reconstruction—Five ironclads of the older type are to be finished, and two more to be advanced sufficiently to be finished in 1893-94.

This is independent of the contract-built ships of the Naval Defence Act, nine of which will be completed after delivery this year, and fifteen are to be materially advanced.

Very recently (October, 1892), the Admiralty have decided on the construction of 14 torpedo-boats, 10 of which are to measure 140 feet by $14\frac{1}{2}$ feet, with a guaranteed speed of 23 knots, and 4 are to measure 180 feet in length by $18\frac{1}{2}$ feet in breadth, and are expected to attain a speed of 27 knots, or a little over 31 statute miles.

building of the ships has reversed the old order of things, and, so far from ships being useless for want of guns, the guns await the ships on which they are to be mounted. In 1891, 396 heavy guns* were completed, as against 240 in the preceding year, and the number of guns ready for ships on December 31, 1891, was 1,623. As the great powers have adopted smokeless powder for war purposes, our Navy will be supplied with cordite, the new explosive, which is now manufactured on an extensive scale at Waltham Abbey.

The following is a retrospect of the work of the six years between 1886 and 1892:—

	1886.	1892.
ORDNANCE :—		
Breech-loading guns (afloat and in reserve)	499	1,868
Light quick-firing guns (afloat and in reserve)	33	1,715
Torpedoes (afloat and in reserve)	820	2,874
SHIPS:—		
In Commission—		
At home—Excluding coast defence ships, gunboats, and torpedo-boats	15	21
Displacement tonnage	110,000	154,500
Abroad—Total of all classes	96	110
Displacement tonnage	205,800	307,000
Complements—	18,100	23,350
In Reserve (ready for Commission)—		
Excluding coast defence ships, gunboats, and torpedo boats—		
Fleet Reserve—		
Division A	—	6
Division B	—	11
Old 1st Class Steam Reserve	10	2
Displacement tonnage	25,700	82,200
Ships of 15 knots speed and upwards (afloat and building), all classes except torpedo-boats	57	140
PERSONNEL :—		
Establishments of officers and men (active list)	61,400	74,000
Numbers of Royal Naval Reserve (officers and men)	18,300	23,500

* The following are the heavy ordnance in use in our Navy :—
16·25-inch, of 110 tons; 13·5-inch, of 67 tons; 10-inch, of 29 tons; 9·2-inch, of 22 tons; 8-inch, of 14 tons; 6-inch, of 5½ tons.

During the past two years there has been a gradual increase in the *personnel* of the Navy. The vote for 1891-92 was for a total force of 71,000, and for 1892-3 for 74,000, including 14,000 marines. But this number will require augmentation by at least 2,000 men. Of the total strength the Blue-jackets, who, with the Marines, form the actual fighting strength of the Navy, number little more than 20,000. England, during the first decade of the present century, with a population of 11,000,000, mustered 85,000 seamen in her fleet, besides 35,000 marines, and this at a time when her Colonial Empire, with the exception of Canada and Cape Colony, had no existence, and her commerce was not one tithe what it now is. This vital consideration "should give us pause," for vain is all our wealth, useless even our ships, without seamen to fight them.

It has been the custom until recently to regard the Channel fleet as a training squadron, composed of old and, in some instances, quite ineffective ironclads; but a change has been introduced, and this part of our naval defences, which for centuries had always been regarded as the most important, and was kept in the highest state of efficiency, is now composed of four first class battle-ships and two belted cruisers, all of modern type. In addition, there are nine ironclads in commission in connection with the coastguard system, which can be made ready for use in forty-eight hours. The ships of the First Class Steam Reserve in the home ports, and the coast defence vessels, with gun-vessels and torpedo-boats, can be prepared for sea, as has been proved by actual mobilization, in five days, and some in less time. Again, the Mediterranean Fleet, always kept in a state of the highest efficiency, has been raised to a strength of ten battle-ships and two armour-plated cruisers. From this *resumé* it will be seen that, while much remains to be done to maintain the ancient supremacy of our Navy, important steps in advance have been taken during the past few years. The strength of a navy, as of a nation, depends upon its reserve power, and the value of that reserve, in a great measure, on its readiness for active service.

In addition to the new vessels constructed under the Naval Defence Act and the annual shipbuilding vote, the old armoured ships have been renovated, and the depot-hulks at the naval ports have been replaced, as we have already observed—at Sheerness, Portsmouth, Plymouth, Queenstown, and Pembroke—by such sea-going ironclads as the *Northampton, Nelson, Swiftsure, Alexandra,* and *Triumph,* which form a considerable accession to the reserves ready for immediate service. An equally satisfactory change has recently been made with regard to the ships in reserve at the dockyards. These are now all placed conveniently together in the basins, ready coaled, with armaments

ROYAL NAVAL ARTILLERY VOLUNTEER.

on board, stores set apart, and skeleton crews told off to keep them in order. A similar policy of preparedness has been pursued with reference to obtaining on the shortest notice the very large extra quantity of coals and sea stores which would be required on the outbreak of war.

Then there is the new force of mercantile armed cruisers, whose value it would be difficult to overestimate, for the initiation of which the credit is due to Mr. Ismay, the Liverpool shipowner. There are now retained thirteen merchant steamers, of an aggregate displacement of 100,000 tons and 150,000 indicated horse-power. Such a tonnage built for the Navy would cost over £6,000,000, and the payment made by the country to secure the call for their services is only £60,000 per annum, which includes, free of charge, fifteen other large and fine steamers, and of the entire number, seventeen are commanded by officers of the Naval Reserve.

During 1891 the country lost the services of the Royal Naval Artillery Volunteers, which had been given the option of disbandment or being handed over to the War Office. Although it seemed an ungracious act, still it was, we think, the wisest course to adopt, as there seemed no prospect of increasing their numbers. There were, however, more important reasons for the adoption of this step, as it is clear that an addition of 2,000 really efficient seaman-gunners would be of no slight value to the defensive power of the country; but these men were in no sense sailors, and could not have been drafted for service in the fleet.

From Parliamentary Returns it appears that the Royal Naval Artillery Volunteers, which, at the time of their abolition, numbered 1,947 of all ranks, were recruited from no fewer than "254 different professions and trades," and moreover, it is shown that the class most fully represented was that of the clerk, of whom there were 439, while of the whole number, those connected, however remotely, with the sea, numbered only 150.

The Royal Naval Artillery Volunteers were first called into existence in 1873, when Mr. Goschen was First Lord of the Admiralty. At first they were no expense to the nation, but in the year following their enrolment, £1,000 was voted with a strength of 1,000 members, and this was gradually increased until 1891, when £6,685 was voted for less than 2,000 efficients, exclusive of the value of stores and ammunition supplied, the cost of maintenance and repairs of the *Frolic*, in the Thames, and other vessels, and the incidental expenses incurred by the use of gunboats.

The chief difficulty is now, as it has ever been in the past, the manning of the

Navy. During the great war, the pressgang was called into requisition to make up the complement of ships under orders to sail—a mode of recruiting which would, doubtless, in the event of war, be replaced by conscription among the seafaring classes. It is patent that this deficiency of seamen, not to speak of stokers as well, will have to be faced when the country is involved in war with a great maritime power, and some way found, either by this method or higher pay, to raise the number of seamen requisite to man the vast fleet we are constructing with such rapidity under the Naval Defence Act. Ships without sailors, or rather seamen-gunners, are no more use than an army with skeleton battalions such as we now possess, and if we are unable to find crews for the ships commissioned in peace time, with diminished crews, how shall we hope to man all the battle-ships and cruisers passed into the Reserve?

Without doubt those seamen we have are quite equal in physique to the gallant race that gained our victories under Howe and Nelson, and in intelligence they are vastly superior, while their training leaves nothing to be desired. Our officers, too, are not inferior in knowledge of their duties, among which seamanship no longer holds a place, to their predecessors, but of both officers and men the numbers are deficient. Some three hundred lieutenants are still needed, notwithstanding an augmentation to complete the number necessary for torpedo-vessels and other duties, and our reserve of seamen is notoriously and admittedly insufficient, and "dangerously small" (as the late Admiral of the Fleet, Sir A. Ryder, said) "in comparison with that of France." Other distinguished officers, Admirals Phillimore, De Horsey, and Lord Alcester, have written and expressed themselves to the same effect, but the country appears indifferent. Our mercantile marine has ceased to be a chief source of supply of seamen, for it is mostly manned by Norwegians, Swedes, Danes, and Lascars. Thus, although the *personnel* of the Navy has been greatly increased within the last few years, it is still below our requirements.

The authorised strength of the Naval Reserve is 20,700, divided into first and second class, in almost equal numbers, and lately recruiting has been so rapid that the total enrolled exceeds that number. Of these, the 10,000 second class, or fishermen, are always at hand, and of the 10,000 of the first class, or seamen, about 7,000 are also immediately available, being engaged on short and home voyages. Estimates have been made of the further possible increase of the service, and without undue pressure doubtless 10,000 men in the two classes could be obtained, which would raise the total strength to 30,000 men out of the 80,000 British seamen and 70,000 fishermen who form the supply. It is a disquieting fact, however, that whereas in fifteen years the merchant tonnage has increased by 1,750,000, the number of British seamen has diminished by 20,000, while the foreigners in our ships have increased by 6,000.

The officers of the Royal Naval Reserve, drawn from the mercantile marine, number 135 lieutenants, 250 sub-lieutenants, 200 midshipmen, and 100 engineers and assistant-engineers. Of these, a certain portion, which it may be hoped will be increased in succeeding years, have had a year's naval training. By being thus brought into actual contact with their naval brethren on board ships-of-war, and experiencing the conditions of naval life and discipline, those officers of the Reserve who have taken advantage of these facilities have really increased their value in the event of war.

With regard to firemen and stokers, the number in the Reserve does not increase, and additional inducements will have to be held out to them to join, as a ship-of-war of our day is as much a mechanical as a fighting machine.

An excellent system of annual mobilisation of the fleet has been adopted within the last decade, and with satisfactory results, not only in giving valuable practice to officers and men and the Intelligence Department, but as showing the weak points in our harness. We have said that the reserve of 20,000 men is totally insufficient to man all our ships, built and building, under the Naval Defence Act, which are passed into the Reserve, and to provide for the drain of war. But it is different in France, where the conscription prevails. There the navy, with fewer ships, has a *personnel* of far greater strength. The recent augmentation in officers has been great, as the following numbers will show. There will be 3 vice-admirals, instead of 1 as hitherto; 11 rear-admirals, an increase of 5; 56 captains, instead of 42; 106 commanders, instead of 71; 519 lieutenants, in place of 408; and 329 *enseignes de vaisseau*, instead of 277.

The total number of *equipages* (officers and men), which was, in 1891, 36,623, was raised in 1892 to 40,620, of whom 34,879 are regularly afloat, 2,058 in reserve, and 3,688 ashore. The number of ships in commission was also increased as follows:—Ironclads of all types, thirty-one instead of eighteen; cruisers, twenty-eight instead of twenty; and torpedo cruisers, fifteen in place of five, exclusive of sea-going torpedo-boats. The Mediterranean Fleet was increased from twenty-six to fifty ships; and the Channel Fleet, or *Escadre du Mid*, from eight to eighteen. The French *troupes de la marine* — who are supposed to be the same as our Royal Marines, but only garrison the military ports and the colonies, and do not serve afloat—number (infantry and artillery) 25,500, of whom some 15,000 serve in the French ports, and 10,000 in the colonies. The *inscrits*, or **reserve** of French seamen, are no less than 114,552, a number which contrasts favourably with our meagre Naval Reserves of all classes. The newly organised French Reserve, which corresponds with Division A of the British Fleet Reserve, consists of ships manned by three-fifths of their effective complements. The vessels are anchored in the roads of the various ports, and are kept filled up with ammunition, torpedoes, coal, and stores. Once every three months they proceed to sea to execute their quarterly firing; and it is ordered that no repairs shall be undertaken that would prevent the ships from sailing within 24 hours. The vessels in this class at Toulon alone include nine ironclads, four cruisers, one torpedo cruiser, one torpedo gun-vessel, and four torpedo-boats, besides thirty-nine equally ready torpedo-boats, which belong to a special reserve. In addition, there is in commission at Toulon, the Mediterranean squadron, consisting of nine ironclads, four cruisers, two torpedo cruisers, three torpedo gun-vessels, and five torpedo-boats, a number likely to be increased in all the ports since the recent development of this branch of the French war marine, on which that nation places such reliance. Thus it is the present policy of France to keep as many vessels of all classes as possible in readiness for immediate service.

It therefore behoves our rulers and people not to delude themselves with the fallacy that, having built many more ships than the country with which in the past we have mostly waged our wars, we have fulfilled our duty and may rest on our oars. Not only may new inventions and novel developments revolutionise war on the sea, as we have actually seen happen within the last thirty years, but all this array of ships which fills our dockyards, is of small account if we cannot procure a sufficient supply of competent British seamen to man them.

INDEX.

A.

Abyssinia, expedition to, iii. 281
Achille, capture and services of the, ii. 105, 113; iii. 9
Achilles, her services, i. 256, 294
Acre, defence of, by Sir Sydney Smith, ii. 260
Acre, attack on, by the British fleet, iii. 225—228
Active, services of the, ii. 331; iii. 78, 86, 88, 177, 284
Aden, capture of, iii. 242
Œolus, services of the, i. 258, 309; iii. 33
Africa (Spanish), capture of the, i. 203
„ services of the, ii. 184, 349; iii. 17, 64, 195
Africa, service on the coast of, iii. 255, 281
Africaine, loss, capture and recapture of the, ii. 309; iii. 81
Agamemnon, services of the, under Nelson, ii. 81, 90, 145, 149, 164—166
Agamemnon, services of the, under Berry and others, ii. 287, 289, 344, 349
Agamemnon, services of the, in the Russian war, iii. 17
Ajax, services and loss of the, ii. 299, 344, 348; iii. 17, 51, 78
Alceste (late *Minerve*), her capture and services, iii. 47, 60, 87, 88
Alcester, Lord, iii. 252, 287—292
Alcide, two captured and one lost, i. 318; ii. 148; iii. 140
Alcmene, services of the, ii. 269, 270, 276, 286, 289
Alexander, lost and recaptured, ii. 135, 140; iii. 139
Alexander, services of the, ii. 231, 237, 240, 248
Alexandria, bombardment of, iii. 287—292
Algiers, bombardment of, iii. 209—213
Alicant, reduced by Sir John Leake, i. 87
Amazon, services of the, ii. 169, 187, 188, 288, 291; iii. 38
Amboyna, capture of, iii. 83
Amelia and the *Arethuse*, iii. 92
Amethyst captures the *Thetis* and *Niemen*, iii. 64, 65
Amphion, services and loss of the, ii. 184, 319, 342; iii. 73, 74, 78, 86, 270
Andromache, services of the, ii. 216, 281, 308; iii. 245

Anson, Lord, circumnavigates the globe, i. 173—178
Anson, Lord, his victory off Finisterre, i. 198
Anson, Lord, his career, i. 320—322
Anson, services and loss of the, ii. 219, 226, 229, 254; iii. 46, 53, 188
Apollo, services and loss of the, i. 317; ii. 8, 337; iii. 52, 70
Arctic exploration, iii. 258—264
Ardent (French), capture of the, i. 197
„ loss and recapture of the, ii. 14, 41, 44
Ardent, services and loss of the, ii. 7, 85, 121, 213, 215, 286, 289
Arethusa, services of the, ii. 124, 129, 183, 218
Arethusa (French), capture of the, ii. 257
Argo captures the *Santa Teresa*, ii. 268
Ariadne, services of the, ii. 329
Armada, description of the Spanish, i. 13
„ its defeat and dispersion, i. 14—20
Ashantee, the expedition to, iii. 281
Ashby, Sir John, his services, i. 57, 67
Astræa, services of the, ii. 154; iii. 89, 93
Ayscough, Sir George, his services, i. 28, 30, 42, 45, 54

B.

Baker, Admiral, his services, i. 159
Balchen, Sir John, his services and death, i. 63, 185, 266
Ball, Sir Alexander, his services, ii. 232, 248; iii. 207
Baltic, operations in the, iii. 270
Banda Islands, surrender of the, iii. 83
Bantry Bay, action off, i. 57
Barcelona, events at, i. 62, 85, 87
Barfleur, services of the, i. 72, 141, 182; ii. 39, 109, 139, 200, 344; iii. 192, 193, 197, 198
Barlow, Captain, his services in the *Phœbe*, ii. 187, 219, 279, 309
Barnett, Commodore, in the East Indies, i. 187, 189
Barrington, Admiral, his career, i. 256; ii. 15
Bart, Jean, his career, i. 63, 72
Bathurst, Commodore, his services and death; iii. 63, 215, 219

Beauclerk, Lord Aubrey, death of, i. 264
Beaufort, Sir Francis, gallantry of, ii. 283
Belleisle, services of the, ii. 335, 349; iii. 6, 23, 42
Belleisle (French), capture of the, i. 258
„ (French), late *Formidable*, capture of the, ii. 140
Belleisle, reduction of, i. 294
Belle Poule, her capture and services, iii. 38, 87
Bellerophon, services of the, ii. 100, 107, 237, 239; iii. 8, 23, 74, 151, 226
Bellerophon, Napoleon surrenders on board the, iii. 95
Bellona takes the *Courageux*, and other services, i. 298; ii. 286, 289; iii. 42, 123, 190
Bellone (French), captured by the *Vestal*, iii. 197
Bellone, capture of another; ii. 227, 285; iii. 83
Benbow, Admiral, his services and death, i. 62, 64, 73—75, 124—128
Berkeley, Lord, his services, i. 62, 97, 138, 149
Berkeley, Sir William, his death, i. 54
Berry, Sir John, anecdote of, i. 134
Berry, Sir Edward, his services, ii. 205, 243, 277, 349; iii. 17, 207
Beresford, Lord Charles, his services, iii. 289, 302—308
Berwick, services of the, i. 182, 328
„ lost and recaptured, ii. 143
Bickerton, Sir Richard, joins Admiral Hughes, ii. 50, 75, 231
Blackwood, Sir Henry, his services, ii. 276, 347, 349; iii. 51
Blanche, Captain Faulknor, takes the *Pique*, ii. 151; iii. 130
Blanche, her services and loss, ii. 181, 322, 340; iii. 37, 46, 128
Blake, Admiral Robert, his career, i. 27—40
Blake, his action with the Dutch off Dover, i. 29
Blake enters Calais Harbour, i. 30
„ engages Van Tromp in the Channel, i. 31
Blake, his battle off Cape La Hogue, i. 33
„ his victory at Tunis, i. 36
„ at Malaga and Cadiz, i. 37
„ his victory at Teneriffe, i. 38
„ his death, i. 39

Blenheim, services and loss of the, ii. 37, 200, 323, 336; iii. 38, 182, 246
Blonde, services of the, iii. 75, 246
Bodley, Commodore, his action off Elba, i. 31
Boreas, services of the, i. 246, 251, 252; iii. 161
Borneo, the pirates of, iii. 249
Boscawen, Admiral, services of, i. 168, 194, 244, 253
Boscawen, sketch of his career, i. 314—320
Bourne, Admiral, serves under Blake, i. 29, 30
Bowen, Captain Richard, his services and death, ii. 131, 134, 179, 211; iii. 131—137
Boyne, services and loss of the, i. 171; ii. 15, 130—133, 158; iii. 93, 132
Brenton, Sir Jahleel, his services, ii. 269, 302, 320; iii. 54, 73
Brett, Sir Piercy, his career, ii. 64, 188
Bridport, Lord, his services, ii. 37, 96, 115, 139, 256, 273; iii. 194—196
Brisbane, Sir Charles, iii. 40, 46, 53
Brisbane, Sir James, ii. 288; iii. 209, 244
Britannia, services of the, i. 261; ii. 81, 144, 202, 349; iii. 18, 126
Broderick, Admiral, his career, i. 216, 241, 339
Broke, Captain P., of the *Shannon*, takes the *Chesapeake*, iii. 103—107
Brunswick, action with the *Vengeur*, ii. 110; iii. 120
Buckingham captures the *Florissant*, i. 238, 333
Bunker's Hill, battle of, iii. 192
Buonaparte, Prince Jerome, as a sailor, iii. 42
Buonaparte (see also "Napoleon").
Burmah, our wars in, iii. 242—245, 250—253
Bushire, capture of, iii. 256
Byng, Sir George, his services off Malaga, Alicant and Toulon, i. 82, 87, 90
Byng, Sir George, his victory off Cape Passaro, i. 139—147
Byng, Sir George, his career, i. 151—155
Byng, Admiral, his indecisive action and death, i. 206—212
Byron, Admiral, his career, i. 174, 251, 311; ii. 7, 15, 65—68

C.

Cadiz, expeditions to, i. 12, 24, 25, 26
,, Lord Nelson at, ii. 209
Cæsar, services of the, ii. 106, 231, 302, 305, 347; iii. 33, 66
Calcutta, recapture of, i. 222
Calder, Sir Robert, his career, ii. 202, 297, 344
Calvi, Nelson at, ii. 123; iii. 165
Camperdown, battle of, ii. 213—216
Canada, abortive attempt on, i. 107
Canadian Lakes, actions on, iii. 108, 113, 114
Canopus (late *Franklin*), her capture and services, ii. 240; iii. 25, 41, 52, 205, 213
Cape of Good Hope, capture of, ii. 159; iii. 40, 48
Cape Breton Island, capture of, i. 187, 204, 318
Captain, services of the, i. 141; ii. 85, 145, 165, 166, 200, 203, 278; iii. 166—169
Caraccas, attack on, repulsed, i. 180
Caroline, services of the, iii. 48, 83
Carraccioli, Prince, execution of, ii. 258
Carthagena, in Spain and West Indies, Blake and Vernon at, i. 11, 167
Casse, Admiral Du, his action with Benbow, and other services, i. 73—75, 105, 109
Cato, loss of the, ii. 69
Centaur, career of the, i. 319; ii. 44, 335, 340; iii. 45, 47, 57, 166, 199
Centurion, services of the, i. 173—178, 199; ii. 8, 161, 184, 324, 326
Cerbere, cutting out of the, ii. 282
Cerberus, services of the, ii. 270; iii. 65, 78, 86
Ceres, services of the, ii. 183
Ceylon, operations in, ii. 48—52, 162
Cherbourg, expedition to, i. 243
Chesapeake (American), captured by the *Shannon*, iii. 103—107
Chesapeake Bay, fighting in, iii. 108, 111
Chevrette, the cutting out of the, ii. 314
China, our wars with, iii. 245—249, 277—281
Churchill, Admiral, career of, i. 129
Cinque Ports, their ships defeat the French, i. 5
Cleopatra, her services and loss, ii. 308; iii. 35, 71
Cleopatre (French), her capture, ii. 87
Clue, Admiral de la, his defeat by Boscawen, i. 319
Cockburn, Sir George, ii. 165, 181, 298; iii. 95, 108, 111, 115, 167
Cochrane, Lord, his career, ii. 310; iii. 44, 65, 66—69
Cochrane, Sir Alexander, ii. 155, 298, 301, 333, 343; iii. 40, 76, 113, 115
Codrington, Sir Edward, at Trafalgar and Navarino, ii. 349; iii. 17, 215—225
Coghlan, Lieutenant, his gallantry, ii. 282; iii. 36
Cole, Captain, services of, ii. 187; iii. 83
Collingwood, Lord, his career, i. 257; ii. 204, 347; iii. 2, 23, 56, 70, 77, 191—194
Colossus, services of the, ii. 139, 200, 206, 248, 349; iii. 8, 23
Conflans, Admiral de, career of, i. 198, 254, 331
Constitution (American) captures the *Guerrière*, iii. 98, 101, 116
Cook, Captain James, his discoveries, i. 312
Cooke, Captain John (of the *Sibylle*), his services and death, ii. 216, 251, 264
Cooke, Captain John (of the *Bellerophon*), his services and death iii. 8, 150—152
Copenhagen, Sir George Rooke at, i. 64
Copenhagen, Nelson's attack on, ii. 287; iii. 172
Copenhagen, its capture in 1807, iii. 49
Cornish, Admiral, his career, i. 283, 304.
Cornwall, services of the, i. 203, 304; ii. 8, 22
Cornwallis, Admiral, his services, ii. 21, 41, 94, 120, 137, 318, 327, 343, 346; iii. 160, 177, 204
Corsica, conquered and abandoned, ii. 84, 121, 166; iii. 165, 198
Cotton, Sir Charles, his career, iii. 205
Courageux, her capture, services, and loss, i. 298; ii. 85, 146, 147, 278; iii. 33, 123, 197
Crescent, services of the, i. 257; ii. 90, 128, 161, 272
Culloden, services of the, i. 319; ii. 120, 148, 167, 200, 201, 211, 237, 248; iii. 48, 178—181
Cumberland, services of the, i. 218—226, 232, 262, 282, 322; ii. 148; iii. 70
Curaçoa, capture of; iii. 53, 188

D.

D'Aché, Count, his actions with Pocock and Stevens, i. 231—235, 281—287
Dædalus, services of the, ii. 266; iii. 86, 129, 133
Dance, Commodore, his action with a French squadron, ii. 325
Danae, mutiny of the, ii. 279
Darby, Admiral, relieves Gibraltar, ii. 34
Dardanelles, Duckworth forces the, iii. 51
Dart, Captain Campbell, gallant deed of the, ii. 281; iii. 286, 289
Deane, Admiral, death of, i. 34
Defence, services of the, ii. 109, 147, 237, 239, 280, 288, 349; iii. 19
Defence, her loss, iii. 85
Defiance, services of the, ii. 66, 73, 171, 199, 205, 286, 289, 344, 349; iii. 19, 66
Delaval, Sir Ralph, at La Hogue, i. 59, 128
Demerara, capture of, ii. 182, 323
Denmark, her fleet defeated by Ethelred, i. 4
Denmark lays an embargo on the Armada, i. 14
Denmark coerced by Rooke, i. 64
,, war with, ii. 287; iii. 64, 85
Devonshire, destruction of the, i. 93
,, services of the, i. 200, 272, 275, 328
Diamond, services of the, i. 164, 189; ii. 129, 136,155, 168, 169, 223, 315
Diamond Rock, loss of the, ii. 333
Dido, services of the, ii. 156; iii. 249
Dilkes, Sir Thomas, his career, i. 77, 82, 91, 92, 131—132

Dominica, capture of, i. 294
Donabew, repulse at, iii. 252
Donegal (late *Hoche*), services of the, iii. 24, 41, 66
Doris, services of the, ii. 188
Dorsetshire, services of the, i. 142, 241
Douglas, Sir Andrew, his career, iii. 137—139
Douglas, Sir James, his services, i. 252, 294
Drake, Sir Francis, his expedition to Darien, i. 10
Drake, Sir Francis, circumnavigates the globe, i. 11
Drake, Sir Francis, his expedition to Corba, i. 11
Drake, Sir Francis, destroys shipping at Cadiz, i. 12
Drake, Sir Francis, his death and character, i. 21—22
Dreadnought, services of the, i. 238, 337; iii. 18
Droits de l'Homme, loss of the, ii. 188
Duckworth, Sir Thomas, his services, ii. 249, 257, 340; iii. 40, 51, 205
Duff, Captain, his services and death, ii. 349; iii. 152—156
Duguay-Trouin, Admiral, his career, i. 93, 94, 97, 98, 102
Duguay-Trouin (or *Implacable*), capture and services of the, ii. 320; iii. 18, 34
Dumanoir, Admiral, services of, ii. 302; iii. 18, 33
Duncan, Lord, his victory at Camperdown, ii. 213—216
Duncan, Lord, his career, iii. 143—147
Dursley, Lord, defeats Duguay-Trouin, i. 98, 102 (see also *Berkeley*)
Dutch fleet assists England against the Armada, i. 14
Dutch, our wars with the, i. 28—56; ii. 26, 159, 182, 213—216, 263, 273, 323

E.

Eagle, loss of the, i. 92
  " services of the, i. 158, 199, 200; i. 7, 50, 51; iii. 140, 150
Edgar, destruction of the, 107
  " services of the, i. 287; ii. 286, 289
Edward I., his fleet defeats the French, i. 6
Edward III., his victory at Sluys, i. 7
Edwards, Commodore, his loss of a squadron, i. 93
Egypt, expedition to, ii. 299; iii. 52, 287—300
Elphinstone, Sir George (see *Keith*)
Elliott, Commodore, defeats Thurot, i. 258
Emerald, services of the, ii. 231, 249, 280; iii. 59, 68
Endymion captures the *President*, iii. 116

Epervier captured by the *Peacock*, iii. 110
Erie, Lake, fighting on, iii. 109
Essex, her services, i. 142, 294
Essex (American) captured by the *Phœbe*, iii. 110
Euryalus, services of the, ii. 347, 349; iii. 112
Eurydice, services of the, ii. 128, 223
Excellent, services of the, ii. 200; iii. 65, 192
Exeter, services of the, i. 185, 197; ii. 47, 51
Exmouth, Lord, his career, ii. 87, 129, 136, 187, 188, 254, 273; iii. 48, 93
Exmouth, Lord, his bombardment of Algiers, iii. 209—213

F.

Fairborne, Admiral, services of, i. 72, 76, 88, 96, 132, 133
Farmer, Captain, of the *Quebec*, death of, ii. 17
Fatshan Creek, the action at, iii. 277
Faulknor, Captain, his career and capture of the *Courageux*, i. 298; iii. 123—126
Faulknor, Captain (his son), his career and capture of the *Pique*, ii. 86, 131, 151—154; iii. 126—131
Fisgard (late *Résistance*), her capture and services, ii. 217, 229, 280, 315 ; iii. 53
Flora captures *Nymphe* and *Castor*, ii. 25, 33
Flora, her services, ii. 124, 253
Flushing, bombardment of, iii. 70
Foley, Captain Thomas, his career, ii. 200, 236, 248, 286; iii. 207
Forbin, Admiral de, his career, i. 93
Foreland, the North, Blake's victory off, i. 30
Formidable (French), capture of, i. 255; ii. 140; iii. 34
Formidable, her services, ii. 11, 39
Forrest, Commodore, his services, i. 238, 336
Forte, capture of the, ii. 264
Foudroyant, capture and services of the, i. 240; iii. 37, 131, 132, 203
Foudroyant, services of the new, ii. 226, 228, 257, 258, 276, 300; iii. 38, 184, 207, 214
Fougueux, captured by Hawke and Nelson, i. 201 ; iii. 6, 7, 18
Fox, Commodore, his services, i. 199, 201
Franklin (afterwards *Canopus*), capture of the, ii. 240
Franklin, Sir John, his career and fate, iii. 260—264
Fremantle, Captain, services of, ii. 210, 287, 349; iii. 16, 207
Frobisher, Admiral, engaged with the Armada, i. 16
Frolic captured by the *Wasp*, iii. 99
Frolic (American), her capture, iii. 110

G.

Galatea, services of the, ii. 130, 168, 175, 339; iii. 53, 89
Galissonnière, Admiral De, engages Byng, i. 207
Gambier, Lord, his career, ii. 96, 109; ii. 49, 66
Gardiner, Captain, death of, i. 240
Gardner, Lord, his services, ii. 93, 96, 101, 114, 139; iii. 189—191
Généreux, her career and capture, ii. 241, 243, 276
Genoa, surrender of, ii. 275
Gheria, capture of, i. 217—219
Gibraltar, capture of, i. 77—79, 114
  " relief of, by Sir John Leake, i. 84
  "   " by Sir John Jennings, i. 151
  "   " by Lord Rodney, ii. 18
  "   " by Admiral Darby, ii. 34
  "   " by Lord Howe, ii. 37; iii. 141
Glatton, services of the, ii. 173, 286, 289
Gloire, capture of the, i. 275 ; ii. 154
Gloucester, services of the, i. 174
Gordon, Captain James, services of, iii. 60, 86, 88
Gordon, Captain Alexander, services, iii. 111
Goree, surrender of, i. 242
Grafton, services of the, i. 141, 213, 273 282—288, 325; ii. 24, 77; iii. 196
Grafton, capture of the, i. 193
Grasse, Admiral De, his defeat by Howe, ii. 39
Graves, Lord, his services, ii. 30, 96, 108
Graves, Admiral Thomas, his services, ii. 286, 290; iii. 142
Grenville, Sir Richard, his death, i. 23
Griffin, Admiral, in the East Indies, i. 193
Guadaloupe, events in, i. 247; ii. 132—134; iii. 65, 129
Guerrière, her capture and loss, ii. 320; iii. 46, 98
Guichen, Admiral de, defeated by Rodney, ii. 21
Guillaume Tell (renamed *Malta*), her career and capture, ii. 241, 276, 344

H.

Haddock, Admiral, his career, i. 141, 163, 178, 179
Hamilton, Sir Charles, his services, ii. 231, 254
Hamilton, Sir Edward, services of, ii. 270, 310
Hannibal, loss and services of the, ii. 155, 302, 304; iii. 94
Hardinge, Captain, his services and death, ii. 337; iii. 58, 182—187
Hardy, Sir Thomas, his services, i. 109, 137
Hardy, Sir Charles, his services, i. 185; ii. 60

Hardy, Sir Thomas Masterman, his career, ii. 181, 232, 257, 287, 319
Harfleur, the fleet relieves, i. 7
Harland, Admiral, his career, i. 200; ii. 11
Harvey, Captain John, of the *Brunswick*, his career and death, ii. 110; iii. 119—122
Harvey, Captain Eliab, of the *Téméraire*, ii. 129, 131; iii. 1, 11
Havannah, reduction of, i. 302
Hawke, Admiral Lord, his services, i. 182, 209, 215, 241
Hawke, Admiral Lord, his victory over Conflans, i. 254
Hawke, Admiral Lord, his career, i. 327—332
Hawkins, Admiral, engaged with the Armada, i. 14—20
Hawkins, Admiral, death of, i. 21
Hebe, services of the, ii. 183, 329; iii. 148
Hector, services of the, ii. 187, 199, 298; iii. 192
Hector (French), captured and lost, ii. 41, 44
Heligoland, acquisition of, iii. 51
Henry III., his fleet defeats the French, i. 5
Henry V. at Harfleur, i. 7
„ VII. builds the *Great Harry*, i. 8
Herbert, Admiral (Lord Torrington), his services, i. 57, 64—67
Hercule, her capture by the *Mars*, and services, ii. 221, 340; iii. 149
Hercules, services of the, i. 257
Hermione, career and loss of the, ii. 135, 199, 220
Hermione, recapture of the, ii. 270—272
Hero, services and loss of the, ii. 51; iii. 85
Hewett, Sir William, his services, iii. 267, 282
Hoche, capture of the (renamed the *Donegal*), ii. 227
Hogue, Cape La, battle of, i. 59
Holland, our wars with, i. 28—56; ii. 213—216, 263, 273, 323
Holmes, Sir Robert, takes Cape Coast Castle and New York, i. 41
Holmes, Sir Robert, his services, i. 47
Holmes, Admiral, his services, i. 213, 249, 251, 294
Hood, Lord, his services, i. 256, 296; ii. 29—43, 81—85; iii. 161, 196—198
Hood, Sir Alexander (see *Bridport*)
Hood, Sir Samuel, his services, ii. 211, 238, 246, 302, 323, 340; iii. 45, 47, 53, 57, 197—199
Hood, Captain Alexander, his glorious death, ii. 221; iii. 147—150
Hope, Sir James, his services, iii. 254, 278
Hopson, Admiral, at Vigo, i. 71
Hornby, Captain Phipps, services of, iii. 86
Hornet (American) captures the *Peacock* and *Penguin*, iii. 102
Hoste, Commodore, his victory at Lissa, iii. 86

Hotham, Lord, his career, i. 256, 309; ii. 37, 81, 124, 142, 144, 150
Howard, Sir Edward, death of, i. 9
Howard of Effingham, Earl, his services, i. 14—20, 22
Howe, Lord, his early career, i. 205, 215, 242; ii. 3, 7—9
Howe, Lord, relieves Gibraltar, ii. 37; iii. 141
Howe, Lord, his great victory off Ushant, ii. 96—118
Howe, Lord, further services of, ii. 137; iii. 201—202
Howe, Lord, his career, iii. 139
Hughes, Sir Edward, his battles in the East Indies, ii. 47—51
Hughes, Sir Edward, his career, ii. 71—75
Hydra, services of the, ii. 223, 224; iii. 55

I.

Immortalité, capture and services of the, ii. 229, 328; iii. 47
Impérieuse, her services under Lord Cochrane, iii. 65, 66, 88
Implacable (late *Duguay-Trouin*), her capture and services, ii. 320; iii. 57, 74, 214
Impregnable, ii. 96, 109, 110; iii. 210, 212
Indian Mutiny, services of the Navy in the, iii. 273—276
Invasion of England, French plans and attempts for the, ii. 222, 327, 343
Invincible (French), capture of the, i. 275
„ services of the, ii. 101, 109; iii. 288
Ionian Islands, surrender of the, iii. 70, 77
Iphigenia, services of the,. ii. 91, 183; iii. 79, 83
Ireland, French expedition to, ii. 186, 225, 231
Isis, services of the, i. 297; ii. 7, 9, 49, 286, 289

J.

Jamaica, capture of, by Penn, i. 36
James, Sir William, at Gheria, i. 217
Jason, services of the, iii. 71
Java, reduction of the island of, iii. 89
Java (late *Rénommée*), capture and loss of the, iii. 89, 99, 101
Jaux (Dutch ship), capture and loss of the, iii. 48
Jennings, Sir John, his services at Alicant and elsewhere, i. 87, 101, 109, 151
Jennings, Sir John, his career, 155—158
Jervis, Sir John (*see* St. Vincent, Earl)
John, King, his fleet defeats the French, i. 5
Johnstone, Commodore, repulses De Suffren, ii. 31
Jones, Paul, captures the *Serapis*, ii. 16
Jonquière, Admiral De, his defeat by Anson, i. 199, 315

Jordan, Sir Joseph, his services against the Dutch, i. 49
Jumper, Sir William, his services at Gibraltar and elsewhere, i. 160—161
Junon, capture and loss of the, iii. 71, 75
Jupiter, services of the, ii. 267

K.

Keats, Sir G., his services, ii. 130, 175, 226, 302, 306; iii. 40, 51, 57
Keith, Lord, his services, ii. 82, 159, 256, 275, 300, 307; iii. 199, 208
Kellett, Captain, in the Arctic Regions, iii. 261
Kempenfeldt, Admiral, his services and death, i. 305; ii. 33, 61—64
Kent, her services, i. 103, 141, 155, 199, 201, 218—226, 298; iii. 78, 147
Keppel, Lord, his services, i. 242, 295, 303, 308; ii. 10, 52, 53—57
Keppel, Sir Harry, his career, iii. 249, 269, 277
Killigrew, Captain, his death, i. 63
Kishm, operations at the island of, iii. 236
Knevit, Sir Thomas, death of, i. 8
Knowles, Sir Charles, his services, i. 164, 168, 169, 180, 201—203, 216, 341

L.

Laforey, Admiral, his services, ii. 93, 182, 223, 349; iii. 18, 177
Latona, services of the, iii. 71, 72
Lawson, Sir John, his services under Blake and later, i. 33, 34, 35, 41, 42
Lawson, Sir John, his death, i. 43
Leake, Sir Andrew, his career and death, i. 81, 130—131
Leake, Sir John, relieves Gibraltar and Barcelona, i. 84, 87, 95
Leake, Sir John, reduces Alicant, Majorca, Sardinia, and Minorca, i. 87, 88, 95, 96
Leake, Sir John, memoir of, i. 121—124
Leander, services of the, ii. 210, 241; iii. 36, 117
Leander, her capture, ii. 243; iii. 210, 211
Lestock, Admiral, his career, i. 167, 168, 179, 182—184, 196
L'Etenduer, Admiral, defeated by Hawke, i. 200
Leviathan, services of the, ii. 107, 184, 249, 280; iii. 17, 23, 91
Levison, Sir Richard, destroys the Spanish galleons, i. 25
Linois, Admiral, his services, ii. 302, 306, 323; iii. 25, 38
Lion, her services, i. 104, 188, 199; ii. 64, 276; iii. 160
Lissa, Hoste's victory at, iii. 85
Loire, capture and services of the, ii. 229, 279, 320; iii. 36, 71

London, services of the, ii. 139, 278, 286; iii. 38, 143, 266
Lorient, failure of expedition to, i. 196
Louis, Sir Thomas, his services, ii. 232, 259, 329; iii. 41, 200, 204
Louisburg, capture of, i. 244, 318
Lowestoft, battle off, i. 42
Lowestoft, services of the, ii. 85, 156; iii. 159
Lutine, loss of the, with other ships, ii. 264
Luttrell, Captain, gallantry of, ii. 46
Lydiard, Captain, his career and death, iii. 46, 53, 187—189
Lyons, Lord, services of, iii. 265, 269

M.

McClintock, Captain, in the Arctic Seas, iii. 262
McClure, Captain, in the Arctic Seas, iii. 261
Macedonian, captured by the *United States*, iii. 100
Macnamara, Captain, services of, ii. 157, 173, 270; iii. 187
Madagascar, action off, iii. 89
Madagascar (late *Néréide*), capture of the, iii. 89, 90
Madras, loss and recovery of, i. 191, 196
Magicienne, services of the, ii. 220; iii. 76, 79, 272
Majestic, services of the, ii. 237, 239
Majorca, capture of, i. 88
Malabar Coast, French losses on the, i. 290
Malacca, capture of, ii. 163
Malaga, Blake at, i. 37
  ,, Rooke's action off, i. 79—82, 115—117
Malcolm, Captain Pulteney, his services, ii. 252; iii. 24, 41
Malta, its capture and loss by the French, ii. 232, 248, 276, 278
Malta (late *Guillaume Tell*), her capture and services, ii. 241, 276, 344
Manilla, capture of, i. 304; iii. 205
Marengo, her career and capture, ii. 224; iii. 38
Marlborough, services and loss of the, i. 182, 265, 303; ii. 40, 108, 274, 320; iii. 108
Mars, services of the, ii. 138, 221, 349; iii. 7, 46, 47, 148, 150, 154—156, 206
Martin, Sir Thomas Byam, his services, ii. 171, 229, 276, 280; iii. 57
Martinique, the fighting at, i. 300; ii. 93, 131
Matthews, Admiral, his career, i. 178, 180—184
Mauritius, events at and capture of, iii. 79—82
Maxwell, Lieutenant Keith, cuts out the *Chevrette*, ii. 314
Melampe and *Melampus*, their services, i. 256; ii. 124, 155, 226, 250
Melpomene, services of the, ii. 231, 253, 307, 328; iii. 74

Mercury, services of the, iii. 60, 73, 74
Miller, Captain, his services and death, ii. 205, 211, 260, 262
Milne, Sir David, his services, ii. 253, 284; iii. 209, 210, 212
Minerva and *Minerve*, services of the, i. 296; ii. 94, 156, 167, 181, 200, 298, 299; iii. 45, 167, 195
Minorca, events at, i. 96, 208, 311; ii. 52, 249
Minotaur, services and loss of the, ii. 237, 239, 248, 259, 275, 281, 349; iii. 18, 200
Mitchell, Sir David, career of, i. 129—130
Mocha, reduction of the forts of, iii. 242
Mohamrah, action at, iii. 256
Moluccas, capture of the, ii. 163; iii. 83
Monarch, services of the, ii. 47, 51, 159, 214, 286, 289; iii. 47, 114, 288
Monk, Admiral, his battles with the Dutch, i. 31, 44
Monmouth, services of the, i. 159, 199, 240; ii. 47, 51; iii. 142
Monson, Sir William, destroys some Spanish galleons, i. 26
Moore, Sir John, his career, ii. 57—59
Muscat, the Imaum of, as an ally, iii. 235—241
Myngs, Sir Christopher, his death, i. 55
Mutiny in the Fleet, ii. 188—198

N.

Nagle, Sir Edward, his services, ii. 129, 168
Naiad, services of the, ii. 270; iii. 84
Namur, services and loss of the, i. 182, 196, 253, 315, 317; ii. 39, 200; iii. 33, 190
Napier, Sir Charles, iii. 88, 112, 225—228, 269
Naples, Nelson and Trowbridge at, ii. 257; iii. 171, 181, 199
Napoleon the First at Boulogne, iii. 84
  ,, ,, his plans for the invasion of England, iii. 222
Napoleon the First surrenders to Captain Maitland, iii. 95
Narborough, Sir John, his services, i. 53
Navarino, battle of, iii. 214—225
Navy, present condition of the, iii. 311—344
Neale, Sir Harry, his services, ii. 216, 268; iii. 38
Nelson, Lord, in the *Agamemnon*, ii. 81, 90
  ,, ,, at Corsica, ii. 122
  ,, ,, in Hotham's action, ii. 145
  ,, ,, in the Mediterranean, ii. 165, 166, 167, 182, 198, 231, 257
Nelson, Lord, takes the *Sabina*, ii. 181
  ,, ,, at St. Vincent, ii. 203—205; iii. 168
Nelson, Lord, boat action at Cadiz, ii. 209
Nelson, Lord, at Teneriffe, ii. 210
  ,, ,, at the Nile, ii. 234—247; iii. 170
Nelson, Lord, at Copenhagen, ii. 287—294; iii. 172

Nelson, Lord, in the Channel, ii. 296
  ,, ,, in the Mediterranean, ii. 319, 330
Nelson, Lord, in the West Indies, ii. 332—335
Nelson, Lord, in England, ii. 347
  ,, ,, at Trafalgar, ii. 349; iii. 5, 21, 26
Nelson, Lord, a sketch of his career, iii. 157—176
Neptune, services of the, ii. 349; iii. 16
Néréide, capture and services of the, ii. 219, 279, 340; iii. 79
Newcastle, services and loss of the, i. 282, 288, 323
New Orleans, the repulse at, iii. 115
New York captured by Sir Robert Holmes, i. 41
New Zealand, the war in, iii. 257
Nicaragua, Nelson and Collingwood at, iii. 160, 192
Nile, battle of the, ii. 234, 247; iii. 198
Nile, expedition to the, iii. 302—308
Norfolk, services of the, i. 167, 182, 284, 288, 305; iii. 142
Norris, Sir John, career of, i. 103, 137, 138, 147, 148, 149, 162, 179, 181, 260—263
Northumberland, loss of the, i. 186
Northumberland, recapture of the, ii. 105
  ,, services of the, i. 276, 333; iii. 40, 90, 95, 295
North-West Passage, attempts to discover the, iii. 258—264
Norway, her fleet defeated by Harold, i. 4
Norwich, services of the, i. 164, 166, 180
Nottingham, services of the, i. 199, 201, 213, 341
Nova Scotia, capture of, i. 105
Nymphe captured by the *Flora*, ii. 25
  ,, takes the *Cleopatre*, ii. 87
  ,, her services, ii. 124, 216; iii. 60, 151

O.

Ogle, Sir Challoner, his services, i. 149, 166, 167, 180
Onslow, Sir Richard, ii. 213
Ontario, Lake, fighting on, iii. 108, 113
Orestes, services of the, ii. 223
Orient, destruction of the, ii. 240, 242
Orion, services of the, ii. 139, 200, 231, 237; iii. 17, 205, 294, 296
Orpheus, services of the, ii. 163
Ostend, capture of, i. 88
Owen, Commodore, his services, ii. 328

P.

Pallas, services of the, i. 258; iii. 44, 68
Palliser, Sir Hugh, and Lord Keppel, ii. 12
Parana, the forcing of the river, iii. 253
Parker, Sir Hyde, his services and death, i. 305; ii. 26, 68

Parker, Sir Hyde (his son), his services, ii. 37, 81, 144, 150, 286; iii. 205
Parker, Sir Peter, his services, ii. 2, 4, 24; iii. 159
Parker, Sir Peter, death of, iii. 113
„ Sir William, his services, iii. 38, 207, 247
Parker, Richard, the mutineer, ii. 188
Parry, Sir Edward, iii. 258
Passaro, Cape, Byng's victory off, i. 139—146
Peacock captured by the *Hornet*, iii. 102
„ (American) her captures, iii. 110, 117
Peiho Forts, the repulse at the, iii. 278—280
Pelican, Drake in the, i. 11
„ takes the *Argus*, iii. 108
„ loss of the, iii. 192
Pellew, Sir Edward (*see* Exmouth)
„ Sir Israel, ii. 88, 184, 308, 349
Pembroke, services and loss of the, i. 104, 187, 196
Penelope, services of the, ii. 135, 276, 328; iii. 288
Penguin, captured by the *Hornet*, iii. 117
Penn, Admiral, his services, i. 30, 33, 36, 42
Persian Gulf, operations in, iii. 229—241, 256
Petropaulovski, repulse at, iii. 271
Peyton, Commodore, his failure, i. 190
Phaeton, services of the, ii. 138, 176; iii. 39, 138
Philippine Islands, expedition to, i. 304
Phœbe, services of the, ii. 187, 219, 279, 309, 332; iii. 89, 110
Phœnix, services and loss of the, i. 31, 152; ii. 8, 24, 94, 171, 298; iii. 33, 39, 177, 205, 226
Phœnix (Spanish) captured by Rodney, ii. 18
Pique, captured by the *Blanche*, ii. 151—154; iii. 130
Pique (late *Pallas*), her services, ii. 279, 340; iii. 44, 225, 271
Plassey, our sailors at, i. 229
Pocock, Sir George, his services in India, i. 218—235, 280—284
Pocock, Sir George, takes Havannah, i. 302
Pocock, Sir George, his career, i. 322—327
Pointis, Admiral de, defeated by Sir John Leake, i. 73
Polyphemus, services of the, ii. 188, 286, 289
Pondicherry, sieges and capture of, i. 194—195, 286—289, 317; ii. 95
Popham, Sir Home, his services, ii. 223, 301; iii. 49, 50
Portobello, Vernon's capture of, i. 163—166
Portugal, expedition to, ii. 52, 57, 206
President (U. S. ship), actions and loss of the, iii. 96, 116
Prince George, loss of the, i. 340; ii. 200, 206
Proserpine, loss of the, ii. 264; iii. 71

Psyche, capture and services of the, iii. 35, 48

Q.

Quebec, capture of, i. 247, 347
Quebec, loss of the, ii. 17
Queen, services of the, ii. 101, 114, 139, 332; iii. 25, 191, 195, 267
Queen Charlotte, services and loss of the, ii. 101, 103, 139, 274; iii. 139, 200, 213

R.

Rainier, Admiral, services of, ii. 161, 184, 324
Raisonable, services of the, ii. 8, 344; iii. 37, 76, 157
Raisonable (French), capture and loss of the, i. 241, 300
Raleigh, Sir Walter, at Cadiz, i. 25
Ramillies, services and loss of the, i. 207; ii. 24, 290, 293
Rangoon, capture of, iii. 243, 250
Ras-ul-Khymah, the pirates of, i. 229—241
Rawson, Commander, death of, iii. 299
Redoutable, capture of the, i. 254, 319; iii. 5, 11—15, 23
Regent, loss of the, i. 8
Reindeer, services and loss of the, iii. 36, 110
Renown, services of the, ii. 278, 380
Repulse, services and loss of the, ii. 274, 344
Resistance, services and loss of the, ii. 163, 184
Resolution, loss of four ships of that name, i. 45, 89, 104, 255, 312
Revenge, Drake's flagship, i. 16
„ her capture under Sir Richard Grenville, i. 23
Revenge at Trafalgar, ii. 349; iii. 19
„ her services elsewhere, iii. 68, 226
Reynolds, Admiral, his services and death, ii. 187, 188
Richard I., his fleet, i. 4
Rivoli, her capture and services, iii. 91, 95
Robust, services of the, ii. 226, 330; iii. 197, 199
Rochefort, failure at, i. 215—217
Rochelle, expedition to, i. 27
Rodney, Lord, his services, i. 200, 259, 300
Rodney, Lord, relieves Gibraltar, ii. 18
„ „ engages De Guichen, ii. 21
„ „ defeats De Grasse, ii. 39
, „ his career, ii. 75, 79
Rome occupied by the Navy, ii. 259; iii. 181
Romney, services and loss of the, i. 89, 92; ii. 301; iii. 142
Rooke, Sir George, at the battle of La Hogue, i. 59, 69
Rooke, Sir George, at the Baltic, i. 64

Rooke, Sir George, fails at Cadiz and succeeds at Vigo Bay, i. 71
Rooke, Sir George, captures Gibraltar, i. 77
Rooke, Sir George, his victory at Malaga, i. 79—82
Rooke, Sir George, his career, i. 111—117
Rosas, operations at, iii. 65, 70
Ross, Sir James Lockhart, his career, ii. 69
Ross, Sir John, his services, iii. 258, 261
„ Sir James, his services, iii. 258, 259
Rodney, Admiral, his services, i. 179, 182, 188; ii. 15, 22
Rowley, Admiral, his services, i. 179, 182, 188; ii. 15, 22
Rowley, Commodore, Josias, ii. 344; iii. 37, 76, 79, 81, 82, 93
Royal George, services and loss of the, ii. 33, 70, 77, 96, 101, 115, 139; iii. 51, 195
Royal Oak, services of the, i. 93, 94
Royal Sovereign (see also *Sovereign*), services of the, i. 67; ii. 108, 137, 332, 344; iii. 2, 6, 23, 143, 193
Royal Sovereign, description of the new, iii. 332
Russell, Admiral, defeats the French off Cape La Hogue, i. 59
Russell, Admiral, relieves Barcelona, i. 62
Russell, Admiral, his career, i. 67—70, 102, 136
Russia coerced by Sir John Norris, i. 138, 148
Russia coerced by Sir Charles Wager, i. 150
Russia coerced by Lord Nelson, ii. 286, 295
Russia allied with us, iii. 90, 215—220
„ war with, iii. 265—273
Ruyter, Admiral De, his battles with Blake and Monk, i. 30, 44, 46
Ryddel, Captain, beats off a French squadron, i. 98

S.

St. Domingo, events at, ii. 135, 323; iii. 54, 40
St. George, her services and loss, i. 40, 52, 156, 241; ii. 81, 144, 286, 294; iii. 85
St. Malo, expedition to, i. 243
St. Paul, Count, death of, i. 85
St. Vincent, Earl, his services, ii. 37, 130, 150, 257; iii. 43, 203
St. Vincent, the battle off Cape, ii. 200—208; iii. 168
Salisbury, services of the, i. 105, 153, 218, 232, 282
Sandwich, the Earl of, his services and death, i. 41, 48
San Fiorenzo (formerly *Minerve*), her services, ii. 216, 268; iii. 35, 58, 185—187
San Josef, her capture by Nelson, ii. 205

INDEX.

San Nicolas, her capture by Nelson, ii. 204
Sanspareil (French) sunk, i. 69
  "   " capture of the, ii. 115
  "   " services of the, ii. 139; iii. 265, 273, 278
Santiago, Admiral Vernon's failure at, i. 170
Santissima Trinidada, her career, capture, and loss, ii. 37, 203, 207; iii. 3, 16, 25
Sardinia, island of, surrenders to Sir John Leake, i. 95
Saumarez, Captain, killed in action, i. 201, 341
Saumarez, Admiral Lord, his services, i. 90, 128, 231, 246, 302; iii. 77
Saunders, Sir Charles, his services, i. 247, 313, 346-348
Seahorse, services of the, i. 305; iii. 61, 111, 158, 176
Sebastopol, attack on, iii. 266
Seine captures the *Vengeance*, ii. 284
Senegal, reduction of, i. 242; iii. 76
Seymour, Captain Michael, captures the *Thetis* and *Niemen*, iii. 64, 65
Seymour, Captain George, his services, iii. 68
Seymour, Sir Michael, his services, iii. 272, 273, 277
Shannon, loss of the, ii. 323
  " captures the *Chesapeake*, iii. 103—107
Shannon, her services in India, iii. 273
Shortland, Captain, his services and death, ii. 254; iii. 75
Shovel, Sir Cloudesley, his services, i. 54, 57, 59, 67, 72, 76, 80, 85, 90, 117—120
Shovel, Sir Cloudesley, his loss off the Scilly Isles, i. 92, 121
Shrewsbury, services and loss of the, i. 156, 167; ii. 298
Sibylle, her capture and services, ii. 129, 251, 264, 308
Sidon, capture of, iii. 225
Sluys, British victory at, i. 7
Smith, Sir Sydney, his career, ii. 129, 136, 155, 168, 169, 259, 299, 327; iii. 43, 51, 52, 200—201
Solebay, battle with the Dutch off, i. 47
Soudan, operations in the Eastern, iii. 300, 308
Southampton, services of the, ii. 157, 173, 200; iii. 92, 187
Sovereign of the Seas, our first three-decker, i. 26
Spartan, services of the, iii. 54, 73
Spartiate, her capture and services, ii. 237, 242, 333; iii. 18
Spragge, Admiral, his services and death, i. 46, 50, 51—52
Stevens, Admiral, in India, i. 231—235, 284
Stopford, Sir Robert, his services, ii. 138, 176; iii. 41, 66, 90, 225—228
Strachan, Sir Richard, his services, ii. 94, 124, 155, 223; iii. 33, 42, 56, 70
Suakin, operations near, iii. 300, 308
Suckling, Captain, his services, i. 238; ii. 59—60; iii. 157

Suez Canal, seizure of the, iii. 294—266
Suffolk, her services, i. 103, 180; ii. 161, 184; iii. 144
Suffren, Admiral De, his career, ii. 31, 46—51
Sultan, services of the, ii. 15, 47, 51; iii. 177, 190, 288
Sunderland, services and loss of the, i. 187, 282, 288
Superb, services of the, i. 141, 187, 274; ii. 47, 51, 302, 306, 335; iii. 40, 41, 210, 212, 288
Surat, capture of, i. 236
Surinam, surrender of, ii. 273
Sweaborg, bombardment of, iii. 272
Sweden, war with, i. 137, 138, 147, 154; ii. 286, 295; iii. 77
Swiftsure, services and loss of the, i. 294; ii. 127, 183, 237, 240, 249, 280, 349; iii. 19

T.

Téméraire (French), capture of, i. 254, 319
Téméraire, services of the, i. 294; iii. 1, 10, 15, 23, 288
Teneriffe, Blake and Nelson at, i. 38; ii. 210; iii. 169
Terpsichore, services of the, i. 309; ii. 134, 179, 210, 231; iii. 62, 133—137
Terpsichore (French), capture of the, iii. 95
Thames lost and recaptured, ii. 90, 171, 257, 306
Thames, services of the, iii. 78, 88
Theseus, services of the, ii. 210, 236, 260, 340; iii. 169
Thetis, services of the, ii. 155
  " (French), capture of the, i. 152; iii. 64
Thunderer, her services and loss, i. 298; ii. 24, 141, 349; iii. 19, 51, 225, 226
Thurot, his defeat and death, i. 254, 257
Tiger, services of the, i. 53, 220—226, 282—286, 325; iii. 265
Tigre, capture and services of the, ii. 140, 259, 262; iii. 25, 52, 70
Tollet, Captain, defeats Duguay-Trouin, i. 97
Tonnant, her capture and services, ii. 241, 242, 349; iii. 7
Toulon, Sir Cloudesley Shovel at, i. 90
  " Hood at, ii. 81—85
Trafalgar, battle of, ii. 349; iii. 1—25
Tribune, wreck of the, ii. 219
Trinidad, surrender of, ii. 219
Tripoli, the British fleet at, i. 53
Triumph, flagship of Frobisher and Blake, i. 16, 31, 33, 35.
Triumph, her services under Hood, Duncan, and Calder, ii. 29, 60, 213, 215, 344
Triumph, her other services, iii. 158, 193
Troubridge, Sir Thomas, his services, ii. 97, 167, 201, 211, 237, 257, 259; iii. 38

Troubridge, Sir Thomas, a sketch of his career, iii. 176—182
Tunis, Blake at, i. 36
Tyler, Captain, his services, ii. 349; iii. 7, 183
Tyrrel, Admiral, his services, i. 238, 333—336

U.

United States, war with the, iii. 97—117
United States (American) takes the *Macedonian*, iii. 97, 100

V.

Valiant, services of the, i. 294; iii. 63, 68, 144
Vanguard, services under Blake, i. 32
  " in the West Indies, ii. 133
  " Nelson's flagship at the Nile, ii. 231, 239, 248; iii. 170
Vanguard, her services, ii. 320
Van Tromp, his career and death, i. 29, 30, 33, 34, 35
Venerable, services of the, ii. 213, 302; iii. 92, 145—147, 199
Vengeance, services of the, i. 296; ii. 133
Vengeur, her action with the *Brunswick*, ii. 110
Vernon, Admiral, takes Portobello, i. 163, 166
Vernon, Admiral, fails at Carthagena and Santiago, i. 167—172
Vernon, Admiral, his career, i. 268, 272
Victorious, Captain Talbot, captures the *Rivoli*, iii. 91
Victory, Hawkins' flagship against the Armada, i. 16
Victory serves under Blake, i. 31
  " commanded by Sir John Jennings, i. 155
Victory, loss of the, under Sir John Balchen, i. 185, 266
Victory, Lord Keppel's flagship, ii. 10
  " Sir Charles Hardy's flagship, ii. 61
Victory, Lord Hood's flagship, ii. 81, 121
  " Admiral Man's flagship, ii. 147
  " Sir John Jervis's flagship at St. Vincent, ii. 200
Victory, Lord Nelson's flagship at Trafalgar, ii. 319; iii. 1
Victory, Sir James Saumarez's flagship, iii. 57
Victory, a brief history of the, iii. 26—32
Vigo, expeditions to, i. 71, 147
Villaret-Joyeuse, Admiral, his career, ii. 91, 136; iii. 76
Villeneuve, Admiral, his career, ii. 167, 330, 333, 343, 346, 349
Volage, capture and services of the, i. 250 iii. 86

W.

Wager, Sir Charles, his services, i. 98, 99, 136, 138, 149, 150, 162, 263
Wager, loss of the, i. 174
Walcheren, expedition to, iii. 70, 75, 76
Wallis, Sir Provo, iii. 107
Walton, Sir George, his services, i. 142, 150
Warren, Admiral Sir Peter, his services, i. 187, 199, 273
Warren, Sir J. Borlase, his services, ii. 124, 129, 136, 139, 141, 168, 226, 278
Warrior, description of the, iii. 314
  ,,   services of the, ii. 344
Warspite, services of the, i. 319
Warwick, loss and recapture of the, i. 213, 272
Wasp (American) takes the *Frolic*, *Reindeer*, and *Avon*, iii. 99, 110, 111
Washington, capture of, iii. 111
Watson, Admiral, his career, i. 200, 217—230, 275—279
West, Admiral, his services, i. 207—212, 272
Westcott, Captain G. B., his services and death at the Nile, ii. 96, 109, 239
West Indies, French losses in the, i. 301
  ,,   ,,   hurricane in the, ii. 23
  ,,   ,,   events in the, ii. 93, 130—135, 182, 323; iii. 65, 76, 96, 127, 161—163
Weymouth, her services, i. 160, 282, 288, 323
Whitaker, Sir Edward, his services, i. 78, 95, 100, 101, 159
Williams, Sir Thomas, his services, ii. 25, 188
Willoughby, Sir Nisbet, his services, ii. 323, 340; iii. 79, 80
Wishart, Sir James, his career, i. 158
Worcester, services of the, i. 146, 164, 171; ii. 49; iii. 150, 159

Y.

Yarmouth, services of the, i. 161, 199, 200—201, 233, 282; ii. 65
Yeo, Sir James, his services, iii. 77, 92, 109, 113
York, H.R.H. the Duke of, his battles with the Dutch, i. 42—47

Z.

Zulu War, iii. 284—286